COMHAIRLE CHONTAE ÁTHA CLIATH THEAS
SOUTH DUBLIN COUNTY LIBRARIES

CASTLETYMON BRANCH LIBRARY
TO RENEW ANY ITEM TEL: 452 4888

Items should be returned on or before the last date below. Fines, as displayed in the Library, will be charged on overdue items.

"Margaret A. Salinger is an artful and accomplished writer."

—*The Toronto Sun*

"Peggy Salinger has become a sort of dream catcher herself."

—*NPR's Morning Edition*

"Utterly riveting in its narrative and its hard-won conclusions."

—*The Globe and Mail* (Toronto)

"Imagine finding your father not at home but through his books. That's the journey Salinger's daughter details in this remarkable piece of writing."

—*Pittsburgh Post-Gazette*

"*DREAM CATCHER* exposes the cracks in the façade of the Salinger mystique."

—Salon.com

"Margaret A. Salinger's work shows the brilliance of what can happen when a woman's way of seeing is adroitly applied to a man's writing. . . . Rarely does a memoir do so much to make readers reconsider a body of fiction by a well-known writer. . . . This memoir has become one of the best books to surface in the world of Salinger criticism."

—*Academic Writing Review*

"By fathering Margaret, or Peggy, America's best-known creator of precocious fictional siblings begot a daughter with a level of brilliance and moral fiber that has proved capable of taking on both the challenge of the flesh-and-blood J. D. Salinger and the mystique he has gone to vast lengths to cultivate. . . . A master interpreter of her father's work, Peggy skillfully balances her incisive readings of the stories with her father's motives and behaviors. What makes it so remarkable is the brilliance with which, in describing the process of winning her own salvation, the author deconstructs the Salinger myth."

—*Richmond Times-Dispatch* (VA)

"Peggy's diverse achievements and experience make *DREAM CATCHER* unlike any memoir . . . darkly comic."

—*The Jerusalem Report*

"Salinger's writing is vivid and strong."

—*The Telegraph* (UK)

"I found myself gaining personal insights from this book that applied to me both as a son and as a father. I could not ask for much more than that. There are, I believe, lessons here for all of us."

—*Buffalo Art News*

Dream Catcher

A MEMOIR

Margaret A. Salinger

POCKET
BOOKS

LONDON • SYDNEY • NEW YORK • TORONTO

First published in Great Britain by Scribner, 2000
First published by Pocket Books, 2010
An imprint of Simon & Schuster UK Ltd
A CBS COMPANY

1 3 5 7 9 10 8 6 4 2

Simon & Schuster UK Ltd
1st Floor
222 Gray's Inn Road
London
WC1X 8HB

www.simonandschuster.co.uk

Simon & Schuster Australia
Sydney

A CIP catalogue record for this book is available from the British Library

ISBN: 978-0-74320-969-4

Printed and bound in Great Britain by
CPI Cox & Wyman, Reading, Berkshire RG1 8EX

For my family

Contents

❧❦❧

PART THREE

BEYOND CORNISH

Introduction

❧❧❧

Dreams, books, are each a world . . .
with tendrils strong as flesh and blood . . .
—"Personal Talk," William Wordsworth

I GREW UP IN A WORLD nearly devoid of living people. Cornish, where we lived, was wild and woody, our nearest neighbors a group of seven moss-covered gravestones that my brother and I once discovered while tracking a red salamander in the rain, two large stones with five small ones at their feet marking the passing of a family long ago. My father discouraged living visitors to such an extent that an outsider, looking in, might have observed a wasteland of isolation. Yet, as one of my father's characters, Raymond Ford, once wrote in his poem "The Inverted Forest"*: "Not wasteland, but a great inverted forest, With all foliage underground." My childhood was lush with make-believe: wood sprites, fairies, a bower of imaginary friends, books about lands somewhere East of the Sun and West of the Moon. My father, too, spun tales of characters, both animal and human, who accompanied us throughout our day. My mother read to me by the hour. Years later, I read that my father's character Holden Caulfield had dreamt of having children in such a place someday; "we'd hide them away," he said, in his little cabin by the edge of a forest. He and his wife would buy them lots of books and teach them how to read and write.

---

*"The Inverted Forest," *Cosmopolitan* 123 (Dec. 1947): 73–109.

In real life, however, it was a world that dangled between dream and nightmare on a gossamer thread my parents wove, without the reality of solid ground to catch a body should he or she fall. My parents dreamt beautiful dreams, but did not have the skill to wrest them from the air and bring them to fruition in daily life. My mother was a child when she had me. She remained a dreamer, and, like Lady Macbeth, a tortured nightwalker, for many years. My father, a writer of fiction, is a dreamer who barely can tie his own shoelaces in the real world, let alone warn his daughter she might stumble and fall.

Fiction, other worlds, other realities, were, for my father, far more real than living flora and fauna, flesh and blood. I remember once we were looking out of his living room window together at the beautiful view of field and forest, a patchwork of farms and mountains fading into the far distance. He waved a hand across it all as if to wipe it out and said, "All of this is *maya,* all an illusion. Isn't that wonderful?" I didn't say anything, but for me, who had fought long and hard for anything resembling solid ground, the idea of its vanishing from underneath me in one fell swoop was anything but wonderful. *Vertigo, annihilation, terror,* are words that come to my mind, certainly not *wonderful.* This was the dark side of the Inverted Forest.

I grew up in a world both terrible and beautiful, and grossly out of balance. It is, perhaps, part of the human condition that children, as they grow to adulthood, must disentangle themselves from who their parents dreamt they might be, in order to figure out who they really are or hope to be. For my mother, for my father's sister, and myself, this task brought us near to drowning, so entangled were we in tendrils, strong as flesh and blood, fantastic garlands of my father's dreams.

Laertes	Drowned! O, where?
Queen	There is a willow grows askant the brook,
	That shows his hoar leaves in the glassy stream.
	Therewith fantastic garlands did she make. . . .
	When down her weedy trophies and herself
	Fell in the weeping brook. . . .

Which time she chanted snatches of old lauds,
As one incapable of her own distress,
Or like a creature native and endued
Unto that element. But long it could not be
Till that her garments, heavy with their drink,
Pulled the poor wretch from her melodious lay
To muddy death.

(*Hamlet*, IV, vii, 189–208)

My father once told a friend that for him the act of writing was inseparable from the quest for enlightenment, that he intended devoting his life to one great work, and that the work would be his life—there would be no separation. In real life, when he chooses to make himself available, he can be funny, intensely loving, and the person you most want to be with; however, for such *maya* as living persons to get in the way of his work, to interrupt the holy quest, is to commit sacrilege. I was nearly middle-aged before I broke the silence, broke the family idol guarding generations of moldy secrets, both real and imagined, and began to shed some light and fresh air, wholesome and life-giving as Cornish breezes.

After my son was born, I felt an urgency to make my way through the magic and the miasma alike, through both history and fiction, to figure out what is real and what is not, what is worth saving and passing on to my son as his precious inheritance, and what I want to filter out, as the Native American dream catcher that hangs over his bed filters out the nightmares in its web and lets the good dreams drip down the feather onto his sleeping forehead.

Although I thought that, as Holden said in the opening of *The Catcher in the Rye*, "my parents would have about two hemorrhages apiece if I told anything pretty personal about them . . . especially my father," I'm surprised and grateful about how generous the women in our family, my mother and my father's only sister, have been with their stories when I finally worked up the nerve to ask. I also took my father's advice to a young lady, an English student, many years ago, when he told her that he thought she'd do much better on her paper without any active cooperation by him. He was very polite and said he appreciated her good will; nevertheless, he told her, the biographical facts you want are in my stories, in one form or another, including the traumatic experiences you asked about. So with the help of my reflections on our life together, my reading and research into my father's life and work, and many long conversations with my aunt and my mother, I managed to piece together a story of how the Salinger family "was occupied and all." It may resemble a crazy quilt, but perhaps that's appropriate, too.

PART ONE

A FAMILY HISTORY:

1900–1955

"How my parents were occupied and all before they had me"

❧❦

> Four gray walls, and four gray towers,
> Overlook a space of flowers,
> And the silent isle imbowers
> The Lady of Shalott. . . .
>
> There she weaves by night and day
> A magic web with colors gay.
> She has heard a whisper say,
> A curse is on her if she stay
> To look down to Camelot.

—"The Lady of Shalott," Alfred, Lord Tennyson

1

"Sometimes Thro' the Mirror Blue"*

❧❀❧

"Now, Kitty, let's consider who it was that dreamed it all. This is a serious question, my dear, and you should not go on licking your paw like that—as if Dinah hadn't washed you this morning! You see, Kitty, it must have been either me or the Red King. He was part of my dream, of course—but then I was part of his dream, too! Was it the Red King, Kitty? You were his wife, my dear, so you ought to know—Oh, Kitty, do help to settle it! I'm sure your paw can wait!"

—Chapter 12, "Which Dreamed It?"
Through the Looking-Glass, Lewis Carroll

MAMA SAID THAT WHEN SHE WAS A LITTLE GIRL, before her house in London was bombed, she would often creep out of her bed at night and open the door between her nursery and the·top of the back staircase that led down to the kitchen. She'd tiptoe downstairs to make sure the door was closed and no servants were around. Then, spreading her white nightgown around her and slowly rising off the ground, she would fly up and down the passageway. She knew she hadn't been dreaming because when she awoke on mornings after flight, there would be dust on her fingertips where she had touched the ceiling.†

---

*"And sometimes thro' the mirror blue, The knights come riding two and two: She hath no loyal knight and true, The Lady of Shalott."

†[Franny, age seven] went on at beautiful length about how she used to fly all around the apartment when she was four and no one was home. . . . He said she

My mother was a child hidden away. She, like many upper-class and upper-middle-class English children of her day, was raised by staff in the nursery. I grew up hearing grim tales of nursery life. The one brief, bright spot was a nice governess, Nurse Reed, who took little Claire home with her on visits to her family. Nurse Reed's replacement, a Swiss-German who, among her many delightful qualities, used to force Claire, after lunch, to sit on the toilet until she "produced," or until suppertime, whichever came first, was more the norm. I knew, too, that she was sent to convent boarding school when she was only five years old and that she was taught to bathe her little body under a sheet so God wouldn't be offended by her nakedness. I used to think about that when I was a little girl sitting in the tub, how scary a wet sheet over you would feel, as if you'd get caught under the immensity of it and sucked down the drain. Once, when I was in the hospital with poison ivy, my mother told me that when she was at the convent and got poison ivy, the nuns scrubbed her head to toe, beneath the sheet of course, with a bristle brush and lye soap to remove the evil ivy boils.

What I didn't understand was *why* she was there. I didn't wonder about it when I was little and assumed that things just happen to children as inexorably as the catechism. But now, as an adult, it no longer made sense to me, and I asked her about it. My mother explained that at the time, in the fall of 1939, the fact that loomed largest in most Londoners' lives was that there was a war on. During the Blitz, parents with the means and "any *sense* at all," she said, took their families out of London and went to stay with friends or relatives in the country. The Douglas family had both country relations and money; nevertheless, Claire and her brother, Gavin, were packed on a train, unaccompanied, "with all the poor children," and evacuated to a convent at St. Leonard's-by-the-Sea. St. Leonard's had the unfortunate geographical attribute of being opposite Dunkirk, and they were soon evacuated again, this time inland to a sister convent in what my mother only remembers as a red-bricked city. She was five years old.

---

surely just *dreamt* that she was able to fly. The baby stood her ground like an angel. She said she *knew* she was able to fly because when she came down she always had dust on her fingers from touching the light bulbs" (*Raise High the Roof Beam, Carpenters*, p. 9).

There was no comfort to be found in her elder brother, who, at seven, had a well-developed penchant for torturing animals and small girls. "He liked to cause pain, poor boy, it confused him terribly." "Why?" I asked, grateful that she had never let "the poor boy" anywhere near *her* daughter while he was alive. "Mom, what was *wrong* with Gavin?" The answer came back flat and blunt: "The man my mother got her black market meat from was a pederast. When he came to the house, he bothered me a couple of times, but it was mostly my brother he was interested in, not me, thank God. I don't think he ever recovered from it."

In the fall of 1941, as Jerome Salinger had his first story, "The Young Folks," published, Claire, age seven, and her nine-year-old brother, Gavin, were put on a train to Southampton, where they were met by a governess. She informed them that their family's house had been bombed and had burnt to the ground. The Douglases had been out for the evening when the bomb struck, but Claire's beloved kitten, Tiger Lily, was nowhere to be found. The governess deposited Claire and Gavin on a ship, the *Scythia,* offering the children no explanation. Her duty accomplished, she turned and marched off the ship.

The ship was packed with stunned, weeping children headed for the safety of the United States to sit out the war. One bit of contact, which Claire clung to like a life preserver, was to stand on the deck each day and wave to the children on the deck of their sister ship, *The City of Benares,* which carried the same cargo of unaccompanied children and sailed alongside them in close convoy. The children would wave back to her. Several days out of Southampton, as Claire was exchanging waves, a German torpedo ripped into the side of the *Benares*. It exploded into flames. Claire watched in mute horror as it sank, children screaming and dancing as they burned.

The *Scythia* disembarked at Halifax, Nova Scotia. From Halifax, Claire and Gavin traveled alone by train to Waycross, Georgia, to meet their first host family. They were in Georgia when, on December 7 of that year, the Japanese bombed Pearl Harbor. Before the war's end, they would be removed from eight different American foster homes because of Gavin's behavior. "And you know what happens to little girls in foster care . . . ," my mother said, as though we were both in on some kind of secret not to be mentioned, only hinted at.

Their second placement was in Tampa, Florida. She remembers being terribly sunburned and attributes her midlife melanoma to her Tampa stay. The next stop, about the time Staff Sergeant Jerome Salinger was preparing to take Utah Beach on D-Day, was Wilmington, Delaware, where she attended the Tower Hill School for about a year. This was followed by placements with families in Allentown, Pennsylvania; Sea Girt, New Jersey; and Glens Falls, New York.

I never heard about these places growing up. My mother didn't have to think for two seconds, though, to remember. The towns, and the order in which the placements occurred, were literally at her fingertips as she ticked them off, counting on her fingers the way my son, at age four, might display his mastery of the days of the week. "Waycross, Tampa, Wilmington . . ."

"Where were your parents?" I asked, assuming they must have been unable to leave England. She told me that her father, an art dealer, came to America shortly after she did, in 1941, to sell some pictures in New York. He was stuck there while the shipping passage was blocked by German U-boats. When it opened, he sent for his wife and they spent the duration of the war in New York City building up the business at Duveen Brothers* and getting established.

When the war ended, the foster program ended, too, and the Douglases had to collect their children, at which point Claire was sent off to the Convent of the Holy Child in Suffern, New York, where she stayed until the end of eighth grade; Gavin went to Milton Academy. "How were they able to have their children taken care of by American families on that war program when they were in the country themselves?" I asked her as she told me this story. She shook her head and said, "God only knows what story my mother told them."

She stayed with her parents in their New York apartment on the oc-

---

*A privately owned art gallery in Paris and Manhattan, specializing in Old Masters. Edward Fowles and a partner inherited the business when Lord Duveen died in 1939. My grandmother married "Uncle" Edward, as we called him, after my grandfather died. Uncle Edward's memoir, *Memories of Duveen Brothers: Seventy Years in the Art World,* is a wonderful resource for anyone interested in the wheelings and dealings of the art world—its patrons, saints, forgers, and other colorful people.

casional school holiday, sleeping under the dining room table—for reasons unknown and probably unquestioned. In eighth grade, she refused to go back to the convent. "They were doing a number on my head, trying to coerce me into becoming a nun. The whole school was ordered to shun me, not to speak to me, until I had declared my decision. I was going mad." Her parents did not, or could not, force her to return, and in the fall of 1947 they enrolled her, instead, at Shipley, a girls' boarding school in Bryn Mawr, Pennsylvania.

Three years later, in the fall of 1950, she met a writer named Jerry Salinger at a party in New York given by Bee Stein, an artist, and her husband, Francis Steegmuller, a writer for *The New Yorker*. Claire's parents lived in the same apartment building as the Steegmullers on East Sixty-sixth Street, and through their shared interest in the arts, they had become good friends as well as neighbors. Claire was sixteen and had just begun her senior year at Shipley. She arrived at the party looking strikingly beautiful, with the wide-eyed, vulnerable, on-the-brink look of Audrey Hepburn in *Breakfast at Tiffany's* or Leslie Caron in *Gigi*, a movie my father loved so much that he bought a reel-to-reel copy and played it for us so many times when I was growing up that, to this day, I can still sing the lyrics beginning to end. As a child, I never heard the names Holden Caulfield or Seymour Glass, but even now I can't hold a glass of champagne without hearing in my mind the song "The Night They Invented Champagne" from *Gigi*.

Our shared world was not books, but rather, my father's collection of reel-to-reel movies. During the long winters, our human visitors were, essentially, supplied courtesy of MGM. My father would set up the screen in front of the fireplace in the living room, and I'd lie on the rug watching Hitchcock's *The 39 Steps, The Lady Vanishes, Foreign Correspondent;* Laurel and Hardy; W. C. Fields; and the Marx Brothers; to name a few of our favorites. The neat, plastic videocassettes he now owns are a sterile substitute for the sensuous delight I remember then. My father would take the reel from the round metal case, as though unwrapping a present, and place it on the projector spindle. I watched him thread the film through the maze of the projector in a lovely over and under hide-and-seek; his hands knew the special moves and codes for each location. When I threaded my old treadle Singer sewing machine for my 4-H class, I felt the same thrill of competence, of secrets mastered.

When he secured the tail of the film in the empty reel, he was ready for me to turn off the lights. A thin blue stream of light beamed from the projector, widening as it moved toward the screen, smoke and dust playing in the flickering light. First the leader tape passed through with its strange hieroglyphics of bull's-eyes and numbers and scratches, absent the dire modern video warnings about the FBI, imprisonment, and fines written in legalese. Then the title appeared with the movie's music and opening credits.

Most of his movies were on two or three reels, so in the middle of the movie we had to stop, turn on the lights, and wait while my father rewound the spent reel and threaded the next. I liked the sound of the film at the end of each reel slapping against my father's hand as it pulled free of the projector. I'd never stick my hand in the midst of all that flapping. He wasn't scared of getting cut at all, even when he had to stop the movie and splice the film together where it broke.

Rewinding the film at intervals was also a chance for me to rewind, have a drink of juice or some peanuts, reassurance that the world, as I knew it, still existed. Some of the Hitchcock movies scared me half to death, and not in a fun way. Much to my father's disgust, I always had to leave the room in the middle of *Foreign Correspondent* and put my head under a pillow to block out the screams of that sweet old man, Van Meer, when the Nazis tortured him in a windmill, offscreen, to get him to talk. Of my flights to the next room, my father would say, "Christ, all you and your mother want to see are sentimental pictures about Thanksgiving and puppy dogs." In my father's vocabulary, *sentimental* was a very damning word indeed.

Old Hitchcock movies, especially, became our secret language. As late as my senior year of high school, I'd receive a postcard saying simply, "There is a man in Scotland I must meet if anything is to be done. These men act quickly, quickly"—signed, in my dad's handwriting, "Annabella Smith, Alt-na Shelloch, Scotland" (from *The 39 Steps*). When my brother was at boarding school, I received many a letter from him signed "Huntley Haverstock" *(Foreign Correspondent)*. In short, we'd all light on the choice of Leslie Caron or Audrey Hepburn, rather than some literary character, to describe the young Claire when they first met.

Claire wore her chestnut hair smoothed back from her lovely forehead. Pretty mouth, fullish lips, and the kind of high cheekbones that promise a beauty that does not fade with youth. Claire's large eyes are a limpid, liquid blue that reflect the ambient world, the way only hazel or green eyes are supposed to do. On a stormy day her eyes look gray and wind-tossed; on a bright day at the beach, like blue sea glass and white sails. When her eyes became the color of a burnt match, it was a signal to her children to run and hide, fast. When her eyes became opaque, like those of a dead fish belly-up at the pond, it was time for me, the elder of her children, to take charge and do whatever needed to be done to survive, because she could no more see us than a dead fish can see the flies buzzing around its eyes.

> Those little eyes so helpless and appealing,
> one day will flash and send you crashing through the ceiling.
> ("Thank Heaven for Little Girls," from *Gigi*)

The night my parents met, her eyes shone like a beacon across the room. She was wearing a mid-blue linen dress with a darker blue velvet collar, simple and elegant as a wild iris. *"God,* I loved that dress. I was a model for a designer called Nan Duskin that summer in New York. She let me keep it at the end of the season . . . said it was made for me. And it was, it matched my eyes perfectly. I've never worn anything more beautiful in my life."

> "You wore a gown of gold . . ."
> "I wore blue that night, and the month was June."
> ("I Remember It Well," from *Gigi*)

Jerry, at thirty-one, was nearly twice her age and was quite simply, or rather, quite complicatedly, tall, dark, and handsome. My father captures his own image, refracted through the eyes of his beloved, fictional Glass family. Under the guise of Buddy Glass as the purported author of *Seymour: An Introduction,* he writes that several members of the Glass family, including himself, have eyes that "could all be rather bashfully described as extra-dark oxtail in color, or Plaintive Jewish Brown." What I can tell you as his daughter, without the bashfulness of a male narrator, or the self-consciousness of a person looking at his own image in the mirror, is that my father's eyes are absolutely beautiful, with thick, long, black eyelashes—inherited by my brother and, a generation later, by my son; the kind that women in the park, peeking into a carriage, click their tongues over and say, "Why is it always the *boys* who get those gorgeous long lashes?"

Buddy, continuing to describe or "introduce" his revered, dead brother, Seymour, writes: " . . . he had very wiry black hair. The word is almost kinky, but not quite; . . . It was most exceedingly pullable-looking hair, and pulled it surely got; the babies in the family always au tomatically reached for it, even before the nose, which, God wot, was also Outstanding."

❧

WHEN JERRY AND CLAIRE saw each other from across the room at the Steegmullers' party, Claire was dumbstruck.* They had each brought a date to the party, "so we couldn't really talk much," she told me. Every time she looked up, though, their eyes seemed to meet and she felt herself blush, afraid he might think she was rather forward. The next day Jerry phoned the hostess to thank her, and to ask her about that beautiful girl in the blue dress. She gave him Claire's address at Shipley.

The next week, Claire received a letter from Jerry. She wrote a letter to him in return, agonizing over it, afraid she might not sound clever

---

*The wife of a New York editor told Ian Hamilton about meeting Jerry a year or two later: "I met Jerry Salinger at a party given, I think, by or for his English publisher. . . . I was not prepared for the extraordinary impact of his physical presence. There was a kind of black aura about him. He was dressed in black; he had black hair, dark eyes, and he was of course extremely tall. I was kind of spell-bound" (Ian Hamilton, *In Search of J. D. Salinger* [New York: Random House, 1988], p. 124). The author Leila Hadley, who went on a few dates with him just before *The Catcher* was published, recalls a similar reaction. She speaks of his "extraordinary presence—very tall, with a sort of darkness surrounding him. His face was like an El Greco."

enough to a real writer. He telephoned and wrote to her off and on throughout the 1950–51 school year. She knew from his letters that he was hard at work finishing a novel. She thinks he changed the school that Holden's friend Jane Gallagher attended to Shipley for her. "It was the sort of thing he'd do, but I was too in awe and on my best behavior to ask."

She knew, too, that Jerry was seriously considering becoming a monk. He had become friends with Daisetz Suzuki and meditated, he told her, at a Zen center in the Thousand Islands. The next year, when *The Catcher in the Rye* was published, he abruptly switched to Vedanta* and often studied with Swami Nikhilananda at the Vedanta center in the East Nineties. But he had already met Claire.

> "That's right," Teddy said. "I met a lady, and I sort of stopped meditating." He took his arms down from the armrests, and tucked his hands, as if to keep them warm, under his thighs. "I would have had to take another body and come back to earth again *any*way—I mean I wasn't so spiritually advanced that I could have died, if I hadn't met that lady, and then gone straight to Brahma and never again have to come back to earth. But I wouldn't have had to get incarnated in an American body if I hadn't met that lady." ("Teddy" in *Nine Stories,* JDS)

When Claire came home to New York from Shipley for the summer, they started seeing each other. This was soon interrupted when each left for Europe, Jerry to the British Isles, to avoid being in America for the publication of *The Catcher.* "It's a goddam embarrassment, publishing," he once said to a fellow writer. "The poor boob who lets himself in for it might as well walk down Madison Avenue with his pants down."

Claire went to Italy, to be with her dying father. It did not come as a surprise to anyone who knew her father that old age finally caught up with Robert Langdon Douglas, or RLD as he was called by friends. He was nearly seventy when Claire, the last of his fifteen or so children, was born in 1933. Baron's *Knights and Peerage* records nine of them. By the time she can remember him, he was suffering from senile dementia. She

---

Vedanta: a system of Hindu monistic or pantheistic philosophy founded on the Vedas *(Webster's).*

told me once, at an age when I, too, would have "died" of embarrassment, that in the middle of a formal dinner party at their home in London, he boomed across the table in his plummy churchman's voice, "Claire, have you moved your bowels today?"

RLD's final years were characterized by similar occurrences of progressive unpredictability; however, his decision to repair to Italy to spend his last days rather than to the Black Douglas Clan's lair in Scotland was well considered. Two divergent paths of his long life led him, at the end, to San Girolamo, a convent and nursing home for retired clergy, high in the hills above Florence. He had been an Anglican priest and had had a parish in Oxford, England, for a time. Several wives and even more offspring later, it was thought best that he find some other mode of employment, and he began his second, highly successful career as an art dealer and historian. "Your grandfather," I've been told, "was largely responsible for putting the early Italian Masters, especially the Sienese, back on the map." He wrote a lovely book on Fra Angelico, and though RLD was dead long before I was born, I used to take great comfort falling asleep beneath Giotto's dark-skinned *Madonna and Child* when, as a young girl, I visited my grandmother in New York. Perhaps RLD did, too; toward the end of his life he converted to Catholicism.

When he died, he was awarded a hero's funeral in Siena, where he is entombed in a great wall. My mother said the whole city turned out in medieval procession that day, with costumes, trumpets, and pageantry, to pay homage to the man who, through his work, had restored such honor to their city. My mother gave me his funeral proclamation by the city of Siena, a two-foot-by-three-foot document worthy of an honorary Italian.

After the funeral, Claire returned to New York. Jerry was back as well and had settled into an apartment on Fifty-seventh Street. When Claire first saw it, she was speechless. It was, she told me, "one of those partly underground, ground-floor places, very underwater feeling. The whole apartment was black and white. I was appalled, frightened, excited, bug-eyed at the black sheets on his bed. They were the height of sophistication and depravity to me. For Jerry, though, I think the black sheets and the black bookshelves, black coffee table, and so on matched his depression. He really had black holes where he could hardly move, barely talk."

Claire would stay the night with him on those black sheets, but they were not intimate. Jerry was very involved with Vivekananda's Vedanta center at the time, she told me, and as his character Teddy said, meeting a woman was heading in the wrong direction for enlightenment. Sri Ramakrishna, Swami Vivekananda's guru and predecessor, expressed the same opinion, though more forcibly, in his book *The Gospels of Sri Ramakrishna* (which my father sent to his British publisher, Hamish Hamilton, as the *only* thing worth reading), saying:

> A man may live in a mountain cave, smear his body with ashes, observe fasts, and practice austere discipline, but if his mind dwells on worldly objects, on "woman and gold," I say, "Shame on him!" "Woman and gold" are the most fearsome enemies of the enlightened way, and woman rather more than gold, since it is woman that creates the need for gold. For woman one man becomes the slave of another, and so loses his freedom. Then he can not act as he likes.

When a disciple of Ramakrishna's confesses that he has been enjoying sexual intercourse with his wife, Ramakrishna replies, "Aren't you ashamed of yourself? You have children, and still you enjoy intercourse with your wife. Don't you hate yourself for thus leading an animal life? Don't you hate yourself for dallying with a body which contains only blood, phlegm, filth, and excreta?"

The summer after her freshman year at Radcliffe, Claire was back in New York, where she had a summer job as a model for Lord & Taylor. She was careful to hide this from Jerry: "Your father would *not* have approved, all that vain, worldly, women-and-clothes stuff. . . . I didn't dare tell him."

Around the time Jerry began seeing Claire, he went on a couple of dates with Leila Hadley, a writer, whom he met through his friend S. J. Perelman. When Ms. Hadley saw that same apartment on East Fifty-seventh Street, she described it as "extremely bare":

> There was just a lamp and an artist's drawing board. He used to do rather good sketches, and when I read "De Daumier-Smith's Blue Period," I was sure he had based the hero on him-

self. On the wall of his apartment there was a picture of himself in uniform.*

In contrast to the young Claire, who was "too in awe and on my best behavior to ask" any personal questions, Ms. Hadley was confident enough, mature enough, to ask him questions and offer her own opinions rather than reflect his own. She said that Jerry "never talked about himself and he resented any personal questions—about his family, or his background. . . . [He] was not easy to be with." Their relationship was a brief one.

❈

THIS RESENTMENT OF QUESTIONS about family and background, about connections from island to mainland, runs like a mother lode through our family. (Recall the opening of *The Catcher in the Rye:* "If you really want to hear about it, the first thing you'll probably want to know is where I was born, and what my lousy childhood was like, and how my parents were occupied and all before they had me . . . my parents would have about two hemorrhages apiece if I told anything pretty personal about them. They're quite touchy about anything like that, especially my father.") My aunt Doris—Daddy's only sister—and I were talking recently about being raised not to ask any questions, and most especially, not to ask questions about one's background, or as Holden put it, how one's parents "were occupied and all before they had" you. Doris told me that by the time she was about seven, shortly after her brother was born, she had "learned enough about the birds and the bees" to figure out that her mother, Miriam, must have had parents. One day she said, "Mother, you *must* have a mother and daddy somewhere. Where are they?"

Her mother snapped, "People die, don't they?"

That's it. That was all she said. Doris heard from one of her aunts on the Salinger side that Miriam was heartbroken when, years later, her mother actually did die. Miriam never said a word about it to Doris though. Later that same year Doris saw her mother packing a box full of their baby clothes. Thinking they might be for her mysterious family,

---

*Hamilton, *Salinger,* p. 127.

Doris asked her whom she was sending them to. "It is none of your business," she was told with a glare.

"Well, I just shut up and took it like I always did," Doris told me.

> She has heard a whisper say,
> A curse is on her if she stay
>> To look down to Camelot.

2

Landsman

❧❧❧

Landsman: *(Yiddish) someone who came from the same town or village or* shtetl *in Europe as you. A kinsman in foreign lands of "gray walls and gray towers." A kindred spirit.*

M Y HUSBAND AND I WENT to visit Aunt Doris after our son was born to show her the baby while she still retained some of her eyesight.* Perhaps because of the presence of new life, questions of where do we come from, who are we, and where are we going pressed upon me. My aunt is no longer one to just "shut up and take it," and she graciously provided me with some vital connections to the mainland as it were; she spoke to me as though it were naturally my business to wonder about our family. After offering us tea and sitting down, she paused and brushed some imaginary crumbs off the couch in her one-bedroom "assisted living" unit in the Berkshires. She is nearly blind now and partially deaf, but even my father, the recipient of several heated conversations and letters in which she accused him of neglecting her and the rest of his family, admits her mind is sharp. Knowing this, I respect her silences and don't try to "bring her back" as one might with a person whose mind wanders off, the years gobbling up the crumbs left behind as a trail to find one's way home through the dark forest. She was deep in thought. "You know, Peggy, your father and I were the best of friends

---

*In her old age, she suffers from macular degeneration.

growing up. I used to take him to the movies with me when he was very little. In those days, you know, the movies were silent and had subtitles that I had to read to him out loud. Boy, he wouldn't let you miss a single one. The rows used to empty out all around us!"

Doris told me that when she was a very little girl, before my father was born, the family lived in Chicago where Sol, her father, ran a movie theater and her mother, Miriam, took the tickets and sold concessions. "Of all those Jews in the business at that time," Doris said, "Daddy was the only one who didn't make it big." Instead, Sol went into the food importing business for J. S. Hoffman and Co. based in Chicago. He was successful, so much so that Hoffman asked him to manage the New York office. Sol took the promotion and moved the family to New York, where my father was born.

Doris said that her upbringing was very different from her brother's. "We had some money by the time Sonny* was born. That made a *big* difference." There were six years between them, because their mother had had two miscarriages. When she was hospitalized with pneumonia during her sixth month of pregnancy, the doctors said that there wasn't much hope for the baby. But on New Year's Day, 1919, out came a nine-pound baby boy, Jerome David, nicknamed "Sonny." "That was really something special," Doris said. "In a Jewish family, you know, a boy is special. Mother doted on him, he could do no wrong. I thought he was perfect, too." Although she spent a lot of her time looking after her little brother, she didn't mind. "Mother was very good about not asking me to baby-sit when I had friends over or some other plans." Interrupting her own train of thought—permission to change course without explanation or self-consciousness is a gift only old people seem to have the grace and authority of years to give themselves—she said, "Did Mother ever tell you the Little Indian story about Sonny?" I shook

---

*My father's nickname, Sonny, was given to him at birth by his parents. Ian Hamilton, in his book *In Search of J. D. Salinger,* claimed that it was at the McBurney School, which my father attended in ninth grade, that "he was nicknamed 'Sonny' by his chums, perhaps with a hint of sarcasm." Please, *chums?* On the West Side of Manhattan, perhaps? Several of my dad's army buddies in the foxholes and bloody battlefields of World War II were referred to, by the same scholar, as his *colleagues.* "Let me confer with my colleague, Rocco," Jerry said. "Oh, Rocco, would you be so kind as to pass me the ammo?" "Right-o, Sonny old chum," Rocco expostulated laconically. . . . I can't stand it.

my head. "Well, one afternoon I was supposed to be taking care of Sonny while Mother was out shopping. He couldn't have been older than three or four at the most. I was about ten. Well, we had a big fight about something, I forget what it was about, but Sonny got so mad he packed his suitcase and ran away. He was always running away. When Mother came home from shopping a few hours later, she found him in the lobby. He was dressed from head to toe in his Indian costume, long feather headdress and all.* He said, 'Mother, I'm running away, but I stayed to say good-bye to you.'

"When she unpacked his suitcase, it was full of toy soldiers."

❦

MY AUNT'S RETELLING OF THIS FAMILY STORY brought to mind one of my father's characters, Lionel, in a short story called "Down at the Dinghy" (reprinted in *Nine Stories*), who is about the same age as the Little Indian, Sonny. As the story opens, Lionel, like Sonny, has run away again. The housekeeper, Mrs. Snell, and the maid, Sandra, are talking about it:

> "I mean ya gotta weigh every word ya say around him," Sandra said. "It drives ya loony." . . . Sandra snorted . . . "A four-year-old kid!"
>
> "He's kind of a good-lookin' kid," said Mrs. Snell. "Them big brown eyes and all."
>
> Sandra snorted again. "He's gonna have a nose just like the father."†

Lionel's mother, Boo Boo Tannenbaum, née Glass (sister of Seymour, Franny and Zooey, Walt and Waker, and Buddy Glass), enters the room, which silences their unpleasant exchange, but leaves it unclear

---

*My aunt would later send my son an Indian costume, complete with suede leggings and feathered warbonnet, for his fourth birthday.

†In the early twenties, when Lionel and Sonny were young, many of the notices by maids seeking employment in the newspapers specified Gentile households only. "Colored woman wants week work; neat; with references; no Jewish people" (Leonard Dinnerstein, *Anti-Semitism in America,* Oxford University Press, 1944, p. 205). One maid interviewed said, "If the Jews killed the Lord and Master, what won't they do with a poor nigger like me" (Dinnerstein, p. 198).

why he has run away. Boo Boo finds Lionel down at their dinghy. He is wearing a T-shirt with a "dye picture, across the chest, of Jerome the Ostrich," hiding his head in the sand, as it were. After a long conversation in which Lionel refuses to tell his mother what happened to make him break his promise never to run away again, Boo Boo climbs into the dinghy and tries to say something comforting. She is interrupted by his sobbing outburst: "Sandra—told Mrs. Smell—that Daddy's a big—sloppy—kike."

After a little while, she asks him, "Do you know what a kike is, baby?"

Lionel was either unwilling or unable to speak up at once. At any rate, he waited till the hiccupping aftermath of his tears had subsided a little. Then his answer was delivered, muffled but intelligible, into the warmth of Boo Boo's neck. "It's one of those things that go up in the *air,*" he said. "With a *string* you hold."

✥

AS I STARTED TO tell Aunt Doris a story about my son, she interrupted me and said, "Peggy, make sure you have a job or something when your son is a little older. Don't let him become your whole life. It's no good. Mother lived through her children. She was very lucky that Sonny is as successful as he is. It was always Sonny and Mother, Mother and Sonny. Daddy got the short end of the stick always. He never got the recognition he deserved."

I asked her if their father was around much during their childhood, or if he was at work most of the time, like all the offstage, absent fathers in my father's stories, from Holden's attorney father, whom we never meet, to "Les" Glass. She said, "Oh, no, he played with us a lot, especially when we went on vacation to the shore during the summers. When we were very little, Daddy used to hold Sonny and me around our middles, out in the waves, and say, 'Keep your eyes peeled for the bananafish.' Boy, did we look and look."

Aunt Doris said that she has only one "real complaint" about her upbringing. What still troubles her wasn't the general silence regarding their family stories and background, so much as the way her parents kept one particular fact hidden from their children, then finally disclosed it in a revelation that Doris, a very levelheaded woman, given to understatement rather than to drama of any sort, said she could only describe as "traumatic." It was so awful, she said, that she can't even remember just how it happened, only that her parents "handled it terribly." When Doris was nearly twenty, shortly after Sonny's bar mitzvah, their parents told them that they weren't *really* Jewish. Their mother, Miriam, was actually named Marie, and she had been "passing" as a Jew since her marriage to Sol.

Until that moment, I never knew that my father grew to adolescence believing both of his parents were Jews. He has often told me that he writes about half-Jews because, he says, that's what he knows best. Unlike my aunt, however, I grew up knowing that my granny, their mother, was Catholic. But beyond the fact that nuns were somehow involved, I had no idea, nor did I question, what being Catholic meant. Daddy said that Granny sometimes told people she was "high Episcopalian" because it sounded "tonier," but she was actually a Catholic girl from County Cork, Ireland. Aunt Doris told me that she was surprised to hear this. She said, in typical New Yorker fashion, she had always thought her mother was born in "Iowa, or Ohio, one of those places," and wasn't sure about the Catholic part even now. However, she said, Sonny probably knew better than she did. "He was more persistent at asking questions than I was, and also he got away with a lot more than I did, being a boy." After they were told that their mother wasn't Jewish, she remembered something her mother had said, and guessed, in hindsight, that her mother *might* have been Catholic, but Doris never asked. "Mother suffered from chronic jaw pain, you know. She once mentioned to me that it was because when she was a little girl, the nuns at her school used to take a wooden mallet and hammer her teeth once a week to cure an overbite." I remember Granny rubbing her jaw and wincing. I always assumed it was out of irritation, though, because my dad makes the exact same gesture whenever someone asks him anything personal or begins "picking his brains," as he calls it.

Doris and I inherited the family overbite, and something else, too: it was Doris's aunts and uncles—Sol's brothers and sisters—who passed on the family stories and told her something of her family history after she was grown up. It was they who told her that her parents had met at a county fair near Marie's parents' farm (presumably in Ohio since Sol was there for the day from Chicago). Marie had beautiful auburn hair that hung down to her narrow waist. She turned heads when she passed by. "She was a real looker, your mother," Doris was told by her uncle. Sol was a tall, handsome young man from the big city. When they eloped, he was twenty-two, she was seventeen. Marie Jillich became Miriam Salinger* and was never to speak to her parents again.

As with most families, it's difficult to sort out who isn't talking to whom. One can be certain, however, that in those days an Irish Catholic young woman did not marry a Jewish man with impunity.† Nor could a Jew marry out of his religion without a stir, but over time, Doris said, Sol's mother grew to love Miriam as if she were one of her own daughters. When his mother died, Sol went to temple every day for a year. Doris believes that he did so because he felt guilty for marrying a non-Jew, even though his mother had accepted his choice. Who knows. From his mouth to God's ear.

What I do know is that the whole subject of Jewishness is something my father is very touchy about indeed. The only way I can think of conveying a sense of this touchiness is to liken it to the way my son, at around four years old, behaved when the subject of bottoms came up (about a thousand times a day, if I recall rightly). It was a mixture of giggly interest, the "butt" of jokes, a swirling confluence of attraction and repulsion, the precious mystery withheld, and the flushed piece of himself. Totem and Taboo. In my father's house, the arousal level occasioned

---

*There is something rather lovely about taking the name of the prophetess Miriam, who sings the triumphant song in Exodus 15:21: "Sing to the LORD, for he has triumphed gloriously; the horse and his rider he has thrown into the sea." The *Oxford Annotated Bible* dates this song fragment to the time of an eyewitness to the event in which Pharaoh's army drowned in the Red Sea while pursuing the Jewish people escaping to freedom from slavery under Pharaoh. Scholars agree it is one of the oldest surviving fragments of Scripture. The name Miriam is thought to mean "revolution."

†For comprehensive yet wonderfully readable documentation see chapter 4: "Racism and Anti-Semitism in Progressive America, 1900–1919" in Dinnerstein, *Anti-Semitism in America*. See also the memoir of an Irish American woman who married a Jew from Chicago: "The Experience of a Jew's Wife," *The American Magazine* 78 (December 1914): pp. 49–86.

by the mention of anything Jewish was matched only by the degree of occlusion of the real facts of life.

I heard, or rather felt, the pitch of emotion surrounding things Jewish when he told me stories about his childhood, but I never knew what to make of it. One story was about the time his grandfather from Chicago came to visit them in New York and my father, then a young boy, nearly died of embarrassment as his grandfather called out each street number on the Madison Avenue bus they were riding. "Forty-feef Street, Forty-seex Street," my father would call out in a loud voice with a heavy Yiddish accent as he told the story.*

As with most things deeply embarrassing in our family, this story was transformed into a sort of running family joke. In sixth grade when I went away to camp, for example, Daddy wrote a letter kidding me that his grandfather, the one who called out the street names, would be joining me at camp, as a cabin-mate. Not to worry about pajamas, he didn't really care for them anyway. Even though I was only nine at the time, I knew this was a little joke within a joke, a bit of shared snobbery about language, that some people think it sounds "tonier" to say I don't "care for" pajamas when you mean I don't *like* pajamas. I should just *enjoy* him, Daddy said.

This is not to say, however, that painful or embarrassing things were treated as humorous at the time they happened. I remember once my father, face flushed with emotion, looked up from a letter he was reading. He told me that he had been corresponding with a small group of Hasidic Jews for whom he felt real affection. This feeling of kinship, of finding landsmen, has been, in my father's life, as precious as it was rare. He said he even sent them a little money from time to time, because they were quite poor. In the letter he was holding, the rebbe had asked him what was his mother's maiden name.† "I'll cut them off," he said, slashing the air with his hand. "I'll never speak to them again." I knew he

---

*Holden talks about his "grandfather from Detroit, that keeps calling out the numbers of the streets when you ride on the goddam bus with him" (*Catcher*, p. 154)—*shanda fur die goyim,* to do something embarrassing to Jews in a place where non-Jews can observe it.

†According to Orthodox law, you are not Jewish unless your mother is; the inheritance is matrilineal. One way of trying to find out without asking bluntly "Are you Jewish?" is to ask what your mother's maiden name is.

was as good as his word; I'd seen it happen too often not to know he spoke with the finality of a man sitting *shiva* for a living son.*

❦

WHEN I FOLLOWED MY FATHER across the boundary from daily life into fictional life, I'd hoped to find, in his published stories, some clarification of the confusing, powerful feelings that things Jewish, and questions of background in general, evoke in him time and again. I came across this kind of exchange many times in my father's fiction, this vetting of your true landsman status. However, in every story except "Down at the Dinghy," the one about the four-year-old boy Lionel, the Jewishness at the heart of the matter is disguised, raising, until I spoke to my aunt, more questions than were answered. For example, whereas Daddy's grandfather in real life had a loud, embarrassing Yiddish accent, his character, Les Glass, Seymour's father, has an embarrassing Australian accent. (Australia, Gracie?) In my father's last published story, "Hapworth," the young Seymour writes from camp advising his father, a vaudeville singer, to lose the accent next time he makes a recording if he wants it to be a success. Seymour assures his father that the family is fond of his accent, but "the general public will not share that affection."

In *The Catcher in the Rye,* this touchy subject comes up several times in regard to Holden's religious background. In the scene in the train station where Holden has a pleasant conversation with two nuns at a breakfast counter, he tells them he really enjoyed talking to them. He tells the reader he really meant it; nevertheless, he would have enjoyed it more if he hadn't been sort of afraid, the whole time he was talking to them, that they'd all of a sudden try to find out if he was Catholic. It happens to him a lot, he tells us, because his last name is Irish. Actually, Holden's father had been an Irish Catholic until his marriage to Holden's mother, at which time "he quit." Holden tells the reader another story colored by the same anxiety about a conversation wending its way to questions of his background. He and a nice boy from Whooton were talking about tennis

---

*Sort of like excommunication, or the WASP favorite, disowning or disinheriting, but more to the bone, *sitting shiva* is to perform the ritual seven days of mourning following a funeral: it is a declaration that the person is dead.

when the boy asked if he had happened to notice a Catholic church in town. Here, again, Holden tells us, it didn't "ruin the conversation exactly," but he knew the boy would have enjoyed it a lot more if Holden had been Catholic. "That kind of stuff drives me crazy."

In the mirror of fiction, the Salingers switch places: my father's Irish Catholic mother becomes, instead, Holden's father, who quits his religion when he marries. The subject of anxiety changes from questions vetting one's Jewishness to whether one is Catholic or not. Reading my father's work recently, I wondered, Why the disguise? Why would the central character of his first book, which he had told friends would be an "autobiographical novel,"* not be half-Jewish? Why would the Glass family, openly half-Jewish, wish to disguise an *Australian* accent? Why does my father get touchy in his fiction and in real life when the subject of background, especially Jewish background, arises?

Had I been born in my father's generation, or had I been told what life was like for Jews of my father's generation, I wouldn't have asked these questions. The answer would have been as plain as the nose on my face. My aunt set me straight:

> It wasn't nice to be part-Jewish in those days. It was no asset to be Jewish either, but at least you belonged somewhere. This way you were neither fish nor fowl. Mother told me—she shouldn't have, it was wrong of her—but she told me that when a woman from a finishing school in Dobbs Ferry that I had applied to came to interview the family, she said, "Oh, Mrs. Salinger, it's too bad you married a Jew." People talked like that in those days, you know. It was hard on me but it was hell on Sonny. I think he suffered terribly from anti-Semitism when he went away to military school.

"People talked like that in those days, you know." In fact, I *didn't* know. What people? I had always associated outspoken anti-Semitism in this country with the lunatic fringe, familiar TV news images of fat, unemployed guys with more guns than teeth ranting about how it's the

---

*Also documented in a letter to Elizabeth Murray (Salinger letters archives, Library of Congress).

Jews' fault he has no job and no teeth, a few disturbed adolescents vandalizing Jewish cemeteries, and the occasional neo-Nazi weirdos, heiling Hitler in their pine-paneled basement rec rooms. How I managed to reach the age of forty with such a mix of ignorance and snobbery is something I'm not proud of. It is truly frightening what you miss when you don't ask the right questions and when whole subjects, such as your family history, are taboo. Never mind the ancient Greeks and Romans I learned about as a history major at Brandeis; better late than never, I set out to learn something about my own family's story, and especially that off-limits subject: what life was like when my father was growing up. With my mother, I found out in middle age, rather like Dorothy and her ruby slippers, that all I had to do was ask and she'd take me to her childhood home, she'd bring to light all those things she'd been silent about that had come to me in nightmares for so long. With my father, I first turned to written stories rather than spoken ones for answers.

Oh, what a breath of fresh air a good library is! I know, *musty* is the usual adjective that is attached to libraries, but not for me. In a free country, one does not have to just "shut up and take it," as my aunt was told by her mother, remaining in ignorance. All that information there, just for the asking! No one slaps your hand at the card catalogue, or tells you to shut up about your questions as you browse the stacks. I spent several glorious months in the library, finding answers to questions I'd never have dared ask a family member. What I found was that my experience of a conspiracy of silence, an unspoken agreement not to talk about vital parts of our history, the feeling, like the Lady of Shalott, that a curse will fall upon you should you look out from your island to the mainland from whence you came, and connect your story to the web of community, is an experience I share with many of my generation. As I read more and looked more deeply into the history of this country during the early to mid part of the twentieth century, I kept asking friends of mine, well educated, both Jew and Gentile, "Did you know about this? Did your parents tell you about these things?" The silence was deafening. For me, as one who grew up in a world where fiction and dreams held sway, facts, things that really happened, are more than a breath of fresh air; they saved me from suffocating from those "tendrils strong as flesh and blood."

I HAD ASSUMED THAT THE TOUCHINESS about background was an idiosyncrasy of Salingers (and Caulfields). A few facts were particularly helpful to me in changing this mistaken assumption. When I began looking at Jewish American life in the early part of the twentieth century, around the time my grandparents met and married, I found that many Americans were very much occupied with the vicissitudes of anti-Semitism at that time, and as my aunt said, "talked that way" shamelessly. Prior to 1890, only 2 percent of the approximately 16 million immigrants to America were Jews, the majority of whom were from the more prosperous northern, central, and western parts of Europe. The turn of the century saw a huge increase in immigration, especially of poorer southern and eastern Europeans, including over a million and a half Jews—about 10 percent of the new immigrants.* Not unlike today, there was much talk at the time about the "problem" of immigrants, whether America could absorb such "barbarian hordes" and retain its values (not to mention preserve the status quo social and economic structure). While New York and New England patricians "generalized about the negative worth of most of the newcomers from Europe and Asia, their most severe racial animus was directed toward the Jews."†

In mainstream magazines, such as those in which my father published his first stories, as well as in daily newspapers and other forms of mass entertainment, anti-Semitism ran rampant. That bastion of the mythical "good old days" Americana, *The Saturday Evening Post* (which would later publish several of my father's early stories), published a series of articles from 1920 to 1921 alleging that the Jews of Poland (such as my grandfather) were, among other things, "human parasites . . . mongoloids not fit to govern themselves."‡

In the interwar years, being identifiably Jewish—having a Jewish name, for example—was generally a great economic and social disadvantage in dealing with wider Gentile America. Many Jewish college

---

*From 1890 to 1914, a total of 16.5 million people immigrated to America.

†Dinnerstein, *Anti-Semitism*, p. 59.

‡"Why Europe Leaves Home" by Kenneth L. Roberts appeared first as a series of articles in *The Saturday Evening Post* before it was published as a book in 1922.

students changed their names before they were graduated. One study of name changes in the 1930s in Los Angeles, where Jews were 6 percent of the population but 46 percent of name changes, found that most applicants were married, prosperous Jewish males who lived in mixed Jewish and Christian neighborhoods. Even in the entertainment business, an area in which Jews could find work, Jewish names were often changed for business reasons.

Jews were alleged, by their detractors, to control not only Hollywood but the media in general, and newspapers in particular. At the *New York Times,* many writers believed that publishers Adolph Ochs and Arthur Hays Sulzberger were so sensitive to such anti-Semitic accusations that they encouraged writers with identifiably Jewish names to use initials instead of their given names in bylines. Thus we read stories by A. (Abraham) H. Raskin, A. H. Weiler, A. M. Rosenthal.*

My father's first byline in a published work, "The Young Folks" in *Story* magazine, was Jerome Salinger. By the next piece, a short story called "The Hang of It," in *Collier's,* he was J. D. Salinger. This was something I wondered about growing up, since all his friends called him Jerry as a nickname, not J.D. I knew he thought Jerome was an ugly name, but I thought it was just a matter of personal taste. Jerome is not on my list of top ten beautiful names for boys either, but I chose his middle name, David, for my son's middle name. *"Terrible* name," my father said, scowling, when he heard the news. He often said how much he hated giving his beloved characters "terrible" (*"Jewish*-sounding" remained unsaid) names, such as Seymour, but that's just what Seymour's parents would have done, he said, so he *had* to do it even though it "nearly killed him."

The self-esteem of many Jews, most especially those in mixed neighborhoods of middle-to-upper incomes, not surprisingly, suffered.† One such man, speaking for many, wrote how "embarrassed he had been by other Jews who spoke English badly, who used gestures to emphasize their points, and who interspersed Yiddish words or expressions in their

---

*Dinnerstein, *Anti-Semitism,* p. 126.
†Beth S. Wenger, *New York Jews and the Great Depression* (Yale University Press, 1996), especially her chapter "The Spiritual Depression," about the assault on Jewish self-image during these years.

speech."* Which brings me back to my great-grandfather Salinger calling out street names on the Madison Avenue bus, "Forty-feef Street, Forty-seex," and likewise, to Holden's grandfather from Detroit, "that keeps calling out the numbers of the streets when you ride on the goddam bus with him."

As my aunt Doris said, "It wasn't nice to be half-Jewish in those days. It was no asset to be Jewish either, but at least you belonged somewhere." My great-grandfather could have been on dozens of bus lines throughout greater New York and fit right in. He might have been joined in his joyful recitation by busloads of landsmen who talked the same way. On the Madison Avenue bus, however, he was met with icy or embarrassed stares. There were places a Jew was at home in New York and places he was not.

When my father was growing up, many buildings and even whole areas such as Park Slope and Brooklyn Heights were restricted, as the infamous signs in windows read: "No Catholics, Jews, or dogs allowed." The courts upheld the right of landlords to restrict until 1948 in *Shelly v. Kraemer,* when such exclusions were held unenforceable in courts of law. However, the informal effect of being unwelcome, or as my aunt said, "how people talked in those days," is often, in reality, indistinguishable from legal banning in outcome.†

Kurt Lewin, the psychologist, advised American Jews of that time how and when to inform their children of the situations they might encounter:

> The basic fact is that child is going to be a member of a less privileged minority group, and he will have to face this fact. Do not try to avoid a discussion of the subject of anti-Semitism because

---

*"I Was a Jew," *The Forum* 103 (March 1940): p. 10. See also "I Married a Jew," *The Atlantic Monthly* 163 (January 1939): pp. 38–46; "I Married a Gentile," *The Atlantic Monthly* 163 (March 1939): pp. 321–26. Also, Dinnerstein, *Anti-Semitism,* p. 293.

†Helen Reid, the wife of the owner of the *New York Herald Tribune,* for example, expressed her fears of Jewish migration and its effect not just on property values, but on the values held by her sons: "I hate the thought of [my] Whitelaw and Brownie growing up with nothing but Jewish neighbors around" (Dinnerstein, *Anti-Semitism,* p. 93).

the problem is bound to arise at some time. The child might not be called a "dirty Jew" until about the fourth grade [later than my father's unlucky character Lionel, who heard the dirty word *kike* at age four] . . . he or she could expect to be invited to parties of their Gentile peers until adolescence when the invitations would cease, and both boys and girls, after their high school years, will face discrimination in colleges and in the work place.*

Most Jewish young people in New York during the 1920s and 1930s, however, would experience the rise of anti-Semitism, discrimination, and the Depression from within the closely woven fabric of Jewish community. Such neighborhoods provided a buffer zone from the impact of wider Gentile society. One woman, reflecting on her childhood in a New York neighborhood that was well over 80 percent Jewish, said she didn't even know she was a member of a minority group until she left high school and tried to find work outside the community. She grew up thinking the whole world was Jewish.†

My father's childhood Upper West Side neighborhood, for example, was over 50 percent Jewish at the time and, by 1929, was a thriving community with scores of kosher butchers and bakers and restaurants, and ten synagogues. I knew that my father did not attend Jewish religious services as a child and that his family, in fact, celebrated Christmas, so I assumed, even after I had learned that he had grown up thinking he was Jewish, that their sense of belonging to the Jewish community was limited. In fact, I found out that the Salinger family's lack of religious attendance was not unusual. In 1929, approximately 80 percent of Jewish youth in New York City were found to have had no religious training at all.‡

My father attended Upper West Side public schools until the end of

---

*"Bringing Up the Child," *The Menorah Journal* 28 (winter 1940): pp. 29–45.
†Wenger, *New York Jews,* p. 85.
‡Wenger, *New York Jews,* p. 184. Another contemporary survey found that in 1935 more than 75 percent of New York Jewish youth had not attended any religious service in the past year. Before the Depression, a minority of Jews was affiliated with a synagogue, and even fewer attended regularly. When synagogues tried to attract new members during the Depression, Jews were appealed to in ethnic rather than specifically religious terms: membership, they were told, was "essential to fortify Jewish self-respect in the face of anti-Semitism."

eighth grade, where well over half of his classmates were Jewish. The following school year, 1932–33, the family moved to a Park Avenue neighborhood that was less than 4 percent Jewish, and he started high school at McBurney, a private Young Men's Christian Association movement school. In January he turned fourteen, and at about the same time that Hitler was sworn in as chancellor of Germany, Jerome David Salinger had his bar mitzvah. Sometime within the next year, he and Doris found out their mother was not Jewish. His records at McBurney state that Jerome "was hard hit by adolescence with us this year." Hard hit indeed.

At the end of tenth grade, when Jerry was fifteen, he transferred from McBurney to Valley Forge Military Academy, in Wayne, Pennsylvania. I'm sorry to say, I don't know how the whole idea of military school arose. There is a certain poetic symmetry with the Little Indian running away with a suitcase full of toy soldiers, but I just don't know. It seems like a case of out of the frying pan and into the fire to me. What I found out about military schools of the day certainly supports what my aunt told me, that she thought anti-Semitism at Valley Forge was "hell on Sonny." Central Pennsylvania, where Valley Forge was located, was rated by a U.S. army war board survey as an epicenter of anti-Semitism in America.* Regardless of location, hazing at military academies was particularly brutal for the few Jews who chose to apply.† Admiral Hyman Rickover, one of the nine Jews to graduate from the Annapolis Naval Academy in 1922 out of an entering class of nineteen Jews, indicated that it was hell. In this "fun" class, the senior photograph of a Jewish cadet, who graduated second in his class, was printed on perforated paper so his face could be torn out of the yearbook.

The choice of school and place is a mystery to me. But that is not how my father tells it. Once, when I complained about having been sent away to boarding school at a young age (twelve), my father said he just couldn't understand my attitude. He was *delighted,* he said (at sixteen),

---

*The 1943 Office of War Information report found widespread anti-Semitism in half of the forty-two states surveyed and described intense anti-Semitism and "unreasonable hate" particularly among the middle class in Pennsylvania (Dinnerstein, *Anti-Semitism,* p. 136).

†Ibid., p. 87. See also Norman Polmar and Thomas B. Allen, *Rickover* (New York: Simon and Schuster, 1982), pp. 51, 52–53; Robert Wallace, "A Deluge of Honors for an Exasperating Admiral," *Life* 45 (September 8, 1958): p. 109.

to be away from home, out from under his parents' wing. He almost always spoke of his mother's overprotectiveness as he did most uncomfortable subjects, by kidding around, and not just with family. In the letter he wrote to "Papa" Hemingway from a hospital bed at the end of the war, he jokes about telling the staff psychiatrists the usual details about his normal childhood, such as how his mother walked him to school every day until he was twenty-four—you know how dangerous streets in Manhattan can be, he said.

When we visited my grandparents in New York, Daddy's reaction to Granny's well-meant questions—benign things such as asking me about school—seemed to me, even as a little girl, to be *way* out of line. He'd snap, "Stop that now, Mother! That's enough, leave them alone, for crying out loud!" I felt sorry for Granny and could see that these little questions gave her pleasure, and I certainly didn't mind. But what really shocked me was the way it seemed he could do no wrong where she was concerned. I would have been "knocked into the middle of next week," as he used to say, if I'd spoken that way to my mother or father. Near the end of Granny's life, when I was in my teens, he was still behaving as if her small questions were giant probes. When he returned from his first visit to see his mother in over a year, he spoke of being "bombarded" with her questions, and how he narrowly escaped a few hours later, hoarse and exhausted. He indeed sounded like, and even had the haggard look of, a man who had survived a particularly grueling interrogation session. Yet he still had the energy to kid around as he reported, straight-faced, that Granny had asked him, "How tall is Peggy? Did she like the navy-blue cardigan screwdriver we sent for Christmas? How tall is Matthew [age eleven or so]? Does he need any more Play-Doh or finger paints?"

This sense of maternal intrusion—a thing so strong it had a bodily feel to it—and the dark humor with which he typically expressed it, runs right down the middle of his fiction as well, especially in the character of Bessie, the matriarch of the Glass family.

> Re-seated, Mrs. Glass sighed, as she always sighed, in any situation, when cups of chicken broth were declined. But she had, so to speak, been cruising in a patrol boat down and up her children's alimentary canals for so many years that the sigh was

in a sense a real signal of defeat . . . she had the particular facial expression that her eldest daughter, Boo Boo, had once described as meaning one of only two things: that she had just talked with one of her sons on the telephone or that she had just had a report, on the best authority, that the bowels of every single human being in the world were scheduled to move with perfect hygienic regularity for a period of one full week.

(Zooey, pp. 184–85)*

In my father's fiction, there is never any doubt of the love the Glass children feel for their mother, Bessie. Nor did I ever doubt for a moment that in real life my father loved his mother; he was quite clear about that even though she sometimes drove him crazy. He would often tell me, in a tone of voice he reserved for those whom he respected, that Granny, though uneducated, "was no dope," his way of acknowledging someone's intelligence. He'd tell me stories of her good sense or her good taste; often, I might add, told by way of contrast to his father, whom he considered a great big dope, and never, to my knowledge, spoke of him with any respect. The report is unanimous from my aunt to my mother, to Grandpa's business partners and my father's classmates interviewed for various books and myriad articles: his mother "obviously adored her only son." "They were *very* close." As my aunt told me, "It was always Sonny and Mother, Mother and Sonny. Daddy always got the short end of the stick." Perhaps there is such a thing as too close, "too close for comfort" as the saying goes, and hence the sense of intrusion, and the "delight" he remembers of "getting out from under their wing" and going away to school.

The one thing I know for certain about his going to military school is that it was not something that was forced on him against his will. He was not *sent* there. First of all, Granny wouldn't force her son to do anything of the sort; it's dangerous at military school—all those sabers and guns. Second of all, she wouldn't have let Grandpa force him to go ei-

---

*See also *Zooey,* pp. 73 and 75, for similar language of intrusion. Here, Bessie Glass is perched on a closed toilet seat while her grown son Zooey is trying to take a bath. He looks around the shower curtain and sees that she is holding a package that "appeared to contain an object roughly the size of the Hope diamond or an irrigation attachment. . . . Mrs. Glass had undressed the package and now stood reading the fine print."

ther. There was no doubt, my aunt said, about who "wore the pants" in their house.

Once he decided he wanted to go, the mechanics of the move are less of a mystery. Hamilton, in his biography, notes that it was Mrs. Salinger and not her husband who took Doris and Sonny to look at the school, and it was she who met with the school representative when he came for a home visit. He cites this as evidence of tension between father and son. Certainly there was tension; however, I think the fact that she alone met with the school officials presents evidence as to the social climate rather than the familial one. It seems far more likely that she dealt with school officials for the same reason that I, alone, dealt with real estate agents and landlords when searching for an apartment in Boston during the mid-seventies when I was, briefly, married to an African American. I'd tell them that my husband was, unfortunately, out of town on business until the end of the month, and I'd sign the necessary papers. While I share my grandmother's propensity to control things, let's just say I doubt Granny felt it would be a great asset to her son's chances of getting into Valley Forge for him to wear a great big sign on his backside that said, "Kick me, I'm Jewish."

The stories he told me about his life at Valley Forge were about "characters" and "types" and little adventures. They were stories, in hindsight, devoid of affect. I heard about the time he, like Holden, lost the fencing team's gear on the subway, and the time he and his friend Bill Dix sneaked out of the dorm to have breakfast in town. The pain and suffering I would later read in the story of Holden's experience in boarding school were not mentioned in the stories my father told me (although, as I said, he told a friend at the time he was working on *The Catcher in the Rye* that he was writing an autobiographical story).

In the version my father told me of his world at seventeen, he knew he wanted to be—knew he *would* be—a writer. His mother was the "good guy" in the story, supporting her son in his wishes, whatever they might be. His mother knew her boy to be a genius; as Doris said, from his birth, Sonny was thought "perfect" and "could do no wrong." History proved his mother right about his talent; however, at the time he was to finish high school, her belief was a matter of faith, rather than reason. My father often told me growing up that his father pressured him to learn the business of J. S. Hoffman and Co., importing Polish meats and other high-end foods. This was always said with resentment, as well as with varying degrees of derision, further proof that Grandpa was a dope. I believed this unquestioningly.

When I became an adult, however, and began to delve into our family history on my own, I found out that Grandpa wasn't quite the big dope my father always said he was. There was a plethora of good reasons for his concern. I certainly understand that when you're a teenager who wants to devote himself to writing, and your father doesn't understand and hassles you to spend a little time learning the family business, you think your father is a big dope. And it is really galling that you have to live at home because you can't support yourself yet, and that makes him an even bigger dope and a "policeman," as my father described to me his feelings, as a boy, about his own father, especially when it came to money. But most of us gain some perspective. I'm sure my grandfather asked him some really "dopey" questions such as how a young man, half-Jewish, during the depths of the Depression and heights of anti-Semitism,* with no college degree, no training, no trade, would support himself, let alone a family.

Economically, this was a particularly bad time to be what my aunt called "neither fish nor fowl." Contrary to the myth of America's history of continual progress toward greater opportunities for its citizens, for Jews the clock was running backward in the twenties and thirties. In the 1920s, although Jews made up 26 percent of the population of New York City and were also by far the best-educated group in the community, 90 percent of white-collar openings went to non-Jews.[†] As opportunities for employment narrowed for Jews in the Gentile world, Jewish professionals opened Jewish offices, with largely Jewish staff, serving primarily Jewish clientele. Large loans for businesses were obtained through Jewish sources, such as the Jewish "Bank of the United States" and the

---

*From 1933 to 1941 over one hundred anti-Semitic organizations were created, as contrasted with perhaps a total of five in all previous American history.

[†]Another study, of twenty-seven thousand openings, also found that 90 percent went to non-Jews. Discriminatory newspaper ads for jobs proliferated, reaching a peak in 1926. Public utilities, banks, insurance companies, publishing houses, engineering and architectural firms, advertising agencies, school districts, major industrial companies, civic bodies for art and music, hospitals, universities, and law firms routinely rejected Jewish applicants. Humble Oil, Eli Lilly, and Western Union, for example, developed official policies of zero acceptance of Jews (Dinnerstein, *Anti-Semitism*, p. 89).

Hebrew Loan Society. For the vast majority of Jewish immigrant working classes, however, the main source of assistance were societies called
landsmanshaftn (hometown societies). These grassroots associations were
organized according to immigrants' European towns of origin, and provided a wide variety of religious, social, and cultural activities along
with a range of relief services, financial assistance, and sick benefits. In
their heyday, more than three thousand such hometown societies existed
(the vast majority still recorded their committee minutes in Yiddish
throughout the 1930s). *Landsmanshaftn* offered their members a source
of community on American soil and an economic lifeline—the difference between hunger and food on the table, rags and clothing, homeless-
ness and shelter—during hard times.*

My grandfather had ample reason to be concerned that his son go to
a good college and train to be a professional (e.g., a doctor, lawyer, ac-
countant) with real career opportunities or go straight into the family
business.† I knew how my father felt about the family business; he'd occasionally tell me stories about it. His reaction to the entire subject of
higher education was something else again—no half-joking stories
here—and the whole notion of "getting into a good college" has always
been a minefield. He would, indeed, as he once said, "break out with a
strange and hideous rash" at the mere mention of anything Ivy League.
Truth be told, I thought he was a big bore on the subject, which struck

---

*It is difficult, I think, to underestimate the intensity and depth of the mean-
ing of this word, *landsman,* in its historical context. When I read in Joyce Maynard's memoir that during her first visit to Cornish, meeting my father in person
after months of correspondence by letter, he took her hand and said, "We are
landsmen, all right," I wondered if she understood the weight of this declaration.

†He was, however, a bit out-of-date in his view of opportunities for Jews to become professionals. Doors were slamming shut. From 1920 to 1940, for example,
the percentage of Jews at Columbia University's College of Physicians and Sur-
geons fell from 46 percent to 6 percent. At CCNY, the percentage of Jewish grad-
uates admitted to any medical school dropped from 58 percent to 15 percent. Law
schools followed the trend as well. In 1935, 25 percent of all American law students were Jewish; by 1946, that number had fallen to 11 percent. When New
York State passed a law in 1948 banning tax exemptions to nonsectarian colleges
and universities that employed racial or religious criteria in selecting students for
admission, the number of Jewish students in New York medical schools rose
from 15 percent in 1948 to approximately 50 percent by 1955 (Dinnerstein, *Anti-
Semitism,* pp. 158–60).

me, as a child and as a teenager, as a weird thing to get all het up about—like raving about state capitals or something—especially since it wasn't so much about colleges in general as it was focused on the "good" ones or "prestigious" ones, most especially the Ivy League. He spoke of Ursinus, for example (a small college he attended for a year or so), with affection. I dismissed his "thing" about the Ivies as one of Daddy's idiosyncratic hot spots, just one more in a man with quite his share of them. Common sense made me avoid the subject around him the same way you don't wave a red flag at a bull.

When I finally read my father's stories, there it was again: those villainous Ivy Leaguers, bastions of phonydom, one-dimensional, successful, cocksure, anti-landsmen; *goyim* like Lane Coutell, boyfriend of Franny Glass, or Tupper, her contemptible English professor, both of whom undermined her sense of place in the world and, ultimately, threatened her sanity. I was fascinated to find out that there were some real roots to this reaction of his. History doesn't necessarily excuse, but it certainly provides a context and explanation. It turns out that when my father was growing up and coming of an age to consider college, some of the most outspoken, eloquent, egregious examples of people who, as my aunt said, "talked that way" about Jews were positively bedecked with Ivy. Dean Frederick Paul Keppel* of Columbia University, for example, wrote of his concern that too many Jewish immigrants make Columbia "socially uninviting to students who come from homes of refinement." Dartmouth president Ernest Hopkins[†] said, "Any college which is going to base its admissions wholly on scholastic standing will find itself with an infinitesimal proportion of anything else than Jews eventually."[‡] It was Harvard, however, whose Jewish population had grown from 6 percent of the student body in 1908 to 22 percent in 1922, that took the lead in proposing a solution to the "Jewish problem." A. Lawrence Lowell,[§] President of Harvard, announced the establishment of numerical

---

*Frederick Paul Keppel, Dean of Columbia College, 1910–18; Assistant Secretary of War, 1918–19; President of the Carnegie Corporation, 1923–42.

[†]Ernest Martin Hopkins, President of Dartmouth College, 1916–45.

[‡]Quoted in Harold S. Wechsler, *The Qualified Student* (New York: John Wiley and Sons, 1977), p. 135. Also Dinnerstein, *Anti-Semitism,* chap. 5, "Erecting Barriers and Narrowing Opportunities, 1919–1933."

[§]Abbott Lawrence Lowell, President of Harvard, 1909–33.

quotas to lower the numbers of Jews at the university. Once Harvard took the lead, many of the nation's most prestigious colleges and universities followed and established their own limits of no more than 3 to 16 percent Jews admitted to the entering class.*

Sarah Lawrence College, in Bronxville, New York—a town that kept Jews out until after the New York State Commission for Human Rights intervened in 1962—asked on its application, "Has your daughter been brought up to strict Sunday observance?" Columbia asked the applicant's religious affiliation, if he or his parents had ever been known by another name, parents' place of birth, mother's full maiden name, and father's occupation.

How one takes for granted today the precious words "without regard for race, creed, color, or national origin." In my father's day, it was equally taken for granted that these things were to be major factors in deciding an applicant's suitability for housing, jobs, colleges, clubs, loans, and so on. Even when a Jew made it over the quota hurdle and gained admission to these colleges, he or she was confronted with a row of additional hurdles and barriers stretching to the vanishing point. Max Lerner (Yale, BA, 1923) said he and other Jewish classmates were basically "kept out of everything."† A contemporary wrote that at social gatherings such as the prom or the class-day tea, "the presence of Jews and their relatives ruins the tone which must be maintained if social standing is not to collapse."

Myriad examples of anti-Jewish sentiments abound in statistics, articles, speeches, and conversations of the day. Yet what I found to be the most revealing and affecting when I read them were not the statistics nor the diatribes, but rather, the way people talked when they tried to say something *nice* about a Jew. We have on record, for example, professors' letters of recommendation for historians Oscar Handlin, Bert Lowenberg, and Daniel Boorstin, then students, for jobs in higher education. They contain phrases like "has none of the offensive traits which people associate with his race," "by temperament and spirit . . . measures up to the

---

*These included Columbia, Princeton, Yale, Duke, Rutgers, Barnard, Adelphi, Cornell, Johns Hopkins, Northwestern, Penn State, Ohio State, Washington and Lee, and the Universities of Cincinnati, Illinois, Kansas, Minnesota, Texas, and Washington. New York University discriminated on its Bronx campus but not at Washington Square (Dinnerstein, *Anti-Semitism,* chap. 5).

†Jews were barred from most clubs and fraternities.

whitest gentile I know," and "He is a Jew, though not the kind to which one takes exception." A professor at the University of Chicago wrote of his student, "He is one of the few men of Jewish descent who does not get on your nerves and really behaves like a gentile to a satisfactory degree."*

English departments, for which my father reserves his most caustic vitriol, in both his real life and in his fiction, considered themselves to be bastions of Anglo-Saxon culture and, as such, were the least welcoming to Jews. When, for example, Max Lerner informed a college instructor with whom he was on *good* terms that he'd like to teach English at a university, the instructor replied, "Max, you can't do this. You can't teach literature. You have no chance of getting a position at any good college. You're a Jew." In 1939, when my father was taking a writing course in the evenings at Columbia, Lionel Trilling became the first Jew appointed to a tenure-tract position in English there. His wife, Diana Trilling, later wrote, "It is highly questionable whether the offer would have been made" had her husband borne the surname of his maternal grandfather, Cohen. When Trilling became assistant professor, a colleague stopped by to chat and expressed the department's hope that the new appointee would not use this opportunity "as a wedge to open the English department to more Jews."†

Such was the atmosphere when my father was graduated from military school. Ian Hamilton writes blithely of that time in my father's life as if there were no constraints, only matters of choice and taste:

> At this point, Salinger's conception of a writing career was focused on these two key citadels: New York and Hollywood. It was a conception that had more to do with the world of mass entertainment (movies, plays, big-circulation weeklies, even radio) than with the world of Letters as this would have been perceived by, say, the editors of *Partisan Review* or by most university English departments. Partly by accident, partly by inclination, Salinger's literary route was from the outset established as metropolitan, not academic. And this separation had mattered quite a lot. To grasp how much, we need only wonder

---

*Dinnerstein, *Anti-Semitism,* p. 88.
†Diana Trilling, "Lionel Trilling, a Jew at Columbia," *Commentary* 67 (March 1979): pp. 44, 46.

what Salinger's writing life would have been like if he had gone to Harvard or Yale. So maybe the arithmetic report [a bad grade in high school] does matter after all. Certainly, his career might have been very different if his first stories had been aimed not at *Collier's* but at *Partisan Review*.   (Hamilton, *Salinger*, p. 37)

Jerome David Salinger, Regis Professor of Literature at Sarah Lawrence. We need only wonder. He could have changed his name, but there was still the little problem with the nose and that darkness. In 1936, my father began his freshman year at NYU. That spring, regardless of his father's objections and of the economic realities of the day, he dropped out of college and took a job on a cruise ship. In the fall, however, Grandpa's wishes prevailed and my father went to Vienna, ostensibly to learn the family business, and to polish up his high school German and French by doing some translating for one of Hoffman's partners. I heard little, growing up, about the family business other than as a joke his dopey father got him into. The Jewish family he stayed with in Vienna, however, was another story. He *loved* this family.* And from all accounts the feeling was mutual. He often told me the mother used to call him Jerrila and explained that this was a Yiddish way of expressing affection. I'd have been called Peggila, he told me. I wish I had met them, but they all were killed in concentration camps before I was born.

⊰⊱

AUSTRIA FELL TO HITLER ON MARCH 12, 1938. My father was probably out of Vienna by February, but there is no way he could have been unaware of the Nazi gangs that raided the Jewish quarter where he lived that winter. He only told me about the loving family, not the horror.

I don't know how he was occupied that summer, but in the fall of '38 he attended Ursinus College, in Collegeville, Pennsylvania. The college was founded in 1869 by the German Reformed Church and served the

---

*See JDS story "A Girl I Knew," *Good Housekeeping* 126 (Feb. 1948): pp. 37, 191–96.

Christian, middle-class Pennsylvania Dutch from nearby suburban areas. Go figure. My father had only good things to say about Ursinus and its lack of pretension. I never thought to ask why he left after one semester.

In the spring of 1939, he enrolled in a Friday-evening writing class at Columbia taught by Whit Burnett, the editor of *Story* magazine. Burnett supported the young writer's aspirations and gave him his first break. His story "The Young Folks," a piece about some debutante "types" home from college for the holidays, attending a house party, appeared in the March-April 1940 issue of *Story*. Making a living as a short-story writer in those days was a long shot, but by no means an impossible dream. Even during the Depression, entertainment sold, and magazines were paying what Brendan Gill called a "king's ransom" for stories. He said, "It's hard for writers nowadays to realize how many magazines were vying for short stories in the thirties and forties; hard too to realize how much they paid." *Collier's, Liberty,* and *The Saturday Evening Post* were paying around $2,000 (about $26,500 in today's dollars) for a short story.

In the summer of 1940, my father was out of town and spent time on the Cape and in Canada. He wrote to a friend, Elizabeth Murray, the sister of a boy he had gone to school with, that he had started work on an autobiographical novel. The following summer he sold a one-page story called "The Hang of It" about an army brat coming of age and following in his father's footsteps, which appeared in the July 12 issue of *Collier's*. *Esquire* followed with "The Heart of a Broken Story." *The New Yorker* bought his short story introducing Holden Caulfield, "A Slight Incident off Madison," then changed their minds about publishing it, holding the story until 1945.

The next story to appear in print was a shot aimed directly at the heart of New York WASP "Society" with its exclusive, exclusionary clubs, charity balls, colleges, and social life. "The Long Debut of Lois Taggett" appeared in the September-October 1942 issue of *Story* magazine, Whit Burnett's domain. It follows almost as a sequel to "The Young Folks" in tone and character, but it is many shades darker. A New York debutante-type phony is put through purgatory, a hazing as it were, by the author of the story, who at story's end allows Lois, cleansed and purged, to join the elite club of non-phonies, Salinger's *landsmanshaftn*. It seems a reversal, or inverse reflection of the true facts of anti-Semitic culture of the day, where Jewish academics, such as Boorstin and Lerner, were deemed acceptable only if "purged" of their Jewishness. It begins:

> Lois Taggett was graduated from Miss Hascomb's School . . . and the following autumn her parents thought it was time for her to come out, charge out, into what they called Society. So they gave her a five-figure, la-de-da Hotel Pierre affair, and save for a few horrible colds and Fred-hasn't-been-well-lately's, most of the preferred trade attended. . . . That winter Lois did her best to swish around Manhattan with the most photogenic of the young men who drank scotch-and-sodas in the God-and—Walter Winchell section of the Stork Club. . . . In the spring, Lois' Uncle Roger agreed to give her a job as a receptionist in one of his offices. It was the first big year for debutantes to Do Something.

Lois Taggett breaks one of my father's personal "ten commandments," which I grew up hearing about in many an emotional hellfire-and-brimstone lecture from him: Thou shalt not "dabble" in the arts. I cringed as I read about Lois's amateur foray into a course or two at Columbia. My father, in real life, could be brought to the point of almost foaming incoherency when confronted with anyone, but most especially an Ivy League "type," usually a woman, amusing herself by taking a course in literature or art. It is sacrilege, defiling, to approach this sacred domain with other than a monk's dedication.*

Quite unexpectedly, Lois falls in love with a man outside her own circle, "tall handsome Bill Tedderton, a press agent." They marry, she for love, he for her money.

---

*See also "Pretty Mouth and Green My Eyes" reprinted in *Nine Stories:* "Brains! Are you kidding? She hasn't got any goddam brains! She's an animal! . . . You want to know who I'm married to? I'm married to the *greatest living undeveloped, undiscovered act*ress, *nov*elist, psycho*an*alyst, and all around goddam unappreciated celebrity-genius in New York. . . . Christ it's so funny I could cut my throat. Madame Bovary at Columbia Extension School. . . . Madame Bovary takes a course in Television Appreciation. . . . *Brains.* Oh, God, that kills me!"

The Taggetts didn't do very much about it. It wasn't fashionable any longer to make a row if your daughter preferred the iceman to that nice Astorbilt boy. Everybody knew, of course, that press agents [or writers] were icemen. Same thing.

Several months into the marriage, Bill Tedderton discovers to his astonishment that he has fallen in love with Lois. After a short interlude of marital bliss, he finds himself burning her with a cigarette, loving her deeply; and a few weeks later, never loving her more, smashing his golf club down on her foot.* He pleads passionately with her to take him back, he'll see a psychiatrist, he didn't know what he was doing. Lois divorces him.

She eventually marries a dull, unattractive guy with all the right society credentials. Once again, a year or so later, danger arises in the form of emotional attachment, when she finds herself head over heels in love with her baby. We are treated to a scene of baby and mommy bliss, broken suddenly by the voice of the narrator, who, like the voice of God's judgment, pronounces: "Then finally she made it." Her long debut has come to an end, she has come out of it and is no longer a phony. "Everybody seemed to know about it," the narrator tells us. "Women in general began to look more closely at Lois' face than at her clothes. . . . It happened about six months after young Thomas Taggett Curfman tossed peculiarly in his sleep and a fuzzy woolen blanket snuffed out his little life."

❦

THE PRICE OF ENTRY into this writer's chosen elect, the elite *landsmanshaftn* of non-phonies, involves neither money nor background nor education: he requires the sacrifice of her firstborn son. Something about this story gave me the creeps as I read it, as though a cold hand had somehow reached across the boundary of fiction into our life as a family. It was with a vague sense of foreboding that I continued to search out our family stories. I was beginning to feel like one combing the woods for missing persons, dreading lifeless, forensic success as much as the failure of continued unknowing.

---

*Like young Seymour, who throws a rock at a beautiful girl in the sunshine (scarring her for life) "because she looked so beautiful" (*Raise High the Roof Beam, Carpenters,* pp. 41, 89).

3

Tinker, Tailor, Soldier, Spy

❧❧

I N THE SPRING OF 1942, Jerome David Salinger was drafted into the United States army. He, along with thousands of other young men from all over the country, reported for induction and began the metamorphosis from civilian to soldier. For the entire time I lived with my father, I saw no going back, no discernible return from soldier to civilian. His civilian occupation as a writer was, at best, a distant concept for me when I was growing up. I still have the note my piano teacher wrote home about how amused she was at my not knowing. The teacher said that before our recital, to ward off nervousness, the children were all talking about what their fathers did for a living. When my turn came, she said, "Peggy spoke up proudly, 'My Daddy, he doesn't do *anything*.'"

What I was never in doubt about was that my father was a soldier. The stories he told, the clothes he wore, the bend of his nose from where he'd broken it diving out of a Jeep under sniper fire, his deaf ear from a mortar shell exploding too near, the Jeep he drove, his oldest friends such as John Keenan, who had been his Jeep partner throughout five campaigns of the war, the guns we used when he taught me how to shoot, his GI watch, the army surplus water and green cans of emergency supplies we kept in the cellar, the medals he showed my brother and me when we begged him to, nearly everything I could see and touch and hear about my father said soldier.

He wasn't the only soldier in the house; I did my best, as a little girl, to be just like him. When I was a teenager and had moved on to boys, I'd forgotten how much a part of his world I had been. Though born in the fifties, I was virtually a child out of time: the forties were far more a present reality to me than whatever the real date was. I was reminded of this when I was sixteen and brought my boyfriend Dan over to Daddy's house for inspection, and my dad took out an old reel-to-reel tape and said to him, "Dan, you have to hear this, it's marvelous." It was a recording of me, age four, singing my entire repertoire: "Mad'moiselle from Armentières"—hasn't been *kissed,* rather than f'd, in forty years, the only nod to my age, . . . hinky dinky parlay voo. The first marine jumped over the fence, parlay voo, the second marine jumped over the fence; "I've Got Sixpence": Happy as the day when the army gets its pay, as we go rolling rolling home; "Don't Sit Under the Apple Tree"—with anybody else but me till I come marching home; "Abdul Abulbul Amir"; "There's a Tavern in the Town." I emerged from World War II when I entered kindergarten and learned a few eensie-beensie spiders and I'm a little teacups. My teacher, Mrs. Perry, was not acquainted with "Mad'moiselle from Armentières."

While the war was often in the foreground of our family life, it was *always* in the background. It was the point of reference that defined everything else in relation to it. When Daddy took pleasure at being warm and dry and cozy by the fire, it was the pleasure of a man who has been truly cold and wet and miserable in his life. There is a quality, among those who have suffered, of not taking things for granted the way the rest of us do. As long as I've known him, my father has never taken being warm and dry and not being shot at for granted. Once, when my mother asked him to join us on an overnight camping trip, he said, outraged, "For Christ sake, Claire, I spent most of the war in foxholes. I will *never* spend another night outdoors again if I can help it, I promise you."

The constant presence of the war, as something not really over, pervaded the years I lived at home. Even as a teenager, when I came home for a visit and he was bugging me about *some*thing, the way parents of teenagers seem to do, I said graciously, "Dad, will you quit interrogating me already!" He said, "I can't help it, that's what I am." Not in the past tense, but in the present as though he were still in counter-intelligence uniform, interrogating prisoners. "That's what I am." Scary. He still drives his Jeep like a nutcase, or a sane person being shelled, same regulation haircut, only gray now.

※

PRIVATE SALINGER, ASN 32325200, age twenty-three, reported to Fort Dix, New Jersey, on April 27, 1942. From there he was sent to Fort Monmouth, New Jersey, for a ten-week instructor's course with the Signal Corps. He applied to Officer Candidate School, and Colonel Baker, head of Valley Forge Military Academy, wrote him an excellent recommendation. He was accepted, but not called up. By July, most of the Signal Corps class were transferred to Signal OCS at Fort Monmouth. He was assigned, instead, to an instructor's job with the Army Aviation Cadets and posted to the U.S. Army Air Force Basic Flying School at Bainbridge, Georgia.

My father told me a number of stories about being stationed in the South. The one that came up most frequently—or perhaps, being a kid, I just remember it best—was about bugs. He told me that, in Georgia, there are these bugs called chiggers that burrow under your skin, and they itch like madmen. The only way to get them out is to burn them out by holding a cigarette near the surface of your skin. The trick was to find the exact spot where it was too hot for the chiggers but not hot enough to burn your skin. They itched so badly, though, that the men often settled for burns.

I collected useful information, such as how to get out chiggers, the way most kids collect marbles or dolls or other precious objects. My dad seemed to know all the best stuff, like the fact that jewelweed grows right next to poison ivy and is a natural antidote. On our long walks together, times I treasured, he showed me which mushrooms were poisonous, such as the beautiful *Amanita muscaria,* and which were delicious in an omelette, such as morels and boletus. Big soldier to little soldier, practical tips for survival were passed on. Like the fact that anyone could turn out to be a Nazi—your neighbor, your baby-sitter, the man at the post office—anyone. And anyone could be a hero; you never knew until it happened, who would be a hero and who would be a coward or traitor.

My father's kind of hero was not the handsome, fearless guy so often seen in the movies of the day, an image that he, through his characters, disparages at length in his war stories. One of the men he admired most in the army was a nameless sergeant who did the right thing simply because it was the right thing to do. Private Salinger had applied to Officer Candidate School and was awaiting his orders to transfer to a language and intelligence corps. One Friday, late in the day, his orders came through. He was told to report for duty at some mechanical repair corps. He knew a mistake had been made (our whole family cringed anytime Daddy so much as touched a tool—we knew it meant something was going to break, usually him—several ribs, a finger, and so on), and he went to the desk sergeant in charge of such things. It was late in the afternoon and the man, as Daddy describes him—I can see him as if I had been there—had his hair all slicked back (Daddy passes his hand over the side of his head slicking back his hair as he tells the story), shoes polished, all ready to go out for a night on the town. This was the army, a war was on in Europe soon to be joined by us, and this clerk had a date to meet in town. Private Salinger showed him his papers and said there was some mistake, and the man quietly took off his overcoat, sat down, and spent the next hour or more diligently getting to the bottom of it, for no recognition, no personal benefit, just because it was the right thing to do. By the time he detected the error and corrected it, he had missed his train into town. My father will never forget him.

The stories my father wrote for the magazines during the war have the same ring to them. As in real life where new recruits were learning life-or-death tips for survival, the characters in his stories, too, reflect this change from civilian concerns to those of a soldier. Gone from his writing is the overt preoccupation with civilian society's saints and sinners, the in-crowd and the out, the phonies and the elite. These concerns appear in an indirect way, or, may I say, a more subtle, effective way. Perhaps this is his daughter speaking, as one sensitive to being lectured by a parent; but even his characters express an awareness of this didactical tendency. Zooey acknowledged of his whole family, "We don't talk, we hold forth. We don't converse, we expound. At least *I* do. The minute I'm in a room with somebody who has the usual number of ears, I either turn into a goddam *seer* or'a human hatpin."* I had heard my father say this about himself long before I ever read *Zooey,* but, as each ac-

---

Zooey, p. 140.

knowledges, it's not something he can control. My father's remorse, the morning after, for an evening of this kind of behavior rings much as a confirmed alcoholic's regret for his behavior. A mixture of sadness, embarrassment, apologies made, but without the hope or promise of turning over a new leaf. There is a real sense in his Glass stories, as in his real life, of its being something beyond his control, a flaw that is part of his being. Not that his judgment or lecture is flawed, mind you, the embarrassment is due to the fact that he can't keep his mouth shut about it.

In his early army stories, however, there is much more story than lecture, and, as I said, a new subtlety, or gentleness really, with which his usual concerns are brought forth. Most striking of all, to me, is that in those army stories, the characters actually have real friends. There is "Babe" Gladwaller, who, in "Last Day of the Last Furlough,"* tells his friend and fellow soldier Vincent Caulfield, "I never knew about friendship until the Army," or Philly Burns, in "Death of a Dogface,"† who tells his wife Juanita, "I met more good guys in the Army than I ever knowed when I was a civilian." In my father's books, however, one finds instead of friendship, relations between guru and seeker, as in "Teddy" and the later stories about Seymour, or between the living and the dead, as in *The Catcher in the Rye* where Phoebe challenges her brother, Holden, to name anyone he likes who's living, or when Franny similarly charges Zooey with the same question, and both are forced to admit that outside the immediate family they can't name a single living person— though the list of dead people they'd give their right arm to meet is full up. My father has, himself, on many occasions told me the same thing, that the only people he really respects are all dead.

The other thing that amazed me, as a person who had grown up hearing from my father a relentlessly pessimistic view of the possibilities of happiness in marriage—any marriage—as well as the worse-than-dismal state of his relationship with my mother, is the brief appearance,

---

*"Last Day of the Last Furlough," *Saturday Evening Post,* July 15, 1944, p. 26.

†When it appeared in the April 13, 1944, issue of the *Saturday Evening Post,* the editors had taken it upon themselves to change the title from "Death of a Dogface" to "Soft-Boiled Sergeant." You can imagine how pleased he was about that—and the Norman Rockwell–like drawings that accompanied the story. But a young writer has no control over these things, as my father would, later, when his reputation was established.

in just two stories, "Wake Me When it Thunders"* and "Death of a Dogface," of a husband and wife who see eye to eye, imperfectly, humanly, but they like what they see. What I didn't realize on first reading them is that, in each of these stories, the husband and his wife are both intelligent but uneducated. The dialect, flawless as usual, makes clear their social status without any sense of making fun of it. That, too, is very like my father; he never lacked respect for local farmers who had something to teach him even though their language might be full of *ain't*s and the like. He was merciless, however, on those who tried to make their language sound "tonier" by using, or rather misusing, words that have a sophisticated sound to the unsophisticated ear. "Always use the simplest word possible to say what you're trying to say" was his adage. Only use a less simple word if you *really* need to in order to describe accurately what you're talking about.

Flawed couples, human couples, in these two stories manage to work toward mutual understanding, love, and respect. Philly Burns, for example, is back from the war and explains to Juanita, his wife, who loves going to Hollywood war movies, why he can't stand them. He tells her the story of his real-life experience of war, and how the movies are a lie. In Hollywood stories, he says:

> You see a lot of real handsome guys always getting shot pretty neat, right where it don't spoil their looks none, and they always got plenty of time, before they croak, to give their love to some doll back home, with who in the beginning of the pitcher, they had a real serious misunderstanding about what dress she should ought to wear to the college dance. . . . Then you see the dead guy's hometown, and around a million people, including the mayor and the dead guy's folks and his doll, and maybe the President, all around the guy's box, making speeches and wearing medals and looking spiffier in mourning duds than most folks do all dolled up for a party.

---

*"Wake Me When it Thunders" (renamed "Both Parties Concerned" by the *Saturday Evening Post,* February 26, 1944), came out a few months before "Death of a Dogface."

Philly tells his wife a real story about a real hero, his sergeant, who happened to be a particularly ugly guy (hence the original title, "Death of a Dogface"), not Hollywood material at all, whose men respected him above all others. When he died, he had his jaw blasted off and he received four other terrible, ugly holes in various places, trying to save some new recruits during the bombing of Pearl Harbor. As the story ends, Philly tells us:

> He died all by himself, and he didn't have no messages to give to no girl or nobody, and there wasn't nobody throwing a big classy funeral for him here in the States, and no hot-shot bugler blowed taps for him.
>
> The only funeral Burke got was when Juanita cried for him when I read her Frankie's letter and when I told her again what I knowed. Juanita, she ain't no ordinary dame. Don't never marry no ordinary dame, bud. Get one that'll cry for a Burke.

This kind of respect and meeting of the minds between husband and wife never again appears in my father's stories. As he turns to the middle-class characters of his novels, it seems that education somehow works as an impediment to being landsmen; the elite world of prep schools and Ivy League colleges creates islands of isolated strangers who can't connect, lonely men who can't find a landsman, certainly not in a lover or spouse.

Reading the stories my father wrote when he was a soldier had, for me, the bittersweet poignancy of a Requiem Mass. Something very human bloomed briefly and died,* and although his work and life passed on to other realms such as those of the prescient, *Herrlichkeit* Teddy and Seymour, whom we meet walking open-eyed to their deaths, the change to his preoccupation with *Übermenschen* both in his fiction and in his life left behind no human lap to sit on, no precious walks and talks, soldier to soldier, no warm arms to hold me, no familiar Daddy smell—a mingling of applewood smoke from the fireplace in his study, old woolen sweaters, and his Balkan Sobranie pipe tobacco—to comfort

---

*Denn alles Fleisch es ist wie Gras und alle Herrlichkeit des Menschen wie des Grases Blumen. Das Gras ist verdorret und die Blume abgefallen—"Then all [the glory of the] flesh is like grass and all godlikeness [the illusion of being as God, or *hubris* if you like] of men, like the grass's flower. The grass withers and the bloom falls" (I Peter 1:24, quoted in Brahms, *Ein Deutsches Requiem*).

me. When I read his novels, the soldier, the father I knew and loved and admired—no that's not right—*worshiped* as a child was missing. It was such a pleasure to discover his old stories, those he said he chose to let "die a natural death" in these old magazines. I read them with affection and recognition: that's the Daddy I like to remember.

❦

EARLY IN 1943, Salinger was posted to a cadet classification squadron at a base near Nashville, Tennessee. He wrote to Colonel Baker again to ask his help with Officer Candidate School, telling him that he'd been accepted but still hadn't been called up. That fall, he was assigned a job in public relations at Patterson Field in Fairfield, Ohio. His orders finally came through, and in October of '43, he was transferred to Fort Holabird, Maryland, to train as a special agent in counter-intelligence, where he would put to good use his own intelligence and the German and French he'd learned at Valley Forge, and please, God, for the Allies' sake, no tools.

A story my father told me many times is about what happened when he went home to say good-bye just before shipping out for England, where he and eight hundred other special agents would receive specific D-Day training and their assignments to fighting units. He didn't want anyone to accompany him to the ship for an emotional good-bye. He just wanted a quiet leave-taking at home and forbade his mother from coming down to the ship to see him off. Later, as he was marching with his battalion on the way to the ship, he suddenly glimpsed her. She was following along, hiding behind lampposts so he wouldn't see her.

While in England, he sold two stories to the magazines about a GI's last visit home and leave-taking before shipping out. Here, my father gets a chance to "fix" things and rewrite history the way he would have wanted it to happen. And, of course, in one of the great joys of fiction writing, he also gets to control his mother: no more hiding behind lampposts.

The first story of leave-taking is called "Once a Week Won't Kill You."* We are now in typical Salinger territory: husbands and wives who have no meeting of the minds whatsoever, and the search for a landsman within the man's boyhood family. The story opens with the man packing to ship out for the war in the morning. Despite his pretty,

---

Story, November–December 1944.

blond wife's babbling presence, he is essentially alone. The real connection and important leave-taking is between the man and his aunt, who is his closest relative since his parents died when he was a young boy. She is terrific, one wants to read more about her, but it's a short story. They have a marvelous conversation, then he has to tell her that he has to go to war. He's nervous about how she'll take the news.

" 'I knew you'd have to,' said his aunt, without panic, without bitter-sentimental reference to 'the last one.' She was wonderful, he thought. She was the sanest woman in the world." The conversation takes a slightly disturbing turn, and as he leaves to go, he makes his wife promise once again to take his aunt to the movies. "Once a week won't kill you," he tells her.

The second story about leave-taking, "Last Day of the Last Furlough," is much longer, and with a different cast of characters, but in one central way it is the same: the mother, like the aunt, takes the news on the chin. In this story we see the last appearance in his fiction of friendship and brotherhood, a *landsmanshaftn* of equals beyond the glass confines of one's own family. I wish that this had survived and flourished in my father's own life; our life as a family would have been so much richer. This was not to be. Instead, his search for landsmen led him increasingly to relations in two dimensions: with his fictional Glass family, or with living "pen pals" he met in letters, which lasted until meeting in person when the three-dimensional, flesh-and-blood presence of them would, with the inevitability of watching a classic tragedy unfold, invariably sow the seeds of the relationship's undoing.

In "Last Day of the Last Furlough," John F. "Babe" Gladwaller Jr., same rank and serial number (ASN 32325200) as Jerome "Sonny" Salinger, is about to be sent overseas. Babe's army buddy Vincent Caulfield is visiting. Vincent has just received notice that his kid brother, Holden, the one "who got kicked out of all those schools," is missing in action. Vincent tells Babe's ten-year-old sister, Mattie, that he, too, has a sister just her age. Vincent kids around with Mattie in a really nice, funny scene—just the way my father kids around. Later, in Babe's room, Vincent says:

> "It's good to see you, Babe. . . . G.I.'s—especially G.I.'s who are friends—belong together these days. It's no good being with civilians anymore. They don't know what we know and we're no longer used to what they know. It doesn't work out so hot."

Babe nodded and thoughtfully took a drag from his cigarette. "I never really knew anything about friendship before I
was in the Army. Did you, Vince?"

"Not a thing."

At dinner, Babe lambasts his father for romanticizing war the way
they do in the movies and goes into a typical long and emotional
Salinger diatribe (for which Babe, again typical of my father, later feels
embarrassed). Babe, in a sentiment similar to that expressed by Philly
Burns, tells him that war will continue until we stop making it look
heroic, "instead of the stupid, bloody mess it really is."

Searching for a landsman, Babe goes into Mattie's room, where she
is sleeping, to wake her up and talk to her. In a scene very like Holden
waking his sister, Phoebe, who guesses he's been kicked out of school
again, Mattie guesses, correctly, that Babe has received his orders to ship
out. Mattie, like the aunt in the previous story, is terrific about it. He
kisses her good-night and leaves her room, finally at peace with himself
about going to war.

. . . this is where Mattie is sleeping. No enemy is banging on our
door, waking her up, frightening her. But it could happen if I
don't go out and meet him with my gun. And I will, and I'll kill
him. I'd like to come back too. It would be swell to come back.
It would be—

His mother, too, guesses that he is going overseas. She tells him
calmly that she is not worried. "You'll do your job and you'll come back.
I have a feeling." The story ends with him feeling happy, following her
suggestion to wake Vincent and go down to the kitchen for some cold
chicken.

Babe appears again in two more stories, one set on a battlefield in
France, the other set just after the war ends and it's not so swell to be
back suffering from "battle fatigue."*

Babe found some peace about going to war, as well as some peaceful
good-byes. I don't know how my father felt until he got on board the

---

*Today we'd call it post-traumatic stress disorder. They did not mean "tired."

ship. His bunkmates, he told me, were having a farting contest and laughing like hyenas about it. He lay back on his bunk and sank into utter despair.

❈❈❈

STAFF SERGEANT SALINGER WAS IN ENGLAND for the next few months occupied in much the same way as is his character Staff Sergeant X, in the story "For Esmé—with Love and Squalor." The fictional X, like my father, attended a planning and training course for Counter-Intelligence Corps agents in the south of England in preparation for the D-Day invasion. X is sitting in a tea shop, having a lovely conversation with Esmé, a young girl of about thirteen, and her little brother, Charles. When queried, X tells Esmé that he is a writer of short stories by profession. Like my father, X is assigned to the Twelfth Infantry Regiment (combat) of the Fourth Division. "I landed on D-Day, you know," he'd say to me darkly, soldier to soldier as it were, as if I understood the implications, the unspoken. Although he said it a number of times when I was a child, he never once elaborated beyond the stark statement. I found out, among other facts, in a terrific book by their regimental historian, Colonel Gerden F. Johnson, *History of the Twelfth Infantry Regiment in World War II,* that it was Utah Beach their regiment hit that day.

My father's story "For Esmé—with Love and Squalor" goes abruptly silent when Sergeant X leaves England's shores, the way his saying "I landed on D-Day" stood for a million things unsaid, bodies and body parts strewn across beach and field and town, miles of white crosses, the slaughter and misery of war. In the story, the scene shifts abruptly from pre–D-Day England to somewhere in Germany shortly after VE day (victory in Europe and the surrender of Germany). Staff Sergeant X is sitting on a bed, vomiting into a wastebasket:

> His gums bled at the slightest pressure of the tip of his tongue, and he seldom stopped experimenting; it was a little game he played, sometimes by the hour. He sat for a moment smoking and experimenting. Then, abruptly, familiarly, and, as usual, with no warning, he thought he felt his mind dislodge itself and teeter, like insecure luggage on an overhead rack.

The war that left him that way is entirely offstage. It's a tremendously powerful way to tell the reader that something terrible has happened without telling you what. It's left to your imagination, which for most of us is a pretty spooky place to be left. Especially when you aren't allowed to ask further questions.

As I began to fill in the pages that had been crossed out of my own family's personal history during the war, things my father never told me, and I never asked, I was, once again, rather horrified to find that I shared with many of my peers a general view of our American story that was missing vital pages. Much like the myth of perpetual progress and widening opportunities for all Americans in the twentieth century, I had been taught that we, as a nation, went to war to fight Hitler and the evil values and practices—genocide of the Jews being the most glaring example—for which he stood. I found out, I'm ashamed to say, that in actuality anti-Semitism in America appears to have been at its apogee from 1939 to 1945. It was a real slug in the stomach to find out how many Americans supported the war *despite* Hitler's view on the Jews, with which many agreed. In a 1938 poll, for example, taken of Americans about ten days after Kristallnacht, it was found that the majority believed that Jews were "partially or entirely responsible for Hitler's treatment of them," and four separate polls revealed that 71 to 85 percent of Americans opposed increasing immigration quotas for refugees. Scores of anti-Semitic leaflets circulated on American military bases stateside. A typical bit of such excreta I came across was allegedly written by a U.S. marine, before he had something useful with which to occupy his time:

The Parable of the Shekels

I. And it came to pass that Adolph, Son of Abitch, persecuted the tribes of Judea and there was war.

II. And when the war was four years, many tribes came to the help of the Jews, but the Jews took up arms not.

III. They took up arms not lest in so doing they would take from their pockets their hand and it would come to pass that they would lose a shekel.

IV. And the Gentiles came up in great multitudes from all the lands to fight for the Jews and the Jews lifted up their voices and sang "Onward Christian Soldiers." We will make the uniforms.

V. And the Jews lifted up their eyes and beheld a great opportunity and they said unto one another "the time has come when it is good to barter the junk for pieces of silver" and straightaway it was so.

VI. And they grieved not when a city was destroyed for when a city is destroyed there is junk and where there is junk there are Jews and where there are Jews there are money [sic] [and sick].*

Such overtly anti-Semitic incidents and leaflets were most prevalent at points of induction.† Secretary of the Navy Frank Knox and Secretary of War Henry Stimson issued orders forbidding the circulation of such anti-Semitic publications at all naval and military posts. It is hard to outlaw or legislate attitudes, but the experience of service together changed the attitude of many a soldier. When the Army publication *Yank* magazine asked soldiers, in August of 1945 just before the Japanese surrender, what changes they most wanted to see made in postwar America, the majority of GIs surveyed agreed that "above everything else, the need for wiping out racial and religious discrimination" was their major hope.‡ Whether this was due to the experience of Jew and Gentile fighting side by side or to the witnessing "up close and personal" of anti-Semitism put into practice, it is impossible to say. Perhaps it is as my father told me when I was a little girl: "You never really get the smell of burning flesh out of your nose entirely, no matter how long you live."§

---

*Lois J. Meltzer, "Anti-Semitism in the United States Army During World War II" (master's thesis, Baltimore Hebrew College, 1977), p. 101. Quoted in Dinnerstein, *Anti-Semitism,* p. 141.

†Ibid., p. 42.

‡Sociologist E. Digby Baltzell acknowledged that he and many of his fellow naval officers returned home from World War II "far less willing to tolerate the traditional, often dehumanizing, ethnic snobberies of our prewar years" (ibid., p. 151).

§As a counter-intelligence officer, my father was one of the first soldiers to walk into a certain, just liberated, concentration camp. He told me the name, but I no longer remember.

It was particularly depressing to find how much the virtual elimination of the Jewish GI's story continues to this day in current histories of World War II. *Citizen Soldiers,* a critically acclaimed book that was on the *New York Times* best-seller list for many months as I was writing my own book, purports to be the story of the American soldier from D-Day to VE day. The author, Steven Ambrose, is a noted writer of best-sellers—*Undaunted Courage* and *D-Day* as well as multi-volume biographies of Presidents Eisenhower and Nixon—and founder of the Eisenhower Center and president of the National D-Day Museum in New Orleans. Two years ago, before I asked questions about what things were like in my father's day, I'm not sure I would have noticed the virtual X-ing out, the elimination by silence, of all but the Gentile GI's stories. In an otherwise fascinating book, bringing to life the GI's experience of battle, this stuck in my craw. I'm not speaking of the author's motivations, but of the *effect* of "talking that way." It's not dissimilar to the tradition of referring to all human beings as "men": someone's story gets overlooked, devalued, or silenced. When you're talking about a war of genocide, something more than being politically correct is at stake when you tell the American citizen soldier's story in a way that excludes Jews. (He devotes a chapter to the African-American soldier.) Imagine you are a Jewish war veteran, or the surviving friend or relation of a soldier who didn't happen to be a Christian, and reading the beginning of chapter 9 of Ambrose's book:

> During Christmas season of 1944 there were some four million young soldiers on the Western Front, the great majority of them Protestants or Catholics. They said the same prayers when they were being shelled, directed to the same God. . . . In World War II, no hatred matched that felt by Americans against Japanese, or Russians against Germans, and vice versa. But in Northwest Europe, there was little racial hatred between the Americans and the Germans. How could there be when cousins were fighting cousins? About one-third of the U.S. Army in ETO were German-American in origin. The Christmas season highlighted the closeness of the foes. Americans and Germans alike put up Christmas trees . . . the men on both sides of the line had an image of a manger in Bethlehem in their minds.

Or this, the opening of the chapter entitled "Victory, April 1–May 7, 1945":

> Easter came on April 1 in 1945. In many cases the celebration of the Resurrection brought the GIs and German civilians together. . . . The GIs were surprised to find how much they liked the Germans. Clean, hardworking, disciplined, cute kids, educated, middle-class in their tastes and life-styles—the Germans seemed to many American soldiers to be "just like us." . . . They were regular churchgoers.

Rabbi Roland Gittelsohn, an Army chaplain at the time, writes in his memoirs an account of the day before Easter, in 1945, when he went to ask his superiors to reconsider an order that all soldiers on base be required to attend Easter services. He was met with hostile incredulity and told that the Jewish soldiers had a choice of Protestant services or Catholic. "We all stand in formation to salute a General and show respect, what's wrong with being required to show respect for our Savior?"

"What's wrong?" Where to begin? Perhaps with a version of the Bible issued to service men and women in 1943 that included such section titles as "The Jews Are a Synagogue of Satan" and "Israel's Fall: The Gentile's Salvation." It wasn't until the 1980s that prominent Catholic and Protestant theologians began to address systematically the problem of how to have a Christian identity that isn't profoundly anti-Jewish.*

Let's just say that attending Easter services in 1945' might not have been a big morale booster for Jewish service men and women.

Citizen Soldiers ends with a John Doe sketch of the typical everyman GI:

---

*Centuries of Christian teachings that the Jews killed our Savior and that Jews suffer because God is punishing them, as a race, for this sin have been rescinded only in the past twenty years or so by prominent Protestant theologians, who say we must stop "bearing false witness against our Jewish neighbors" (Krister Stendhal, Harvard Divinity School). Pope John XXIII in the Second Vatican Council specifically "exonerated" Jews for Christ's death, which means it is now against the teachings of the Catholic Church and false dogma to hold that the Jews are responsible for killing Jesus.

There is no typical GI among the millions who served in Northwest Europe, but Bruce Egger [meet John Doe] surely was representative. . . . He served out the war in almost continuous front-line action. He never missed a day of duty. He had his close calls, most notably a piece of shrapnel stopped by the New Testament in the breast pocket of his field jacket, but was never wounded. In this he was unusually lucky. G Company had arrived on Utah Beach on September 8, 1944, with a full complement of 187 enlisted men and six officers. By May 8, 1945, a total of 625 men had served in its ranks. Fifty-one men of G Company were killed in action, 183 were wounded, 166 got trench foot, and 51 frostbite. Egger rose from private to staff sergeant.

My father, too, rose from private to staff sergeant, landed on Utah Beach—on D-Day, June 6, 1944, however, not in September— never missed a day of service, was on or near the front lines with the Twelfth Infantry Regiment of the Fourth Division from D-Day to VE day, from Utah Beach to Cherbourg, on through the battles of the Hedgerows and bloody Mortain to Hürtgen Forest, Luxembourg and the Battle of the Bulge. He, too, was lucky. The Twelfth Infantry landed on D-Day with a company of 155 officers and 2,925 enlisted men. By June 30, less than a month later, in fighting from Utah Beach to Cherbourg, the total casualties for officers was 118, or 76 percent, and for enlisted men, 1,832, or 63 percent.

"Last Day of the Last Furlough" was published on July 15, but its author couldn't have known about it until, at the earliest, the seventeenth, when, outside of Deauville, he and the other men of the Twelfth Infantry had their first shower and change of clothes since leaving England on June 5. On the day the story was published, these soldiers were in the midst of some particularly nasty fighting in hedgerow country about six hundred yards east of Saintenay, France. The Twelfth Infantry had recently finished what was basically hand-to-hand combat, clearing out the city of Cherbourg, building by building, street by street, body by body. They were now painfully gaining territory, one miserable field at a time, each bounded by nearly impenetrable hedgerows (the United States had not figured on this feature of the terrain, and the tanks were nearly useless) behind which a German panzer division and parachute regiment were well defended. Each field was gained at a tremendous cost of human life. A day's fighting often yielded only a few hundred yards of ground. Colonel Gerden F. Johnson of the Twelfth Infantry wrote, "The carnage was frightful. . . . The next morning it took three two-and-one-half-ton trucks to remove all the German bodies" from the field where they fell.

After a brief rest, shower, and regrouping outside Deauville, Colonel Johnson tells us that the men of the Twelfth Infantry "climbed from their slit trenches to watch one of the war's greatest dramas unfold in the skies west of St. Lô." Three waves of fighter bombers—350 planes in the first wave, 350 in the second, and 1,300 in the third wave—"as far as the eye could see . . . rolled out a lethal carpet of bombs on the terror-stricken Germans, saturating every field and hedgerow from one end of the bomb pattern to the other. . . . As suddenly as this hellish inferno had begun, it ceased, and the silence that followed was eerie." There were far more dead bodies than trucks to handle them, and they lay where they were. The entire Fourth Infantry Division (of which the Twelfth Infantry Regiment was part) began a night march on a narrow road jammed with tanks and vehicles and dead bodies. A breakthrough had been accomplished, and the need to exploit it was urgent. The road they were on came to a dead end in a swamp. The intelligence officers went on ahead and succeeded in locating a new route. They were headed to Mortain, a battle General Bradley said involved the most critical decision he had to make during the entire war.

In four and a half days of fighting at "bloody Mortain" the Twelfth sustained 1,150 casualties, bringing the division's death totals for June, July, and first weeks of August to 4,034, that is to say about 125 percent of the original 3,080 men. Nasty. The few men who lived through it were left with much to sicken them, body and soul.

I remember standing next to my father—I was about seven at the time—for what seemed like an eternity as he stared blankly at the strong backs of our construction crew of local boys, carpenters building the new addition to our house. Their T-shirts were off, their muscles glistening with life and youth in the summer sun. After a long time, he finally came back to life again and spoke to me, or perhaps just out loud to no one in particular, "All those big strong boys"—he shook his head—"always on the front line, always the first to be killed, wave after wave of them," he said, his hand flat, palm out, pushing arc-like waves away from him.

❧

ON AUGUST 23, the Twelfth Regimental Combat Team started the 165-mile march toward Paris. It was slow going; trucks slipped off the wet, treacherous roads into ditches, and the convoy was forced to stop every three hours to let the cramped, soggy troops stretch. On August 25, they entered Paris. They were the first large military force, the first American troops, to enter the city. The Parisians went berserk. My father told me that when he and his Jeepmate John Keenan arrested a suspected collaborator, the crowd spotted the man, tore him from their arms, and beat him to death on the spot. My father said there was nothing, short of gunning down the entire crowd, that they could have done to stop them.

In Paris, he was able to get away from his duties long enough to pay a visit to Ernest Hemingway. Hemingway was, at the time, a war correspondent attached to the Fourth Division. They had never met, but according to John Keenan, when my father heard that Hemingway was at the Ritz, he suggested they go and see him. Their visit was, apparently, a warm one. Hemingway asked to see my father's most recent work, and he showed him "Last Day of the Last Furlough." Hemingway had read it and said he liked it very much.*

Their stay in Paris was brief, and what followed was what the regimental historian could only call a "mad dash" through France and Belgium. In less than a month (they had reached Paris on August 25; Germany on September 12), they would cross the border into Germany. My father gives voice to one soldier's exhaustion at this time in a story called "A Boy in France."†

Until I read this story, published only in an old issue of *The Saturday Evening Post,* I was left, along with all readers of "For Esmé— with Love and Squalor," only to wonder what had happened to that

---

*My father never mentioned this visit with Hemingway to me, but I read about it in his letters on file at the Library of Congress.

†"A Boy in France," *Saturday Evening Post*, March 31, 1945, p. 21.

soldier between D-Day and the war's end. Here we meet up with Sergeant Babe Gladwaller, last seen in the story "Last Day of the Last Furlough," now on a battlefield somewhere in France. It is an extraordinary piece of writing, I think, haiku-like in its brevity and evocative power. Babe, nearly dead on his feet from exhaustion, is searching a rain-sogged, blood-soaked battlefield for someplace to sleep. He finds a foxhole with a stained "unlamented" German blanket in it and begins, leadenly, to dig out the "bad spots," the bloody places at the bottom of the hole. He takes out his GI bedroll and "lifts this bed thing, as though it had some kind of spine to it," into the hole. He is filthy, wet, cold, and the hole is too short to fully stretch out his legs. My father, at six feet two inches tall, encountered this same problem all too often. An ant bites Babe, and as he swats it, he scrapes the place where his fingernail had been torn off in the morning's battle.

What Babe does next is something that grabbed me almost bodily when I read it. It is something my father has done to deal with pain and suffering for as long as I have known him. My strong hunch is that this pattern of coping became part of his being during the trauma of war, but, as I said, it's a hunch, not a certainty, since, of course, I didn't know him before the war.*

Babe examines his throbbing finger and then puts his whole hand under the blanket

with the care more like that proffered a sick person than a sore finger, and let himself work the kind of abracadabra familiar to and special for G.I.'s in combat.

"When I take my hand out of this blanket," he thought, "my nail will be grown back, my hands will be clean. My body will be clean. I'll have on clean shorts, clean undershirt, a white shirt. A blue polka-dot tie. A gray suit with a stripe, and I'll be home, and I'll bolt the door. I'll put some coffee on the stove, some records on the phonograph, and I'll bolt the door. I'll read

---

*My aunt has said she didn't notice him dabbling in anything "strange" medically or religiously before the war, nor does any such "abracadabra" appear in his pre-war writings, but I can't be sure.

my books and I'll drink the hot coffee and I'll listen to the music, and I'll bolt the door. I'll open the window, I'll let in a nice, quiet girl—not Frances, not anyone I've ever known—and I'll bolt the door. I'll ask her to walk a little bit in the room by herself, and I'll look at her American ankles, and I'll bolt the door. I'll ask her to read some Emily Dickinson to me—that one about being chartless—and I'll ask her to read some William Blake to me—that one about the little lamb who made thee—and I'll bolt the door. She'll have an American voice, and she won't ask me if I have any chewing gum or bonbons, and I'll bolt the door."

Babe takes out of his pocket a handful of newspaper clippings. They are full of vacuous gossip about celebrities and fashions, obscene in the context of war. He crumples them into a ball and lies back in despair. At last he reaches for a letter in his pocket, clutching it for dear life, rereading it for the hundredth time. It's a simple, beautiful letter from his sister Mattie. She tells him she misses him and asks him to come home soon. The story ends as Babe falls "crumbily, bent leggedly, asleep."

About this time, the men of the Twelfth, including my father, received a similar, much-needed letter written by a young Belgian girl to the parents of a Twelfth Infantry man. He was killed in action and the letter was sent on to *The Big Picture,* the Twelfth Infantry regimental newspaper, which, in the October lull, had a chance to turn out a few issues on location. The Twelfth Infantry historian writes of this letter, "Its simplicity so clearly plumbs the depths of heartfelt thanks that it will always remain among the treasures of the Twelfth Infantry as a reminder that its sacrifices were not made in vain."

> Rue De La Conversarie
> Saint Hubert
> Ardenne, Belgique
> 21ˢᵗ October 1944

To Family Bill,
    I know just a few words of english and it is from a very little Belgium town, they will start for to express our grateful

to you Americans, for the liberation of our Country by your Sons (the 8th September).

My thanks to you in particular because we have been happy that Bill to be our liberator. He is first American soldier we have seen, we will always remember this nice and lofty fighter, may God keep him throughout the future years and words can never say how in our gratitude towards you and yours.

When you write to Bill said to him I always think very much to him and if he can come in Saint Hubert, I shall be very happy to see him again.

Said to him also, I am always waiting him and he writes with me when that is possible and you also.

Excuse my english. I can explain me very well but I hope you understand me.

Sincerely Yours

I was thrilled to find this letter in the regimental archives. What I find so interesting is the way in which a unique human voice—my father's story for example—gives voice to a feeling, a condition of suffering shared by many.* And then reading how others, each in his unique way, gave voice to their shared experience as each wondered whether anyone back home knew, or cared to know, the hell they were going through and the losses they were suffering. I read somewhere that a biographer of my father's, interested in his story "For Esmé—with Love and Squalor," went on a pilgrimage, of sorts, all over that part of England posting notices in local papers in search of the "real" Esmé, just as a reporter had tried, earlier, to find the "real" Sybil from the story "A Perfect Day for Bananafish." I'm not entirely certain why, but that sort

---

*Another soldier wrote a letter home voicing a similar despair as he wrote of a buddy's death: "He wasn't twenty years old. . . . Shrieking and moaning, he gave up his life on a stretcher. . . . Back in America the race tracks were booming, the night clubs were making record profits, Miami Beach was so crowded you couldn't get a room anywhere. Few people seemed to care . . . we wondered if the people would ever know what it cost the soldiers in terror, bloodshed, and hideous, agonizing deaths to win the war" (Private Daniel Webster of the 101st, quoted in Ambrose, *Citizen Soldiers,* p. 417).

of thing leaves me cold. Perhaps it's because the idiosyncratic, the isolated, the almost mythological aspects of my father writing alone in his tower have held sway for so long.

※※※

WINTER BROUGHT THE CONDITIONS of the Twelfth from unbearable to unspeakable. Their numbers had been increased by 2,228 replacements, bringing its original 3,080 to 3,362. A terrible month of fighting in Hürtgen Forest saw 1,493 battle casualties, and a loss of an additional 1,024 men from non-battle causes, mainly from freezing to death in foxholes, half full of icy water, dug in the alternately frozen and wet ground, snow and mud, with no winter boots nor warm coats, nor an adequate supply of dry blankets for a bedroll in the foxholes.

The normally terse reports from headquarters issued a commendation on December 17, 1944, to the commanding officer of the Twelfth Infantry. It reads in part:

Unseasonal precipitation and damp, penetrating cold were a constant detriment to the health and well being of the personnel, rendering their day by day existence well nigh unbearable. The terrain was characterized by densely forested hills, swollen streams and deep, adhesive mud, which retarded all movement of troops and vehicles.

The enemy had prepared. . . . extensive mine fields and well placed booby traps, in particular, exacted a heavy toll of casualties during the advance. . . . Inasmuch as natural conditions precluded the employment of adequate aerial and motorized support, the burden of neutralizing frantically defended enemy fortifications fell heavily upon the shoulders of the foot soldier. It is with extreme approbation that I commend your officers and men. . . . The deeds of the 12th Infantry Regiment shall not be forgotten as long as bravery and valor are honored and respected.

Major General R. O. Barton
U.S. Army Commanding
[p. 377 /AG 201.22]

While the "burden of neutralizing frantically defended enemy fortifications fell heavily on the *shoulders* of the foot soldier," it fell even more heavily on their feet. The leather combat boots soaked up water in a thaw and froze solid in the cold nights. Waterproof, insulated L.L. Bean–type boots were available, but to the "everlasting disgrace of the quartermasters and all other rear-echelon personnel," who were nearly all wearing them by mid-December, not until late January did the boots get to where they were needed. Three days before the Battle of the Bulge, a colonel of the Ninetieth Division noted that "every day more men are falling out due to trench foot . . . [they] can't walk and are being carried from sheltered pillbox positions at night to firing positions in the day time." During the winter of 1944–45, forty-five thousand men were taken off the front line because of trench foot.

My father said that no matter what, he will always be grateful to his mother, who knit him socks and sent them to him in the mail, each and every week, throughout the war. He told me it saved his life in the foxholes that winter; he was the only guy he knew with dry feet. "Saved my life"—I used to think this was in the same category of language as a well-fed American boy asking his mother what's for supper and saying, "I'm starving." I was too young to realize that there can be extreme situations in life where language is stripped of the cloak of hyperbole. Narrative breaks down and becomes the language of the body, a moan, a wrung breast, vacant eyes, living skeletons. I understand in many ways why the story "For Esmé" falls silent when it does. If one does recover language, it is not narrative with its Aristotelian wholeness of beginning, middle, and end; but rather, a poem—midway between a moan and a story—reflecting the shape of shards and fragments of life blown apart.

It was during that awful winter that Louise Bogan, poetry editor for *The New Yorker* during the war, wrote to William Maxwell telling him that "a young man, J. D. Salinger, has been bombarding me with poems for a week or so."*

As the poet Lord Byron wrote:

---

*Elizabeth Frank, *Louise Bogan: A Portrait* (New York: Alfred A. Knopf, 1985), p. 338.

No words suffice the secret soul to show,
For truth denies all eloquence to woe.
                              —"The Corsair,"
                    Canto iii, Stanza 22, line 551

❦

EXHAUSTED FROM THE TERRIBLE HÜRTGEN FOREST, the Twelfth scarcely had a breath before it was once again in the thick of things in the defense of Luxembourg and the Battle of the Bulge.* So bad were the losses at Echternach that Salinger's friends and family feared him dead or captured.† December 26 brought a call to Mrs. Salinger with the news that "Salinger is all right."‡ New Year's Day, 1945, was Staff Sergeant Salinger's twenty-sixth birthday. Of this day and the following three months, the division commander writes:

> On those days, melting snow revealed the bodies of both German and American soldiers upon the ground where they had been frozen into weird shapes after they had fallen in the winter battles. Hundreds of dead cattle littered the fields and destroyed vehicles lined the roads along with the carcasses of the horses that had been used to pull enemy supply vehicles. Most of the small towns had been either partially or completely destroyed and the wreckage lay untouched where it fell. Human excreta was deposited in the corners of rooms where the fighting had been at such close quarters that even leaving the buildings was an invitation to death. This part of Germany, just north of the point where the borders of Germany, France and Belgium meet, was the filthiest area the 12th had ever fought through.§

---

*The Twelfth Infantry Regiment was awarded the Distinguished Unit Citation for its defense of Luxembourg.
†Collection of letters of Whit Burnett, Library of Congress.
‡Ibid.
§Colonel Gerdon F. Johnson, *History of the Twelfth Infantry Regiment in World War II,* p. 309.

In April, the Twelfth Infantry Regiment was assigned to "mopping up." This meant, among other tasks, that all units picked up many prisoners of war in their areas and were constantly alert for resistance from small groups of bypassed enemy. (As a counter-intelligence agent, one of my father's jobs was the interrogation and processing of POWs and suspects.)

The last action to be fought by the Twelfth Infantry Regiment in World War II took place May 2, 1945, between Company A and SS troops on Tegernsee. On May 5, the Twelfth Regiment opened its command post in Hermann Göring's castle at Neuhaus. The area was secured, and the Twelfth began carrying out its occupation duties. Nazi civil authorities often fled the towns as the Allied forces moved in, and local government was in chaos. Thousands of liberated displaced persons, Allied prisoners of war, and German political prisoners posed a threat to the security of the captured areas, and counter-intelligence officers such as Staff Sergeant Salinger were kept extremely busy.

News of the German surrender reached them on May 8. On the fourteenth of May, the entire Fourth Infantry moved to an area west of Nürnberg in the general vicinity of Ansbach and continued its duties keeping order. Sometime during these next few weeks, my father was taken to a hospital just outside Nürnberg and admitted for battle fatigue. He wrote to Hemingway in July, making light of it, joking about the questions the psychiatrists asked him about his family life and background. What is clear in the letter is that he did take one thing seriously: he was adamant in his resolve to fight any attempt to give him a psychiatric rather than an honorable discharge. He was successful, and the army doctors sent him back to his duties a few weeks later.

A man should receive a medal of honor, I think, for holding off cracking up until after the war with the Eskimos.* Sergeant X, too, held off cracking up until the battle was won. At the end of the war, he, like Sergeant Salinger, is newly released from a hospital. He is "a young man who has not come through the war with his faculties intact." Both sergeants extended their stay after the armistice by signing a six-month civilian contract to help with the de-Nazification of Germany, bringing in suspected Nazis for interrogation and sentencing. Sergeant X is in his room, "and for more than an hour he had been triple-reading para-

---

*"Just Before the War with the Eskimos," title of JDS story in *Nine Stories*.

graphs, and now he was doing it to the sentences." He opens a book that belonged to a "low-level official in the Nazi Party, but high enough, by Army Regulations standards, to fall into an automatic-arrest category."

> X himself had arrested her. Now, for the third time since he had returned from the hospital that day, he opened the woman's book and read the brief inscription on the flyleaf. Written in ink, in German, in small, hopelessly sincere handwriting, were the words "Dear God, life is hell." Nothing led up to or away from it. Alone on the page, and in the sickly stillness of the room, the words appeared to have the stature of an uncon-testable, even classic indictment. . . . [X] wrote down under the inscription, in English, "Fathers and teachers, I ponder 'What is hell?' I maintain that it is the suffering of being unable to love." He started to write Dostoevski's name under the inscription, but saw—with fright that ran through his whole body—that what he had written was almost entirely illegible. He shut the book.

The change in my father's handwriting in the letters (which I read in the Library of Congress collection) he wrote to friends and family stateside after his release from the hospital at Nürnberg is truly spooky. His handwriting, almost as distinctive and familiar to me as his face, be-comes something *totally* unrecognizable.

Sergeant X's friend, Corporal Z, who like John Keenan, was his "Jeep partner and constant companion" throughout the war, comes in the room. He notices that X's face is jumping and twitching. Z tells him that he wrote to his girl back home, a psychology major, and told her that X had had a nervous breakdown.

> "You know what she said? She says nobody gets a nervous breakdown just from the war and all. She says you probably were unstable like, your whole goddam life."
>
> X bridged his hands over his eyes—the light over the bed seemed to be blinding him—and said that Loretta's insight into things was always a joy.

Later, alone, he thinks that there "might be some quick, however slight, therapy in it" to write a letter to an old friend in New York, but his fingers shake so violently he can't roll a sheet of paper into his typewriter. He knows he should get the vomity wastebasket out of the room, but instead puts his head down and closes his eyes sleeplessly. "A few throbbing minutes later" he opens his eyes and notices a letter he hasn't opened. It is from Esmé, the young girl he had met in England. It's a lovely, plain letter much like the one Mattie wrote to Babe, or the girl in Belgium wrote to "Family Bill." The story ends:

He just sat with it in his hand for another long period. Then, suddenly, almost ecstatically, he felt sleepy.

You take a really sleepy man, Esmé, and he *al*ways stands a chance of again becoming a man with all his fac—with all his f-a-c-u-l-t-i-e-s intact.

4

Detached F-a-c-u-l-t-i-e-s

Wild Nights—Wild Nights!
Were I with thee
Wild Nights should be
Our luxury!

Futile—the Winds—
To a Heart in port—
Done with the Compass—
Done with the Chart!

Rowing in Eden—
Ah, the Sea!
Might I but moor—Tonight—
In Thee!

—Emily Dickinson*

THE WAYS IN WHICH MY FATHER SOUGHT to reattach himself and characters to their moorings, before I was born, the ways he found to save them and himself from hell—"the suffering of being unable to love"—is of central interest to me, as his daughter and as a person who also has experienced her own mind "suddenly lurch and

---

*This is the poem that Babe, in "A Boy in France," wished for as he withdrew his hand under the blanket and created, in his battlefield foxhole, a dream in which he imagines himself clean, at home, and with a girl: "I'll ask her to read some Emily Dickinson to me—that one about being chartless. . . and I'll bolt the door."

teeter like insecure luggage on the overhead rack." When and how my father and his characters reached out in a moment of personal crisis and re-established connection, or instead, did the reverse and bolted the door, became something I now looked at closely. How my father dealt with the real-life traumas of war, of anti-Semitism, of family; the vicissitudes of suffering, and his attempts at resolution throughout his life and work, began to reveal some familiar patterns.

I found out that in real life, Sergeant Salinger did not receive a re-demptive letter or a hand out of hell from a young girl. Instead, he, like Sergeant X, met a young woman who, like the woman in the story, was a "low-level official in the Nazi party, but high enough by Army Regulations standards to fall into an automatic-arrest category." Sergeant Salinger, himself, had arrested her. She and Jerry were married by summer's end.

Given my father's sense of duty and honor, as well as his deeply suspicious nature—he was indeed well cast in his role as interrogator—Sylvia, his first wife, must have been, as my mother said, an extraordinary woman. My aunt described Sylvia to me as a tall, thin woman with dark hair, pale skin, and blood-red lips and nails. She had a sharp, incisive way of speaking and was some sort of a doctor. My aunt said, "She was *very* German," and gave me a dark look, chin tucked in, eyebrows raised as if she were peering over the top of bifocals and directly into my eyes for emphasis. My father told my mother that Sylvia, in contrast to Claire, was a real woman who knew her own mind and had accomplished something at a young age. He also vilified her as a terrible, dark woman of passion, an evil woman who bewitched him. My mother said he told her that Sylvia hated Jews as much as he hated Nazis, and she let him feel it. Their relationship, he said, was extremely intense, both physically and emotionally. As happened with many wartime marriages, their passion did not survive transplanting to America, where they moved in with his parents. Sylvia went back to Europe for good several months later. Aunt Doris said, "Mother didn't like her."

I knew my father had a war bride whom he jokingly referred to as "Saliva," instead of Sylvia, but otherwise he was pretty untalkative about his homecoming, scattering a few details such as the hell of his hay fever at the time, as he held a handkerchief to his maddeningly itchy nose and eyes during allergy season each summer. "It was like this only worse over there," he'd tell me, blowing his nose and digging at his reddened eyes. More of the feelings, rather than the details, emerge in his story "The Stranger" (*Collier's,* December 1, 1945) in which he tells us about Babe's homecoming. Babe is suffering acutely from hay fever and battle fatigue. He is home physically, but can't make the transition back to civilian life in his mind and emotions.

You don't need to be the Regis Professor of Poetry for the poetry of this story to hit you squarely between the eyes. He uses language, here, like Basho's frog*—a few words, and an image unfurls in the mind and the five senses, like the little clamshells we had when we were kids and you'd drop them, plop, into a glass of water, and the shell would open and a colored paper flower, hidden inside, would unfold and rise blooming, filling the glass.

Babe's friend Vincent Caulfield has been killed in action. Babe, unlike Vincent, has made it home alive, and he decides to visit Vincent's girl, bring her a poem Vincent wrote for her, and to tell her how he died. His sister Mattie, who is still ten years old, as she was in the story "Last Day of the Last Furlough," set several years before when Babe left for war, accompanies him. He stands at Vincent's girl's door thinking that he shouldn't have come at all.

The maid answers the door and goes to get Vincent's girl. While they wait for her in the living room, Babe looks through a pile of records beside the phonograph.

His mind began to hear the old Bakewell Howard's rough, fine horn playing. Then he began to hear the music of the unrecoverable years . . . when all the dead boys in the 12th Regiment had been living and cutting in on other dead boys on lost dance

---

*Basho (1644–94)   *Furu ike ya!*   The old pond, ah!
                     Kawazu tobikomu,   A frog jumps in:
                     Mizu no oto.   The water's sound!
Or, Sengai's (1750–1863) response to the beloved and revered old master:
                     Ike arabe,   If there were a pond [around here],
                     Tonde basho ni   I would jump in, and let Basho
                     Kikasetai.   Hear [the plop]!

floors: the years when no one who could dance worth a damn had ever heard of Cherbourg or Saint-Lô or Hürtgen Forest or Luxembourg.

Isn't that just brilliant? She comes in the room and Babe introduces himself. They all go into her bedroom where the light is better. Vincent's girl and Mattie sit on her bed, Babe in a chair facing them.

Babe crossed his long legs as most tall men do, laying the ankle on the knee. "I'm out. I got out," he said. He looked at the clock in his sock, one of the most unfamiliar things in the new, combat-bootless world, then up at Vincent's girl. Was she real? "I got out last week," he said.

He starts to tell her about Vincent's death, feeling the same urge that Philly Burns did in trying to explain to his wife, Juanita, that guys don't really die all handsome and Hollywood, the way they do in the movies: it's a lie, it wasn't like that, and the lie isn't fair to the men who suffered. Babe was there when Vincent was blown to pieces by mortar fire. When Vincent's girl asks Babe what a mortar is, he's torn between wanting to tell civilians the truth and keeping quiet about the whole damn thing. He gives up and hands her the poem Vincent wrote about her. He starts to apologize, but she tells him she's glad he came anyway. Babe heads for the door quickly because he, too, is crying. He calms down in the elevator with Mattie, but outside on the street things are worse again:

The three long blocks between Lexington and Fifth were dull and noonish, as only that stretch can be in late August. A fat, apartment-house doorman, cupping a cigarette in his hand, was walking a wire-haired along the curb between Park and Madison.

Babe figured that during the whole time of the Bulge, the guy had walked that dog on this street every day. He couldn't believe it. He could believe it, but it was still impossible. He felt Mattie put her hand in his. . . .

"Babe," she said.

"What?"

"Are you glad to be home?"

"Yes, baby."

"Ow! You're hurting my hand."

He relaxes his grip. The story ends, once again, with a hand stretched toward him helping him out of his private hell. He watches his little sister Mattie. "With her feet together she made the little jump from the curb to the street surface, then back again. Why was it such a beautiful thing to see?"*

Why indeed? Just as the rage expressed by my father—both in his fiction and in real life—at WASP "Society," country clubs, Ivy League schools, debutantes, and the like, becomes less a personal, private Salinger idiosyncrasy when looked at in the context of his life as a Jew or half-Jew growing up in New York in the twenties and thirties, so, too, I think, his wartime experiences and stories of Staff Sergeant Babe Gladwaller and Staff Sergeant X provide a context for *The Catcher in the Rye*. I'm not saying that the reader needs to know the background of the story to appreciate the book, I'm saying something much smaller, that *I* needed to understand the context and the connections to begin to make sense of the frightening, life-or-death emotional intensity evoked in both my dad and his character Holden by things that seem like minor aesthetic issues. I needed to understand how logic and proportion could go so awry sometimes in my relationship with him.

-----

*In a similar scene, Holden spots a family walking ahead of him and tells us the parents were paying no attention to their little boy:

> The kid was swell. He was walking in the street, instead of on the sidewalk, but right next to the curb. . . . I got up closer so I could hear what he was singing. . . . The cars zoomed by, brakes screeched all over the place, his parents paid no attention to him, and he kept on walking next to the curb and singing "If a body catch a body coming through the rye." It made me feel better. It made me feel not so depressed anymore. (*Catcher*, p. 115)

When I read this passage as a mother, rather than as I first did, in my twenties and single, I was outraged. I thought, how nice for you, so glad you're not feeling so blue and have had your Dostoevskian "ability to love" restored, but would somebody please get that child off the street and out of traffic so he doesn't get killed?

After reading the war stories, what had once seemed like foreign territory in *The Catcher* became, in many ways, a familiar story. While the traumas of war and death and dislocation are displaced in *The Catcher*—Nazis are replaced by "phonies" as the enemy—their ability to destroy lives and to wreak emotional havoc upon the survivors diminishes not a whit when storm troopers' black uniforms are exchanged for professors' tweeds.* The battlefield is gone, but when Holden calls out to his dead brother, Allie (who died at ten from leukemia), "Save me, Allie, save me!" as he feels himself "sinking down, down, down" into an abyss, terrified he won't live to reach the curb at the far side of the street, he is in as desperate a fight for his life as was the boy in France. The ways in which Holden seeks to re-establish connection, to find a port in the storm, are familiar as well. When he decides to run away, like the "Little Indian" story of Sonny and like Lionel in "Down at the Dinghy," he waits to say good-bye to his ten-year-old sister, Phoebe; and she, like Mattie for Babe, Esmé for X, and perhaps Sylvia for my father, gives him something to love, a way to reattach and go home again—"a beautiful thing to see."

❦

DURING THE TIME MY FATHER was finishing *The Catcher in the Rye* and working on "De Daumier-Smith's Blue Period," a story about an artist on the verge of a breakdown, he was, like his character, in a dark place, with his faculties only loosely intact. He was living in the apartment my mother described as dark and underwater-feeling, with black sheets and black furniture that, she said, seemed to match his depression. My mother said that, at the time, Jerry sank into "black holes where he could hardly move, hardly talk."†

---

*This was true in our family life as well. To give but one instance, typical of hundreds, when I was about nine I asked—begged—my dad for a pair of white go-go boots. The swirl of emotional invective that rained down upon my unsuspecting head might have been appropriate to my having been asked if I could join the Nazi party and wear those cute jackboots. Wild Nights—Wild Nights!

†My mother's language here reminds me of the language my father uses in the scene where Holden fears he'll sink down into oblivion and cries out for Allie to

Leila Hadley said that when she read "De Daumier-Smith's Blue Period," she was sure he had based the hero on himself. To say that my father based the hero on himself is a bit too straightforward, too linear and logical for the way this story is a reflection or refraction of my father's life in the mirror world of his fiction; but I know what Ms. Hadley means. When I read this story, it rang so true, so much like my father, that it had the uncanny feeling of being real, a story about an uncle of mine or something, rather than a piece of fiction.

This story, "De Daumier-Smith's Blue Period," is a veritable template upon which a lifetime of my father's and his characters' likes and dislikes, their struggles to connect and their increasingly dreamlike, disconnected, abracadabra, otherworldly solutions to suffering are etched, indelibly, with an artist's alchemy whereby stone takes life, and life turns to stone. It is in this story that I saw "as through a glass darkly" the makings of our inverted forest.

The young man in "De Daumier-Smith's Blue Period" is an artist who has just returned to New York after living in Paris for most of his life thus far. He is not adjusting well to being back and, like Babe, feels like "The Stranger." The young man's mother, with whom he was very close, has died, and he is sharing a hotel room with his stepfather, who is also bereft and floundering. He spends the fall doing a series of eighteen oil paintings, seventeen of which are self-portraits. When he comes across an ad in the paper for an art instructor at a Montreal correspondence school of the "Draw Binky" type, on impulse he applies and is accepted. As with Sergeant X, we never learn

---

save him. Also where Holden describes his brother, D.B. ("a writer by profession," which is how both Sergeant X in "Esmé" and Buddy in *Seymour: An Introduction* describe themselves), when he returned from the war after having spent, as did my father, four years in the army and landing on D-Day; when he came home, all he did was "lie on his bed, practically." See, too, my father's last published book, *Raise High the Roof Beam, Carpenters and Seymour: An Introduction,* in which he speaks of the period of time after the war and through the publication of *The Catcher in the Rye,* saying that he/Buddy wrote the short story "A Perfect Day for Bananafish" "just a couple of months after Seymour's death, and not too very long after I myself, like both the 'Seymour' in the story and the Seymour in Real Life, had returned from the European Theater of Operations. I was using a very poorly rehabilitated, not to say unbalanced, German typewriter."

his name, only his pseudonym—de Daumier-Smith—which he takes on when he applies for the art school job, claiming to be a nephew of Daumier. He is accepted, assigned three students, and given their application packets.

The first two students are an embodiment, almost a caricature, of what Sri Ramakrishna, whose work my father was studying deeply at the time, referred to as the excreta of "woman and gold." The first is a young housewife who has given herself the professional name "Bambi." She includes in her application a large pinup-style photo of herself in a bathing suit. Her sample drawings, desperately bad both in choice of subject and workmanship, are attached "rather subordinately" to her photo. She writes that her favorite artists are Rembrandt and Walt Disney.

The second student is a society photographer, R. Howard Ridgefield, who said that his wife thought he should get "into the painting racket."* His painting, obscene in subject and rendering, depicts a young woman with "udder-size breasts" being sexually assaulted in church.

Nearly overcome with despair, he opens the third envelope. It is from a nun named Sister Irma. She teaches cooking and drawing at a convent elementary school. Instead of a photograph of herself, she sends a snapshot of her convent. Her hobbies are "loving her Lord and the Word of her Lord" and "collecting leaves but only when they are laying right on the ground." She was assigned to teach the children to draw when another sister died. The children, she writes, like to draw people when they are running and she asks his help because she doesn't know how to do that. She wants to work hard to improve and sends some paintings—unsigned. Her work is described as that of a "true artist." He stashes Sister Irma's envelope in his breast pocket where "neither thieves [nor his employers] could break in. . . . I didn't care to risk having Sister Irma taken away from me. . . . That evening, however, with Sister Irma's envelope warm against my chest, I had never felt more relaxed."†

---

*See "Hapworth," where Seymour requests many books, "preferably containing no excellent photographs." My father goes ballistic at the suggestion that photography is an art.

†Babe, too, stashed in his breast pocket a letter from his little sister Mattie to keep his faculties intact in his terrible foxhole, as does Sergeant X, just out of a

That night, he stays up working on Sister Irma's sketches and writing to her a long, "almost endless" letter, which he describes as both passionate and chaste. The next day he wonders "in a real panic" how he'll manage to keep his sanity until her next envelope arrives. He doesn't. As he stands outside the window of an orthopedic-appliance shop,

> something altogether hideous happened. The thought was forced on me that no matter how coolly or sensibly or gracefully I might one day learn to live my life, I would always at best be a visitor in a garden of enamel urinals and bedpans, with a sightless, wooden dummy-deity standing by in a marked-down rupture truss.

He somehow makes his way back to his room, where he lies in bed shivering for hours, sleep eluding him, until he forces himself to concentrate on the image of Sister Irma, and of his visiting her at the convent. He imagines her behind a high fence, coming to meet him. In his mind she is

> a shy, beautiful girl of eighteen who had not yet taken her final vows and was still free to go out into the world with the Peter Abelard–type man of her choice. I saw us walking slowly, silently, toward a far, verdant part of the convent grounds, where suddenly, and without sin, I would put my arm around her waist. The image was too ecstatic to hold in place, and, finally, I let go, and fell asleep.

The following day, in front of the same orthopedic-appliance store, he has a mystical vision, a reversal of the one that so upset him where he saw everything, including himself, turned to excreta and its paraphernalia. Now, suddenly, in a whirl of light, the enamel urinals and bed-pans are mystically turned into a shimmering garden of "twice-blessed flowers."

---

military hospital, a letter from a young girl, Esmé; in all three stories the fragile mental stability of the man is held together by a thin letter. As Mattie's letter sustains Babe amidst the obscene carnage of the battlefield, Sister Irma's sustains de Daumier-Smith through the long afternoon of correcting Ridgefield's nudes, male and female "sans sex organs" that he had "genteely and obscenely drawn."

IT IS UNCANNY HOW CLAIRE, a shy, beautiful girl, fresh from convent school, should walk into my father's life as if on cue, shaped into reality from the mists of his dream, the way Cornish would appear as if in response to Holden's dream of a little cabin somewhere right at the edge of a forest. When Jerry came to visit her, she said it was blissful. They took long walks by the river and talked late into the night. But she also remembers long stretches of time that year when he neither called nor visited, leaving her feeling, once again, bereft, and at sea.

5

We'll Bolt the Door

❧❦❧

I am not One who much or oft delight
To season my fireside with personal talk,—
Of friends, who live within an easy walk,
Or neighbours, daily, weekly, in my sight:
And, for my chance-acquaintance, ladies bright,
Sons, mothers, maidens withering on the stalk,
These all wear out of me, like Forms, with chalk
Painted on rich men's floors, for one feast-night.
Better than such discourse doth silence long,
Long, barren silence, square with my desire;
To sit without emotion, hope, or aim,
In the loved presence of my cottage-fire,
And listen to the flapping of the flame,
Or kettle whispering its faint undersong.
—"Personal Talk," William Wordsworth

MY AUNT DORIS, Daddy's sister, told me, some forty-odd years later, how the two of them found their way to Cornish. In the fall of 1952, during a glorious Indian summer, Doris and her brother decided to take a holiday. She told me that he had some money in his pocket from the publication, the previous summer, of *The Catcher in the Rye* and wanted to look for a little place in the country where he could live and work without the distractions of the city. Doris was what was called in those days a career girl. She was divorced, thirty-eight, living at home with her parents in Manhattan, and busy traveling back and forth to Europe as a buyer for the Green Room at Bloomingdale's. Nevertheless, when he suggested that she come with him, she said she dropped everything and "jumped" at the chance for a pleasant drive in the country with her beloved brother.

They drove up the New England coast and stopped at Cape Ann, an area north of Boston, with its old seafaring towns of Essex, Ipswich, and Gloucester. They loved Cape Ann. He would have bought a place and settled there, in Melville's old stomping grounds, but after looking at houses for a few days, he realized he couldn't afford it. No one at the time, least of all he, expected *The Catcher in the Rye* to take off the way it later did.

They headed inland and north along the Connecticut River valley and stopped for lunch in Windsor, Vermont. A local real estate agent, Hilda Russell, struck up a conversation with them at the town diner. After lunch, she drove them across the covered bridge that spans the Connecticut River between Windsor, Vermont, and Cornish, New Hampshire, and up a rough, steep, dirt road, miles into the hills and woods. They passed a dairy farm, cows perched, as they do in the Alps, on impossibly steep pastures. Like their cows, the dairy farmers up in the hills maintained a precarious existence. Many spent winters working over at the split ball-bearing factory in Windsor, or at the Goodyear rubber plant before it closed. Others left for months at a time, signing on with winter fishing boats that sailed from Gloucester, while their wives and children held the fort at home.

The road took a sharp turn just past the farm and climbed straight up between two steep pastures, the fields humming with the Indian-summer colors of goldenrod, Queen Anne's lace, Indian paintbrushes, and black-eyed Susans, and the songs of birds, bees, cicadas, and grasshoppers. As they reached the crest of the hill, the pasture faded softly into woods, and they continued upward at a gentler pace, through birch trees, pines, old maple, and oak. Along this stretch of the road, the only sign of human existence was a group of seven rough, unmarked gravestones concealed in a tangle of underbrush and green moss.

After another mile or so, they approached a clearing in the woods. There, at the highest point of the hilly road, stands a small barn-red house. It is perched on the edge of a meadow that falls sharply downward for about an acre or so to the brook below. The meadow is so steep, in fact, that if you go over the edge, you have to hold on to strong weeds to pull yourself back up. The brook, and the remaining few feet of old pasture at the bottom, disappear into a forest of tall pine trees that slopes steadily downward to the Connecticut River valley many miles below. Beyond the river, Mount Ascutney rises up from the floor of the valley to the sky like a dark blue pyramid. To the right of the mountain, a patchwork of green and brown dairy farms spreads over the valley. Above and behind the farms, rows upon rows of smaller mountains fade to lighter and lighter blue as they roll like waves across Vermont, spilling into New York State.

The realtor said that on a clear day, you could see the Adirondack Mountains hundreds of miles away. The living room windows faced due west, the perfect spot, she said, to view the sun setting over Mt. Ascutney. Doris agreed that the view was magnificent, but the house itself was another story. "It wasn't a house, Peggy, it was a *disaster*." She felt rather insulted at having been shown the place at all. There was no running water, and no bathroom facilities to speak of. The kitchen was a hovel. The rest of the house consisted of one small, water-stained bedroom, and a living room that resembled a barn, two stories high, with exposed beams and an arched wooden ceiling. A large family of squirrels had set up housekeeping in the living room rafters. "Vermin," said Doris. Away from the view, on the east side of the living room where it shared a wall and chimney with the kitchen, was a blackened fieldstone fireplace. Beside the fireplace, a rickety wooden staircase, built along the wall, led up to a little loft.

Doris could not believe that her brother would even consider buying the place—this was well before the days of rustic chic; livestock, not writers, lived in barns. She knew that Sonny had just enough money to buy the house "as is," with nothing left over to repair it, or, as Doris thought more appropriate, to raze the thing and build something decent from the ground up. But she hadn't been listening very carefully to Holden's dream:

> . . . I'd build me a little cabin somewhere with the dough I
> made and live there for the rest of my life. I'd build it right near

Aunt Doris and Granny before my father was born, around 1916.

Doris and "Sonny," the future J. D. Salinger, August 1920. "You know, Peggy, your father and I were the best of friends growing up."

Left to right: Two friends, Doris in background, Sonny, and their mother, Miriam. "In a Jewish family, you know, a boy is special," Doris said. "Mother doted on him. He could do no wrong. I thought he was perfect too."

Doris as a high school senior. "Mother told me that when a woman from a finishing school in Dobbs Ferry that I had applied to came to interview the family, she said, 'Oh, Mrs. Salinger, it's too bad you married a Jew.' People talked that way in those days, you know. It was hard on me but it was hell on Sonny. I think he suffered terribly from anti-Semitism when he went away to military school."

Sonny at Valley Forge Military Academy.

My father describes, in his fiction, exactly what I witnessed of his real-life visits with Granny, Grandpa, and Aunt Doris: "Sometimes...when I come in the front door, it's like entering a kind of untidy, secular, two-woman convent. Sometimes when I leave, I have a peculiar feeling that both M. and her mother have stuffed my pockets with little bottles and tubes containing lipstick, rouge, hairnets, deodorants, and so on.... I don't know what to do with their invisible gifts." (*Raise High the Roof Beam, Carpenters*, p. 69)

In the spring of 1936, my father dropped out of college and took a job on a cruise ship.

Salinger rose from private to staff sergeant, landed on Utah beach on D-Day, was on or near the front lines with the Twelfth Infantry Regiment of the Fourth Division from D-Day to VE Day, from Utah beach to Cherbourg, on through the battles of the Hedgerows and bloody Mortain, to Hürtgen Forest, Luxembourg, and the Battle of the Bulge.

Entered: Class IV; Vice-President IV; Vice-President III; President II; Junior Dramatic Club IV; Chorus III; Dramatic Club III, II, I, President I; French Club III, II, I; International Relations Club I; Third Hockey Team IV; First Hockey Team III, II, I; Third Basketball Team IV; First Basketball Team III, II, I; Baseball Squad IV; Tennis Squad III, II, I; Captain Green Team II.

ALISON CLAIRE DOUGLAS
New York, New York

What She Is: Ingenious
Idiosyncrasy: Those eyebrows
Passion: French perfume and records
Animosity: Sophistication
Expression: I've got so much to do
Where Found: On the Honor Roll
Why Can't I: Live nine lives?
Remembered for: Her originality
Destiny: Sarah Bernhardt's successor

*"My heart's in the Highlands;
my heart is not here"*

Seventeen

In the fall of 1950, Claire met a writer named Jerry Salinger at a party in New York. She was sixteen and had just begun her senior year at Shipley.

Jerry, at thirty-one, was nearly twice Claire's age and was quite simply, or rather, quite complicatedly, tall, dark, and handsome.

Claire's mother and stepfather in the Duveen Brothers Gallery, in the 1960s.

My grandfather, Solomon ("Sol") Salinger.

My parents' beloved yogi, Lahiri Mahasaya. When my brother and I were children, my father gave both of us a photograph of a yogi and asked us to tuck his picture away and take it with us wherever we went. Since Daddy never mentioned the yogi's name, I never asked who he was. I just thought he looked a lot like Grandpa with his lush white hair and mustache.

The summer after her freshman year at Radcliffe, Claire was back in New York, where she worked as a model for Lord & Taylor. She hid the fact that she was modeling from Jerry. "Your father would not have approved, all that vain, worldly, women and clothes.... I didn't dare tell him."

When Claire's pregnancy became obvious, she said that Jerry's attraction turned to "abhorrence."

the woods, but not right *in* them, because I'd want it to be sunny
as hell all the time. . . . I'd meet this beautiful girl that was also a
deaf-mute and we'd get married. . . . If we had any children,
we'd hide them somewhere. We could buy them a lot of books
and teach them how to read and write by ourselves.

(*Catcher,* p. 199)

On New Year's Day, 1953, Jerry's thirty-fourth birthday, he moved
into that house in Cornish. Claire spent many long weekends with him
there. This being the fifties, a young lady had to obtain written permission from a respectable person to be away from college for the weekend.
Claire and Jerry made up a certain "Mrs. Trowbridge" and composed
some very funny letters to Claire's mother and to those *in loco parentis* at
Radcliffe, with lots of silly, patrician news about Claire's lovely visits
with the little Trowbridges, and how much we enjoy having her come to
stay with us at our winter cottage.

In a scene straight out of *The Catcher in the Rye,* where Holden on
an impulse asks Sally Hayes to run away with him to the sunny cabin he
imagines right on the edge of a forest, Jerry asked Claire to drop out of
school and come live with him in Cornish. When Claire refused, Jerry
dropped out of sight. She thinks he spent the year in Europe but isn't
sure. In desperation, she borrowed a car and drove up to the house, but
there were no signs of life. Had she been able to contact him, she said,
she would have done anything to be with him. "The whole world was
your father—everything he said, wrote, and thought. I read the things
he told me to read, not the college stuff nearly as much, looked on the
world through his eyes, lived my life as if he were watching me. When I
stood up to him on that one thing, college, he vanished."

Claire was not a person with her faculties intact. When he left, she
collapsed. She was hospitalized with a long bout of mononucleosis complicated by a rather dubious appendectomy. My mother's version of
what happened next has remained remarkably stable over the years in
its instability, like a snapshot of a building collapsing. I could recite it in
my sleep. It begins: "I was sooooo tired. A very nice man from the business school wanted to marry me. He kept coming by my hospital room
and asking me to marry him and finally I said yes. It was such a relief
just to be left alone where it was sooooo quiet."

They eloped sometime that spring; she is fuzzy about the details. The marriage was annulled within the year. The impression I had as a young girl hearing this story was of somebody sleepwalking or in a fevered state. It worried me that such important things could happen to you in a dream or somewhere stuck between dreaming and waking. It also angered me. This quality of depicting herself as a person without will, a marionette almost, in someone else's hands, acknowledging no responsibility for her part in all this, made me a little crazy. It may have been her reality, but mine, as a young child, felt like an almost constant struggle between the often violent urge to shake her into sensibility, hoping she'd be my lost mother, and self-protection—a Pyrrhic victory—as I tiptoed away, invisible, and let sleeping tigers lie.

❧

JERRY REAPPEARED IN CLAIRE'S LIFE during the summer of '54. By the fall, Claire had moved in with him. They drove down to Cambridge each week from Cornish so that she could attend classes Tuesday through Thursday. Jerry took a room at the Commodore Hotel, and she shared an apartment with five other divorced or otherwise "not quite dorm material" girls, as she put it. He became increasingly unhappy with this arrangement and the effect it had on his work, a story that would be called "Franny." This bothers my mother to think about because, as she says, "it wasn't even 'Franny's' story, it was mine, and that's *not* how it happened." In real life, the girl in a blue dress, with the blue-and-white overnight bag slung over her shoulder, was named Claire, not Franny. She still has the order slip from Brentano's Bookbinding Department for "Franny's" book, *The Way of a Pilgrim*.

In January of 1955, "Franny," the thirty-seven-page first part of what would become the book *Franny and Zooey*, was published in *The New Yorker*. During that same month, just after the midyear examination period of Claire's senior year, she said she was given an ultimatum. "The choice was the same as last time, choose Jerry and Cornish, or Radcliffe and a degree."

Just four months shy of graduation, Claire dropped out of college. The story of what happened when Claire, as in the dream of Sister Irma, a young girl just short of her vows, left the verdant grounds of Cambridge with her Peter Abelard, reminds me of one of our favorite movies, *Lost Horizon:* outside the gate of the verdant valley, a blizzard howled. On their wedding day, Claire and Jerry drove, or rather crept, thirty miles through a nearly impenetrable gray, February sleet, from Cornish, New Hampshire, to Bradford, Vermont, to find a justice of the peace. My mother describes the four of them packed into my father's drafty old Jeep, Jerry cursing the road, their witnesses—Bet and Mike Mitchell—in the back, silent, probably petrified, as he is a terrifying driver under the best of circumstances. My father's version of the wedding, oft repeated to my brother and me, usually starts out with him grumbling that he's never forgiven Bet and Mike, friends of his from his Westport days some years before he moved to Cornish, for not "speaking up" and letting him go through with such an obvious mistake.

The gray reality of their elopement contrasted sharply with Seymour's resplendent dream of a "sacred, sacred day." On the eve of his elopement, my father's character, Seymour Glass, wrote in his diary:

> I really called to ask her, to beg her for the last time to just go off alone with me and get married. I'm too keyed up to be with people. I feel as though I'm about to be born. Sacred, sacred day. . . . I've been reading a miscellany of Vedanta all day. Marriage partners are to serve each other. Elevate, help, teach, strengthen each other, but above all, *serve.* Raise their children honorably, lovingly, and with detachment. . . . How wonderful, how sane, how beautifully difficult, and therefore true. The joy of responsibility for the first time in my life.
>
> (*Raise High the Roof Beam, Carpenters,* pp. 90–91)

On his honeymoon, however, Seymour sat down on the hotel bed where his new wife, Muriel, lay sleeping, took out a pistol, and blew his brains out in "A Perfect Day for Bananafish," written around 1947. My father wrote the "sacred, sacred day" passage above, from *Raise High the Roof Beam, Carpenters,* around 1955. He had dropped out of Claire's life in 1953, when he wrote "Teddy," an ode to the renunciation of earthly attachment of any sort, most especially sexual attachment; and then, in 1955, less than two years later, he asked Claire to marry him. What happened? Was it just another impulsive scene in the drama between blissful engagement and blowing one's brains out, attraction and repulsion, attachment and renunciation, bringing flowers and throwing stones?*

I assumed that his off-again, on-again relationship with Claire, before they were married, was just another act in this drama of conflict. Then I found out, in talking to my mother, that something quite different had happened that led to their marriage: my father had found a new guru with a message that appeared to reconcile the conflict between earthly attraction and heavenly renunciation. According to the teachings of this guru, Paramahansa Yogananda, women and gold, the two enemies of enlightenment and karmic progress, were transmuted from Ramakrishna's bags of "phlegm, filth, and excreta" into something potentially holy. Marriage, for the first time in my father's post-war study of religion, was held out as something potentially sacred rather than automatically defiling; Eve and the serpent were no longer ineluctably entwined.

During the fall and winter evenings prior to Jerry and Claire's wedding, they had been reading a miscellany not of Vedanta, as Seymour had prior to his marriage, but rather, Paramahansa Yogananda's book *Autobiography of a Yogi*. My mother told me that what was so appealing to them at the time were the stories about Lahiri Mahasaya, Yogananda's guru, who lived from 1828 to 1895. Lahiri Mahasaya is told

---

*I mentioned earlier that, as a child, Seymour threw a rock at a little girl who was sitting in the sunshine, inflicting serious injury, opening up her forehead and requiring stitches. In the story, everyone in the family understood that it was "because she looked so beautiful" sitting there in the sunshine. I don't understand it, but to the Glass family and their author, it was an almost religious act and made perfect sense. The only way I have of approaching some feel for this is something I learned from my son. We went through a period during the terrible twos where he'd hug me and be really close, and then all of a sudden he'd throw something at me or hit me. It was so weird; he'd only misbehave like that when things were really lovey-dovey, not when he was mad about something. We figured out that at times it (Mommy and me) became too intense for him and that he felt engulfed, in danger of being swamped by me and his feelings for me. He still got put in time-out for doing it, but I could then help him with it by backing off a bit, and encouraging him to use his words, and also by having his dad take over more of the parenting stuff for a while, until he'd regained his equilibrium. It makes me think of my aunt saying, "It was always Sonny and Mother, Mother and Sonny. Daddy never got the recognition he deserved." All I know is that a man who is too close to his mother, who can't separate properly, is as much of a danger sign as one who hates his mother and can't get close to women. It's a tricky thing getting those boundaries right.

that he has been chosen by God to bring the path of the yogi, heretofore restricted to celibate renunciates of the world, to those who desire enlightenment but are "encumbered" by family ties and jobs, or "worldly burdens." His message is that even the highest yogic attainments are open to such a family man.

My mother recently sent me a copy of the book with a note telling me to "look up Lahiri Mahasaya and householders in the index rather than ploughing your way through." She said that I was to read the "sweet passages" about Lahiri Mahasaya and his wife, their duties as "householders"—that is to say, as married persons with children rather than monks or nuns.

My mother said she remembers feeling "full of joy at having found a path," a religious way that said "women can," in contrast to her Catholic upbringing with its male-dominated hierarchy, and in contrast to Vedanta and the Vivekananda center where celibate men were, she said, again the valued ones. She remembered Paramahansa Yogananda's book as tremendously liberating. When I read the book, I wondered if we were reading the same thing, particularly as I read Yogananda's interview with Lahiri Mahasaya's widow, whom he calls the Sacred Mother or Kashi Moni. In this passage, Kashi Moni tells Yogananda that it was years before she realized the "divine" status of her husband. In a vision she saw her husband floating in midair, in the lotus position, surrounded by angels who were worshiping him. As he came back down to the floor of their bedroom, she threw herself prostrate at his feet, begging him to forgive her for having thought of him as her husband.

"Master," I cried . . . "I die with shame to realize that I have remained asleep in ignorance by the side of one who is divinely awakened. From this night, you are no longer my husband, but my guru. Will you accept my insignificant self as your disciple?"

In a ritual gesture he accepts her as a disciple and instructs her to bow before the angels. In divine chorus, the angels sing to her:

"Consort of the Divine One, thou art blessed. We salute thee." They bowed at my feet and lo! Their refulgent forms vanished. . . .

From that night on, Lahiri Mahasaya never slept in my room again. Nor, thereafter, did he ever sleep. He remained in the front room downstairs, in the company of his disciples both by day and by night.

Kashi Moni then tells Yogananda that she will confess to him a "sin" she committed against her "guru-husband," when, several months after her vision and initiation as a disciple, she began to feel "forlorn and neglected."

One morning Lahiri Mahasaya entered this little room to fetch an article; I quickly followed him. Overcome by delusion, I addressed him scathingly.

"You spend all your time with the disciples. What about your responsibilities for your wife and children? I regret that you do not interest yourself in providing more money for the family."

The master glanced at me for a moment, then lo! He was gone. Awed and frightened, I heard a voice resounding from every part of the room:

"It is all nothing, don't you see? How could a nothing like me produce riches for you?"

"Guruji," I cried, "I implore pardon a million times! My sinful eyes can see you no more; please appear in your sacred form."

"I am here." This reply came from above me. I looked up and saw the master materialize in the air, his head touching the ceiling. His eyes were like blinding flames. Beside myself with fear, I lay sobbing at his feet after he had quietly descended to the floor.

"Woman," he said, "seek divine wealth, not the paltry tinsel of earth . . ."

I have to say that reading this, forty years after my parents' engagement, was like reading the obituary of our family before we even became one, or going back to the beginning of a tragedy and this time, with the benefit of hindsight, deciphering the oracle's cryptic prediction of the character's undoing. "Some months after my initiation, I began to feel forlorn and neglected. . . . You spend all your time with the disciples. What about your responsibilities for your wife and children?"* But that was yet to come.

While the relationship of Lahiri Mahasaya and his wife was, in a real sense, a foreshadowing of the state of my parents' married life, I am convinced were it not for the teaching of Lahiri Mahasaya, that neither their marriage nor my birth would have taken place at all, so caught up was my father in the teachings of Ramakrishna. The teachings of Yogananda held out to my father the possibility of having his cake and eating it, too, of marriage as an institution not hopelessly defiling, setting back one's karmic progression many lifetimes (recall Teddy's comment about a woman being responsible for his having been reincarnated in an American body). As a model for a marriage, I find his teachings and life anything but "sweet," but that said, it feels unseemly to speak ill of one whose teachings were so directly responsible for my birth.

Subsequent pregnancies, my mother said, came about because she wanted more babies and, at the right time of the month, would give my father far too much wine at dinner.

❦

AFTER READING *The Autobiography of a Yogi* together in the fall of 1954, they wrote, separately, to the publishers of the book, the Self-Realization Fellowship. Jerry soon asked if the fellowship could recommend a teacher-guru in their area who might consider initiating Claire and him into the fellowship. A member of the fellowship wrote back to say that the nearest disciple he could recommend was Swami Premananda, who had recently established a church of believers just outside of Washington, D.C., and suggested Jerry write to him. He did

---

*When my brother and I were children, my father gave both of us a photograph of a yogi and asked us to tuck his picture away, in our breast pockets where thieves could not break in, as it were, and take it with us wherever we went—off to boarding school and so on. Since Daddy never mentioned the yogi's name, I never asked who he was. I just thought he looked a lot like Grandpa with his lush white hair and mustache. Imagine my surprise to see "our" yogi's photograph in the center of Yogananda's book when my mother sent it to me. It was Lahiri Mahasaya. Yogananda relates several miraculous instances where people were saved from death—lightning bolts repelled, and so on—by the photographic image they had of Lahiri Mahasaya.

so immediately. Swami Premananda wrote back and said he would receive them, after their marriage, and initiate them as householder devotees. They were instructed to abstain from eating breakfast on the day of their arrival and to bring offerings of fresh fruit, flowers, and a little money.

Claire had seen Vivekananda's center off Fifth Avenue and loved its cathedral-like quiet and beautiful high ceilings. Her mind was filled with visions, from Paramahansa Yogananda's lush autobiography, of saffron robes, incense, and refulgent palaces in the sky of the Indian pantheon. When they got off the train, however, she found herself in what she called a lower-middle-class suburban area, "home for porters on the trains and people who bag groceries, that atmosphere. It wasn't my class of people." The church itself was "sweet and storefronty, kind of like a small grocery store." Then, much to my amusement, she summed up the ashram as, "you know, basic apple pie stuff." Laughing, I blurted out, "Ma, on what planet?" With some self-realization, thank goodness, she laughed, too.

As the conversation progressed, the "good girl" patina on the story underwent a sort of reverse transmutation, turning Cinderella's coach and coachmen back into a pumpkin and rats. The *"sweet* church" of her initial version became a "gaudied-up suburban tract house. The altar table had *photo*graphs on it." (This comment is understandable, coming as it does from a young woman who grew up with Giotto and Fra Angelico altarpieces on the walls of her parents' home.) And finally, "I didn't like the low ceilings of this horrid little place."

They were met by "this nice, sweet little Indian man, perhaps in his forties, but it's hard to tell." She said the man had no visible "whirls of glory" around him, as in Yogananda's book. "Without his robes on you'd have never noticed him." Jerry and Claire had a private meeting with the guru after the regular morning service, where the congregation sang "normal hymn tunes, but with funny words. He gave us each a mantra and taught us how to raise the breath and watch it." The Kriya yoga breathing exercises were, she said, very soothing and calming. They were instructed to practice for ten minutes each morning, and ten minutes in the evening. Premananda told them to return for more advanced training if they saw a white light in the middle of their forehead. In my typically enlightened way I said with a big eye roll, "Oh, great!" "No, no," she said. "I did see it, I think it has something

biological to do with the third eye. But I never went back to him. I went elsewhere."

"On the train home to Cornish that evening, Jerry and I made love in our sleeper car. It was so nice to . . . we did not make love very often, the body was evil. . . . I'm certain I became pregnant with you that night."

6

Reclusion

reclusion, n. 1. the condition or fact of becoming or being a recluse.
2. the condition or fact of being in solitary confinement.
—*Webster's*

WHEN CLAIRE'S PREGNANCY BECAME OBVIOUS, she said that Jerry's attraction turned to "abhorrence." There is a point in every woman's pregnancy, excepting perhaps that of the Virgin Mother herself, where the fiction of virginity can be maintained no longer. Gone was the pure novitiate, swept across her convent's verdant meadows by Peter Abelard, as de Daumier-Smith desired so ardently, and so desperately. Claire was no longer pure; her every motive was now suspect and tainted.

My mother told me that before she and my father were married, they had seen a lot of his friends and traveled often to New York and Boston; once married, however, she was increasingly isolated to the point where she felt she became "a virtual prisoner." From the fourth month of her pregnancy on they saw no one.

There is one thing you need to understand clearly. In Cornish, "seeing no one" doesn't mean that you have stopped entertaining formally; it means you do not lay eyes on a living soul, with the exception, perhaps, of Alex White, the man who came to empty our garbage shed once every two weeks or so and take it to the dump, or Mr. McCauley, who delivered the mail to a mailbox at the crossroads, a quarter of a mile down the road from the house, and only came by in person if there was something my father had to sign. My mother is not sure when they finally had a phone line run to the house, but whom would she have called? She had burnt her bridges, at my father's request. She said that he had asked that she not bring with her to Cornish any baggage from her past life as a student at Radcliffe.* She burned all her papers, including some fictional pieces and plays she had written while at college. As for maintaining contact with her school friends and family, I didn't need to be told how he dealt with that; I'd seen, through the years, how he derided any friend she might have had, as well as any contact with her family. It was fine for us to visit his family, but visits to my maternal grandmother were a source of major friction. Even as a little girl, he'd demand to know how I could accept gifts and vacations from someone I didn't "respect," as he put it. To this day he still puts his young wife, Colleen, through the wringer about contact with her family, as if the desire to see her family were a sign of shameful weakness and imperfection. Leave all and follow me.†

My mother, living in virtual isolation with my father in Cornish, didn't see much of him either. During the years when he was still publishing, she told me that he had not yet established the comfortable, regular routine that I remember well of rising at dawn, working until mid to late morning, driving into Windsor for the mail, coming home and doing his correspondence, or what he called "that damn stuff piled up on my desk," and then finishing for the day, leaving the afternoon free for gardening, going for walks, playing with his children or dogs, and doing a few errands. Instead, back then, sixteen-hour days were the

---

*A generation later, a girlfriend of my father's wrote that when he came to pick her up from her student apartment at Yale, to come to live with him and drop out of school, he arrived in his BMW, not his big Chevy Blazer, so that nearly all of her possessions, including her beloved bicycle that she'd had since she was a kid, were left behind. (The girl, Joyce Maynard, was eighteen, he was fifty-four.) She wrote that while she waited for him, she thought about a classmate she had become friends with at Yale and realized that she'd probably never see her again.

†See Jesus to his disciples, Matt. 4:18–23, also Matt. 10:37–39; Mark 1:16–21; Luke 14:26; and especially Luke 5:1–12, "They left everything and followed him."

norm, and often, he'd work all night and through the following day as well.*

When he was around, Claire said she was kept busier and busier. The house was primitive; there was no hot water, and poor heat, but Jerry demanded what she called "Park Avenue service." Much like the great Thoreau, who had his mother deliver lunch to his little cabin in the wilderness, my father required three good "New York restaurant" meals a day to please him, or so she thought. Then, just when she thought she could manage that, "It was decreed that the sheets should be laundered and ironed twice a week—with no hot water, and cold water that left everything rust-colored. It felt very like the fairy tale where, whatever the girl did, another impossible task was added on. . . . I was in despair, trapped. And I was subject to Jerry's constant and lacerating criticism when I failed to come up to his standards."

All was not a wicked fairy tale, however. My mother said she loved the beauty of Cornish, her garden, the peace and quiet. She also loved having the pictures of their Indian gurus around as company. "It was like my pictures of saints as a little Catholic girl." She practiced Yogananda's Kriya yoga faithfully and contentedly, morning and evening. The peace and quiet never lasted very long, however. "I wanted to stay with that [Kriya yoga], but Jerry jumped to Dianetics. He went to L. Ron Hubbard himself, I think. He started to pick on me for any thoughts I might have that weren't Dianetically correct. Such thoughts, he believed, injured you. He soon became disenchanted with that and it was on to Christian Science, and here was I still struggling with the Kriya yoga technique. I dropped it when I became too depressed after I had you."

His radical changes had an alarming pattern to them. When he reached the point of almost finishing up a piece, the "home stretch," he'd leave for weeks at a time and go to New York or Montreal or Atlantic City to work. My mother said that he would go away for several weeks only to return with the piece he was supposed to be finishing all undone

---

*After my brother was born in 1960, my father finally allowed my mother to hire someone (Mrs. Sawyer) to help her with the house once a week. Recently, Mrs. Sawyer said to me, "I just don't know how your mother did it. Your dad, God love him, was never home in those days. I think I was the only person she had to talk to all week."

or destroyed and some new "ism" we had to follow.* These came with every botched or unpublished work: Zen Buddhism, Vedanta Hinduism, 1950s off and on; Kriya yoga, 1954–55; Christian Science, 1955 off and on to present; Scientology, called Dianetics at the time, 1950s; something having to do with the work of Edgar Cayce; homeopathy and acupuncture, 1960s to present; macrobiotics, 1966 through the end of their divorce.

What was so unsettling and made her, for the first time, lose faith in Jerry was "not the abuse, as this at times seemed inescapable, but the lack of logic! I had to completely reject what I had had to completely accept one hundred percent and adopt the next thing one hundred percent, just because this was Jerry's new super-encompassing God. I believe it was to cover the fact that Jerry had just destroyed or junked or couldn't face the quality of, or couldn't face publishing, what he had created."[†]

I think my mother is probably right in identifying the match that ignited these sudden changes whereby a new cult, or "ism" as she called them, rose out of the ashes of a work destroyed. However, not everyone who has problems with writing reacts by worshiping a newly risen phoenix, a new guru. This pattern has had a profound effect on those closest to my father—his flesh and blood family as well as his fictional characters and stories. Why? What made the forest so dry, as it were? Why were the conditions so flammable in the first place?

I understand one aspect of this behavior with every fiber of my being. Even the language of our clichés speaks to the vulnerability of human beings under fire, under terrible stress: "There are no atheists in the trenches." In times of excruciating chartlessness or "detached f-a-c-u-l-t-i-e-s," like the boy in France, Esmé's sergeant, Holden, and my soldier father, I, too, have sought mooring in another human being, as well as heavenly hosts divine ("Jesus, Savior, Pilot Me!" or "Throw Out a Lifeline"[‡]), clinging to them for dear life, sometimes nearly drowning

---

*My mother kept their joint tax returns. I went over them, and sure enough, the weeks at hotels, the travel expenses, the donations to various cults and charities, are all there in black and white.

[†]Like his character Buddy Glass, who had "written and histrionically burned at least a dozen stories or sketches . . . since 1948" (*Seymour: An Introduction,* p. 182).

[‡]Common hymns.

my human rescuers so tightly I clung and thrashed about in panic.*
Human beings, when chartless, seek a stable point of reference, whether
it be the North Star, permitting dead reckoning, or, when all is dark, a
guiding light. This is true whether they be wise men in the desert or
thirsty fools who pass by an oasis in pursuit of a mirage—reckoning
dead wrong.

A few years ago, my mother sent me a book, *Cults and Consequences,*† in response to my questions about my father's involvement in
and donations to everything from Zen Buddhists, Vedanta Hindus, Yogananda's Self-Realization Church, Christian Science, L. Ron Hubbard's
Scientology, followers of Edgar Cayce, George Ohsawa's macrobiotics,
Eastern medicines, and a hodgepodge of practices including drinking
one's urine, speaking in tongues, and sitting in a Reichian orgone box.
This book proved an invaluable starting place for unraveling the mystery
of my father's journeys through the looking glass.

What I began to understand is that the content of what my mother
called isms doesn't matter, it may be truth or absolute rubbish: it's what
a cult does to the mind of a believer as well as the way in which the believer embraces the belief—the particular characteristics of the relation
between believer and belief—that earns it the designation *cult* rather
than *religion* or *belief* or *philosophy.*‡

The existential state of the typical person who, upon encountering a
cult, is likely to become a follower reads like a description of most of my
father's characters, and indeed, of my father himself. Many studies of
cult phenomena have found that the appeal of the cult depends "largely
on the weakness and vulnerability that all of us feel during key stress periods in life. At the time of recruitment, the person is often mildly depressed, in transition, and feeling somewhat alienated."§ One study, in
particular, of those who become involved in cults, speaks directly to the
vulnerability of my father and his characters who "just got out": "Leav-

---

*" 'Ow,' said Mattie to Babe, 'you're hurting my hand.' He loosened his grip."

†Rachel Anders and James R. Lane, eds., *Cults and Consequences* (Los Angeles:
Jewish Federation Council of Greater Los Angeles, 1988).

‡I do not think for a moment that all Buddhists or Hindus are "cultists," any
more than I believe that Christianity, Judaism, Islam, or most any other religion
for that matter are lacking in their share of pernicious cults.

§Robert W. Dellinger, *Cults and Kids* (Boys Town, n.d.).

ing any restricted community can pose problems—leaving the Army for civilian life is hard, too . . . many suffered from depression . . . loneliness, anomie,"* or what can be referred to as "future void." They're standing at the edge, as Holden said, of "some crazy cliff," looking for a catcher, searching for a landsman in whom they can find mooring, before they sink down, down, down. Many of those who join cults find "close relationships with like-minded others."†

My father's troubled characters find landsmen in their ten-year-old sisters (Mattie and Phoebe) and ten-year-old dead brothers (Allie), in Sister Irma (in De Daumier-Smith), in and within the Glass family, siblings of various ages, both dead and alive. As time passes, however, my father and his characters increasingly begin to find landsmen only among the dead. We see it early on when Phoebe challenges Holden to name one thing he really likes, and all he can think of is Allie, his dead brother, and James Castle, the boy who died when he fell from a window at Pencey Prep. In my father's next novel, Franny says of Zooey that "the only people he ever really wants to meet for a drink somewhere are all either dead or unavailable . . . he never even wants to have *lunch* with anybody, even, unless he thinks there's a *good chance* it's going to turn out to be Jesus, the person— or the Buddha, or Hui-neng, or Shankaracharya, or somebody like that." With the story "Teddy," the departure is final. Teddy doesn't seek a landsman even among dead people; he seeks unity with non-being, the dissolution of all separateness and personhood. He wishes to join the vast sea of undifferentiated souls in another, transcendent dimension. This ten-year-old child casually describes his prescient knowledge of his imminent death in order to teach the listener about the virtues of detachment and the absurdity of seeking mooring in this life, which is just *maya,* an illusion.

> "I wish I knew why people think it's so important to be emotional. . . . My mother and father don't think a person's human

---

*Margaret Thaler Singer, "Coming out of the Cults," *Psychology Today,* January 1979.

†A study conducted by the Jewish Community Relations Committee of Philadelphia asked former cult members to list their reasons for joining. The committee found that, in order of relative importance, the number one reason was loneliness and the need for friendship. "More than any other factor, the desire for uncomplicated warmth and acceptance . . . leads people into cults."

unless he thinks a lot of things are very sad or very annoying or very—very un*just,* sort of. My father gets very emotional even when he reads the newspaper. He thinks I'm inhuman."

Nicholson flicked his cigarette ash off to one side. "I take it you have no emotions?" he said.

Teddy reflected before answering. "If I do, I don't remember when I ever used them," he said. "I don't see what they're *good* for."

"It's so silly," Teddy begins as he describes how his little sister may accidently push him into an empty pool where he'll crack his head open and die in a few minutes:

"What would be so tragic about it, though? What's there to be afraid of, I mean? I'd just be doing what I was supposed to do, that's all, wouldn't I?"

Nicholson snorted mildly. "It might not be a tragedy from your point of view, but it would certainly be a sad event for your mother and dad," he said. "Ever consider that?"

"Yes, of course, I have," Teddy said. "But that's only because they have names and emotions for everything that happens . . ."

By the time I read this story, I had already heard similar "sermons" from my father so many times that it was hard not to feel, once again, like a bored child being lectured. In reflecting on this, however, I have come to feel truly sad, rather than annoyed or bored. I think that my father was searching for landsmen, and when he didn't find them amongst the living, he turned his search to other realities. Indeed, this reaction, a desire for an alternate reality or transcendent experience, was found to be the second most common response by those who had left a cult (the first being loneliness and the search for close companionship) to the question of what had attracted them. "The cult offers a path—they would say *the* path—to the unfamiliar realm of transcendence. . . . It stands to reason, after all, that if you are looking for an experience that you have never had before, you should look in places you have never before been to find it."*

---

*Ibid.

The third reason given for the attraction to a cult, the "need for moral authority," strikes even closer to the Salinger home. Middle-class parents, whose children predominantly fill the ranks of cult membership, often seek to overshelter and overprotect their offspring. They want to give their children things they themselves were denied to make them happy.*

> In such circumstances young people often build up dependencies on their parents of which they are not aware until, at the end of adolescence, they are suddenly expected to take charge of their lives and become independent individuals . . . it is not surprising that many young people find this sudden assumption of responsibility burdensome and confusing, especially in today's world. . . . This is where cults come in. . . . They offer lifestyles that are . . . highly structured, with very limited choices and very specific demands. For some such a security blanket is most inviting."†

A blanket that Babe, in "A Boy in France," held in hopes of its magical, restorative powers.

Though I tread lightly here, I suspect that my father's attraction to the authoritarian nature and certitude of cult leaders has something to do with his upbringing. He describes, in a fictional account, exactly what I witnessed of his real-life family during our New York visits with Granny, Grandpa, and Aunt Doris. Seymour says of his visits with the Fedders, his fiancée's family:

> I wish Mr. Fedder were more conversationally active. Sometimes I feel I need him. Sometimes, in fact, when I come in the front door, it's like entering a kind of untidy, secular, two-woman convent. Sometimes when I leave, I have a peculiar feeling that both M. [his fiancée] and her mother have stuffed my pockets with little bottles and tubes containing lipstick, rouge,

---

*Ibid.

†Ibid. Esther Dietz, founder and former director of the B'nai B'rith Cult Education Project, also found that most who become involved are rather naive, middle or upper-middle class, searching for a meaningful spiritual experience.

hairnets, deodorants, and so on. . . . I don't know what to do
with their invisible gifts.   *(Raise High,* p. 69)

The unmet need for an active male presence in a boy's life can lead
to a vulnerability, or an attraction to what is called, in the literature on
cults, an "authoritarian personality." As I read the descriptions and theory of the so-called authoritarian personality, I felt as though the re-
searcher had been a fly on the wall in our home for years observing my
father's strange behavior in the thrall of a new belief. In a way, it was a
relief to find that this disturbing phenomenon was not unique to us. It
was horrifying as well. This was not a mainland to which it was comforting to find our island linked. For me, it was the proverbial "read it
and weep" experience. One article in particular, "Religious Cults:
Havens for the Emotionally Distressed, Idealists and Intellectuals, and
Strongholds of Authoritarian Personalities," could have had the subtitle
"At Home with J. D. Salinger." The author[*] writes:

> First, cult leaders are individuals with authoritarian, charis-
> matic personalities who exude, if for some with reserve and
> indirection, a determined and unshakable conviction in them-
> selves and their religious views. They serve as authority figures
> with whom their converts identify and their views and pro-
> nouncements are presented as infallible.
>
> Next, each cult leader claims that only the religious
> views he espouses are true, as well as being the ideal and
> practical means of resolving the problems afflicting the
> world and those who join cults. The doctrinaire character of
> their statements provides converts with a clear sense of
> meaning, direction, and purpose for their minds and lives,
> thus dispelling the confusion, uncertainty, and self-doubt
> that are characteristics of many of them prior to their conver-
> sion.
>
> Third, cults impose specific, demanding, and often ascetic
> and puritanical rules and regulations that govern most of the

---

[*]Edward Levine, Ph.D., professor emeritus of sociology, Loyola University;
board of directors, Mental Health Association of Evanston.

major aspects of converts' daily lives (e.g., the observation of religious rituals, diets, personal appearance, sexual codes, prohibiting drug use, etc.). Cultists perceive the religious views as true, encompassing explanations about the meaning of life and their role in it, and welcome the inflexible standards as concrete guides for their personal, interpersonal, and social behavior. Both provide them with an alternative of substance to the anomie culture that so bewilders them.

Another way of understanding my father's attraction to such belief systems involves moving away from the realm of individual psychology and looking, instead, at our shared history. I believe that there are things particular to my father's background as a Jew or half-Jew growing up in America that left him, and those with a similar background, vulnerable to what one expert in the field calls "the new religions," a term perhaps less emotionally provocative than *cults*. Rabbi Fine* speaks eloquently of Jews and chartlessness in our society:

> Young Jews . . . wonder, what does it mean to be a Jew, rising out of the ashes of the Holocaust? What does it mean to be one of 3.5 percent of the population in a non-Jewish culture? Those considerations affect Jews as individuals. They cause a person to question and wonder. And when men and women question and wonder inside of themselves, internally they seek resolution. The new religious movements, of course, provide that resolution.

The belief systems that Rabbi Fine cites as particularly attractive to Jews are precisely those to which my father and his characters are attracted. Fine believes that Eastern religions, especially guru movements, "because of their universalist pitch—we will accept and bring in everyone— . . . solve a lot of unique Jewish concerns instantly. . . . You can still be identified more or less (mostly less) with your Judaism, but ac-

---

*Rabbi Yehuda Fine, founder and director of the Jewish Institute; member of the New York Task Force on Missionaries and Cults, and of the Interfaith Council of Concern on Cults.

ceptance is for everybody. You don't have to deal with any of those historical or minority problems because the solution is 'we are one' . . ."*

While Rabbi Fine's view is not true for all, or perhaps even many Jews, when I looked again at my father's writing, I found Fine's argument supported in spades. While my father's early work, time after time, is concerned with chartless young men searching for mooring in the purity of a child, this strategy is transposed, resulting in a sort of Christianized Eastern mysticism, in the story of de Daumier-Smith, who finds his way out of his Blue Period through a vision of purity amid the sea of filth in which he is drowning. First Sister Irma saves him, and then, in a mystical vision, the shit of the world—including himself, his terrible students, and the colon-irrigation devices—is transmuted into twice-blessed flowers. De Daumier-Smith embraces a new unity with the world, reinstates his terrible students, and leaves us with his revelation that *"tout le monde est une nonne"*—all the world is a nun, a sacred sister. He finds mooring in the realization that we are one.

My father's final two novels restate the identical problem and solution. In *Franny and Zooey,* Franny is cracking up, unmoored and battered by the phoniness of life at college. She regains her faculties through the revelation that everyone is Christ. "Don't you know the secret?" Zooey asks her. Each and every one of those phonies, those irrigation devices, "even the terrible Professor Tupper . . . is Christ Himself." The book ends: "For some minutes, before she fell into a deep, dreamless sleep, she just lay quiet, smiling at the ceiling."

My father's last published book, *Raise High the Roof Beam, Carpenters and Seymour: An Introduction,* ends with Buddy realizing that Seymour was right, that the "awful Room 307," Buddy's classroom of college girls just back from Ivy weekends, is really "Holy Ground," and every one of those girls, "even the terrible Miss Zabel, is as much his sister as Boo Boo or Franny."

In each book, the tension is resolved by the revelation, as Rabbi Fine

---

*Esther Dietz confirms that Jews are overrepresented in cult membership. She found that Jews are particularly likely to be drawn to cults based on the Eastern religions—Hinduism in particular: "The Eastern or Hindu-based groups seem to be the most attractive to Jews and to have a relatively high proportion— as much as 25–30 percent (Divine Light Mission, Hare Krishna, Muktananda, Rajneesh, T.M., would be included in this group)."

said, that "we are one." The suffering character no longer has to deal with any of the historical or minority problems that we first saw in "The Long Debut of Lois Taggett," or with Lionel in "Down at the Dinghy," or with Holden's "half-Catholic" background, or with my father, hurt, as my aunt said, by "people talking that way." We are one.

❧

My father's fictional solution falls apart at the boundary of reality, however. It is one thing to merge with humanity, or even just one person, in an ecstatic experience of joy, quite another to live with him or her the morning after, day after day, week after week. Peter Abelard leaves the verdant green of the convent with the pure young girl, just short of her vows, and finds that once outside the gate, she is transformed into a sack of phlegm, filth, and excreta.

In a conversation recalled by one young woman, my father is caught in the web of his own conundrum. She described to him a folk concert she attended:

"For a few minutes it felt as though everybody in the room was *good*. We were all friends. I just looked around and loved everyone. It was such a relief, feeling that way."

"The song ended eventually, I imagine?" Jerry says, with a bitter edge in his voice that takes me by surprise. "There's the catch. You can only go on for so many verses before people start remembering how much everyone else actually irritates the hell out of them."*

My father could not have described any better his real life, as opposed to the world of his fiction. Time and again I've witnessed that his epiphanous experiences of joy and unity with all creation are "like joy, a liquid," rather than "happiness, a solid."† The morning after, they slip through his fingers like the mists of a dream.

Outside of the realm of fiction, my father is able to hold on to his

_____

*Joyce Maynard, *At Home in the World: A Memoir* (New York: Picador, 1998), p. 158.
†"De Daumier-Smith's Blue Period."

"we are one" solution, albeit tenuously, only in reclusion. It is here that the two meanings of reclusion are made manifest, whereby one man's chosen hermitage (the condition or fact of becoming a recluse) becomes another's prison (the condition or fact of being in solitary confinement). For my father to realize the promise that Paramahansa Yogananda held out, and reconcile the reclusive religious life with the life of a married man, the real girls and young women to whom he reaches out must become part of his dream.

To become one with him, each gives up her previous world, as well as her own hopes and dreams, to join his world, and his dream. Recall Yogananda's story of the marriage of my parents' beloved yogi, Lahiri Mahasaya, as his wife tells the story of her vision of the divine nature of her husband:

> "Master," I cried . . . "I die with shame to realize that I have remained asleep in ignorance by the side of one who is divinely awakened. From this night, you are no longer my husband, but my guru. Will you accept my insignificant self as your disciple?"

I often wondered how his wives and lovers, intelligent young women, so full of promise, could become like the mythological Echo, wasting away. Although on reflection, it seems to me that their backgrounds left them vulnerable perhaps to an unusual or extreme degree—certainly my mother's childhood is an ode to the agony of the unmoored, the child adrift and at sea—the trajectory of their entry into my father's world could not be more typical of standard cult entry.

My mother left all and married my father just before the last term of her senior year at Radcliffe. It is during such stressful times of the year—the first week of classes on the college campus, for instance, when new students are often feeling alone and disoriented in a strange new environment, or during finals week and graduation time, when many students are feeling a great deal of pressure and uncertainty about the future—that cult recruiters are especially active and successful on college campuses.*

---

*Jewish Community Relations Committee of Philadelphia, *Challenge of the Cults.* See also Dr. Sandy Andron, youth program director of the Central Agency for Jewish Education in Miami, in Anders and Lane, *Cults and Consequences.*

A key part of the attraction to the cultic relationship at such vulnerable times is what researchers refer to as "love bombing"*—sincere smiles, eye contact, hand-holding, and general expressions of great affection; a kind of total and unconditional love that is hard to describe in its dazzling intensity unless you, too, have been blinded by its light, though few would not understand the appeal. It is certainly understandable that my mother should have been tremendously awed and moved by the attention of an author in his thirties writing letters to her, a senior in high school. What is harder for me to understand is how she came to drop everything and follow him, how she became entangled, in tendrils strong as flesh and blood, even after the criticism began. Here again, I found that the pattern is classic. It is referred to by many names, *milieu control* and *totalism,* for example, but the method doesn't change. The essential element in this seemingly mysterious dance macabre is reclusion. The glasshouse flower of a dream cannot withstand the elements outside protected walls. Such a relationship and belief system cannot withstand a reality check. Therefore, "the probability of conversion is much higher if the cult is able to gain control of the individual's environment and communication channels."† Methods include control over all forms of communication with the outside world, sleep deprivation, change of diet, control over whom one can see and talk to, the message that the subject has been chosen to play a special role in the divine order, the need for purity, and convincing the subject of his/her former impurity and of the necessity of becoming pure or perfect, the introduction of "sacred science," and convincing the subject

---

*Drs. Louis J. West and Margaret Thaler Singer in *Cults, Quacks, and Non-Professional Psychotherapists* include love bombing in their outline of ten key points to cult indoctrination. See also re "love bombing": Arthur Dole, professor of educational psychology at University of Pennsylvania in *Cults and Consequences.* Joyce Maynard records, in her memoir, this early stage of her relationship with my father. She tells him she had signed a book contract, "news that I might have expected to elicit expressions of concern, but he is past censure now. He expresses nothing but pleasure and encouragement to me about my upcoming assignments. . . . As always, the letter Jerry writes to me, after receiving [mine], begins with a warm and loving appreciation of what I have written to him. . . . He calls my letter from Miami beautiful. Reading [her letters], he says, revives in him a deep love of writing that he doesn't often feel these days."

†Arthur Dole in *Cults and Consequences.*

that the control group's (or person's) beliefs are the only logical system and must therefore be accepted and obeyed, and that all who disagree are doomed.* The dissociation of the past, your family, friends, and your own past identity is, according to exit counselor Officer Mark Roggeman, the most important step in maintaining control over the person.†

Leila Hadley—the writer my father dated briefly around the time he met Claire—said, reflecting on their relationship, "I think he liked putting me down. There was something sadistic about it. . . . He was very much like that character of his in 'The Inverted Forest'—Raymond Ford. . . . It wasn't a sexual power, it was a mental power. You felt he had the power to imprison someone mentally. It was as if one's mind were at risk, rather than one's virtue."‡

I think of this as my mother tells me of her early courtship with my father: "The whole world was your father—everything he said, wrote, and thought. I read the things he told me to read, not the college stuff nearly as much, looked on the world through his eyes, lived my life as if he were watching me." When Claire refused to give up college the first time Jerry asked, and he left her, the feeling of abandonment was so terrible, she said she would have done anything to be with him, but she couldn't find him. She wound up in the hospital on the verge of a breakdown and jumped into a marriage with another man.§ When my father did come back into her life, she did indeed try to do everything she could to keep in his good graces, but as time went by, she pleased him less and less. My mother said she felt as though she

---

*Robert J. Lifton, *Thought Reform and the Psychology of Totalism* (Norton Press, 1963).

†Mark Roggeman, police officer, Colorado; national chair, Security for Cult Awareness Network; in Anders and Lane, *Cults and Consequences,* Chap. 3, p. 16.

‡Hamilton, *Salinger,* pp. 126–27.

§Joyce writes of her breakup with my father: "One day Jerry Salinger is the only man in my universe. I look to him to tell me what to write, what to think, what to wear, to read, to eat. He tells me who I am, who I should be. The next day he's gone. . . . Not having Jerry to lead me, I feel left behind and lost, not simply alone physically, but spiritually stranded. I've been well acquainted with the sensation of loneliness all my life. Never like this" (*At Home,* p. 211).

Someone from *Esquire* interviewed Joyce the following winter, after their breakup. The interviewer wrote: "Her purity blows through the room like a draft. . . . She hugs her sides and sits by the fire, rocking . . ." (p. 223).

were trapped in a fairy tale in which every time she met his demands, the standards increased ad infinitum. Although she came to believe, quite early on, that she was incapable of redemption in my father's eyes through any effort of her own, she imagined that by producing a child—knowing how much he loved children—she might, vicariously, regain some lost ground.* She was shocked into a suicidal depression when she realized that her pregnancy only repulsed him, sending him deeper into the forest, where, after countless hours of hard labor, two Glass children came into the world: *Franny,* published in *The New Yorker* in January of 1955, followed by *Raise High the Roof Beam, Carpenters,* in November.

At the end of that same year, on the tenth of December, another child was born, untimely torn as it were, from my father's imagination. I was nearly christened Phoebe, my father's choice of name for Holden's beloved little sister, but my mother prevailed, and at the last moment I was given my own name, Margaret Ann, "Peggy" for short. My father's version of my naming certainly has changed over time. He told me on a visit during the summer of 1997 that if it were not for Claire, "I'd have given you guys [my brother and me] no names at all and let you name yourselves at about twelve years of age." At present, he has three cats whose names are Kitty 1, Kitty 2, and Kitty 3.

⚡

A FULL GENERATION AFTER MY MOTHER BECAME PREGNANT, and I was nearly grown up, I found out that my father was still dealing in dreams, rather than real children. Because I lived through the reality of this as a child, and because I'm now a parent myself, with a very real child, the hardest thing for me to read in Joyce Maynard's memoir was that noth-

---

*Joyce, too, came to believe that she was incapable of the "purity" my father expects, though, sadly, she does not question the standard. "My only hope of redemption," she writes, "is to have a baby. To me, having a baby with Jerry would be a way of experiencing a childhood I never had but longed for. If I cannot be the child myself that he would have wanted, I will be her next of kin anyway. If I can't please him enough for who I am myself—and indications are that I cannot—I will please him by providing him with this other person who will be perfect in all the ways I am not. . . . He will never leave me, because I am the child's mother" (Maynard, op. cit., pp. 167–68).

ing had changed. Regardless of the problem that Joyce mentions of their inability to consummate their relationship due to sexual difficulties, she writes:

> We talk about the baby more and more, and when we talk about the baby, it's always a girl. We don't talk about where we might live, what our days will look like, caring for a baby; we don't discuss how Matthew and Peggy might view any of this, or even where, in this small, crowded house, the baby might sleep and play, though surely these are all the kinds of questions that Jerry has had to deal with before with his wife Claire when Matthew and Peggy were born, and in the years before his divorce when they were very small. I don't ask how we will avoid immunizing the baby, though I know Jerry will be adamant about that. Maybe she just won't go to school.
>
> "I'll make her a dollhouse," I say. "We'll make dolls and furniture, and play food out of cornstarch and salt dough with food coloring." I tell him about the pies my mother used to make for my Barbies. . . .
>
> The problem [their inability to have intercourse] remains unchanged and increasingly, unaddressed, even though the baby plan has continued to the point where a name has been selected for our future child. It's an odd name—not a name at all.
>
> "I dreamed you and I had a baby," he tells me one morning. "I saw her face clearly. Her name was *Bint.*"
>
> He looks the word up in the dictionary. "What do you know?" Jerry says. "It's archaic British, for little girl." From that point on, we refer to our future child by the name from Jerry's dream.
>
> (*At Home in the World: A Memoir,* pp. 168, 177)

My father's current wife, Colleen—Gaelic for "young girl"—whom he met, some fifty years her elder, when she was a young girl in her early twenties, looks up at me with her clear blue eyes, pretty smile, lovely peach skin glowing beneath her reddish gold hair cut pixie style—all that is missing is the Catholic-school uniform—tells me now, in my middle age, that she and my father are trying to get pregnant. I begin to tell her what life is really like for a child in reclusion; I ask, would they move? I mention that my father is nearing eighty. Then, I fall silent, feeling as though I'm talking to a girl, too young to be having sex, about responsibility and consequences, hurling limp reason at a dream glowing in the moonlight.

> She hears me strike the board and say
> That she is under ban of all good men and women,
> Being mentioned with a man
> That has the worst of all bad names;
> And thereupon replies
> That his hair is beautiful,
> Cold as the March wind his eyes.
> —"Father and Child," W. B. Yeats

PART TWO

CORNISH:

1955–1968

❧❧❧

On either side the river lie
Long fields of barley and of rye,
That clothe the wold and meet the sky;
And thro' the field the road runs by . . .
The island of Shalott. . . .

Four gray walls, and four gray towers,
Overlook a space of flowers,
And the silent isle imbowers
The Lady of Shalott.

—"The Lady of Shalott," Alfred, Lord Tennyson

7

Dream Child, Real Child

❦

"I almost wish I hadn't gone down that rabbit-hole—and yet— and yet—it's rather curious, you know, this sort of life! I do won- der what can have happened to me! When I used to read fairy tales, I fancied that kind of thing never happened, and now here I am in the middle of one! There ought to be a book written about me, that there ought! And when I grow up, I'll write one—but I'm grown up now," she added in a sorrowful tone: "at least there's no room to grow up any more here."
—Chapter 4, "The Rabbit Sends in a Little Bill"
Alice's Adventures in Wonderland, Lewis Carroll

AS THE RABBIT SAID, I think the trouble may have started because I was late. I was three weeks overdue when I finally arrived, yellow with jaundice and my hair all black. The nurse took me in to show to the proud father. He bellowed at her, "You've brought the wrong baby! Can't you see this one's Chinese?"

Later, when I was able to go home, he was in for another shock. Sit- ting on the couch, holding me gingerly, my father suddenly cried out and tossed me up in the air. My mother said that it was sheer luck that I landed on a cushion. This event was to be passed down for posterity in the following family verse:

> Fire! Fire! False alarm.
> Peggy peed on Daddy's arm.
> Daddy said that wasn't nice.
> Peggy said I'll do it twice.

In the opening paragraph of *Raise High the Roof Beam, Carpenters,* published a month before my birth, in a passing of the torch, as it were, Franny Glass is no longer college-girl Claire's age, as she was in *Franny,* but an infant. Baby Franny awakens, crying, at 2 A.M. Her eldest brother, Seymour, who had warmed a bottle and fed her less than an hour ago, begins to read a Taoist tale to quiet her. Franny not only stops crying instantly, but years later "swears she remembers it." The author tells us he chose to reproduce the Taoist tale, in its entirety, in the opening paragraphs of the story, "not just because I invariably go out of my way to recommend a good prose pacifier to parents or older brothers of ten-month-old babies."

I was on a collision course with my father's fiction. This baby was anything but "mute," and the impossibility of "hiding me away somewhere," as Holden dreamed, was beginning to turn into a nightmare. My father told my godparents, Judge and Mrs. Learned Hand,* that the first month was terrible—the panic of having an infant in the wilderness, the incessant crying: we nearly gave her away. My father began construction of his own place, nearly a quarter of a mile into the forest. Soon he was spending several days at a time in his one-room cabin, leaving my mother and me alone, in his dream house at the edge of the forest.

My mother, I'm alive to testify, managed not to destroy her less than perfect creation. But she came very, very close. She was determined not to repeat with me what had been done to her by various nannies and governesses in the nursery. I would be read to, sung to, breast-fed, and gently toilet trained. She had great hopes and dreams of childhood being different for me than it was for her, and it was, but it's hard to make the dream a reality with no help or instruction, no neighbors or friends, alone in the woods, especially when you have not been cared for adequately. It is well nigh impossible to reach the standard she had set for herself when the mother is as deeply, suicidally depressed as she was.

She doesn't remember many details about that first year of my life. It's mostly a dark blur. What she does remember is that, in general, as my

---

*(Billings) Learned Hand, 1872–1961. In a fifty-two-year career as district judge, appeals court judge, and chief judge (1939–51) of the second U.S. Court of Appeals, he issued some three thousand opinions touching virtually every area of law. His opinions were so highly regarded that he became known as "the tenth judge" of the U.S. Supreme Court (excerpted from *Who's Who in America*).

father became enchanted with me (by the time I was four months old and smiling he told the Hands, "We grow more overjoyed every day"), my mother continued to lose ground. She admits that her jealousy and rage over my replacement of her in my father's affections would continue to give, for years to come, a particularly serrated edge to her punishments.

My father complained to the Hands of my "constant illness" and told them we had seen no one all winter. But what he doesn't tell them is that I had not been brought to a doctor. He had suddenly embraced Christian Science, and now, in addition to being forbidden any friends or visitors, doctors were out.* There was absolutely no one to see or hear if I was left alone, for great pits of time, while my mother disappeared into depression's oblivion.

My father was off in the woods writing *Zooey,* the sequel to *Franny,* which would end with Franny on the couch, at home, having had a nervous breakdown, looking up at the ceiling smiling, rising from her litter, as it were, healed by Seymour's revelation that we are all Christ Himself.

Back at the Red house on the edge of the forest, my mother was lying on the couch, too, but she was not smiling up at the ceiling. She was in serious trouble, and no abracadabra revelation of Seymour's was forthcoming. By midwinter of '57, when I was about thirteen months old, my mother's mental grip, tenuous at best, teetered over the edge. With the "adamantine logic of dreamland,"† she began to make plans to murder me and then commit suicide.‡

A few weeks later, my mother had sorted out the details of our murder/suicide. It would happen during a brief trip in town for a *New Yorker* gathering, a "summons to Rome" that my father was not yet in a position to refuse. She planned to accompany him. It would be she,

---

*I reviewed their income tax returns documenting payments to Christian Science practitioners who, presumably, prayed for me long distance.

†James Russell Lowell on Samuel Taylor Coleridge's poem "The Rime of the Ancient Mariner."

‡This is not something I grew up knowing about. She, generously, told me on a "need to know" basis when I was grappling with my own teetering luggage. The doctors who evaluated me noted that the bizarre symptoms I exhibited were common to the community of what they called "torture babies," infants who had experienced repeated and sustained trauma over time.

Claire, not the fictional Seymour, who'd go bananas and leave guts spattered across the hotel room for the horrified spouse to witness. Dumb luck? Grace? A sudden flash of mothers' life force? Lahiri Mahasaya? *Some*thing intervened and whispered into her ear. While my father was out of the hotel room, my mother decided, suddenly, on impulse, to pack me up and run away instead.

Her stepfather arranged for an apartment and a nurse to care for me while she saw a psychiatrist three times a week.* My mother said that life would have been very different for her, and for me, had my father not come to New York, four months later, to convince her to return. She was far from "cured," but following the advice of her "paternalistic, sexist, Freudian psychiatrist," Claire went home to her husband. It was better for the child, she was told; how could she deprive her child of a father? She wishes now that she had had the courage to remain in New York, and to separate from a relationship she felt was destructive. Nevertheless, the four months of therapy, as well as the rest she had gained by having a nurse to take me to the park, gave her the strength to insist that if she were to return to my father, it would be under the following conditions: I was to have some friends to play with, *she* was to have some friends to play with, he was to build a proper nursery and a lawn—a contemptibly bourgeois trapping—and she was to be allowed to take me to a regular doctor for regular check-ups and when I got sick. He agreed.

When Claire returned to Cornish in the summer of '57, the lawn and the nursery were well under way. Although the nursery was Claire's idea, its execution was pure Jerry. He didn't trust the integrity of the builders who had good credentials. He often equates honesty with ignorance, purity with educational virginity. Here, he preferred the "purity" of some guys whom my mother called "absolute rubes" and who had little or no skill as carpenters. They built a flat roof, which of course had to be shoveled off, by my mother, every time it snowed. Throughout the long winters, buckets were placed strategically around the room to catch dripping water from the ceiling. The cream-colored ceiling tiles soon became dappled, like the concentric circles of rain on the surface of our

---

*The names of M.D.s and amounts charged were listed on the following year's income tax return as my father paid back "Uncle" Edward, as we called my widowed grandmother's new husband.

pond, with rust-colored rings from the leaks. The nursery was built of concrete cinder blocks and was not insulated. It had electric baseboards and was, my mother said, "hell to heat, but, at least I had someplace to put you."

In writing to the Hands that summer, my father mentioned nothing of the winter's events. But it's clear that a certain amount of reality had penetrated Shangri-La. His response, however, was not actually to *do* something about it, but to trade one dream, one wish, for another. He told the Hands he wanted to move the family to Scotland. Living in Cornish was hard on Claire, he said, particularly during the long winters, and he wished that they lived just outside a little Scottish village, where they might walk to visit the vicar and have tea-time visits to and from people in the village. As for me, he said, my Peggy dances slowly and thoughtfully to jazz on the radio, solo, with her teddy bear tucked under one arm.

※

I WAS TOO YOUNG to understand the isolation in which my mother and I lived, but with an intensity born of long hunger, I savored the visits of the few human beings who came to Cornish. After my mother's negotiated return to my father, her "revolt" as she calls it, a handful of people were on what my mother called the "authorized list," who, as such, were allowed to trespass. The first visitor I remember was Father John, a priest and the only man my father allowed to stay the night in our house during the ten years that he and my mother were married. I was not yet three, and it was past my bedtime when Daddy took me down the road in his Jeep to the station in Windsor, Vermont, to meet Father John's train. This was something special, I knew, because breaching my mother's bedtime rule required nothing short of a papal dispensation.

I held my father's hand tightly as we walked through the train station toward the platform. I remember being nearly blinded by bright sunlight, but it must have been fluorescent light since it was nighttime. I felt a little dizzy watching the sea of legs around me opening and closing, opening and closing. Shafts of light pierced the openings like sunlight seen from watery depths. I was tossed, like seaweed, in a sleepy reverie as I watched the movement around me. Suddenly a whistle exploded in my ear and the train came screaming through the walls of the station, smashing the vision to smithereens. I was knocked off my feet and lifted into the air. I came to rest wedged between my father's jacket and his chest. The last thing I saw before it went dark was a swirling tornado of legs and suitcases and people. As the screaming train reached my daddy's jacket, it paused and, instead of crushing us, wisely went around, having met its match.

In years to come whenever we would hear the train whistle from deep in the valley below our house, my father would tell the story of Peggy and the Nighttime Train. Only in his version, when the train whistle blew, I leapt into his arms and flung myself under his jacket and wouldn't come out. Not ever. But before he got to the part where he would make a low, rumbling whistle, I'd hide my head under his jacket and press my ear to his chest and listen to the rest of the story in that safe place with no words, where my father smelled like applewood smoke from the fireplace in his cabin, and Balkan Sobranie pipe tobacco, his voice a lullaby.

The next morning I woke up, and hearing voices, I followed the unfamiliar sound. Father John was sitting in the kitchen talking to my mother. He turned and said hello to me. I remember clearly that he waited quietly as I moved closer to him, the way I'd been taught to approach creatures in the wild. "I've brought you a little present. Perhaps you'd like it now?" I nodded. Mama said, "Yes, *please,* Peggy." I said, "Yes, please," and sat down and unwrapped the present by myself. There, in the folds of tissue paper, sat a beautiful, fragile, little blue-and-white china bowl. Something beautiful and delicate for me. When he placed it in my clumsy, oft-slapped hands, they were anointed and, in that moment, washed clean, more graceful than slow-falling snow.

I loved Father John, without reflection, without hesitation; the way plants turn toward the sun, it was a response of the soul. I loved him, as the children's hymn about loving Jesus says, so simply, "because He first loved me." There would be only a few more visits over the years until I was five and Father John was sent to the South Seas. I never saw him again. I had forgotten, until my mother reminded me recently, that he continued to send me strange little gifts from time to time, things carved from coconuts and sea grass. But I've never, ever forgotten that he loved me.

HUMAN VISITORS WERE FEW and far between. Besides Father John, there was but one other person who seemed to come and go as she pleased. Old Mrs. Cox (the mother of Archibald Cox* and a formidable woman in her own right) used to spend summers in Vermont, but after her husband died, she lived year-round in Windsor. She had a handsome, weathered face, and thick gray hair that she wore swept back in a sensible bun at the back of her head. Mrs. Cox had been a visitor even when visitors weren't allowed. When she heard from someone that my mother was all alone up in the hills with a new baby, she set her broad Yankee jaw, donned woolen skirt and sensible shoes, and marched over to pay a social call on the new mother. My mother said that Mrs. Cox had a way of simply blustering past Daddy, paying no attention to his nonsense.† My mother was not allowed to return Mrs. Cox's visit, however, until her "revolt." After that, she and I were invited to afternoon tea with Mrs. Cox on occasion, and I remember well the smoky smell of Lapsang souchong tea, her beautiful silver tea set with its sugar bowl piled high with little white cubes, forbidden at home, that Mrs. Cox permitted me to take with little silver tongs and drop one-by-one into my milky cup of tea. I have no idea how she, her tea set, or her beautiful house with its formal gardens and statuary arrived in working-class Windsor. I think she willed it and they simply materialized.

Such was the force of her person that, ever since I can remember, my father was unable to refuse Mrs. Cox's invitations. While she lived, he obeyed her summonses and faithfully attended her seasonal rituals: Fourth of July picnics, Labor Day softball games, Christmas eggnog, and so on. My father *hates* holidays. All of them put him in a foul mood, even Sunday because the mail doesn't come. Summer, being an extended sort of holiday, never fails to depress him. He said

---

*Archibald Cox, born 1912. Professor of law, Harvard, 1946–61 and 1965–84. Solicitor general of the United States under Presidents John F. Kennedy and Lyndon B. Johnson (1961–65). He became widely known as director of the office of the Watergate special prosecution force (1973) and was fired when he demanded that President Richard Nixon turn over possibly incriminating tapes. In 1980 he became chairman of Common Cause.

†Not unlike the matriarch of my father's fictional Glass family, Bessie Glass, in her behavior toward her privacy-loving boys.

it "always reminds him of a red-haired, freckle-faced kid eating an ice-cream cone." And then he shivers with the willies at the image. (Sometimes when I'm angry at him, I imagine a whole host of such "freckle-faced" Norman Rockwell characters coming to life and appearing at his doorstep.) Mrs. Cox's were the only holiday gatherings I recall him attending during the entire time we lived together as a family.

One family, with girls around my own age, was on the "approved list" from about the time I was three years old until I was five or so, and that was Bill and Emmy Maxwell* and their children, Kate and Brooke. My mother said it was mutually agreed that it would work out better for all concerned that we visit them at their summer place, rather than having them come see us. She said I loved our visits to the "bear's cabin," as I apparently called their summer place.

My father's Jeep partner throughout all five campaigns of World War II, John Keenan, visited a few times, but Judge and Mrs. Hand were the only people we entertained with any regularity. They lived in New York but spent summers in Cornish. Once a week, they would come to our house, or we would go to theirs. We would have an early dinner, then my parents and the Hands would read aloud, sometimes well into the night. I remember the voices, light and happy, instead of the dark, angry ones I often heard when I fell asleep at home with a knot in my stomach. I'm sad to say I don't remember Mrs. Hand much except that she was old and Daddy read to her. But I loved loved loved Judge Hand. On these evenings I'd often fall asleep on the Judge's lap. My mother remembers those visits as "delightful." She said, "Jerry and Bee [Judge Hand] loved to talk literature together; they'd read aloud from one of Constance Black Garnett's translations of Tolstoy's novels. I liked to ask him questions about history, Roosevelt, life in New York, his past. Mrs. Hand was very quiet but liked wit in all its varieties, but in good taste."

My mother and I went to tea at the Hands' every Thursday afternoon during the summer. She told me, "This is when Judge Hand got to

---

*William Maxwell, writer, editor. He worked at *The New Yorker* for a long time, which is how he and my father became friends.

know you well. He liked you very much and found in you a kindred spirit." He used to call me The Dynamo.

Judge Hand often took long walks with me. He'd ask me what I'd been thinking about lately and tell me what was on his mind as well. He listened with care and real understanding, person to person, from the heart and from the mind. I didn't have all the words for it at the time, but he gave me the feeling that I was a unique self who had a mind and feelings worth paying attention to, and worth the hard work of growing and thinking for myself, rather than becoming someone else's dream. I was not surprised, years later, to come across a famous quotation by Judge Hand: "The spirit of liberty is the spirit which is not too sure that it is right."

My mother says she remembers coming upon us in the living room discussing a drawing I had done. She quietly backed out of the room so as not to disturb us at work. I wish I could remember the particulars of our conversations, but I recently came across a short poem that expresses beautifully how friendship with an old man could mean so much to a young child—how we would be landsmen. It is called "The Little Boy and the Old Man" by Shel Silverstein:

> Said the little boy, "Sometimes I drop my spoon."
> Said the little old man, "I do that too."
> The little boy whispered, "I wet my pants."
> "I do that too," laughed the little old man.
> Said the little boy, "I often cry."
> The old man nodded, "So do I."
> "But worst of all," said the boy, "it seems
> Grown-ups don't pay attention to me."
> And he felt the warmth of a wrinkled old hand.
> "I know what you mean," said the little old man.

Judge Hand died when I was five, the year Father John was sent to the South Seas. I miss him still. When I was a college student at Brandeis studying history and law, I often imagined conversations with him, wishing he were there to talk to, to share my excitement. Both he and Father John left a warm place in my life, though, not an empty one, the way the mouse in Leo Lionni's book *Frederick* saves the colors of summer in his mind to sustain him through the long, dark winter.

❦

THE WINTER OF '59 was a long, gray, sleepless night. Even my father longed for spring when the sunlight returned and Judge and Mrs. Hand once again warmed our lives with their good company. In a letter to the Hands, my father writes of the endless winter, and how he misses them terribly. He tells them he wished they lived in Cornish year-round. But my father, at least, had escaped the snow and ice for many weeks at a time. He'd been in Atlantic City hotel rooms trying to finish a final draft of *Seymour: An Introduction*.

While my father was away, a terrible thing happened. It remained locked away, buried deep within my body, until nearly thirty-five years later, when all hell broke loose during the birth of my son. I had been in hard labor for some thirty-four hours when, suddenly, my water broke on the delivery table and I began to disappear. A three-year-old girl took my place at the window of my eyes and told the nurses what she saw. "I didn't kill it, I didn't kill the baby, I didn't mean to," she screamed, pleading with the nurses to believe her.

I'm three years old and terrible sounds are coming from the bathroom, sounds like the ones I hear in my ears now. My mother is in the bathroom, and I have to pee. I don't dare knock on the bathroom door. I'm hiding in my room and stuffing my fingers in my ears, which doesn't help. The noise stops. I hear the door shut and Mama's footsteps fade down the hall to their bedroom. When the door is shut, I creep out quietly and steal into the bathroom. I haven't peed in so long I just had to go in there or risk sitting in cold, wet clothes until somebody finds me. You never knew how long that could be. Just short of forever. I dash in and barely make it, plunk down on the toilet and pee. I get up and flush like a good girl. Mama's shrieks reach me, too late. "Don't flush the toilet. Don't flush it!" I look and there in the toilet is a baby, all watery and bloody, but a small, real baby. And I'd killed it.

The attending nurse clicked her tongue and said in an Irish brogue, "It's terrible, just terrible the things children see." I asked her if we could all pretend that I was expelling a tumor, that there wasn't any baby, any *real* baby that could die, that I might kill by accident. That helped until the god of mercy came, Epidural is thy name.

After my son was born, I asked my mother about what I'd seen, the flashback in the delivery room. She confirmed that she did indeed have a miscarriage well into her sixth month of pregnancy and there was a baby in the toilet. She said she was saving it for Dr. Balantine to examine. She had no idea that I'd known anything about it.

My own "not knowing" about it until childbirth when the experience broke through into my consciousness with the force of a tidal wave was not, in hindsight, watertight. It leaked through in dreams. Throughout my entire childhood, I was plagued with recurring nightmares, some of which visited me regularly for years. One that's been with me nearly my whole life is my waterbabies dream and variations. I'm on a beach trying to rescue babies from a tidal wave. It is a gray day with blackish clouds on the horizon. I see tens, sometimes hundreds, of babies playing on the sand, their parents oblivious to the wall of water, the great tsunami casting a shadow of death across the sand. I yell, try to warn them, but to no avail. I'm the only one who sees it coming. I rescue several, grabbing their arms, legs, whatever I can reach, and carry them off the beach. I often rescue many of them successfully, but never all of them. Sometimes, after the storm passes, I'm in a flooded beach house, water up to my knees, and a baby, horribly jellyfish-like, and not-put-togetherable-again, swirls by my legs in a pinky puddle. One I missed.

❦

SHORTLY AFTER MY FATHER came home from Atlantic City, with the text of *Seymour: An Introduction* cradled in his arms, my mother became pregnant again. My brother, Matthew, was born on February 13, 1960.

Daddy and I drove to the hospital to pick up Mama. I moved to the back of the Jeep and watched as Mama sat on a red rubber inner tube in front. I asked what the tube was for and she said it was because of stitches. It wasn't until we were nearly home that I heard a squeaky noise and leaned forward, between the seats, to see what it was. I was stunned to see a baby's face poking out of the bundle of blankets she was carrying. I knew she went to the hospital to have a baby, but it never occurred to me that she'd actually bring one home.

My mother said she noticed that I seemed to go into a profound depression after my brother was born. She said I seemed afraid that I'd injure the baby somehow. She was concerned about it but didn't know what to do. My father saw in me only the apple of his eye, his little soldier, his "Dynamo." He told the Hands, "Matthew is an intelligent and smiley baby. . . . He doesn't have his sister's toughness and bounce. But who does?"

TOUGHNESS AND BOUNCE: BE A SWELL GIRL, a good soldier. This message penetrated my being so intensely that I can remember the first time it was put into words. Once, when I was still at the age where I could pull my father's nose and ears and get away with it, I wandered into the bathroom as he was preparing to shave. Daddy lifted me up so I could see better. I was perched on the little counter beside the sink, my favorite spot from which to witness the mysteries, the morning ablutions, of shaving. He dipped his hands in a basin of hot water, heated on the stove in a big pot by my mother, and splashed the water on his face. Then he took the lathering brush from its special stand. The stubby brush had a chunk of jewel-like glass on top that fit snugly into a half ring of metal and clicked perfectly back into place when you were through playing with it. Daddy made a beard of white lather. As he drew the razor down his face, neat strips of pink appeared beneath the lather. I thought about the strips of ice, beautiful skateable ice, that emerged from underneath his shovel as he cleared the deep, powdery snow off our pond a few weeks before.

I wasn't sure where the razor came from or went to. I knew it was dangerous and not to be touched; I thought it might slice my eyes if I looked at it, but I never saw it except when he was holding it. I heard it scritch across his face as he shaved off each strip of lather. I only liked to watch the down part. The up part, under his chin, sometimes left little blood droplets; also it unnerved me to see him with his head bent unnaturally to the side. Daddy disappeared and all I could see was a bent neck, like the necks of unlucky birds or chipmunks that dangled from our cat's mouth as she slunk past me emitting a weird, throaty growl to warn me off her prey.

Under the nose was last. Unlike the smooth, steady strokes on the rest of his face, lots of little scrapes happened so fast that he had to hold his nose out of the way with one finger of his other hand so that it didn't get in the way of the razor. He rinsed his face, splashing up water with his hands and patting, and then we both paused and looked in the mirror to see what was there.

The reflection was all wrong. "Daddy, you don't really look like that," I said. He almost staggered, his knee bent as he looked at me with a smile as loud as a shout.* I could see in his face that I must have done something wonderfully good. But I flinched inside the same as I did when my mother came at me suddenly—bad, bad girl; any notion of what I'd done obliterated in the blizzard of her anger. I disappeared in the fog of the bathroom.

Years later he recounted *his* version of that story to me and said to me, with relief, that that was the moment when he knew I was going to be a *good* girl. It became clear to me, with the second or third telling, that he thought I had been being kind to him, in the opaque way of a child, telling a homely guy that he didn't really look like that, that he really was the handsomest of all, and the mirror was wrong. I always thought, and still think, my father to be very handsome indeed; but that wasn't what I'd meant at all. He has a very asymmetrical face: his big nose slants markedly to the left, his lips likewise are off-center. So when you look at him in the mirror, he really does look a lot different in his reflection than in person because all the off-center things are reversed, creating a very different-looking image. I was making a factual observation, not weaving a kind fiction about his appearance in the mirror. Although I realized he'd misunderstood me, I kept quiet, feeling like a liar.

He repeated this story to me many times growing up. After the part where I say "Daddy, you don't really look like that," he says, with as much relief at a disaster narrowly skirted as pride in the achievement,

---

*In his story *Seymour: An Introduction,* published that year in *The New Yorker,* he wrote, "In 1959 . . . I think on the quantities of joy they [their youngest sister and brother] brought Seymour. I remember Franny, at about four, sitting on his lap, facing him, and saying, with immense admiration, 'Seymour, your teeth are so nice and *yellow!*' He literally staggered over to me to ask if I'd heard what she said" (pp. 165–66).

"*That's* when I knew you were going to be a good girl." A "swell girl," as his character Babe Gladwaller put it while he looks at his ten-year-old sister, Mattie, sleeping. Babe thinks about how short a time it is to be a child, to be ten; "all of a sudden little girls wear lipstick, all of a sudden little boys shave and smoke." He wants her to "try to live up to the best that's in you."

> If you give your word to people, let them know that they're get-
> ting the word of the best. If you room with some dopey girl at
> college, try to make her less dopey. If you're standing outside a
> theater and some old gal comes up selling gum, give her a buck
> if you've got a buck—but only if you can do it without patron-
> izing her. . . . You're a little girl, but you understand me. You're
> going to be smart when you grow up. But if you can't be smart
> and a swell girl, too, then I don't want to see you grow up. Be a
> swell girl, Mat.   ("Last Day of the Last Furlough")

I didn't read these words until I was long grown up, but the message—if you can't be smart and a *swell* girl, too, then I don't want to see
you grow up—was imprinted in the marrow of my bones. It became
part of the curse whispered in my ear, my personal *Semper Fi,* do or die.
Whatever happened, I wanted to be a swell girl.

With my increase in rank to "big sister" came the responsibility
for those under my command. Sometimes it nearly broke my back.
One hot August evening, my brother, Matthew, now seven months
old, and I were put to bed as usual long before dark. Matthew had
learned to pull himself up in the crib. He was holding, teeteringly, on
to the crib rail with one hand and throwing his precious bottle out of
the crib with the other. He began to wail "ba-ba," which was his word
for bottle.*

Mama swept into the room in a tight-lipped fury, plunked the bottle
back in his bed, and said to him, "Next time it will stay on the floor till
morning." At seven months old, he didn't know that she meant it, but at
four and a half years old, I was sure as hell smart enough to know she did.

---

*Ba-Ba was also his name for me. It predated Mama or Dada, who were
nameless at the time, by a wide margin and lasted for years, it seemed, until the
unfortunate months of "Baggy" finally changed into "Peggy."

I watched him with the horror of watching someone who can't read the danger sign walk into a trap. Again, he laboriously pulled himself up and threw the bottle out of the crib. He began to wail. When Mama didn't come, he threw out his teddy, his blankie, his socks—one by one the contents of his world, as if on some life-or-death fishing expedition where you gamble all you own, including the last of your food, in hopes of hooking the big one. I got it instinctively: I understood the game and understood just as well that Mama did not. I knew he just wanted to know, *had* to know, that if he threw something away, it would come back. I knew that was all he wanted and that, however many times it took, at some point, he'd finally be satisfied, he'd know he could keep the bottle and drink it and go to sleep.

He needed to know that it was safe to love it because it comes back. I didn't say all the words in my mind, but I knew. My parents used to joke about my knowing what he wanted when they didn't have a clue. They'd say, "How come Peggy is the only one who can speak his language?"*

I didn't think it was at all amusing or cute. It *enraged* me that they could be so obtuse. I also began to have a sense, which grew rapidly into conviction, that I was the only grown-up in the house. Oddly, though, the fact that I often knew better than my mother what the baby wanted gave me a great gift, a compass of normalcy as it were: I became aware that something was wrong with her that wasn't wrong with me.

Matthew threw his bottle out of his crib again and, of course, began to cry. I knew she'd think he was just being naughty and punish him. So I snuck out of bed and tiptoed across the room, frightened that she might relent and come back into the room and we'd both be in big trouble. I picked up the bottle and, as quietly as I could, dragged a chair up to the crib so I could reach him. He took the bottle and put it in his mouth. Through his residual sobs, he watched me pick up the blanket and teddy and socks one by one. I climbed down and put the chair back, but before I could get into bed, out came the bottle, out came the blankie, and the socks. This may go on all night, I thought, but I was

---

*As an adult, I am, of course, aware that this is a little fiction many parents tell their children, hoping to make them feel special, and perhaps, to mitigate the intrusion of a new baby brother or sister. In the "Inverted Forest" of our family, however, this was not comforting fiction, but rather, the awful truth.

grimly determined not to let her come in and spank him. The second time I retrieved the contents of his crib he smiled. The third time he laughed, the fourth time he laughed so hard that I was afraid she'd hear us. "Shhh! It's our secret."

I stood on the chair on tiptoes, my arm hanging over the crib rail, and was prepared to pat his head until he dropped off to sleep or until my arm dropped off—whichever came first. Luckily, he drifted off, and I crept back into bed.

As my brother lay sleeping in his crib, from my bed I could hear his snuffly breathing. He always had a cold, it seemed. Or was crying, one or the other. As his breath deepened, I let mine out. I knew by the sound that he would not wake up again soon. I listened to the night noises gathering, the songs of the grasshoppers and evening orioles as they faded seamlessly into the deeper night songs of crickets and owls, the world a monastery where the treble chant of the novices as they fall asleep is overtaken by the bass voices of the elders of the night watch.

The night-light in our room cast a gentle glow. I pretended that I lived on the ceiling. The ceiling tiles were my floor and I imagined walking around on them. After playing in the corner for a while, I tried to get down off the ceiling, but my bed had disappeared. The tiles disappeared, too. All I could see was gray, like a thick fog. I opened my eyes and I tried to get a breath of air. I was horribly hot. My sheets were all around me, tucked in so tightly that I couldn't lift them off. I sort of breaststroked forward, and they only became tighter and tighter. I tried every direction but, like a lost traveler, I began to turn circles. My skin prickled with heat and panic. If I yelled for help, I'd wake my brother. Finally, I gave up, stopped struggling, and lay there, a "swell girl," resigned to suffocate.

Mama came in around midnight to check on us. She undid the sheets and found a dripping-wet, glassy-eyed four-year-old girl.

"How long have you been like this?" she asked me.

"I don't know, Mama," I whispered.

"Why didn't you call me when you got stuck in the sheets?"

I thought I was in trouble, but I had to answer or I'd be in worse trouble. I said, "Because I can't wake up Matthew."

She bit her lip, and the weather, the prevailing winds behind her eyes, shifted. She took my hand gently and brought me outside onto the lawn bathed in the moonlight. I had never seen the world by moonlight, and like the little raccoon in my book by Garth Williams, *Wait Till the Moon Is Full,* I "wondered." I drank in the clear night air. She led me up to the low stone wall that was built to keep the children playing on the lawn from falling down the steep side of the meadow. I looked over the wall, and there, in the valley below, were hundreds of tiny twinkling lights dancing the entire breadth and height of the meadow. Fireflies.

8

Babes in the Woods

❦

. . . Fairy Elves,
Whose midnight revels by a forest side
Or fountain some belated peasant sees,
Or dreams he sees, while overhead the moon
Sits arbitress . . .
      —*Paradise Lost,* book 1, lines 781–85, Milton

MY CHILDHOOD HOUSE IN CORNISH sits high on a hill near the forest and is situated in such a way as to welcome little people and deter large ones from visiting. Miles of often impassable, never-signposted dirt roads served as a modest moat of mud in the spring; dust, bumps, and washboard in the summer; and ice and snow in the winter. Autumn simply dazzled and bewitched people, like cows drunk on fallen apples, into losing their way. It was sheer kismet, or perhaps Holden's homing instinct, that permitted my father to find Cornish at all.

A child, especially a lonely one, one "hidden away," is sometimes permitted a glimpse of the little people who inhabit these remote places. These creatures shun the limelight and the intrusion of large humans, preferring to dance, in field and forest, by the light of the moon. Deep within the old forest of tall pines at the foot of the steep meadow below our house is a small clearing where the sun shines through onto the forest floor. It smells wonderful as the sun warms the dry pine needles that lie in a carpet several feet thick on the ground. As a little girl, I visited this spot every few weeks to make a house for the fairies who lived there. First, I'd form the castle wall of pine needles in a circle. Next, some smaller walls for separate rooms. In several of these rooms, I'd put soft bits of green moss for their beds and leaves for coverlets; in others, twigs for chairs and tables. But the largest room of all I just swept flat and clean of all debris. This was their dancing room. On moonlit nights they gathered here from all corners of the forest for the dance. It went on so late and so long that they danced the walls down. I could tell because whenever I returned, the outline of the walls remained but they always needed to be built up again with more pine needles. And the bedding, of course, needed changing as well.

The other place the fairies lived was beneath a large fungus that grew on a fallen maple tree beside our pond. The fungus was big enough for me to sit on, had I been so ill-mannered as to sit on someone's house. I never saw the woodland fairies, since they only came out at night when I had to be in bed. I knew of their existence the way I knew of Santa Claus, by thrilling evidence of what was left behind—Santa's half-drunk glass of milk I'd left for him, the pine-needle walls worn down by hundreds of tiny dancing feet. Once, though, I heard Santa's sleigh land on the flat roof of my nursery as I lay in bed on Christmas Eve. I held perfectly still for several minutes, listening. Then I heard a loud woosh as it took off again. I told my mother about it in the morning. She solemnly and completely believed me. Were you to ask her today if it happened, I'm sure she would swear to it.

What I shall go to my grave swearing to is that, when I was little, I saw a house fairy. She was caught by the sunrise long after she was supposed to be gone. I woke up in my bed, and all I can say is that I felt a presence. I turned over, and there she was on my bed. She was as tall as my hand, and like a ballerina in stage lights, she was all movement and light and gossamer tulle. I watched as she twirled, spinning round and round, becoming smaller and smaller until she gradually faded into nothingness. Like a morning star, there was no identifiable time, no exact point dividing here and gone. Being and unbeing blended seamlessly into each other, and after a while I realized that only the afterglow remained etched, for a time, on my retina. A profound sense of otherness remained with me, and I told myself never to forget.

The scarcity of both woodland creatures and human friends, especially during the long winters, was equaled only by the abundance of fictional ones. Like the celibate monk in his dark cave, I sometimes was blessed with visions of paradise and wonder dancing before my eyes. Mama read books to me by the hour. Beautiful books with tales of other worlds, lands with no snow, where there were playmates and magical transportings, and dogs with eyes big as saucers, and princes riding up glass pyramids after golden apples. The Little Lame Prince imprisoned in a tower escapes through the window on a magic carpet and soars over the countryside; the lonely orphan girl discovers a secret garden and brings it back to life and in so doing finds a friend and family.

Daddy didn't read to me very often; he made up stories instead. The only book I remember him reading aloud was not one of mine, but an old children's book that he'd kept from when he was a little boy. That, in itself, made it magical. It was called *The Weather Children*. As the story opens, Mattie and her little brother are playing in a field when a strange old man flies down from the sky. He is so tired he sits against a tree and asks the children if they would guard his satchel while he takes a rest. He tells them that he is The Weatherman and opens his satchel to show them just a few of the capes he wears as he flies through the sky creating the weather. There is a beautiful peach cape for sunrise, pale yellow for the morning sunshine, sky blue for a summer's afternoon. He said the children might slip these over their shoulders and try them out, but they mustn't put on any of the capes that wouldn't be right for a summer's day. Some of the others, he warned, are tricky to handle, and they shouldn't even unfold them to look or they might get into trouble.

The children were delighted to soar above the countryside on a beautiful day, looking down upon picnics and farmers. After a while, though, they couldn't resist peeking deeper into the satchel. They unfolded a deep violet cape with silvery flashes, and the farmers and picnickers below were dismayed at the big thunderstorm that seemed to come out of nowhere on a day that was supposed to be sunny and clear. The children were so blown about, they could not fold the cape neatly back into the bag as they had been shown. The trouble really started when they spotted, toward the bottom of the satchel, the most magnificent cape they had ever seen. It was midnight blue with frosty silver swirls and snowflake patterns. Had The Weatherman not woken up in the cold and caught up with them, there's no telling what trouble they might have caused the world. The Weatherman decided never again to take a holiday.

My father, too, created worlds and seasons and weather for me. As he cast his spell, the smoke of applewood fires and Balkan Sobranie rose, weaving tendrils of stories over the land. His early stories were not separate tales confined to nursery or bedtime; they intermingled freely with our daily life. They wove in and out as we fed the birds, went for the mail, took our afternoon walks, and so on. The content, too, was often rather spur-of-the-moment, depending on his mood.

A group of characters my father made up became friends who accompanied me throughout my childhood. There was Irving and Julius Grosbeak, who came to our bird feeder, year after year, when the grosbeaks returned to Cornish for the winter. They spoke with heavy Brooklyn accents and always came to the window the morning of their arrival and asked my father, "Say, Mack, who's dat pretty little goil in da plaid bat[h]robe?"

"It's Peggy," Daddy told them.

"No! You don't say. Boy, she sure has gotten pretty!"

Some were cautionary tales that cropped up as my behavior perhaps warranted. My favorite imaginary character was "that naughty little girl Lucia Ferenzi" and her toy lion, Samba. These stories usually began, "You're not going to believe what that naughty little girl Lucia Ferenzi did!" And a tall tale would unfold that bore a striking resemblance to something that Peggy, who just happened to have a toy lion named Simba, had done. Of course Daddy and I knew that *I* would never do anything like that.*

The stories he told changed over time, from the ones in the fifties he told me throughout the day, to those he told my brother at bedtime in the mid-sixties. The later stories were much more organized. The longest, which continued each night at bedtime for many years, was,

---

*Like Seymour in "Bananafish," talking to his four-year-old friend, Sybil: "You probably won't believe this, but some little girls like to poke that little dog with balloon sticks."

like the wonderful "Laughing Man" in *Nine Stories,* a tale of high adventure. These were the travels of Cap'n Bruno and his mates as they sailed around the world on their submarine. My brother's favorite mates were Dead-eye Dick, who always talked out of the side of his mouth in very gruff tones, and Hultch, who was so tall he had to lie flat along the bottom of the entire submarine to accompany them.

In the fifties, however, the boundaries between story and life were so fluid, so entwined, that not only did the characters accompany us throughout the day in Cornish, they even ventured beyond the boundaries of Cornish itself and followed us down the mount into town. I often went with my father as he drove into Windsor to get his mail from the post office.* Part of our routine, as we rode down the hill in his Jeep, was that I'd ask him at a particular stretch of the forest, "Daddy, what are the mosquitoes saying?" The mosquitoes, I had decided for reasons I no longer remember, resided among a dark thicket of trees we passed beneath, just before emerging into sky and open highway by the Connecticut River. "They're saying, 'Look, there's Peggy and Daddy going for the mail. We understand that Peggy is going to visit Mrs. Hand tomorrow. Do you think she'll bring Sootie and Kertiss Icebox (my toy bear and squirrel respectively) with her?' " It was our version of "Talk of the Town."

Two of our make-believe friends, Mr. Custe and Mr. Curzon, lived in Windsor and wore brown felt city hats like the ones Daddy wore when we went to New York. They always asked for me when Daddy went into Windsor alone. We never seemed to run into them, though, when we went into town together, not even at the diner where they usually ate lunch. I'm sure I would have spotted them; no one else in Windsor wore those hats. Sometimes Daddy and I would sit at the lunch counter and have jelly omelettes. I'd twirl my stool while he chatted with the girls behind the counter and gave me nickels to play my favorite song, over and over, on the jukebox:

> Walk right in, sit right down,
> Daddy let your hair hang down.

---

*I don't know when he started getting his own mail at a P.O. box in Windsor instead of our family mailbox down the road.

Everybody's talking 'bout a new way of walking,
Do you want to lose your mind?

(The Roof Top Singers)

❧

BY THE TIME I WAS FIVE AND A HALF, in the summer of 1961, I no longer had to wait at home for Daddy to make an appearance; I was finally big enough to breach his tower. It was a special treat to walk all by myself through the woods to the cabin where my father worked and bring him his lunch. One day my best friend, Viola, came over to play while her mother cleaned our house. My mother packed our lunches and we took one paper sack for us and one for my father and set off down the path through the field on the other side of the house.

Just past the juniper bushes that concealed one of my secret forts, the path reached the woods and dropped off sharply. There, my father had set into the hill large, beautiful stepping-stones, so getting down was easy even for little legs. Beside the path, dappled sunshine fell on the thick blanket of pine needles. As we reached a clearing, the path leveled off and you could hear the stream and a little waterfall. The path stopped beside a deep, fresh spring. There were clumps of wild purple iris on the banks of the stream and iridescent dragonflies, but by far the most beautiful thing, magical almost, to us was deep within the spring. If you knelt down on the path and reached down into the cold water, you could pull out green glass bottles of Coca-Cola that Daddy put there to keep cool.

My father had built a simple wooden footbridge, about ten feet long, across the stream, just high enough that we could sit on it and dangle our feet in the water. Viola and I sat down on the footbridge in the sunshine and opened our lunch. My mother was good at packing lunch boxes and presents. She knew how to make things special and pretty, the way kids like them, with separate compartments for things—like my beloved roll-top wooden pencil box that had a special place for everything one might need. Viola and I ate our lunch and drank our Cokes and imagined swimming in the stream and wondered if there were any fish in it (yuck!) and what happened to them if they swam near the edge where the stream dropped out of sight. Viola's shoe fell in the water and floated away. We knew we were in trouble, but for now it was so funny we nearly fell in after it. We went on our way one shoe lighter.

The last part of the path I only liked once a year when the gauntlet of brambles on either side turned to blackberries. In the next clearing was Daddy's Green house. It was built of cinder blocks painted dark green like the pine trees around it. It had just one small room inside and a big overhang outside where he stored cords of wood to feed his wood-burning stove in the winter. He used to pat the stacked wood with his hand, the way a farmer might pat his prize heifer on her plump flanks, or a farmer's wife her plump jars of tomatoes and preserves put up for the winter.

We knocked on the door. I was always a little nervous, though I'm not sure why. Daddy opened the door, surprised, but happy to see us. We came in and sat on the army cot that took up almost the entire wall. There were bookshelves above the cot with cool things on them like tins of salty corn parchies, and glass honey jars full of silver coins or peppermints. Lots of my drawings were taped up on the wall. Opposite the cot was the wood-burning stove. At the far end, way up in the air where I couldn't reach it, was an old, brown leather car bench seat that my father used for a desk chair. (I guess he had a tall platform built underneath it, but from my child's-eye view, it seemed suspended in the air.) He showed me how he sat, lotus position, legs crossed beneath him. Even at the flexible age of five I couldn't copy him. On the plain slab of wood he used for a desk was an old manual typewriter, which he used in his self-taught two-fingers-only style. Light shone onto his desk from a milky skylight above, a thing that positively delighted my father. Lots of small yellow pieces of paper with notes written in dark, soft-lead pencil were taped, here and there, to almost every surface within reach of the desk—the wall, the lampshade, and so on. I never had to be told not to look directly at his desk, nor did I ever read any of those notes. I even avoided looking in their direction just to make sure I didn't read something by mistake.

He shooed us outside, but came out and talked to us for a while. He was always so nice to my friends when I was very young. And he wasn't like most other grown-ups who talked to you about stupid stuff like what *grades* you were getting in school. He talked about things that we kids might talk about with each other. I've lost that touch now that I'm grown up. I often catch myself asking kids about things that I thought were dumb then. It also occurs to me now that his Green house was cool the way a kid's tree fort is cool, not the way I, or other adults I know, would build a study.

I'm not sure why, but I'm glad he had that Green house in the woods. It feels like a loss somehow that, after my parents were divorced, he built a real house just down the road, with a study that seems just another room with bookshelves. He still uses the same old car seat and typewriter though. My old drawings from kindergarten and grammar school, like Tuffy the Tooth, who whitely cautioned him to "watch out for between-meal treats," also made the move and stood guard over his work until they were burned, together with the dogs Daisy and Tillie, in a house fire in 1992.

9

Border Crossing

❦

URING THE FALL OF 1961, two of my father's Glass children, Franny and Zooey, ventured beyond the safe confines of *The New Yorker* and were introduced to the readership of the world at large. It was a big move from magazine to book. Another big move into the world occurred that fall as Viola and I entered the first grade of the Plainfield elementary school. I don't think either of my parents saw Cornish and the next town over, Plainfield, except "Thro' the Mirror Blue," through the reflection of their own dreams. I saw clearly that these towns were not the creations of a New Yorker's dream, such as Rockefeller's Woodstock, Vermont, or stage sets for Fred Astaire, Bing Crosby, and Marjorie Reynolds in *Holiday Inn* or for Danny Kaye, Bing Crosby, and Rosemary Clooney in *White Christmas*. They were the real McCoy. And Hatfield. The sublime and the squalid coexist in a way that's hard to believe unless you've lived in a place like that. In the center of town there is a plain and lovely white New England church, a small brick library, one tiny general store with wooden floors, cans of Campbell's soup, Wonder bread, Crisco, and the most beautiful glass case of penny candy in the universe, complete with wax lips that you could both wear and chew, Pixy Stix—straws full of tart sugar that you bit open and sprinkled out on your tongue—and jawbreakers that magically turned different colors as you sucked them. Across the street from the store is the town hall, a square, brick, one-story building with peeling paint on the windowsills. Inside, the citizens of Plainfield held auctions, potluck suppers, and on the stage at the back of the hall, ceremonies of all sorts, such as kindergarten graduations. On the town hall stage, a Plainfield artist had built and painted a three-dimensional backdrop of natural scenery—trees, fields, flowers—which, when you shine different sets of colored lights on it from the projection room, actually changes seasons, from spring to summer to fall and winter. It is glorious, luminous, transcendent; by far my favorite of Maxfield Parrish's works. I saw it again last summer at a school reunion, and it was still a sight to behold.

The distance from the center of town can be measured, I'm sorry to say, in teeth per capita. Rural poverty is not remotely picturesque. It's hungry, cold, and it smells. In school, we didn't make complex distinctions between parents' occupations or things like houses and cars and TVs: it was to the bone; who has B.O. (body odor) and who doesn't. In the city where I live today, poverty seems more to do with *things;* in the country, it had to do with human bodies. The Courdelaine kids all had "wicked B.O." and their bony elbows and knees stuck out of their clothes akimbo like a scarecrow's. My mother once found one of the Courdelaine kids, Ralph, sitting on the playground after school, crying. His front tooth had been knocked out by accident on the playground. It wasn't a baby tooth since, even though he was in the same grade as we were, he was retarded, and so had stayed back a lot. She picked up the tooth, wrapped it in a wet Kleenex as she was taught in first aid, and volunteered to drive him to the dentist. The principal said okay, so off they went. Ralph was smiling.

Mom came home white in the face. She said that when she walked into the dentist's office with Ralph, carrying the carefully wrapped tooth, she was greeted by the front-office nurse, who asked her, "Why'ja bother? All them Courdelaines lose their teeth anyways." The nurse told her to go on home.

❧

PLAINFIELD SCHOOL WAS A FOUR-ROOM SCHOOLHOUSE about the width of a double-wide trailer, which served eight grades, two grades per room plus the retarded kids in the basement, of which there was a high proportion. I believe there were three retarded children in my little class of twelve alone. On the first day of school, Mrs. Corette, who taught the first and second graders in one room, was standing outside to greet us.

She was wearing a pink-striped seersucker dress with two huge green frogs appliquéd on the pockets. I loved her instantly. She started the day, every day, singing, "Good morning to you, good morning to you," as she pointed to each one of us in turn, so no one ever felt left out, "We're all in our places with sunshiny faces, oh, this is the way to start our new day." It was, indeed, a most pleasant way to start our new day. Next, we stood, faced the flag, put our hands over our hearts, and said the Pledge of Allegiance. During the pledge, Boy Scouts and Girl Scouts would get to do this neat-looking two-finger salute instead of putting their hand over their heart. After the pledge, we sang patriotic songs: "The Star-Spangled Banner," "Home, Home on the Range," "America the Beautiful," "Yankee Doodle," and "Over Hill Over Dale," as we march the dusty trail and those caissons go rolling along. Then we took our seats for prayers. We recited Our Father and afterward sang a children's prayer that went:

> Father we thank thee for the night
> and for the pleasant morning light;
> for rest and food and loving care,
> and all that makes our day so fair.
> Help us to do the things we should
> to be to others kind and good;
> in all we do at work or at play
> to grow more loving every day.
> Amen.

The prayer was lovely. More than lovely, it was a lifeline for me as I repeated my prayers in the dark of my room at night, stiff with fear, a talisman against the dark side of our inverted forest, a Grimm's world in which goblins, ghosts, and other unnatural creatures and disembodied terrors existed just as surely as did the good fairies and their gossamer wings, just as surely as I saw, time and again, my parents' eyes cloud with hatred, rage, and terror as they looked at each other. Worse still was when my mother looked my way. Although she complained that pleasing my father was a constantly moving target, to me, it was my mother who was the changeling. What was funny on Monday got you slapped on Tuesday. There was no winning, no staying ahead of that game, because, as I figured out years later, the whole point of the game was to punish you for being a bad girl, so that she could be the good one.

As I look back on this time, I was becoming more a creature of the forest or a fairy tale, of dreams and nightmares, than a visible, embodied, human little girl. Being seen, being noticed, just *being,* was not safe. While I would learn to build secret compartments in my mind to hide thoughts and feelings unacceptable to my father, with my mother the only solution was a full-company strategic withdrawal. I gave up the front line of my body and retreated behind an icy, numbing moat and cold stone battlements in order to survive to fight another day. I still have no memory, tactile or otherwise, of my mother's hands coming closer than about a foot from my body, neither for blows nor caresses. It is as if my memory were stopped at the drawbridge and all instances of bodily contact chopped off by the fortress guards before allowing the rest to pass. The events surrounding such scenes, however, are fully alive. I can look down at my body and see what I'm wearing, smell things around me, hear what is being said, feel the blood rushing to my face and the shame in the pit of my stomach, the feeling that I have to go to the bathroom right now, that I'm going to mess my pants; that terrible, inexorable, hypnotized feeling of "Come here!" and your limbs feel stuck in molasses as in a dream where something horrible is chasing you and you try to run but can't. And then it's blank, hacked off, and nothing exists until the aftermath, when memory resumes.

Most of my strategic retreats were largely reflexive; however, I executed one key maneuver fully conscious of what I was doing. I learned how to cry soundlessly, without tears, silent as the stones of the Wailing Wall. I remember the instant I did it. I was in the room I shared with my little brother. I'd been brought in there to be punished. The door was shut and it began. I didn't feel, or remember feeling, "the four hundred blows." I knew I was being spanked only because I heard my brother's terrified screams coming from the hallway on the other side of the door, and his little fists pounding against it. In a split second, I realized that it must be my cries that were terrifying him. I was the one who explained stuff to him and he believed me, the one who picked up his bottle and teddy over and over when he threw them out of bed at night and no one big came.

She tore open the door he was pounding, and the next thing I knew, he was off the floor dangling by one skinny arm and spinning in the air because she was hitting him so fast. I vowed that never, ever again would I make so much as a peep.

I would soon discover an additional payoff from my newfound skill, this one not just for my brother, but for me as well. Although, at first, my total lack of reaction infuriated her, her rage seemed to burn itself out faster, like a fire with no oxygen, as it were, no drama and noise to fan the flames.

❈

AT HOME, DADDY WAS UNUSUALLY BUSY THAT FALL, or perhaps I was just getting old enough to quantify his absences somewhat. My mother, too, had something with which to occupy herself. We were going to renovate and expand the house, and an architect had made a perfect little dollhouse for her out of graph paper, with movable walls and little pieces of paper furniture. The house would have a separate bedroom for each of us, and an underground passageway to the planned-for garage. Upstairs, above the garage, Daddy would have a little apartment of his own with a bathroom and a tiny kitchen.

While Mama was busy playing with her paper house, I'd sneak up to the open loft above the living room and play a game I'd invented. I swore my brother to secrecy and deputized him as my assistant. Then I began operating. First, I made incisions in my dolls and beloved stuffed animals. Then I'd begin to spank each one, methodically at first, then wildly. My brother joined in, and after an orgy of spanking, we hurled them, one by one, over the balcony to the floor below. After some time, my mother discovered the incisions in my menagerie, and after I explained that I wanted to be a doctor when I grew up and needed to practice, she stitched up the dolls and stuffed animals, without punishing me. I was thrilled with the scars; they looked very swashbuckling. She forbade any more operations, but my brother and I kept up the secret doll-spanking sessions, hurling them over the balcony. The scissors disappeared for good after my mother discovered that Maxer and Pearly, our two cats, had clumps of fur missing.

❈

THE GAMES WE PLAYED AT SCHOOL could not have been more unlike the ones I played, hidden away, at home. Our teacher, Mrs. Corette, taught

142

us wonderful games. The first day of school, we all joined hands in a ring and sang, "Bluebird, bluebird, through my window," as one "bird" began to weave in and out of the circle of children. Then we'd sing, "Take a little girl and tap her on the shoulder," and the "bird" would tap another child on the shoulder. The tapped child took the bluebird's hand and together they'd weave in and out of the circle tapping others at the correct moment in the song, until there was a line of children holding hands where the circle had been. Finally, we would re-form a circle holding hands. The older kids taught us rougher games like Red Rover Red Rover send Peggy right over.

I didn't have B.O., but I said my words queer, like "tomaahto" and "trousers," which was almost as bad. And I came across another distinction that mattered, something most people would call politics, but which ran deeper than that: it had the fervor of religion. At recess, the eighth-grade girls culled me from the pack, and when the playground monitor turned her back to cuff some boy on the ear, the girls linked arms, formed a long gauntlet, and began kicking me, like some pack of feral Rockettes. This happened a lot. The first sentence I ever wrote was a note to Barbara, the worst of the big girls. "YOU ARE A RAT." When I walked into the girls' room to use the toilet, there she was, showing my note to the rest of the pack and laughing.

One day, when I was on the teeter-totter with a boy in my class, his sister Corleen, an eighth grader, came over. Because she was alone for once, I saw my chance. I worked up my courage and asked, "Corleen, why do the big girls hate me?"

"Promise you won't tell them I told you?"

"Cross my heart," I said, gesturing.

"Well, I'm not sure exactly, but I think it's because your father is a Communist."

I had no idea what a Communist was, but I was relieved, somehow, to know there was a reason. I don't know if it's universally preferable to know *why* you're being beaten, even if the reason is wrong. I suspect so. In my case, the reason was dead wrong. My father was probably the most un-Communist, anti-Communist of any of them. He detests Communism. But he also detested McCarthy and that whole un-American idiocy of which New Hampshire in the fifties and early sixties was in thrall. *Communist* meant anyone who looked different, spoke different, and boy, did it mean anyone who was a Jew or had even visited New York City. Communists were why each classroom walked single file down to the basement, where we knelt against the dank green wall and covered our heads with our arms until a teacher blew the all-clear whistle. These "duck and cover" civil defense drills were to prepare us in the event that Communists dropped the bomb on Plainfield. Unlike any other assembly, there was no giggling or fooling around. We were scared, quiet, and in deadly earnest. Weekly we knelt, covered our heads, and silently contemplated our mortality.

❖❖❖

WHEN THE SNOW FELL IN 1961, I was told not to put it in my mouth. This might not seem like a big deal to a city kid, but in Cornish where we drank out of the brooks, tapped maple sap from the trees, boiled it down, and poured it on snow for candy, and ate wild berries and apples by the handful, this was strange and disturbing. My mother said it had "fallout" in it from nuclear bomb testing. I examined great drifts of it that winter, looking for fallout, the deadly black flecks I expected to find sprinkled in amongst the white snowflakes. I never found any until we went to visit Granny, Grandpa, and Aunt Doris in New York City for a long weekend after Thanksgiving. The place was radioactive! Black, sooty flecks and more yellow dog pee than I could stomach.

The trip had not started out well either. We woke up in the dark, which was creepy. (It was a revelation to me, when I became of age to make my own travel plans, that it is, in fact, totally unnecessary to rise before dawn when going on a journey. Nor does one have to get to the airport several hours in advance.) I had a beautiful dress laid out on my bed in the nursery. It was a red print jumper with little smocked flowers across the chest, and underneath a white blouse with the same red print at the border of the cuffs and collar. I got myself dressed, except for the buttons up the back, and went in to use the bathroom. I sat down. Splash! Backwards into the toilet. Daddy had forgotten to put down the lid. Drowning in horror and disgust and panic, things went dark for a while, and then I remember arms wrapping me in "soft pinky," my mohair blanket. I was inconsolable about having to wear a different dress. Life, as we know it, was ruined.

I'm not sure it's possible, but I distinctly remember my grandmother walking out onto the tarmac to meet us as we climbed down the steep, narrow stairs that a man rolled up to the plane door when we landed. Life proceeded to get unruined as Aunt Doris said I could have the beautiful blue butterfly broach she was wearing, for keeps. Her bedroom in my grandparents' apartment at 1133 Park Avenue was my favorite place to visit. She had a beautiful dressing table with a little chair she let me sit on and look into the mirror. But the best thing was she let me look into all the drawers and touch her make-up and jewelry and glass bottles of perfume and soft gloves. I could even take things out carefully and try them on one by one in the mirror. She told me strange and wonderful facts. For example, she called the skin on my face "your complexion" and said I should never wash my face with soap because it dries out your complexion and leads to wrinkles. I should use this pretty-smelling stuff in a jar, pat it on my face with warm water, and then rinse it off with cold water and pat dry.

Did you know water can smell? Water at home is just water, but in New York it smells nice as it comes out of the faucet and into the sink. My mother wrinkled her nose and said, "That's *chlor*ine, dear. It's a chemical." Well, *I* had learned a thing or two myself. Getting ready for bed that evening, I announced to my mother as she began to wash her face, "Soap *ruins* your complexion, you know."

My grandparents had a dining room off the living room. You could see it from the couch, but you had to go through a sort of archway to sit down at the table. In the corner of the dining room stood a big black-and-white television set at an angle where the three of them, my aunt, grandmother, and grandfather, could watch the news throughout dinner. I couldn't see it very well; I think I was too small to see over the table anyway, but I remember the flickering light from the television reflecting across the polished table and the dark, disapproving looks my aunt and grandmother exchanged in silent commentary. I was glad it was someone on television who had been naughty instead of me. I got gingersnaps to dip in whipped cream for dessert.

I only remember the living room at night with the lights on. Grandpa sat in a big chair at one end of the room and listened to the Mills Brothers on a huge Victrola. He had a nice singing voice, and a good ear like me, and I couldn't figure out why his singing made Daddy squirm the way he did when Mama sang off-key. There was also something embarrassing about Granny's prints of the *Life of the Orchid* that hung over the living room couch; I could tell by the way he mentioned them, but I didn't get that either.

I went to sleep with the comforting hum of traffic and city buses a dozen stories below. I loved it that, in the city, the night had people in it. In the country, the night, like the winter, is too solitary, too devoid of human consort.

❦

THE NEXT YEAR, IN THE FALL OF 1962, a wonderful thing happened. The earth opened up and swallowed the big girls. Plainfield and Meriden townships consolidated their school districts: we sent over our sixth, seventh, and eighth graders; they sent us their third, fourth, and fifth. So now, with the exception of first and second grades, there would be only one grade per room. We not only kept our beloved Mrs. Corette for another year, but the playground, in all its glory, was ours.

That winter, we did not take our family trip to Florida, as planned. Instead my mother was going to take my brother and me to spend several weeks in Barbados with her mother, whom my father referred to as "Mummy De-ah," which he always said in a strained, high-pitched voice, mimicking Claire and her mother talking together. Daddy had some business to take care of in New York, I was told. No one mentioned that his book *Raise High the Roof Beam, Carpenters and Seymour: An Introduction* was to be published that January. In fact, I'd venture to say that no title of any of his books was ever spoken in our house; they were like the boxes of books with his name on them, sent by his publisher I suppose, that I discovered in the cellar, stowed away and unmentioned. He used to tell us things his characters said though, quoting them as though he were talking about old friends, like Mr. Custe or Mr. Curzon or Bill Shawn.

He wrote to us in Barbados from his room at "The Sherry Netherland 781 5th Avenue 10022 ELDORADO 5-2800." It was addressed to Miss Peggy and Master Matthew Salinger c/o the Buccaneer Bay Hotel St. James Barbados W.I. He said he loved and missed us and hoped we were having warm weather. He also assured us that he'd pick up Joey, our dog, from the kennel the minute he got home. The next letter included my mother, sort of, beginning Dear Girls and Boy. It was a very funny letter, full of news about our imaginary friend Mr. Curzon. Again he tells us he misses us, but adds that his work is going well so we should just concentrate on swimming and being warm. What I took as my due then, but now strikes me as not exactly *normal,* is that all the lavish expressions of affection in my father's letters to us as a family were directed, almost without exception, solely to me. The last letter we received before returning home from Barbados began Dear Fambly, but ended in boldface type that he was convinced more than ever that Peggy Salingers don't grow on trees. It was signed with about a million XXXs.

I don't remember if I had a good time in Barbados that time or not. I imagine I did, and it seems a bit churlish to report that all I remember clearly about my own experience is that strange blisters appeared on my arms, and I suddenly had the chills and wanted thick blankets on my bed. I was sunburned, my mother told me as she put some kind of salve on my arms. This was quite a blow to my pride. My mother and brother were the fair ones who needed lots of smelly suntan lotion; Daddy and I never burned. The other thing I remember was the smell of sugarcane burning in the evening, which disturbed me greatly. All I knew about were forest fires raging out of control because, as Smokey the Bear warned, someone had been careless with a match. I had no concept of controlled stubble burning as a farming technique, and I lay awake at night terrified the fire would soon reach our hotel, and even more terrified that I seemed to be the only one who was concerned.

What I did notice was that sunning and resting did my mother a world of good. All the nice, playful, pretty things within my mother came out on vacation visits with her mother. She wasn't just well-behaved, she was fun. There was new life in her veins, her face shone, her clothes were bright, Lilly Pulitzer colors, she even smelled different than she did at home. I liked being near her. There were no scenes, no punishments. This other Mama, the lovely one who smelled of Blue Grass lotion and lavender, put in an appearance, a transformation that happened most reliably when we were away from Cornish, and Daddy stayed behind.

My grandmother, too, seemed magically transformed. My brother and I had been forbidden to see her when we were very young, and I still recall clearly the image I created of her in my mind as a wicked witch, with wild hair and bony, jabbing, long fingers. When I met her, here was

this tiny old lady with twinkling blue eyes and soft, curly, white hair, looking for all the world like a fairy godmother. Everything about our visits
with her was enchanting. We left the cold, gray isolation of winter in Cornish and were transported to fairy land: Barbados or Venice, her house in
Mount Kisco with its swimming pool and gardens, her apartment at
Seventy-ninth and Madison with its beautifully scrolled front entrance
door that looked as if someone had blinked and turned a secret garden of
ivy and roses into everlasting metalwork, doormen who knew me and an
elevator stop that was hers alone, and inside were paintings of voluptuous
naked ladies, of people dressed like kings and queens, of Madonna and
child illuminated by sparkling cut-glass lamps, and floors made of hundreds of small wooden rectangles in a rainbow of forest colors from honey
to deep red to darkest brown, all pieced together in patterns that only a
magician's kaleidoscope could have made in its perfection.

For years, I thought of the Metropolitan Museum of Art, just a
block away from her apartment, as a natural extension of the magical
world she inhabited. There, at the museum, most wondrous of all, to
me, was that you could take a tray and fill it with food you could see and
smell, laid out before your eyes for the taking in such abundance it was
like the feasts I'd read about in my books where the king, or some pasha
in silk pajamas, or a Mandarin emperor, clapped his hands and a hundred dishes might be paraded before him and his guests. After making
your choices, you found a table fit for the gods set all around a long pool
of water with various sprites making gentle, musical, sparkling foun-
tains of water turning the air around them into a dance. As Holden said,
I wish you could have been there—it has been renovated since then, if
one can refer to what Mount Vesuvius did to Pompeii as a "renovation."
The pool has been covered over, or removed to make way for more tables, and all too human waiters bring your meal sight unseen chosen
from letters and sentences and numbers on a menu. Gone the magical
grotto, the sound and feel and shimmer of droplets in the air, copper
penny wishes tossed in by children; now the raucous sounds of utensils
and glass and plate, humanity in a hurry, with grown-ups signaling
waiters to bring the check.

The civility I remember of the Metropolitan Museum, the quiet
sanctuary, was similar to the way I felt about the relations between
Granny and my mother. They maintained a formal, perhaps distant ci-

vility—though it didn't strike me as distant when I was a child and thought everyone with an English accent conversed in that manner—that was contagious. Even when I was twelve and the possibility of the barest hint of civility between my mother and me seemed well nigh impossible, we had a lovely, peaceful time together exploring Italy with Granny. It makes me think, now, that my mother was quite right in saying how different things would have been had she stayed in New York and received some psychiatric help and support, rather than going back to Cornish after she ran away.

My father told me that Mummy De-ah was a terrible liar and if I had any self-respect, I'd have nothing to do with such a person. I didn't disagree with him, about the lying that is, but what I didn't tell him is that I enjoyed her, and even some of the lies, or "stories," just the same. Like the whopper she told us about riding on the back of dolphins from the Cipriani, that glorious island hotel, to the dock by Saint Mark's Square in Venice. Although Daddy had a fit about the vacations that my mother, brother, and I took with her, he'd still send me love notes, even in enemy territory.

❦

MRS. CORETTE, WHO HAD PROBABLY never taken such a vacation, refers cheerfully and generously to my absence from school during this time.

[Report card: period 4]

Peggy's reading work continues to be satisfactory this period. With your help during her absences, she has progressed satisfactorily with her group.

Her travel experience must have been richly rewarding as she came back looking so rested and tanned.

Peggy has been a most interesting child with whom to work. She completes her seatwork assignments and is a helper in our room. She has a very nice, sweet little singing voice and she likes to sing for us. Peggy has shown qualities of leadership and her enthusiasm has been most enjoyable. We shall miss her in our room next year.

We want to say a big "thank you" to you for allowing
Peggy to bring so many interesting things to our classroom.
Plants, books, etc. are always appreciated and enjoyed by the
little children.

Sincerely,
Mrs. Corette

❦

WE WANT TO SAY A BIG "THANK YOU" to Mrs. Corette. I revisited the
school playground this year, on a sad trip to Plainfield for the funeral of
my friend Viola's little sister. During the break between the church service and the burial, I walked a block over to the old school, which is now
an auction house. I had driven by there hundreds of times, but I hadn't
been back behind the school, where the playground was, in over thirty
years. I remembered the playground as huge and was curious to see how
big it really was, or rather, how small it might have become to the eyes of
a grown-up after all those years. I rounded the corner of the old school
building and found, for the first time in my experience of revisiting
childhood places, it was even bigger than I'd remembered. It was immense. I have been a city dweller for so long that I now measure what
urban real estate agents call "outdoor space" in square feet, not acres. I
paced off 125 long-legged strides from the back of the building across
the field to the edge of the woods. There were probably twenty feet of
woods, which was part of our playground as well, before it fell sharply
over the forbidden bank into an old dirt pit. In fair weather we ate our
lunch outside in circles of friends on the field. I wish I'd brought my
lunch box and thermos.

I thought about Viola's sister. I'd been with her a few days before
she died from a long battle with brain cancer. Viola and I were forty;
Carol was thirty-one years old. The tumor had devoured most of her
spark. She could still walk a little and sit up with assistance, but the light
was nearly gone from her eyes. The town minister, who had been
Carol's sixth-grade teacher and soccer coach, arrived for a visit. We sat
around talking out back of Viola's house. To include Carol in the conversation, I asked her, "Did you have Miss Chapman, or Mrs. Spaulding?" I was met with a blank look, and her mother answered for her

that she did have Mrs. Spaulding in fifth grade but wasn't sure about Miss Chapman. "You did have Mrs. Corette though, didn't you?" I asked. She smiled, not just with her lips but her dark eyes lit up. "Mrs. Corette," she said slowly. "Mrs. Corette, yes."

A few days later, the pain was outrunning the morphine, and Viola, in her gentle way, told her beloved, feisty little sister that it was time to stop fighting and urged her to turn toward the light and take Dad's hand. Carol died minutes later, sitting up in her easy chair, her family and her cats surrounding her, loving her to the last. It occurred to me that if I ever die (!)—yes, I just wrote that—I mean if I'm scared when I'm dying, which I most probably will be, I hate going anyplace strange (my son was playing with our cheap folding closet doors yesterday and said, "It's just like we're on an airplane, Mommy"—they were, indeed, like bathroom doors on a plane, site of several whopping panic attacks, and just the mention of it made me run to the bathroom to empty my gripping bowels. No, I won't be going gently into the night I think). When I die, I don't really want the Saints or Jesus or any of those big guys to stretch out their hand to me in the light. I'd like to see Mrs. Corette in her pink dress with frog appliqués on the pockets, holding out her hand and inviting me to come and join the circle in the field. "Bluebird, bluebird, through my window, take a little girl and tap her on the shoulder."

Requiem eternam. Recess eternal.

10

Snipers

※&※

I WAS SEVEN YEARS OLD when I entered third grade in the fall of '63, the same age and grade as Seymour was in the story "Hapworth 16, 1924," published in *The New Yorker* a year and a half later, in 1965. The "story" consists of a letter, the length of which took up nearly the entire issue of the magazine, written by Seymour, age seven, from summer camp, to his parents back home. He asks them to send a "few" books for his brother Buddy, age five, and him to read over the summer. His request includes the complete works of Tolstoy; Cervantes' *Don Quixote; Raja-Yoga* and *Bhakti-Yoga* by Vivekananda; all of Charles Dickens, some of George Eliot, William Makepeace Thackeray, Jane Austen, the Brontë sisters; *Chinese Materia Medica* by Porter Smith; some Victor Hugo, Gustave Flaubert, Honoré de Balzac; selections from the works of Guy de Maupassant, Anatole France, Martin Leppert, Eugène Sue; the complete works of Sir Arthur Conan Doyle; and so the list goes on and on.

This is not simply the summer reading list of a peculiar fictional character; it is my father's way of treating the reader to the same advice and exhortation he gave his own real children, though at a slightly older age. With the exception of the foreign-language books such as conversational Italian, and the "two invaluably stupid books" by Erdonna and Baum, there wasn't one of the books on Seymour's list that my brother and I hadn't heard him canonize or declare anathema, using the same language, ad nauseam, I'm afraid. It was hard for me to maintain an adult reference point as I read "Hapworth" in my late thirties—lots of adolescent eye-rolling and tooth-sucking at being lectured—"I *know*, Dad, you've said it about a *million* times already." No one else, that I know anyway, talks like this. Phrases I could recite from memory:

> Both are written by distinguished, false scholars, men of conde-scension, exploitation, and quiet, personal ambition. . . . I would greatly appreciate anything not containing excellent pho-tographs . . . a damned beautifully self-reliant spinster . . . a ge-nius beyond easy or cheap compare! . . . Vivekananda of India. He is one of the most exciting, original, and best equipped giants of this century I have ever run into . . . godsent models of the feculent curse of intellectuality and smooth education running rampant without talent or penetrating humanity . . . preferably unwritten by vainglorious or nostalgic veterans or enterprising journalists of slight ability or conscience . . .   ("Hapworth 16, 1924")

We third graders in Plainfield were pleased to begin reading in the *Junior Classics of the Collier's Encyclopedia*. On the first day of school, pretty Mrs. Beaupre told us to bring the volume home and have our mothers help us cover it in brown paper from a shopping bag, and write the title on the cover, centered, with our name and class in the upper right-hand corner. I remember illustrations of Indians having a lot more fun than the Pilgrims, and being so bored sitting there in class that I used to disappear and walk around in the pictures.

One day just after recess, we all took our seats and folded our hands. Mrs. Beaupre said, "Children, open your desks and take out your *Junior Readers*." Roseanne LaPlante was about to read aloud when Mrs. Spaulding, the principal, entered our classroom. She asked Mrs. Beaupre if she would step into the hall for a moment. Marilyn Percy, one of the front-row girls, was appointed monitor, which meant she was supposed to write down the names of all the children who misbehaved during the teacher's absence and tattle when the teacher returned. Nei-ther Viola nor I, who sat in the back with the boys and could shoot spit-balls with the best of them, was ever appointed monitor, nor were any of the boys, who, in those days, were, by definition, unfit to snitch, being made of "snips and snails and puppy dog tails," as opposed to "sugar and spice and everything nice."

This time, though, not one of us budged. We were all wondering whose father had had an accident at home with the farm machinery, or over at the split ball-bearing factory, and who'd have to get home right away. Mrs. Beaupre looked strange when she and Mrs. Spaulding stepped back into the classroom. She said, "Children, President Kennedy has just been shot."

Bedlam broke out in our classroom as several children stood on their chairs and stomped and clapped and whistled.* I could not have been more shocked than if Mrs. Spaulding had entered our classroom and pulled down her pants. Not about the president so much as that anyone would think that someone being shot was something to cheer about, and that they dared do it in class, in front of the principal.

My mother picked me up at the usual time. I got into the car and she started to tell me about the president. I said I already knew that. During the funeral, Daddy was in front of the television, his face an ashen green, with tears rolling silently down his cheeks as he sat and stared. The only time I have ever seen my father cry in my whole life was the day he watched JFK's funeral procession on television.

I thought, as I watched the procession, I must never forget this. So, for some reason, I set myself the task of memorizing the drumbeat of the long funeral march: dum, dum, dum, da-da-da; dum, dum, dum, da-da-da; dum, dum, dum, da-da-da; dum, dum, da-dum—all those blocks down Pennsylvania Avenue toward Arlington National Cemetery. As I listened, I thought about Granny, sitting by the window in her bedroom overlooking Park Avenue, as she did every morning, hoping to catch a glimpse of little Caroline Kennedy going to school.† She called me in and we sat there together by the window as she told me that Caroline and I were almost the same age and how prettily she was

---

*I often reflect on the chasm that exists between what my urban Democratic friends think is politics—a sort of an extended *Meet the Press,* or *Firing Line*—a basically cerebral if banal activity, and the primal arousal of a crowd at a cockfight, or perhaps the crowd at the Colosseum watching slaves and Christians fight to the death, that arises when people talk about niggers and Jews and Communists. The mob passion these little kids tapped into was and is something not to be underestimated.

†The Glass family apartment was across the street from an exclusive school for girls.

dressed the last time she had seen her. She was thrilled by a "sighting." The little boy, John junior, whom we saw saluting his father's casket, was the same age as my brother. They wound up, years later, at boarding school together.

My mother had already shed tears over the Kennedys the spring before the president was shot. President Kennedy had decided to have a party to honor American writers and artists, and he had invited my parents to the White House. I remember thinking how wonderful, having cake and ice cream with the president. They almost went, such were my father's feelings for President Kennedy (to this day, although I have warm feelings for President Kennedy, I don't know why he was singled out in my father's affections). My father delayed replying to think it over.

Mrs. Kennedy placed a call from the White House to our house in Cornish. Our telephone number at the time was 401. She spoke to my mother, who said she'd love to come but was embarrassed to say that she was having trouble convincing her husband, you know how he is about his privacy. Mrs. Kennedy said let me try. A conspiracy of well-brought-up young ladies. My mother told me, "Jackie got on the phone with him and then again with me. She really wanted him at the dinner. But I must have let on I wanted it. So he said no way to me. Jerry didn't want me to feel I was worth anything, and above all, he wanted to make sure that I be prevented from having a chance to fall into the feminine vice of vanity. . . . I may still have the invitation. I wrote a haiku at the time and kept it for years. It was something like:

> "Having to decline
> The White House invitation,
> She dreams of her gown."

Killing was in the air. My mother told me years later that there was a specific reason for my feeling that the level of danger in the house suddenly became so palpable at the time. My parents had begun to receive bizarre, anonymous notes, in graphic and sexually perverse language, threatening to kidnap the children and do horrible stuff to us. This coincided, most unfortunately, with the rapid rise in my father's fame as well as the mystique of his reputation as a recluse. Occasionally we glimpsed reporters sneaking about, and at least once, one even climbed up a tree. We saw him through the kitchen window. There was no way of knowing if these men were kidnappers, escapees from Windsor Prison across the river, plain old perverts, or reporters. It fanned the pervasive odor of fear and skittishness around the house almost to the choking point.

Worse still, I somehow came across a library book that had photographs of concentration camp prisoners, which is enough to send anyone's terror off the Richter scale, let alone an already frightened seven-year-old girl. I don't remember a time when I wasn't aware that I was one-quarter Jewish and that that was enough to get me sent to the gas chamber had I been in Hitler's Germany. That threat, that fact, was part of my being since the beginning, since I was aware I *was* a being. This is not to say I had any concept whatsoever about what Judaism is or what being a Jew entails. The heart and soul and breadth and depth of what I knew was that it was dangerous. It was passed down to me as the unedited, unsubtitled nightmares of my father, brief things said about the war—such as the fact, he said, that you could live a lifetime and never really get the smell of burning flesh out of your nose—congeries of primal images and emotion, no context, no narrative, no explanations. When I saw the stark, black-and-white photographs of the death camps, a new and terrible fact struck me: these people were mostly naked. With the logic of a child, I concluded that that was what happened to bad little Jewish girls—even quarter-Jewish girls like me—who, like me, thought about sex and naked bodies and pulled my pants down in front of a boy to show him my thing and for him to show me his. Here were whole rows of people being punished and starved and killed for the same thing.

I did not see Catholic depictions of naked, tortured bodies in purgatory or hell (as in that Bosch painting—you know the one—with a devil sticking a bunch of flowers up somebody's backside in a diorama of the tortures of hell) until I was beyond the primal-terror stage: they were somebody else's bogeymen, someone else's bad dream. As a child, when my mother would read the Christmas story to me each Christmas Eve—the flight out of Egypt, the birth in a manger, the star in the east, incense, frankincense, and myrrh—I thought every child in the world heard the same story about that special night that happened so long ago. The story wasn't religion, it was history, and thrilling, and even tonight, the miracle of Santa Claus would fill my stocking without fail and take a bite out of the sandwich I left for him. I had no idea Christmas had anything to do with being Jewish or Catholic and bad things happening to you. My mother never read any stories about bad things happening to Jesus, just the lovely gifts he received from the Magi. I was successfully steered away from images of crucifixion at the Metropolitan Museum. Easter was strictly about coloring eggs and a candy hunt.

Religion, for me, was something my parents said I could choose when I was older, if I had any interest. My mother, I knew, had chosen not to be a Catholic anymore when she grew up. But there was no equivalent choice about the existence of the Jewish blood that was inside of me, about the fact I qualifed for extermination in Germany, or about a documentary photograph of living, or half-living, persons on their way to death.

Try as I might in my teens, when I chose to become a Christian, hoping somehow to be adopted by the Holy Family, I never could quite believe in them with the same depth of faith that I believed in Nazis, or my mother believed in devils as a child. Nazis, not devils, were my bogeymen.*

※

IT WAS AROUND THIS TIME that I began to have problems with the alligators. The ones that lived under my bed. For the longest time, all I had to do to stay out of harm's way was to make sure I didn't dangle any bait over the edge. Arms and legs were held close to my body, tightly under the covers. No child I knew was foolish enough to dangle an arm over the edge even in the hottest weather. But around this time those alligators began to

---

*I have a private theory that a person's background and deep identity can be determined most accurately by one simple question: When you were growing up, who was your bogeyman? I asked a friend I've known most of my life, who is half-Indian and half-Jewish, but who identifies himself as Indian, about his bogeyman. On the Canadian reservation of his tribe, parents (then as now) warned their children, "Watch out, the Mounties will get you!" Though most of the children had never seen a Mountie, the mere word struck dread in their hearts.

act up. At bedtime, I had to run on tiptoe across my bedroom floor, risking as few steps as possible, and leap into bed. After a few nights, they were onto this game. To keep one step ahead of them, I learned to long jump. After brushing my teeth and having one last pee, I'd whisper, "Ready . . . set . . . go!" and spring from the bathroom door; gathering speed as I ran across the hallway, I'd leap from the transom some four feet through the air, clear the footboard, and plunk onto my bed.

Daddy didn't try to talk me out of the alligators; instead, he turned his attention to my breathing. He'd place his hand on my belly to check to see if I was chest-breathing, shallow, tense, and unhealthy, or stomach-breathing, deep and healthful. He taught me the same breathing techniques that young Seymour teaches his family in "Hapworth": you breathe through the left nostril while covering the right nostril for one breath, then switch sides for the next breath. He also suggested that before I fell asleep at night I should say, or think, the word *hong* on the in breath and *sha* on the out breath. Alternatively, I could say, or think, *om* for the entire breath cycle.*

Relaxation and breathing exercises might have helped if my problem had been in falling asleep. I had little trouble with that because, for much of the year, the evening sounds of the field and forest sang me to sleep. The most beautiful of all was hearing the cows from Day's farm driven home for their evening milking. As they walked, single file, along the path, I could identify each one as it passed, for the metal cowbells that hung from an old leather strap around the neck had been hammered, by hand, each to a slightly different pitch from the others; and finally, I'd hear the whole glorious symphony as they made their way into the distance toward hay barn and home.

My secret problem was that once I fell asleep and began dreaming, I became caught in the web it spun, and I couldn't escape and find my way back to consciousness and home. The harder I struggled, the more entangled I became. This was something that so terrified me I'm still not at all comfortable writing about it. I'd always had terrible nightmares, but even worse than the content of the dreams was what began to hap-

---

*These were probably the "hong sau" and "Aum" techniques in Yogananda's book on Kriya yoga.

pen to the structure of them around this time. The boundary between dream and awake, once a firm door I could shut behind me, was becoming grotesquely elastic.* I entered my own internecine Battle of the Bulge as I began to become trapped in my dreams. I'd be in the midst of a terrifying, often physically excruciating nightmare and then find myself wide-awake, or so I thought, lying in my bed, damp hair sticking to my neck like seaweed to the drowned, thankful it was morning and the nightmare was over. After a few minutes, I'd notice something subtle was out of place, something was wrong. Then to my horror, I'd realize I was still dreaming. This hell could go on for five or six or seven permutations; sometimes I'd even brush my teeth and get to the breakfast table before I realized I was still dreaming and the terror would begin again. And again.

My dream life was the Alice-like mirror image of what was happening to me in my waking life. In the face of overwhelming assault, the child, like a good fighting combat unit, jettisons a piece or pieces of the self to save the rest. Some develop full-blown multiple personalities. Others have a collection of fragments, or "shard people" as I call mine, split off from the main body. Apparently, parts of me, little encapsulated personalities jettisoned during retreat, may well have died or are, at least, lost forever. Some of these parts of me died in exile, each on some desolate island since childhood. Some are alive but missing in action. I have spent years, with doctor and friends beside me, cruising the archipelago, calling out, "All-y all-y in come free."

The clue, that there were dead to be identified and mourned, as well as missing survivors out there, came to me in a dream—their message in a bottle, as it were. In my late twenties, not only was I caught in the dream web as I so often had been as a child, but now, for the first time, I actually died. This was quite a shock to me, having heard somewhere, and taken it as an article of faith, that dreamers don't die in dreams, they al-

---

*A psychiatrist once told me that this is indicative of one's ego boundaries breaking down, the next stage being psychosis, where ego and id, dream and reality, form a tidal wave breaking up all semblance of structure and function of anything in its path. I think I prefer my father's words in his story "For Esmé" where he likens his character's mind to unstable luggage "teetering off the overhead rack" on a train.

ways wake up before hitting the bottom of the cliff as it were.* Not so. I was tied to a stake by Nazis who then lit the wood pile underneath my feet. I felt my flesh burning†; excruciating, terrible agony—words fail me here—as the flames burned my legs, higher and higher. When the flames reached my genitals, I smoothly left my body. It was not a traumatic jerk or the kind of wrenching separation one might imagine. It was like swimming in a lake. I glided above my body and watched it burn. I knew I was dead. When I woke up, it seemed so real that I wondered whether some past-life experience, if such a thing exists, had intruded upon the present.

The next time I died in a dream, I was clearly myself even in the dream, and not some "character" from a past life. This convinced me to search my own life for an explanation and for help. I was terrified. I'm captured by two huge metallic beings. They say nothing. They just line up all the humans they've captured, and we walk and walk until we arrive at the top of a hill, and I can see a sawmill poised at the edge of a cliff. The humans are floated in a stream through the mill, end to end like logs, until they reach the edge of the falls where two of the metallic beings operate a whirling saw that decapitates each human in turn. The body drops over the edge, down the flume, and floats out of sight. When

---

*I asked my shrink, a psychoanalyst and medical school lecturer who specializes in such things, and was told that it was, indeed, extremely uncommon, in the general population, even of therapy patients, for a dreamer to die in a dream. However, among a subgroup of persons who were subjected to repeated and severe trauma as infants or young children, it is quite common. This is not to say the physical intensity of the punishments has to have been extreme. I did not go to school with bruises and whip marks as did a number of my classmates. In fact, I used to wish I had scars to point to on my arms or legs to explain, to vouch for the impact on me. I still find it troubling that my psychological symptoms mirror, or are, in some cases, worse than those of friends of mine who suffered broken bones at the hands of their parents. I know, intellectually at least, that the effect of terror does not reside in blows alone, but it's something I struggle with especially when I'm beating myself up—no one used a cattle prod on me, why can't I just straighten up and fly right, and so on. Well, I'm trying my best—no excuses. I'm asking questions to get some terra firma beneath my feet, not for some distant object at which to point my finger, or tq have some name to yell like a rock thrown into an abyss.

†It was also put forth to me that babies left too long in urine-soaked diapers do, in actuality, experience severe blistering and burns on the genitals and down the legs.

I reach the saw blade, I feel it cut my throat all the way through, and as I fall over the edge, I feel the whirly stomach you get on an amusement park ride or drunk in bed when the room starts to swim. As I hit the bottom, my consciousness begins to fade smoothly, slowly, as I float down the stream. I see the surface of the water recede as I sink gently as stars fade at dawn, into nothingness.

11

"However Innumerable Beings Are,
I Vow to Save Them"*

❧❦❧

IN DECEMBER OF '63, I had my eighth birthday. All I can say is, winter birthdays in New Hampshire are really crummy. Viola's is May 11 and there were picnics and games in the field. In December, the few kids whose parents were able to make it up the steep road in the snow played in our garage. It was heated, sort of, but it was no one's idea of a picnic. I don't remember who came, except Viola of course, and the rest of the kids did not notice when I slipped away. I sat at the top of the stairs to my father's garage apartment, and after a while, Viola came and sat with me. I was feeling sick and strange.

Viola went and got my mother, and the next thing I knew I was in a hospital bed in Windsor, Vermont, and told I had bubbles in my ears. I was there for several days, including my real birthday. I vaguely remember opening a present on my hospital bed, but that is all. I specifically remember no pain, but rather a feeling of unreality, as in the dreams I had that mimicked reality and went on forever without escape, like the TV show *The Prisoner.* I would have done much better with a proper explanation; it would have grounded me, feverish and all, in a world of biology like the ponds I loved. Bubbles in my ears; I floated away until, I suppose, they faded into iridescence and popped.

I don't remember coming home from the hospital. It is hard in the best of times to get a firm grip on the earth in the midst of northern December snow and its perpetual twilight of grays and whites and electric

---

*The first of the Four Great Vows recited by Zooey (*Franny and Zooey,* p. 104).

lights turned on shortly after lunch and school beginning and ending in darkness. My mind scattered in dry snowflakes; puffs of air blew the light powder across the hard crust of ice that formed over the packed snow several feet deep on the lawn. Someone may have shown up at school and sat in my seat; perhaps my shadow played in the faded-winter-light recess. Under aging banks of fluorescent lights, the fragments of dancing, twitching glare make my brain feel as if it's skittering even now.

Hibernation. I lay in a liminal state, like a fish in the mud at the bottom of a frozen pond, through the long months of January and February and into March. Then, the world beyond my eyes became a speck of blue frozen light in the distance of a long, long tunnel. Gradually I became aware of a certain dampness. I was awakened by smells of wet wool and deep brown mud.

As the snow melted, I felt an acute sense of urgency, for where there is life, as opposed to suspended animation, there is the specter of death. "However innumerable beings are, I vow to save them." Each spring, Viola and I took up our glass jars and did battle with the grim reaper, that harvester of stranded worms on pavement, fallen birds, caterpillars crossing the road, and frog eggs foolishly laid in drying puddles.

My mother was wonderfully helpful with our rescue missions. She gave us old shoe boxes to make houses for our worms and let us dig up from her garden some dark, rich earth that, for some reason, smelled like coffee grounds. When we brought home a cocoon some boy had broken off a tree, she showed us how to make a home for it. We took an old honey jar, poked holes in the top for air, put green blotter paper on the bottom, dampened it, and put in the stick and cocoon. When we were finished, Viola and I decided to walk up the hill to see what was doing in our secret pond this year. It was now our pond, not Day's pond. Mr. Day, the farmer down the road, had died and somebody had threatened to build a trailer park on the land. My father mortgaged everything we owned and bought it, so we now owned over 450 acres. A walk to the pond was not a casual stroll, but a half-hour climb. We had discovered the pond the previous year while following the trail of an apparition. It first appeared as we walked up the hill, mist rising from the patches of snow under the shade of the juniper bushes, which were always the last to melt. There, in the mist, stood a thick white horse, matted and muddy, and next to him a small brown donkey. They stood still, frozen against the sharp-smelling spruce trees and deep green pines, the only sound the droplets of melting snow dripping off the ends of the pine needles as the sun warmed the numbed, cold bark. I wasn't sure whether the two beasts were real. I looked and could see that Viola saw them too, so we were either both dreaming or both awake. Steam rose from the nostrils of the donkey, and I let out my breath in response, automatically, like catching a yawn, unaware I'd been holding it. If they had walked slowly off a cliff, I'm not sure I'd have awakened. Following them, we stumbled across the secret pond where they stopped to drink.

This year we didn't see the horse and donkey, but I doubt they could have taken a clear drink from the pond this late in the spring. The pond water was way below last year's level, so low in fact that it seemed to be less liquid than alive, teeming with wriggling life. It was too full of things even to wade in. (And we weren't squeamish girls. Behind Viola's house we had swum happily in the forbidden stream reputed to be full of bloodsuckers.) Masses and masses of frog eggs, clear jelly with tiny black dots, were engaged in a life-or-death race against the receding water as they clung to the weeds near the bank. In one tangle of weeds we spotted some exposed, greenish masses with fat red dots that we'd never seen before. We took some of each and put them in our jars, taking care not to tear apart the jelly mass. In another jar, we caught seven newts and brought them home.

I got to keep the eggs and the newts at my house, I think, because my mother didn't mind; Viola's was a bit more squeamish. We set up an aquarium with water and some stones in case the newts needed to get out and turn into red salamanders later. They survived for several months until one morning I came downstairs and saw a dead newt floating at the surface of the water. The next morning, another. The following morning I got up earlier than usual and caught the murderer red-handed. One of my newts, the skinniest one in the tank, had gone mental. He had his back legs wrapped around the neck of a bigger newt and was slowly strangling him to death. I tried, but I could not pry his legs off the other one's neck. Even flicking his head rather sharply with my fingers didn't do it. Squeezing that slimy flesh to the mushing point was something I was incapable of doing. Finally I held his head out of the water for what seemed like hours and he let go. The other newt was staggering—if you can believe a newt can stagger—but alive. I netted the remaining newts, put them in a jar, and carried them back up the hill to release them into the pond. I kept "Killer" in a tank by himself rather than release the Cornish strangler into the wild. He lived an unconscionably long life.

※

THE SUMMER OF 1963 marked the worst year of a seven-year drought. Wells were running dry, ponds drying up. One day, I went to pick some wild watercress from a nearby brook where it always grew this time of year. The brook had dried to a trickle of mud. So I decided I'd better go see how the other brook, farther into the forest in the same direction, was faring. I jumped across the mud and crawled under the barbed-wire fence that separated the woods from the field. There was a lot of old, rusty barbed-wire fencing from previous farms on our property. I have a scar on my calf and many tetanus shots to show for it.

After a few minutes I came to the spot where another brook flows into a little pond that always dries up late in the summer. This spring it was already close to dry. I saw masses of doomed pollywogs. They'd never grow legs before the pond dried up. I had my trusty jar and I knew where there was water in another part of the forest. One little jar and thousands, millions of pollywogs wriggling black and shiny in half-inch pockets of water that would be gone for certain in, at most, a week or two. Like the sorcerer's apprentice, I dashed back and forth, filling my jar with them and running, sweating, dizzy, ten minutes each way, over and over, back and forth from the dying pond to a swampy area where three brooks met. Finally, I dropped to the ground. I couldn't go on. I lay there with the impending deaths of thousands on my conscience.

I passed out flat on the pine needles and slept for I don't know how long. When I awoke, cool and rested, I got up and walked beyond the pond, resolutely not looking at it, and up to the edge of a twenty-five-foot drop of sheer granite where, some twenty thousand years ago, the last great glacier had passed by, laughing at the presumption of rock to be substantial. A brook ran along the narrow valley at the bottom of the cliff, and on the other side, the land rose steeply up again, trees growing between large boulders tossed by the glacier.

In the valley at the base of the slope were two old stone wells and some rock arrangements that were clearly human-made. These thrilled me. My mother had said that the wells were probably from colonial times or maybe even from the Indians. Colonial times and Indians and cavemen and dinosaurs and Jonny Quest intermingled freely in my mind. Whenever I went to that place in the woods, I felt as though I were entering a lost valley. I skirted around the cliff and went down into the valley along the brook that flowed through it. I climbed up the slope on the other side and sat in the great lap of an old birch tree, just where it divided into three strong trees, and from my perch, looked down at the old wells. I imagined I was one of those half-ape, half-human women I'd seen in the Museum of Natural History. My imagination was such that, after a short time, all vestiges of my former life faded from consciousness. Gone was my house, the road, my sneakers, my pink skin, my name; I became a wild, hairy ape-woman. I lived by the cliff for protection. My heart began to pound as I thought of marauders. Then, I heard them coming.

I chose a high point and waited, muscles taut, poised to hurl down a rain of rocks upon their heads. My eyes surveyed the area for possible escape routes in case there were too many of the enemy. I saw them coming over the far ledge. My bowels turned to ice; there were at least twenty heading straight for our wells. I picked up my club and ran noiselessly, just the sound of my pulse and the wind in my ears, fleeing for my life down the path of an old stream bed through the woods. I reached the swampy area where they would lose the scent of my trail and plunged in, weeds whipping my face and making little cuts on my legs. I didn't feel the stinging until after my flight.

I spotted our well-house* and came abruptly to a halt. I was entering forbidden territory. I crept up to the window, daring myself to look in. The thought never occurred to me that the well-house was forbidden

---

*A small, wooden structure, with four walls and a roof, built over a well, presumably to keep animals and debris out of the water. They usually have a windowlike opening so you can check the level of the water in the well.

for my own safety. I thought, or more than half-thought, that someone had been murdered and was floating around in there, which was why we couldn't use the well anymore and the water was rusty-colored and bad. I did not peek in. My club was powerless against bloated corpses.

Beyond the well lay an old logging trail that led to the road. As I emerged into the dappled sunlight of the dirt road, familiar plants, and birches, I metamorphosized back into girl—hairy body became pink, uncovered breasts flattened, matted hair became messy braids, and I thought about a bologna sandwich with mustard.

❦

I WAS OUT IN THE WOODS, as usual, when I heard my mother calling my name. Since it wasn't dinnertime, I raced back to the house to see what was wrong.

"Margaret Ann Salinger, *where* have you been. I've been calling and calling. Oh, never mind, we'll be late for William's birthday party. Just *look* at that hair! Go get changed and bring down the brush. Your pink seersucker is on your bed. And change those socks and shoes, too."

I liked my pink-and-white-striped seersucker dress. It was sleeveless and gathered at the waist, and when the breezes blew, the skirt puffed out nicely. Had I been allowed to wear those scrunchy petticoats that Viola wore, it would have made real hoops. I was also relieved to find out that William's party was going to be held at the Platts', friends of ours, rather than at Saint-Gaudens',* where he lived in the summer because his parents were caretakers. I loved Saint-Gaudens, but William and I always seemed to get into trouble when we played together there. Like the time he suggested that we pick all the flowers, and there were great piles, literally over our heads, of uprooted orange lilies. It was just before a big gallery opening. "You're going to get the spanking of your life when we get home." The summer before that, William's mother and

---

*Augustus Saint-Gaudens, 1848–1907. Considered the major American sculptor in the beaux arts style, honored for his coin designs; *Grief*, his sculpture for the grave of Mrs. Henry Adams; the Robert Gould Shaw Memorial, a commemoration of Shaw's leadership of an all-Negro battalion in the Civil War; and the equestrian sculpture of General Sherman. He maintained a summer home and studio, Aspet, in Cornish, New Hampshire, which became a National Historic Site in 1964.

mine came running out of the caretaker's house, horrified. A group of old ladies on a tour of the grounds had just left *terribly* upset. Apparently two children were swimming buck naked in the goldfish pool in the rotunda, one of whom stood up on the sculpture of the turtle that spits water into the pool and was last seen peeing as far as possible—and it wasn't William. "You're going to get the spanking of your life when you get home." Or the summer before that, when William showed me some shiny three-pointed leaves and told me to rub them all over my body. I landed in the hospital with one of the worst cases of poison ivy— I'd not neglected my genitals—they'd seen. "What were you doing, rolling naked in it?" the doctors asked. Then there was the time our mothers were having a ladies' tea, and when one lady looked out the window, she spied William and me with our pants down playing doctor in the woods. I thought she must have had X-ray vision. We were in a grove miles away from the main house, or so it seemed to me. "I was so . . . hu*mil*iated. You just wait until we get home, you're going to get the spanking of your life." The earliest memory I have of our catastrophic visits is of me sitting on top of a great heap of toys I had piled together, sobbing, but refusing to let anyone play with them. William's brother, still in rubber diaper pants, ran in and told. "How *could* you be so selfish . . ."

All the children at William's eighth birthday party went down to the Platts' field and were told to pile into a cart that was hitched up to a tractor that William would drive. He was to take us for a hayride. He got going pretty fast and turned sharply to the left. The cart tipped over, Stephanie Yatsavich fell on top of me, and I fell on top of my right arm, which was out straight where I had been bracing myself against the cart. No one seemed hurt. Something was terribly wrong with my arm, though. I picked up the strange arm with my good one and cradled it, as if it were a baby. Then I walked across the field to get a grown-up from the house. I noted, sadly, that my nice pink skirt was all red. My arm had changed into an odd purply thing with the inner forearm distended like a pregnant cat's belly. I told William's mother I thought she had better take me to the hospital. Now.

Instead, she drove me three miles up the mountain road to my mother's house to ask her what she should do. I'd already *told* her what to do! I got into our car and Mom drove me up to Hanover, twenty miles away. By Lebanon, despite my best effort to stay in control, to make sure I got my arm to the hospital, I lost consciousness.

Some idiot moved my arm to place it on an X-ray plate. Screaming agony. They did it an eternal hell number of times. I had a compound fracture: one bone was splintered, the other was sticking out and covered with dirt. A mask came over my face. Some nurse, with a cheery stewardess voice, actually asked me to *count!* Jesus. Now?

An instant later (in real time, six hours on the operating table had passed, I was later told), the mask was off my face, and I heard a group of nurses talking and laughing. They didn't know I could hear them I guess, because they looked surprised and a bit flustered when they saw my eyes were open. "This one's waking up." On the table next to me was an old lady with tubes sticking out of her nose and face. *Gross.* That was the last thing I remembered until it was dark and I heard someone moaning terribly and it was me and I had to throw up over and over. (Ether was the anesthesia used in those days, and the aftereffect was pretty wild nausea.) Pain so bad there were no words, no tears. Moaning. My mother was in the room. There was only one bed. Days passed and I was stuck in a dream. When I was finally able to form words, about the time I remembered the taste of ginger ale in my mouth instead of bile, I was so scared I was crying.

My mother said, "What's the matter? Shall I ring for the nurse?" She was standing on the right side of my bed. "Mama, I can't tell whether I'm dreaming or awake." She looked at me and said slowly and calmly, looking right into my eyes, "It doesn't matter." I heaved a sigh, a shudder of relief. I'm not quite sure why, but it was the most useful piece of information someone had given me in my life up to that point. Things weren't so bad after that.

After a week or so I was moved from a private room to the children's ward. I was by the window farthest from the door. The girl to my left rocked her head to get to sleep. I thought that was cool and tried it myself, but it just made me dizzy. The girl across the way had psoriasis and had to have tar all over her, which stank to high heaven. My mom finally went home after insisting on sleeping in the hospital on a chair in my room, much to the annoyance, she said, of the staff. It just wasn't done in those days. She and Daddy began to trade visits. He came one day, she the next, during visiting hours. One day the tarry girl became cross with Daddy and said, "Doctor, how come you only bring *her* presents, it's just not fair."

Ugh! Bedpans and bed baths. The nurse who was giving me my first sponge bath in bed handed me the washcloth in the middle of it, having done much of what I could do myself with one hand. In a singsongy, cutesy voice she said, "Alrighty now. You wash in between." And she left, pulling the curtains closed behind her. In between *what*? Oh . . . Oh, God!

The glorious day finally came when I was allowed to get up and use the bathroom myself instead of a bedpan. I could also walk up the hall to the playroom. Once I was allowed to be up and about, I had the distinct impression that I was invisible. All this business of nurses and doctors and carts and trays went on around me as I walked the halls, and nobody seemed to notice me at all. It wasn't unpleasant actually, it was rather like walking in the woods, animals busily at their work all around me. "However innumerable beings are, I vow to save them."

A person came into view. It was a very little boy wearing a hospital johnny but no diapers or underpants. He was walking toward the playroom looking lost. He was invisible, too, but we could see each other. I took his hand and brought him to the playroom where I spent what seemed like a very long time taking care of him and playing with him. A nurse materialized briefly at one point with some measuring thing he was to pee in. The sign pinned to his johnny said "Do not give liquids. Kidney patient." I didn't know what a kidney was exactly, but it had something to do with pee. I saw why when, at one point, his hospital johnny parted. His penis was shaped more like a tube than a penis (now I realize he was simply uncircumcised, but I'd never seen one like that), and I thought he was in the hospital to get it fixed. He mostly just wanted me to pick him up and walk around with him. I brought him back to my room on one hip, with my good arm around him. I was a little afraid I'd hurt or damage his penis and tried to be careful carrying him, but it didn't seem to bother him in the slightest. I sat him on my bed. I got in, hooked my arm up, and we looked at the books I'd hoarded from the play lady's cart. About suppertime a nurse said, "Oh, there you are," and scooped him up and took him out of the room. He waved to me over her shoulder. The next morning when I awoke, guess who was peeping over the edge of my covers waiting patiently for me to wake up.

❧

THE RIDE HOME WAS TERRIBLE. Mom tried to go slowly but the motion of the car as we went around left turns struck remembered terror in my body of the cart tipping over. I couldn't help it, I was certain the car would flip on its side and land in the ditch. We finally made it home in one piece, and I put on a new pair of pajamas with blue smocking that Mom had bought for me because the top fastened with ribbons at the shoulders and you could easily slip it on over a cast and tie up the bow. They were lovely. As she did the bows, she said, "I just knew something like this was going to happen to you, you've been so bad lately."

12

Glimpses

❧

. . . those two, tantalizing, tiny portals in my mind I mentioned last year are still far from closed; another brisk year or so will probably turn the tide. If it were up to me, I would gladly shut the portals myself; in only three or four cases, such as the present one, is the nature of the glimpse worth the wear and tear on one's normalness and blessed peace of mind . . .

—"Hapworth 16, 1924"

IN HIS LETTER FROM CAMP, Seymour dispenses advice to all and sundry, based on his glimpses into their past or future, rock certain of the correctness, the perfection, of his vision. He tells his mother, for example, not to retire from dancing until a certain date the following year; advises his three-year-old twin brothers on their "chosen career"; discusses advising the school nurse on her virginity and a seven-year-old bunkmate on his past-life weakness regarding alcohol; and so on. Seymour forecasts the ebb and flow of the karmic stream with the certainty of yesterday's news, rather than doing the meteorologist's modest best.

The gap between his experience of glimpses and mine was nearly as great as the difference in our third-grade reading material. I always distrust someone who claims to have a hot line to God, with perfect ears for reception. It has been my experience that most glimpses are as imperfect as the rest of real life. They're more like radio transmissions on the battlefield: you almost never get the message clearly,* or when you do, it's

_____

*When I was in college, for example, I lay down for a nap, but before I fell asleep, I was jolted upright by a vision, a "glimpse," of my roommate jumping off

about weird stuff that doesn't really matter, like the time I glimpsed the depth of our well before it was drilled. After several years of using water that often amounted to little more than a rusty trickle from the faucet, my father had finally agreed to give up on our spring-fed well and drill down into the bedrock for an artesian well. He was not happy about the expense, especially coming on top of building his new house down the road (having found the tiny apartment over the garage to be inadequate). The driller came and said, "We'll probably have to drill down a couple of hundred feet. There's no guarantee, though; you're on a thick ledge of granite, you know."

"Where will you drill?" Daddy asked him.

"Don't know that yet. Have to dowse for it first."

The driller surveyed a couple of our trees and found what he was looking for, a sturdy yet supple Y-shaped branch. He took a jackknife out of his pocket, and cut it down. Then he began slowly, deliberately, but in a relaxed manner, walking across the property, holding the stick, one fork in each hand, parallel to the ground.

My father asked him with the hushed respect of a novice inquiring who is your master, "How did you learn how to do that?"

"My mother was a dowser. Showed me when I was about your girl's age."

The stick began to waggle slightly and the nose slowly pointed down toward the ground. "See that? There's a water vein under there, but it's a weak one. We'll keep moving." After a time he found one he liked and stopped. "Now here's a real good one. Feel it?" He put the stick in my father's hands. "No, not like that, you have to pull out on 'em. Not too much or you'll split the stick, but too little and you won't feel it pulling."

Daddy and I spent several afternoons dowsing the property and felt some really good pulls, sure enough, in the area the driller had chosen.

---

the bridge in town. I leapt up, told my friend James, who was in the room, to grab his parka, and we went running down to the river. We searched up and down the riverbank; no Annie. We went back to the dorm to wait for her to come home. Four hours later, she walked through the door soaking wet. She'd thrown herself off the bridge all right, but when the icy water hit her body, she snapped out of it, grabbed for the nearest branch, and pulled herself up onto the riverbank. She was fine except for a frostbitten toe. Some help my glimpse was! *Bubkes*. The message hadn't come through stamped with the date and time.

He came back with his equipment a few days later and the whole family stood around to watch. He guessed he'd have to go down about two hundred and fifty feet. We each took a guess, and my mother wrote them down to see who'd come the closest. My father guessed three hundred; my mother, two hundred; my brother said four, which, not coincidentally, was also his age; and I said ninety-eight feet.

Ninety-eight feet to the inch later, we struck water. The driller nodded at me, making a "hats off to you, kid" gesture, and said, "Jerry, you've got yourself a little water witch there." What in many families would be considered an amazing hole in one was simply par for the course for the Salingers, myself included; or, as with the dowser and his family, taken for granted that some folks simply have the gift. When you *know* it's going to be ninety-eight feet, it is a shoulder shrug to have it confirmed, just like most of the "experiments" we did in school where we already knew what the outcome was supposed to be. These "glimpses" are not in any way the same experience as the "Eureka!" of discovery, or the thrill of winning a game of chance, as when I guessed—but didn't know—the number of marbles in a jar at a town auction and got to keep them because I came the closest.

One night during the long drought, however, those "portals" did matter. I had had glimpses all that week, a recurring vision of Christmas trees on the lawn bursting into flame. I think there is something about chronic danger that is conducive to developing such sensitivities. You learn to listen with more than your ears. Like a wild animal, I could sense danger approaching by the smell of the ground and the feel of the air. That night, I felt an electricity in the air that made the hair on my arms stand on end. I lay in my bed in the dark and watched.

My mother had set fire to our house. I smelled smoke, ran into my little brother's room, and said firmly, "Matthew, wake up. We have to get out of here." Mom may have shouted "Fire," I don't know. I was focused on the little hand in mine and getting us safely out the front door. I didn't know if Matthew was asleep or awake. Sometimes he was in between and would walk into my room at night and pee against the wall thinking he was in the bathroom or something, so I held him tightly and went by feel down the stairs to the landing near the front door. Flames were coming up the other set of stairs from the kitchen addition below the landing. My mother was on the other side of the flames. She yelled, "Go get Daddy. I have to call the fire department." I remember thinking it was crazy to stay where she was and to make a phone call, leaving no safe passage to the door should the flames spread as they were likely to do. I shooed the cats out the door, and to my great relief, they took off. I followed them into the Indian-summer night, my brother firmly in hand.

My father's new house was about a half a mile away, down a steep and stony dirt road. In the valley between two hills the road became so dark that I saw sparkles in front of my eyes and absolutely nothing else. Country darkness. One of the things I love best about living in the city is that it never, ever gets that kind of blind dark. We were in pajamas and bare feet, and Matthew stepped on a sharp stone and started to cry. I talked to him and sang so he wouldn't be scared. We got to Daddy's house and told him the house was on fire. He went over, and I was told later that he and my mother held a hose on the house; apparently it took over half an hour for the fire engines to get there. At some point that night, Daddy came back from the fire to take us to stay with the Jones family over in Plainfield while he saw about the house. I wasn't sure where my mother was. She later told me she didn't leave the house because she was afraid of burglars ransacking the place. Daddy must have brought me some clothes from the house because I stank when I went to school the next day. My clothes weren't burned but they smelled bad for a long time after.

There were no admissions or accusations. I simply assumed my mother had set the fire. I may have been wrong, she says now that I was mistaken, but at the time, the thought that it could have been an accident *never once* crossed my mind. A few days later I mentioned it in passing to my father, rolling my eyes about her story that she smelled something strange which she assumed were my Creepy Crawlers, those plastic toy bugs you baked in an oven.

Although the firemen determined that the fire had started in the hall closet and ventured a guess that perhaps a lightbulb had touched a sleeping bag and ignited it, and she, herself, to this day denies, perhaps quite rightly, that she had anything to do with it, Daddy shared my point of view, but for a different reason. He thought that she set it because of *where* it started. The hall closet was where her clothes were. He said she set it because she wanted some new clothes and he was unwilling to pay for them. It only confirmed his view of what women will do for vanity.

As soon as the workmen had made some progress rebuilding, Daddy came and collected my brother and me from the neighbors who had taken us in. He dropped us off at the house on the edge of a crazy cliff and went back to his house alone to work.

The ground floor of the house was gutted. The upstairs looked shocking. All the bathroom lighting casements, toothbrushes, and other stuff had melted and formed long pools of black, twisted plastic. Nothing looked the way it was supposed to. The gerbils, I found out, had been trapped in their cage when the fire swept through the room. I thought of them not being able to run and hide.

13

"There She Weaves by Night and Day"

❧

A magic web with colors gay . . .
— "The Lady of Shalott," Alfred, Lord Tennyson

A FTER THE FIRE, I began to read as if my life depended on it. I snuck
books into school and read them behind the dreary, brown-paper-
bag-covered schoolbooks that I was supposed to be reading, wherein
plodded those aggressively unthrilling Pilgrims and drawings of equally
unnaked Indians. Having exhausted the resources of the children's library in Plainfield, my mother drove me twenty miles to the children's
library in Hanover, where, each week, I was allowed to check out six
books. The books I chose were portals to other worlds offering foreign
travel, time travel, psychic travel, intergalactic travel, dream travel. *East
of the Sun and West of the Moon, The Chronicles of Narnia, Five Go Off to
Smugglers Cave, Mystery at the Old South Lake, At the Back of the North
Wind, A Diamond in the Window, The Phantom Toll Booth, A Wrinkle in
Time, Tal,* the *Oz* books. The last even provided a portal out of my own
private nightmares. By some miracle, I was able to bring Dorothy's technique into my dreams, and instead of being stuck in them, I could now
click my heels three times, start spinning around, whirling through the
galaxy, away from the dream, toward earth, then the map, then Cornish
and my rooftop, and finally I'd land with a thump in my bed and wake
up. I now held the keys both into and out of dream worlds.

My fictional Glass siblings with their precocious, grown-up reading lists were robbed, I think, of the wonderful experience of childhood reading.

❦❧

MY FATHER LET ME COME with him to the Dartmouth College Library, where he browsed the stacks and sometimes borrowed books. It was a sanctuary of cool in the summer and cozy warmth in the winter and smelled wonderfully of dust, lemon oil, and old leather. You entered through a revolving door, exciting to begin with, and found yourself in a vast, quiet space with, I couldn't believe it, a huge black-and-white tile floor like an almost endless chessboard. Daddy taught me how to play checkers, which I liked if I won, and chess, which took too long, especially when the only thing I really liked was to move my bishops—tall, oval-headed things with slits for mouths—on the diagonal. While Daddy went about his business in the stacks, I happily played games of patterns on the black-and-white squares.

At the end of the squares, just off the main hall, students sat reading at long tables by lamplight surrounded by a cozy glow. I hopscotched back across the main floor to look at the huge murals on the walls. I think they were of Indians, but I couldn't show too much interest. It would have been a betrayal of the unwritten Salinger code of good taste. My father had made it stingingly clear that murals, as an art form, were beneath contempt. Ditto anything "primitive," like the African art at my friend Rachel's house. For him, there are those such as his "wondrous Chinese, and noble Hindus" with their "fine and subtle minds"* and delicate features; and then there are the primitive, the physically strong, the great unwashed, including Negroes, Hispanics, and the vast majority of Caucasians. He has the taste in physiognomy of an Hasidic Jew: the paler and frailer and more studious looking, the more valued the being. For my father, there is something most definitely suspect—not kosher—about physical robustness. When I brought home an A in Spanish one year, he said, "Oh, terrific, now you're studying the language of the ignorant!"

It's not that in his day these were atypical cultural prejudices, but they are strange attitudes, it seems to me, for someone who considers himself to be well read, to think Spanish-speaking writers and poets and

---

*"Hapworth."

painters, for example, are ignorant. Though my father considers himself to be widely read, I discovered as I grew older that what he is, in fact, is deeply and passionately read in very selected areas. He becomes an expert in whatever he falls in love with, whatever he is passionate about, and leaves the rest untouched.

His worldview is, essentially, a product of the movies of his day. To my father, all Spanish speakers are Puerto Rican washerwomen, or the toothless, grinning gypsy types in a Marx Brothers movie. Once, when he was criticizing me about my black friends in high school—"coarse" was what he called my friends and me—he said that blacks had no subtlety of humor at all. "Wasn't it all that crap?" he said as he put on a big stupid grin and rolled his eyes and waved his hands. I said, "Dad, that's in the movies, they don't do that in real life amongst themselves. That's for the camera, because that is what white people want to see." His expression changed and he said thoughtfully, "No . . . of course you're right. That makes sense." He is by no means a heartfelt bigot who will hold to an idea in the face of evidence to the contrary. But his frame of reference is Hollywood in the twenties, thirties, and forties. When I was a teenager and announced my engagement to my karate teacher, who was black, my father was terribly concerned, but for fictional rather than real-life reasons, of which there were plenty; e.g., you've only known the guy a few months, you aren't out of school, he doesn't have a job except teaching karate and the occasional guitar gig, and so on. Instead, he cautioned me, saying he saw a movie once called *The Jazz Man* or something where a white woman married a black singer and "it worked out terribly."

He used to borrow movies from the Dartmouth film library, and we often stopped there after a trip to the regular library. But someone at the film library apparently let it be known which movies J. D. Salinger borrowed, and he's never since darkened their door. It's not that he had any cause whatsoever to be embarrassed about his choice of movies; it was the violation of his privacy that so infuriated him.

After Daddy finished his business at the libraries, he'd take me to Lou's or the Village Green for a tuna fish sandwich and french fries. Then we'd either go next door to the Dartmouth Bookstore or we'd go to do his marketing at the Hanover Co-op. He loved the fresh food but hated to go there because he stood a good chance of running into someone he knew and, to be polite, would have to stop and talk. The dreaded human encounter. I liked the Co-op better than the local stores because it didn't smell like ammonia and old sour-milk sponges or death at the meat counter, the way the others did, like the old wooden-floored IGA or the Grand Union with its S & H green stamps booklets we filled but never redeemed. When, years later, Purity Supreme, which he referred to as Puberty Supreme, built a megastore in Lebanon, he gave up the Co-op, even though he liked the Co-op's food better. He preferred the impersonal atmosphere.

On the way home from a trip to Hanover, I mostly just looked out the window because if you engaged my father in conversation while driving, he'd turn and look right at you, forgetting he was at the wheel. He'd swerve back onto the road or into his lane at the last instant. It was even worse if you were in the backseat. He'd turn his head all the way around to listen to you. If my brother made a peep, I shot him my most murderous look that said, "Shut up, will you. Do you want to get us all killed?" In an era of two-lane highways—your lane and the traffic coming toward you—he was an absolutely terrifying passer. When someone ahead of us was going too slowly, being a "road hog" (one of his favorite movies was one where W. C. Fields inherits a million dollars and spends it all smashing, one by one, into the cars of offensive drivers), he would pull up to the offending car's bumper, lurk there at forty-five miles an hour or so until he reached what was technically a passing zone, and then pull out to pass. We'd careen down the wrong side of the road heading straight for an oncoming car. He'd duck back just in time. In the Jeep it was always dicey whether it would have enough pickup to pass the car in front before hitting the oncoming one. Terrifying. My hands, he noticed, were never unclenched as we drove. He thought it was just a habit of mine.

Right by the beaver pond, before the Plainfield town line, a solitary road sign said NO PASSING. "Will you look at that," he'd say, "tsking" his teeth. "What would Miss Chapman say? 'No Pissing!' Can you imagine?" I fell out in giggles every time he said it.

❦

MISS CHAPMAN, MY FOURTH-GRADE TEACHER, would *not* have been amused. Before they put in the interstate, we passed her house each way to and from Hanover. It sat at the edge of the road, brown, squat, square, and unlike its neighbors, utterly devoid of any decoration: no flowers, no lawn ornaments, no shutters to soften the severe lines of the house. Miss Chapman, like her house, stood in stark contrast to the lush world of Mrs. Corette and pretty, young Mrs. Beaupre. After a whole year, the only sign of life on my report card was the terse comment "Peggy is often careless in her work. She is capable of better work." I got A's and A-'s in most subjects. My only bad grade was a C- in penmanship, but considering that my right arm was in a cast that term and I had to learn to print with my left, it could have been worse.

The contrast between the worlds, over the rainbow, of my books and the reality of our classroom became unbearable that winter. We sat for endless hours beneath banks of poorly maintained, maddeningly flickering fluorescent lights, buried beneath an endless pile of purple mimeo worksheets made up thirty years prior by a spinster whose motto was "Idle hands are the devil's workshop, active minds the devil's spawning ground." The more you did, the more they came—endless, boring, numbing. I nearly wept in despair.

One dreary day in late February, with yet another endless hurdle to span between boredom and recess, something magical was to happen. Winter meant, for the most part, keeping out of range of the snowball-throwing boys, which was no joke, for more than once I witnessed a boy packing his with a rock in the middle. This was the same boy who slit open live frogs, and whose father tied him to a tree and whipped him with a bullwhip for punishment. Telling on H., even if it hadn't been against my personal code of ethics, was out of the question.

There was one big rule on the playground, and that was we were not allowed to go "over the bank." About twenty feet into the pine forest, the ground fell away sharply, almost straight down. As in old maps before the world was round, that steep bank was where the known world ended. One day, at recess, as I stood at the edge and looked over the bank, I felt a rush of excitement. It suddenly seemed like the wardrobe entrance to Narnia. I hadn't planned to, but, unknown to anyone, I slipped over the edge and entered another world. I was dizzy with the adventure and the peril of what would happen if I was caught. I slid down the bank slowly so as not to slip and fall without stopping. (All those weekends of ski lessons over at Mount Ascutney stood me in good stead; I knew how to do a controlled side-slip.) At the floor of the forest where the bank leveled off was a brook with the most perfectly clear black ice I'd ever seen. It wove like a magical snake through the trees. Most ice is white and bumpy and you need skates to slide well; boots offer too much resistance. Here was skating heaven, even in boots, and it was my secret. I scrambled up the bank to make sure I was back before recess ended and walked back across the field when the bell rang. I had something to live for, I had a secret.

At recess time I went straight across the field and stood at the edge of the pine trees and busied myself with some feigned play and waited, one eye on the playground monitor, until she turned her back and I whisked over the bank. After a few days the enchantment of the secret began to wear off; it needed the added magic of a secret shared. I told Viola and she came, too. Suddenly, from up above, we heard someone shout, "Miss Chapman's coming!"

Miss Chapman, Viola has said in her kindly, generous way, should have retired years before. She was neither mean nor cruel, but she was *fierce*. Perhaps I can say this without being too mean since she is long dead: Miss Chapman looked like a gargoyle perched on the gates to every child's land of nightmares. She had thick, terrible lips that, when she became enraged, were home to great stringy wads of white matter. Her great wrinkled wattle shook and her eyes bulged like a wrung rooster's when she struggled to give breath to her fury at some misbe-having child. At particularly daring moments we whispered under our breath and *well* out of earshot, "The old battle-ax." She was, indeed, old and terrible as medieval weapons. "Miss Chapman is coming!"

She strode across the playground like the Huns across the plains and she was headed straight for us. Somehow, in my mind's eye, I recall see-ing her coming from the point of view of an aerial camera, impossible in real life, panning the entire playground from above. We scrambled up the bank, and like the condemned without the mercy of a blindfold, we saw the whites of her eyes. We knew that she knew. We had gone over the bank.

It was such a huge offense, something I like to think not attempted before nor since the days when Brave Peggy and the Fair Viola walked the earth behind Plainfield Elementary School; my mind simply could not imagine the punishment. Miss Chapman, too, was speechless. She sputtered, but nothing came out. The rage came coursing through her hand as it seized my shoulder, talonlike, to carry her prey back to the nest to be torn to shreds. She shook Viola so hard she wet her pants. She must have shaken me as well, but I don't remember it. As she dragged us—for I can only assume Viola was pinioned on the other side—across the long field, my senses registered only the wind howling in my ears, Miss Chapman's brown wool coat flapping in my face.

There was no principal's office at our school, no detention room, no escape from our dreaded captor. We were hers from 8 A.M. until 2:30 P.M. for an interminably long month of days. There was no morning recess for us. We sat with our heads down on our desks while the rest of the class was excused. No lunchtime with the rest of the school; we ate alone in the room under the watchful eye of herself, bread sticking in our throats. No afternoon recess, again heads down on our desk for the entire period while we listened to her breathe and swallow and clear her throat and smack her thick lips—all manner of terrible intimacy with the bodily functions of the feared one. It was the longest March in the long history of endless rural New England Marches. Mud season. The bowels of Mother Nature.

14

Journey to Camelot

❧❦❧

IT MAY COME AS A SURPRISE, but throughout my childhood, my father was an ideal traveling companion, not just at home on our walks in the woods, but in public as well. When we visited New York, he would let me run down the hotel corridors, ride the store escalators five times, laugh out loud, go to the Central Park Zoo and only visit the seals if that was all I wanted to look at the whole time, visit the Museum of Natural History and head straight for the dinosaurs, with nothing "educational" in between. The New York I knew was Holden's New York: the Museum, Central Park with its zoo and carrousel and lagoon with the ducks, the doormen and the lobbies of good hotels. After my grandparents and aunt moved from Park Avenue to a smaller apartment, we stayed at the Plaza when we were in town. I came to think of "Eloise" as a close relation. Like Eloise, "my absolutely most favorite thing" was room-service breakfast. Plates came with beautiful silver lids on them to keep eggs or pancakes warm, or rested on a bed of ice to chill the grapefruit or melon. Everything had to be opened like a present, even the heavy linen napkins, just the way I imagined the princesses in my fairy books would have breakfast served to them.

It was at the Plaza, in the Oak Room, that my father taught me formal table manners. I'll never forget it, I was so impressed at the time. I still am. He told me that *he* didn't care if I used the proper fork, that was my choice. But he wanted to make sure that it was a choice, and that I never embarrassed myself because I didn't know any better. Or had to feel awkward on a date when I grew up.

After breakfast, we'd walk across the street into the park. Daddy always took me for a ride on the carrousel. I remember how happy my father looked, how he stood there grinning from one big ear to the other, waving to me each time I came around on my horse.

This time, however, we had to cut short our visit to the park because we were going to see Bill at *The New Yorker.* After Judge Hand died, my father asked Bill Shawn, the editor of *The New Yorker,* if he would be my godfather. I had seen him many times before, but never at work. I could tell by the way Daddy talked about it that this was something special. Sort of like being allowed inside his Green house.

I always liked to see Bill. His face looked like an illustration of the old man in the moon in one of my books: kind and round and softly twinkling when he smiled at me, which was often. He moved at a slow, gentle, steady, and sedate pace across my path. His wife, Cecile, reminded me of black twigs blowing across the face of the moon on a windy night. I never really saw her face; it never registered, that is. She was all movement. Where a face might be, I remember a blur of jagged black scribbles and pink and the feeling that someone had just left the spot where she had been standing. She wore a black velvet bow in her hair, which I simply coveted, and beautiful black patent-leather high heels that clicked marvelously when she walked across the floor of their apartment.

We rode up the small elevator, got out, and said hello to a smiling woman at a desk whom my father seemed to know, then walked down a long hall to Bill's office. Even though I was only seven, Bill stood up as though he were in the presence of a young lady, shook my hand, and offered me a seat. This is hard to explain, but I never felt as though he had mistaken me for somebody else, someone older or better-behaved. It was as though he responded to the person I really was inside, beneath the blankets of other stuff, like the ugly wool dresses and scowls I wore, piled on top. I don't mean he saw someone perfect or fictional, separated somehow from the imperfections that are part of who I am. How do I say this? Ah! He was a born editor, a writer's dream catcher.

Daddy and Bill talked while I sat at his desk and looked at his pens and at the greens and browns and shadows and light of the room. It wasn't brightly lit like a classroom or a doctor's office. It was gentle like a pine forest. Bill said he'd join us later for lunch, and Daddy and I held hands as we walked down the hall to see Alastair Reid, who had a son named Jasper. The name fascinated me. My classroom had Butches and Mikes and Herbies and Howards. Jasper. Alastair gave me a book he'd written called *Ounce Dice Trice* and wrote "For Peggy from Alastair Reid" in it with a fountain pen.

Then we came to the artists' room and that's where I stayed. Someone helped me up onto a stool way off the ground. They had easels, like mine at home, only much taller. The paper wasn't paper, but canvas and textured. The paint smelled wonderfully like gasoline in a puddle, and it stayed where you put it, unlike my watercolors, which ran too fast to catch up. These paints gave you time to think and plan things and daydream about the colors. And what colors! The red, yellow, and blue in my school and home didn't resemble any known thing except finger paint and the floury food coloring of homemade play dough. These colors looked like melted flowers. They were shiny and bright and didn't fade into the paper. There were dozens of tubes of paint with beautiful stripes on them; some were squeezed, and everything was used enough so that I wasn't afraid to touch. Someone put a big shirt that smelled like warm horses over my dress. People I'd never met seemed to know me; they smiled and said hello but didn't disturb me. That's Jerry's girl.

We went to the Algonquin for lunch with Bill and Lillian (Ross). We sat in a big round booth built into the wall that felt cozy like a clubhouse. I felt included, but not on display. Bill and Lillian and Daddy talked among themselves, and when the conversation turned my way, it happened naturally; there wasn't the usual huge gap in tone that grown-ups do, suddenly getting all singsongy and poky and intrusive, that would make me sink behind my eyes and start hearing their words as though through watery cotton wool, like the blinding fright and disorientation of a diver's light catching the eyes of a dreaming fish. When I was with Bill, I could inhabit my skin right up to the surface. I didn't know the word for it then, but I relaxed. I enjoyed myself looking around the room at the cut-glass table lamps, taking in all the textures and shapes and smells.

Bill created a world where a tight-lipped little soldier like me could talk, at the lunch table, about the color of fall leaves against the sky. Lillian wrote to me shortly after:

The NEW YORKER,
No. 23 West 43rd Street,
New York, N.Y. 10036
OXFORD 5–1414

October 24, 1964

Dear Peggy,

Those leaves are so lovely to have and to look at, every single one. They arrived in wonderful shape, still damp and fresh and smelling of that ground up there, and a little of the air, too! We've had some blue-sky days here this past week, and I've held the golden leaves up and looked at the blue sky through them just to get an idea of what you described when we had lunch at the Algonquin. Some day I want to come up, with Erik, of course, to visit you and really see what you were talking about. I've never had a more wonderful present than those leaves, and I've been showing them to Erik, one by one. He loves them (and talks to them) as much as I do. Thanks for sending them, Peggy, and a special hug from Erik. And love to all up there from Erik and his Mama.

Love,
Lillian

P.S. I took a picture of the leaves and will send it to you.

L.

And she did, on November 4, enclosing a little note:

I keep the leaves in the little basket shown here.
Erik looked at them so longingly that I gave him a couple.
He loves the way they feel and look.
I hope you'll be able to visit us again soon.
My love to everybody up there.

Love Lillian

❧

MY MOTHER AND I were talking about Bill one day, shortly after he died in 1992. I asked her about something that happened at the Plaza, a detail

I couldn't remember. She floored me by saying that during the entire time they were married, she never once came with Daddy and me on our "first-class" trips to New York. She said that when Jerry traveled alone or with just us children, he went first-class. When he traveled with her, he (himself) called it "third-class in Bulgaria." She said it was all part of his attempt to keep her weak female soul pure, away from the seductive, evil goodies that life with a famous author could bring. Thinking back, I don't remember her there specifically, but it hadn't occurred to me that she wasn't. I simply assumed she was there because these trips to New York were as much a part of my early years as our family trips to Florida each February.

Even at seven years old, I knew the places we stayed in Florida weren't like the fancy ones where we stayed in New York. I didn't care; I just noticed they were different. I assumed that staying in a small, ten-unit, one-level motel with the rooms in an L-shape around the swimming pool, many blocks from the ocean, was part of the game, albeit a serious one, of traveling incognito. After *Time* magazine came out in '61 with my father's face on the cover, it reached even the wilds of Cornish that Daddy was getting famous, and my parents began drilling me about appropriate behavior around strangers, not getting into cars and taking candy and so on, before we went anywhere. When we traveled to Florida, we did so under assumed names. I chose Annabelle; it was like my middle name Ann only *much* fancier. My brother's was Robert because that *is* his middle name and he therefore had a slight chance of remembering it. My father's was John because it was the most anonymous name around. My mother chose Mary to complement his, but my father dubbed her Ruby. I was swell about it, you can imagine: "Ruby red nose! Ruby red nose!"

We left Lebanon airport wrapped in snow and gray and heavy coats and mittens. We changed planes at La Guardia in more of the same and took off for Florida. Mama had us change into other clothes before we landed. When I stepped out the plane door into the sunshine, warm air touched my bare arms, startling me so that I stopped short and looked where it had touched my skin. "People are waiting, dear, hold on to the railing." These days when one "deplanes," one steps directly into a tube connected to the airport building and walks down carpeted corridors that could lead to any one of a hundred cities on several continents. By the time one is outdoors, there's the hustle and bustle of buses, taxi queues, rental car vans, things to be done routinely and expeditiously. The whole muffled process neutralizes or at least mitigates the shock of transition. Back then, the otherness of the place, the climate, the air, the smells, hit one squarely in the face as one emerged from the plane onto the tarmac, like Dorothy emerging after her wind-flown house landed in Oz.

We checked into our motel in Fort Lauderdale. The door of our room opened up onto a cement walkway surrounding a pool. While my mother unpacked and got us "settled in," whatever that was, Daddy and I went for a walk. Each morning, Daddy and I would take a walk together around the neighborhood. I don't remember if Matthew came along or stayed with Mama. As I run through my memories of these walks, I realize that I didn't notice people or cars or buildings much, but instead I noticed the kinds of things that were of my forested world in Cornish. The smells carried on the breeze, the trees and the variegated shade patterns of the palm fronds, were all so unlike the scent of pine and the dappled pattern of oak leaves and maples.

I loved walking on the ledges, like balance beams, adjacent to the sidewalk. As with a sailor's rolling walk on dry land, conditioned from months at sea, my view, and therefore the things I remember, was shaped from a long habit of walking in the woods at home. In the woods, on or off a path, you automatically focus your eyes on the ground a few feet ahead of you so you don't trip over stumps or stones or bumps in the ground. On the flat sidewalks of Florida, I took in little of anything above shoulder height, but not a thing on the ground escaped me. I collected things, a small coconut the size of my fist miraculously dropped within reach, the fleshy head of a red flower blossom rotted off a tree, a bright orange kumquat. The plants and lawns all had the thrilling look of dollhouse toys, or illustrations in books: everything was shaped into neat squares and rectangles between the sidewalk and the lawns, not real-life wild and scraggly all over the place.

My brother and I couldn't wait to go to Wolfie's, where Daddy said they made the best seven-layer chocolate cake in the whole world. Daddy had been all over Europe in the army, so he knew what he was talking about. We made our pilgrimage. Wolfie's restaurant seemed a world unto itself. When we walked in the front door, the lighting wasn't the plain white light of puritan New Hampshire restaurants; it was like a lush stage set. Hidden lights flooded different areas selectively, highlighting some, mysteriously darkening others, and nothing was quite the right color. I think that's where my love affair with bar scenes in science fiction books and movies began. So exciting.

The waitress asked what I'd like to drink, and Daddy suggested a Shirley Temple. Oh my gosh. It came with a whole tower of ice cubes in it, with bubbling fizzy stuff on top and a sweet, slow red layer on the bottom. But best of all was what dangled deliciously on the rim of the glass. A green toothpick in the shape of a sword pierced several triangles of orange slices and a big juicy maraschino cherry that was all mine, and I didn't have to watch some grown-up's drink, like a covetous hawk, sip by agonizing sip, hoping to be offered the olive or cherry at the bottom of the glass. Hanging off the end of the toothpick sword was the treasure, like a ruby in my beautifully illustrated book of Indian tales. A red glass monkey, about one inch tall, hung by his tail from the sword's hilt. You were allowed to keep it.*

Daddy had the seven-layer cake for dessert. We all did, but I don't remember mine; I was watching him, his expression of furtive pleasure, the naughty thrillingness of it all. He devoured it. Said it was "poison."

We went back to Wolfie's several times during our two-week stay, and my brother and I collected the coveted monkeys. I lined mine up on the bureau at the motel to keep me company and give me strength as I slogged through the stygian pile of worksheets my teacher had made me take along in order to be excused from class for two weeks. Mom had to nag me every inch of the way. What was so weepingly awful about it was that it broke the dream, like going to heaven, sitting on a golden cloud, listening to sweet strains of the harp, and an angel suddenly puts a pen in your face and asks you to sign for a package from the IRS. Just a little paperwork.

The evening brought cool relief from the worksheets. I stepped out the door into the night air and behold! Each of the palm trees surrounding the pool was lit from below by floodlights of blue and green and red and yellow. The blue light illuminating its palm tree like some sort of terrestrial moonstone was one of the most beautiful things I'd ever seen. The next day by the pool, I met two sisters, one a year older and one a

---

*I still have one in my old jewelry box, along with my baby bracelet and a few other treasures in storage. Never mind that the monkey is plastic, not glass; it's also garnet-colored, which is even better than red.

year younger than I. After playing together for a while, we were friends, and friends tell each other secrets. Laurie told me something about her mother's hair color. I had a good one, too. I told them that Annabelle wasn't my real name. Nor Smith either. Somehow it got back to my parents via her parents, but my father, strangely, wasn't angry with me.

The following day we took a trip to the Miami Seaquarium. The highway was like a board game: all the roads had signs and names and you could make your way to the Seaquarium just by reading and following the arrows. At home, you navigated by places: Go up the road past Day's farm, take a right, and go about two miles; as with Maine's "Burt and I," if you don't know where you're going, "you can't get theya from heya." Believe it or not, I didn't know the road we lived on had a name until I got a Christmas card from my dad's new wife, about 1994 or so, and she had a little "personalized" address sticker affixed that said Sander Hill Road, Cornish. Our address was always just R.F.D. #2, Windsor, Vt. Our postman, Mr. McCauley, knew where we lived.

We found our way to the Seaquarium without a single fight—"discussion," dear. The first thing we saw after we parked the car and entered the gates was a long, straight brook made out of rectangles of cement. It didn't look deep and you could watch all the fish swimming in the same direction. Oh, boy, *some*thing was winging its way through the water past us, graceful, dark; I held my breath. Someone told us it was a manta ray or stingray. We walked along the brook in the direction the fish were swimming. A few yards ahead, separated from us by the brook, was a bird sanctuary. Flamingos really exist! And they're even brighter and pinker than in books. Parrots. The Froot Loops toucan. At home I'd catch a glimpse of the red epaulet on a red-winged blackbird as it took to the air, or the Baltimore oriole's flash of orange and black, or the goldfinch's bright yellow darting against the pine trees a few times each summer. I invariably missed the scarlet tanager when my mother said, "Look!" Twice in my life I saw a bluebird with its soft reddish chest. The birds that hung around our bird feeder in plain view were all browns and grays, chickadees or nuthatches, or the weird algae-yellow of evening grosbeaks. I was used to bright colors as rare flashes like the northern lights or a shooting star. But here were all the colors I'd ever marveled at stuck together on one darn bird just hanging around to be looked at at leisure. These tropical birds seemed almost motionless compared to the speed of our chilly birds. I almost got sick from the colors, like overeating at a dessert buffet.

A voice on a loudspeaker announced the dolphin show would "commence" in five minutes. The resident stars at the Seaquarium were Flipper and Snowball, a gray and a white dolphin. A series of them, really. I don't remember the dolphin show; I remember my father. I don't know why, not then, not now, but what happened at the end of the show was one of the highlights of my father's life. He still talks about it. The dolphins circled the perimeter of the show tank, and for some reason one of them tossed a ring and my father caught it. He was delighted and threw it back. The dolphin followed him partway around the tank and tossed it back, right into his hands. The dolphin had chosen him. Over and over again they played catch.

What *I* liked best was outside the show tank near the bathroom and concession stand. If you put a quarter or fifty cents in the slot, you could get a replica of Snowball or Flipper in wax. The machine made them right on the spot—you could smell the wax as it cooked—and when the dolphin tumbled out of the bottom like a can of soda, it was still warm and deliciously smelly. I got Snowball in white and Matthew got gray Flipper.

Our Flipper and Snowball souvenirs would later melt when our house burned down. From dust ye came, unto dust ye will go. The first time I studied Ecclesiastes at Harvard Divinity School, planning a sober contemplation of the cycle of life, all I could think about were those darn wax dolphins: Flipper and Snowball. Waxes to waxes, dust to dust. "A little song, a little dance, a little seltzer in your pants."*

❄❈❄

AS A CHILD, I collected myriad bright treasures from the beaches in Florida. The thing I've noticed that has changed the most from when I was a child on the beach, some forty years ago, is the paucity of shells. The difference is huge. On our family trips to Fort Lauderdale, I'd find scores of butterfly shells in pink, purple, yellow, orange, vast riches of shells strewn across the beach. Last year, my husband and I went to the great shelling beach in Florida that runs from Sanibel to Captiva. Per-

---

*From the Chuckles the Clown's funeral episode of *The Mary Tyler Moore Show*. One of our favorites.

haps we were unlucky, but there were mostly clamshells, white, brown, often chipped, few and far between, and none of the bright colors and odd, fantastical shapes.

This day, in Fort Lauderdale, however, I collected the wrong thing at the beach: an aqua blue balloon with long streamers that had washed up on the beach. I showed it to my father and he let me take it back to the motel with me. Within half an hour or so my hand had swollen to the size of a baseball mitt. The doctor from a nearby hotel said it was a man-o'-war jellyfish and told us that their tentacles could stream out twenty feet or more from where you spotted the blue balloon in the water. Swimmers came into his office looking as if they'd been bull-whipped, great long strips of inflamed, angry tissue where the tentacle lashed past them. I seem to recall putting Adolph's meat tenderizer on it (which makes sense, actually; the papaya enzymes in the Adolph's would break down or "tenderize" the tissue and get the poison out). Daddy was very upset that he'd let me carry it. "Da, you didn't know." "But I *should* have, I should have."

Back at the beach the next day, Mama slathered suntan lotion on a wriggling Matthew, while Daddy and I headed straight for the water. He loved swimming in the ocean. On this particular beach, it was easy to get in, but getting out was another story because the waves tried to suck you back under. I tried to ride a big wave in to shore, the way Daddy did. Sometimes it worked; sometimes I'd just get tumbled under the wave and sucked under for longer than I thought was possible for me to hold my breath. It was much too scary. But the thing that got me out of the water for good, scared the daylights out of me, was what I saw as I lay panting on the beach after being underwater for too long and strug-gling against the waves to get onto the shore. I looked up and saw my fa-ther with the same expression of fear on his face that I was feeling. He had been tumbled under, too, and had had the wind knocked out of him. When he saw me looking at him, he put on a toothy grin and said, wow, that was a big one—something meant to reassure a child that Daddy's all right and that this is fun. Too late. I'd seen Daddy looking scared and disoriented, and the sand shook from underneath me and I was sucked into a tumbling whirl of fear.

A FRIGID BLAST OF WINTER AIR snuck into one of our suitcases and came with us to Florida. Muscles tightened, drafts came out of nowhere. My parents fought as they always did, but fighting in a motel room is different from fighting in a house with other rooms and a study to escape to. My brother and I fought, too, as we always did, but in a motel room we were not able to hide it from my father, nor could he hide himself from the realities of us. It made him sick—he, quite literally, would turn green and become nauseated—when my brother and I fought. He was furious at me and deeply disappointed. My perfect, fictional siblings never fought as we did. Allie (Holden's dead brother) "never got mad at anybody. People with red hair are supposed to get mad very easily, but Allie never did." Tough stuff to live up to.

I could avoid most of the things that aroused my father's anger or contempt. But just as I couldn't control fighting with my brother, I couldn't avoid getting sick. This made my father crazy. He was terribly concerned when we were sick, but at the same time absolutely furious with us for having become so. And furious with my mother as well for not having adhered to the regimen of the week, whether it be megadoses of vitamin C, no protein, raw foods, whatever. Or for having followed last week's regimen, now anathema. That was one subject on which my brother and I were united. We would whisper to each other, hiding the telltale Kleenexes as he came in the front door: "Don't tell Daddy I'm sick."*

Most of my father's health regimens, such as drinking urine or sitting in an orgone box, he practiced alone. Homeopathy and acupuncture he practiced on us. When we became ill, or rather, so ill we couldn't hide it from him, he'd go into an angry whirlwind and spend enormous amounts of time and energy investigating which homeopathic medicine

---

*My father wasn't entirely unaware of this trait of his, I realized, when I read *Franny and Zooey* a few years ago. Franny tells Zooey:

"Just get sick sometime and go visit yourself, and you'll find out how tactless you are! You're the most impossible person to have around when somebody's not feeling up to par that I've ever known in my *life*. If somebody just has a *cold*, even, you know what you do? You give them a dirty look every time you see them. You're absolutely the most unsympa*thet*ic person I've ever known. You are!"

"All right, all right, all right," Zooey said, with his eyes still closed. "Nobody's perfect, buddy" (pp. 157–58).

would be correct for what ailed us. If it didn't work, it was back to the books for hours of more research and much irritation at the time spent away from his work.

Homeopathy often seemed to work well for my brother, but seldom, if ever, for me. My father practiced acupuncture with wooden dowels rather than needles. Needles are nearly unnoticeable, I've found out since. Being treated with those dowels, however, was like having a blunt pencil shoved into your skin. It hurt like hell. When my brother caught an unhideable cold in Fort Lauderdale that year, I can still see my father and those damn dowels, pressing a point on the top of Matthew's pinkie fingers. Matthew started crying. Having someone jam wooden dowels into the bones of your pinkie could bring tears to a grown man, let alone a small boy. But my father, predictably, was furious. He strode toward the door yelling, "You, your mother, and your sister have the lowest pain thresholds I've ever seen. You'd think you'd caught a piece of shrapnel, for Christ's sake!" And slammed the door behind him.

My father was often pointedly irritable, or "tactless," in the thralls of his more private fads, but the effect on me was more diffuse. I never questioned his judgment, I just had a pervasive, creepy feeling that something wasn't right, that something disturbing and spooky was going on.

Early that spring, when I was eight, I walked down to his Green house to bring him lunch and heard a terrible sound. He was outside in a little lean-to he had built with reflectors for sunning—another health fad; he was dark brown by April that year. When I came around the corner, he told me he had been speaking in tongues (a form of Christian glossolalia thought to be a manifestation or outpouring of the Holy Spirit). He had been to a charismatic church in New York City, the Rock Church, and was enchanted with the experience. It gave me the creeps.

Some months later, he started to turn a sickly shade of green and his breath smelled like death. That was macrobiotics and fasting. If I think about the odor too much, even now, it makes me gag. I was scared he would die.

15

Boot Camp and Iced Tea

❦

MY FATHER FINISHED his last published work to date, "Hapworth 16, 1924," in the spring of 1965. It appeared in *The New Yorker* in June, a week or two before school let out. I was nine years old and unaware that my father had published a story at all, let alone a story set in a summer camp. Nevertheless, I was all too aware that summer camp was in the air, as the brochures piled up. I was able to stave off the inevitable for a year, but the following summer, between fifth and sixth grade when I was ten years old, it was my turn. I did *not* want to go, any more than I'd wanted to take tennis lessons or sip iced tea on the sidelines with the "summer" people up from New York. My mother, of course, as any well-brought-up young lady, played a good game of tennis and drove me many thankless, sulking miles to Hanover and back for lessons. All I really wanted to do was swim in the pond, catch turtles, and play baseball in the summer, but chances for girls to play on a baseball team were nonexistent. My dad taught me to play, at least the parts you can learn without a team. When the weather was good, he came over almost every afternoon and pitched to me, played catch, and a game we called ball-on-the-roof, which was a variation of a city kid's game played against an apartment building wall. We'd take turns throwing a rubber ball or a tennis ball against the shingles of the garage roof, and the other one had to catch it. To score a point, you had to have your ball land in fair territory (for us it was the exposed, flat cement area that covered the underground passage between the house and the garage) without the other guy catching it first. It provides good training for catching both pop flies and grounders that take an odd bounce, with the added benefit that you don't have to worry about being slammed in the face with a hard ball if you miss. We loved baseball. Tennis was another story. Daddy was quite cutting, as well as right on target in his mimicry of tennis people's (including my mother's, of course) language and all the hidden aggression it masked. (This dates me well before John McEnroe's yelling at the referees and slamming his racket.) "Good try!" he'd mimic in his best upper-class, jolly-good-sport voice. I would later recognize this voice in his fiction, in the Ivy League, Lane Coutell–type (Franny's beau) characters. Back then, lessons notwithstanding, I drew the line at the dopey white skirt with underpants that showed when you bent over. Mom and I reached a compromise with white shorts. Oh, how I hated that desert of red clay, white net, and lines shimmering like a mirage. I longed for the grass-green oasis where guys pledged allegiance and spit and didn't smile a whole lot.

It was the same with riding. My mother drove me at least an hour to a stable for riding lessons each week one summer. I managed, technically, to lose my virginity on the pommel of a western saddle when the damn horse stopped short on the upswing of a trot. That ended as I refused to "get back up on the horse" again. But I did like to go and watch—from a safe distance—the Morgan horse show that my dad used to take me to when it came to a field near Windsor several times a summer. We sat up on the hillside above the ring and ate hot dogs with mustard and watched the horses. They were a sight to behold, deep chestnut bodies gleaming in the sunshine, green fields, wonderful warm smells of hay and manure, leather and sweat.

Although my parents had widely differing ideas about summer camp, the tide of their dreams proved irresistible. My mother told me stories of her happy summers spent at Camp Wyonagonic. She showed me a photograph of a group of girls in swimming costumes lined up the way they do in group photos, a row of little kids on the bottom, the bigger girls standing behind them.* There was little Claire, looking directly into the camera with serious, wide eyes, tummy sticking out

---

*This photo, from *Life* magazine, of the young girls was taken at the Mayfair Swimming Club, in London, not at summer camp, I later realized.

nicely, hair beautifully cut at her chin, parted on the side and held back by a ribbon band. She pointed out various other girls: "There's Princess Margaret and Lady so-and-so."

I was to go to Camp Billings in Vermont, and I can assure you that no princess of any sort had ever set foot on the shores of that lake. Nevertheless, we went shopping for camp as though I were one of the young ladies in my mother's old photograph. They sent a list of required clothing, which my mother taped to the inside of my new trunk. I loved that trunk, with its orderly, private compartments all smelling of cedarwood. My clothes were to be camp colors, navy blue and white, with name tags that said "Peggy Salinger" sewn in. Even in the underpants. I had seven new white underpants, three pairs of white socks and four of blue socks rolled into tidy bundles, five blue shorts, five white shirts with short sleeves, buttons down the front, and a Peter Pan collar, one blue pullover, one white button-down sweater, one pair of sneakers, one bathing suit, and for Sundays, one pleated navy blue skirt and one pair of saddle shoes. My mother placed these into my trunk in neat rows and bundles. I had my own toiletry kit with my own bottle of shampoo, soap, a toothbrush still in its case, and an unsqueezed, perfect tube of toothpaste. The toothpaste was still yucky old Crest that smelled bathroomy instead of the cinnamon-smelling Colgate that my friend Becky got to use. I had asked for the Colgate because it seemed within the realm of possibility, unlike what I really wanted, which was the new fizzy stuff called McCleens that made my tongue go numb when Viola let me taste some. It was really cool and totally out of the question. With the English, there is something at best suspect, at worst French and immoral, about things that taste too good or are too comfortable; plain pudding not fancy pastries, cold rooms with lots of fresh air at night instead of fluffy warmth. It was sensible Crest for me. I probably had slippers, but they are overshadowed by the memory of great plush, fuzzy things, in Kool-Aid pinks and pastels of a forbidden palette, that the other girls in my cabin wore on their feet.

When I arrived at camp, I was shocked by the appearance of my cabin. All those bunk beds stacked against every free bit of wall space. It was dark and dirty and not at all like my beautiful trunk. It was far too much like the photograph I had seen of concentration camp barracks, the prisoners stacked up in bunks. I was afraid one might peer down at me as the skeletal man in striped pajamas peered down at the photographer below. I chose an upper bunk so no one could look down at me with those eyes, although my cabinmates were nine-to-eleven-year-old well-fed girls.

The latrine was dark and filthy and it stank. I don't think I had a bowel movement for a week. I didn't go into the moldy showers either. Blue uniforms notwithstanding, this was not a camp where they inspected you or your bunk for cleanliness, the way Mr. Happy, head of Seymour's camp, bounced a quarter on each boy's bunk to make sure it was made tight, to army regulation. Our counselors barely let the cabin door hit them at night as they ran off to meet boys and go drinking. When I overheard two of them talking about it, I thought they meant sodas, which were no longer allowed in our refrigerator at home, and that sounded really sexy and exciting to me, sneaking off to drink Sprite in the woods with boys at night.

The following day we had general orientation, which meant sitting in the dining hall and listening to the head of the camp tell us about the camp's facilities and rules. Basically, the facilities consisted of the lake and a few boats; the rules, dock safety. On rainy days we would do crafts in the dining hall. I had expected horses and was torn between relief at not having to ride, and disappointment at not being able to just hang around them.*

At Camp Billings, we seemed to spend most of our time in the dining hall at picnic tables singing what I now know to be "Christian" songs, led by the camp director. "Oh, Noah, he built him, he built him an ark-y ark-y; Noah, he built him, he built him an ark-y ark-y; made it out of hick'ry bark-y bark-y; children of the Lord. The animals they came in, they came in by twoseys twoseys; animals they came in, they came in by twoseys twoseys; el-le-phants and kangarooseys-rooseys; children of the Lord." There were hand signals and gestures to go with the various songs such as "Dem Bones Gonna Rise Again," which I can still do to this day. The things that stay with us!

---

*As Holden said of Pencey Prep, "They advertise in about a thousand magazines, always showing some hot-shot guy on a horse jumping over a fence. Like as if all you ever did at Pencey was play polo all the time. I never even once saw a horse anywhere *near* the place" (*Catcher,* p. 2).

We may have been singing about the Lord, but to me, that first meal in the dining hall was as though I'd entered Sodom and Gomorrah. I stared, openmouthed in disbelief, at what they allowed you to do if you didn't like the food. Instead of eating what was served, you could take a slice of white bread, the wonderful spongy kind I was never allowed at home, and you could spread it with softened butter, which I knew to be *crawling* with germs when left unrefrigerated for more than a few minutes, and sprinkle or douse it, as the case might be, it didn't seem to matter, with sugar straight from a big pourer, just like the ones at the diner in Windsor. And then you'd eat this sugar sandwich open-faced so there'd be room for several. I just couldn't believe it. When I tried one, it was like chewing sand, but I thoroughly enjoyed the wickedness of it all. Years later when I read a story about a Jew eating pork for the first time and imagining his father turning over in his grave, I could feel that gritty sugar sandwich in my mouth.

What I didn't enjoy was how the girls in my cabin decided to amuse themselves at quiet time and before bed. They told ghost stories. Seymour, of course, is immune to that sort of thing, but I was scared to death. I put my fingers in my ears and hummed quietly to myself in my bunk to block out the sound. My trunk began to get disheveled; I couldn't make neat rows and sock bundles the way my mother did. The dirty laundry and the clean got all mixed together.

The trouble started on the third day of camp. Barbara B., age eleven going on thirty, sat on the floor rolling her blond hair in curlers. We thought this was the height of sophistication. Most of us had never even had our hair curled by our mothers, let alone knew how to do it ourselves. She had all kinds of stuff in her toiletry case—perfume, curlers, face cream. We sat on our bunks in quiet fascination. Suddenly Barbara looked up and said sharply, "Who stole my shampoo? Someone has used two inches of it." She held up the bottle and made two inches with her nail-polished forefinger and thumb for our inspection. Over the next day or two, other things started disappearing, mostly Barbara's things. She began telling the other girls that I was the thief. Why she chose me, I'll never know. A decree was issued, by her blond self, that none of the girls in the cabin should speak to me. After a day of being shunned, I was approached by Barbara on the path up to the cabin and she pulled me aside. "I'll tell the other girls to talk to you again if you'll help me raid the store."

The store was a shack by the dock that sold combs and toothpaste and candy for about an hour or so a day. I considered stealing to be unimaginably wicked, something rough men were sent to jail for over in Windsor. In Plainfield School, a kid stealing was unheard of. First of all, there wasn't anything much to steal, but I think it was more the ferocious respect for private property in that part of the country that made it so unthinkable. An adult could be shot on sight for trespassing, a child bullwhipped for it. I wasn't incensed; I was scared. But I was more scared of Barbara than of stealing, so I agreed. That night we snuck out and crept over to the shack. She jimmied the lock like a pro, climbed in, and we grabbed handfuls of lollipops and gum and Fritos. We brought the loot back to the cabin and had a big pig-out. Barbara was the hero. In the midst of midnight festivities, one of the girls forgot the ban and spoke to me. Barbara lifted a perfectly polished, mauve fingernail to her lips and said, "Shhhhh!"

The next morning when I awoke, I found a piece of paper folded on my blanket. The message said "I don't think that you took anything, but please don't tell anyone I told you so. Marilyn." A thin, dark girl with birdlike features smiled at me from her perch on the top bunk that stood at right angles to mine. I silently mouthed, "Thanks." A secret friend.*

That evening, Barbara decided we should hold a séance and try to levitate a girl who lay in the center of a circle. I dug down inside my sleeping bag and prayed: "I will fear no evil for thou art with me, thy rod and thy staff they comfort me." I was spooked out of my wits. I wrote to my father and told him what was happening there. He didn't come and get me. Instead, he wrote to thank me for the "terrific" letter I'd written and asked my permission to send it to Bill [Shawn]. Not knowing that he'd just published "Hapworth," a letter from a boy at camp, I didn't understand at all. I had the feeling that he must have mistaken another letter for mine.

---

*Truth being stranger than fiction, I asked a dear friend of mine, whom I'd met at Harvard summer chorus, to read a draft of this book. Marilyn suddenly hooted, "Oh my God! *I* went to Camp Billings, too. Last top bunk on the left-hand side as you walk in the cabin." She remembered a "blond bitch on wheels" who was way bigger than the rest of us. She didn't remember me in particular, she said, she was mostly focusing, with all her energy, on how to get the hell out of there.

It seems odd to me now, though it didn't at the time, that my father was never shocked by anything. It was as if my life were something he was reading in a novel or watching at the movies. "Don't be so silly, Peggy, they're not real, they're actors." *Maya*.

❧❀❧

LATE ONE NIGHT, FROM MY CABIN WINDOW, I saw a red light hovering on the horizon. I watched it moving slowly, growing gradually larger. Then, time jumped; not the way time passes when you're asleep and some internal clock keeps a record, but the way, under anesthesia, the electricity goes out, time stops, and the clock needs resetting. I came to and sat upright in my bed and looked out of the window into the moonlight. Hundreds of small dinner plate–size disks were moving slowly, perfectly spaced, like fat snowflakes on a windless night. I felt a quiet, snowfall-watching reverie; not fear, not curiosity. Then, in a blink of an eye, they were gone. The large red light nearby got smaller and smaller as it slowly joined the stars at the horizon. I swore to myself that I'd remember, remember, remember. I rehearsed it over and over again and then fell asleep. In the morning when I awakened, I asked Marilyn, secretly of course, if she'd seen the UFOs last night. She shook her head; no, she hadn't, and she whispered, "Wake me up if you see them again. Promise?"

Sunday evening, the campers put on a talent show in the dining hall. I'm in awe of people who can get up and put on a show, making up their own lines as they go along, confident that they will be well received. The thought of doing something like that myself is unspeakably impossible and embarrassing, like those endless dreams where you have to go to the bathroom but there is no door to the bathroom, or the toilet you're sitting on is in the middle of a crowded room. The older campers put on funny makeup and did funny things and swirled around me like a circus gone out of control. People laughed in groups and said clever things in group skits, and I couldn't even get a toehold into the glass wall that separated me from them. I sat at one of the picnic tables, shoulders hunched over, in stark contrast to Buddy and Seymour's talented performance of a soft-shoe routine showcased for the campers and the adult guests in "Hapworth," trying to make my weird, unclever, untalented, unpopular self invisible.

I awoke the next day feeling strange. The nurse said I had a temperature of 101. For some crazy reason, or perhaps for no reason at all, they still made me go on the mountain hike scheduled for the day's activity. My father wrote about another absurd expedition inflicted on children at camp. Seymour Glass is seven years old and in the infirmary recuperating and writing a letter home. He writes:

> After breakfast every Midget and Intermediate in the entire camp was obliged to go strawberrying. . . . We drove miles and miles to where the strawberry patches were in a little, ramshackle, old-fashioned, maddening cart, quite fake, drawn by two horses where at least four were required.

The wheel of this cart had a big piece of iron sticking out of it that penetrated several inches into Seymour's leg. He was brought back to the camp infirmary by Mr. Happy, the camp director, on his motorcycle. Seymour reported that he bled all over Mr. Happy's new motorcycle. This situation had "several fleeting, humorous moments. . . . Fortunately, I find that if a situation is funny or risible enough, I tend to bleed less profusely. . . . [He threatened to sue Mr. Happy] in the event that I lost my ridiculous leg from infection, loss of blood, or gangrene."

Unfortunately for me, I did not have Seymour's control of my ridiculous, risible body. Partway up the mountain, my throat closed and I couldn't get a breath in. I heard terrible rasping sounds as I lay down on the dirt path. I looked up at the counselor above me and saw fear in her eyes. That's when I got really scared. She did mouth-to-mouth, and after a while, I got my air back. What I remember, but have trouble believing, is that we kept on walking up the mountain. It happened again, my throat closed up, and the next thing I know I'm in the infirmary, listening to the nurse talking about me to my mother on the phone. She said I had a temperature of 103, but it was probably nothing to worry about; she only called because they were required to notify parents of anything over 102. I got on the phone and asked my mother just one thing: "Get me out of here."

Years later, Mom told me that when she heard the tone in my voice, she was out the door before she put down the receiver. She said it reminded her of her own voice when she called her mother from convent boarding school and told her that bad things were happening to her there and begged her mother to come and get her. Her mother told her she was just imagining things. *My* mother came and took me home.

I brought home with me a Camp Billings Indian stuffed toy, a grotesque caricature with a huge nose and an idiot's tiny, close-set eyes that was the camp mascot. It was a very ugly souvenir of my failure to bridge the gap between what my parents dreamed and the ugly reality I experienced. My friend Marilyn said she came across an identical thing leering stupidly out of a box of old stuff in her mother's cellar one day when she was cleaning. She couldn't remember what it was and threw it away.

❦

SOMETIME AFTER MY ABORTED STAY at camp during the summer of '66, my parents announced they were getting a divorce. Or, perhaps I should say, they *tried* to announce it. It had been in the air for quite some time and came as no surprise to me. In fact, when they called us into the house to say they had something to speak to us about, something they never, ever did—speak to us as a team, I mean—I slumped down in our big red leather chair and beat them to the punch. I rolled my eyes and, with my best ten-year-old ennui, said, "You're getting a di*vorce,* aren't you." "Well, yes, actually, we are," my mother said as she started to deliver her speech about how sometimes when grown-ups can't get along . . .

She was interrupted as my little brother, just six years old, burst into tears and ran out of the house and down the road. On the doorstep, I told my parents in no uncertain terms, "Wait here, I'll talk to him." I found him by the roadside, down a bank, curled up in some leaves and sobbing. "Matthew, stop crying and listen to me." You had to speak a little sharply to him at first because he could get quite hysterical, understandably lost in the swirling storm of rage and fear in and around him. A few months prior to their announcement, he'd been furious at my mother about something, and he had sat on the stairs, giving vent to the obvious tension in the house, screaming down at my father, eyes bulging, blood veins visible in his pale, six-year-old's neck, "Divorce Mom! Divorce her!" I didn't even know he knew the word.

Matthew took his head out of his hands and, snuffling, looked up at me. "Listen," I said, "nothing is going to be any different when they get divorced, except maybe they won't fight as much. They both love you. They just hate each other. Daddy will still live in his house, Mom and you and I will still live in our house, and Daddy will still come over to visit and play ball on the roof and go for a walk with the doggies and everything. All right? It's no big deal." He smiled damply and said, "Okay," and got up. Big Sister had spoken. I put my arm around his shoulder for a second or two as we walked back to the house. I told my parents we were fine now and that I'd explained to him that nothing was going to change except that *you* two won't fight as much, as I glared darkly at them. Then we went back to whatever it was each of us had been doing, alone, before the "family conference."

❦

A FEW WEEKS LATER, I received an invitation to spend the better part of the summer up in Maine with the McAndrew family at their summer house by the sea. My beloved friend Rachel McAndrew and I were in our mothers' wombs when they met. Mrs. Cox, who was related to the McAndrews somehow, introduced them. She thought that Charlotte and my mother would be good company for each other. Although my mother did not see Charlotte with any regularity until my father moved out of the house, Mrs. Cox was correct as usual. I know my mother will always be grateful for Charlotte's friendship. Her calm gentleness and uncommon intelligence were a tremendous help and comfort to my mother as she tried to raise two young children in isolation.

Charlotte was married to a Dartmouth professor, and they lived in a wonderful old house in Hanover during the school year, and another wonderful old house in Maine in the summer. Her daughter Rachel was my best "out of school" friend throughout our childhood and early adolescence. Some of my happiest memories are of time spent with her. And there was the added excitement of having all those older brothers and sisters and their friends around talking about dating and new records and all that cool teenage stuff. I feel lucky to have been an adjunct member of their family for so many years.

My father was woven, albeit loosely, into their family during the years my mother and Charlotte, and Rachel and I, were such close friends. Daddy liked Charlotte and the children very much, but Colin, her husband, was more problematic. Colin was a professor of literature at an Ivy League college, a robust and enthusiastic tennis player and sailor, and an exuberant specimen of what my dad refers to, with some genuine awe I might add, as "that damn WASP confidence." Such was his confidence that he routinely insisted that my father join him in "activities." Nine out of ten times my father refused, but Colin persisted with such good-natured self-assurance that continued refusal would have seemed ill-mannered. Usually my dad's social debt could be erased by the occasional drinks and dinner. The summer of '66 he must have run up a whopper. It was he, rather than my mother, the usual chauffeur, who drove me up to the McAndrews' house in Maine.

Daddy had agreed to go on a sailing trip with Colin and the boys. Can you imagine such purgatory if you're J. D. Salinger? Being confined to a small boat, at sea, for several days, with a Dartmouth professor? *"Why* did you say yes, Da?" I asked him as we drove along. "Oh, Peggy," he sighed, sounding tired, "I said yes because I get so sick and tired of saying no to everything all the time. It depresses me."*

When Daddy arrived back at the McAndrews' from his sailing trip, he could barely walk. Not six hours out of port he had smashed his knee on something and it had swelled up badly. He took some arnica from the homeopathic medicine kit he'd brought on board. Without the arnica, he said darkly, it would have been *very* bad. To make matters worse, they were caught in a choppy rainstorm and everyone, except Colin of course, had been vomiting wildly since Nova Scotia. I would not be at all surprised if, when he got home to Cornish, he knelt and kissed the ground.

I stayed on in Maine, but no sailing trips for me. It was the source of some friction between Colin and me that I refused to go sailing. At one

---

*See *Zooey,* p. 144: "I feel like those dismal bastards Seymour's beloved Chuang-tzu warned everybody against. 'Beware when the so-called sagely men come limping into sight.' He sat still, watching the snowflakes swirl. 'I could happily lie down and die sometimes,' he said." See also Seymour's quotations from sagely men written on his bedroom wall, such as: " 'Don't you want to join us?' I was recently asked by an acquaintance when he ran across me alone after midnight in a coffee house that was already almost deserted. 'No, I don't,' I said."—Kafka point in the summer he was so insistent that I felt it necessary to call my dad, collect, to ask him to tell Colin that I didn't *have* to go on the boat. Tipping scared me senseless after the accident with my arm. My mother insisted I "try it, dear" every year or two, and I'd sit huddled behind in the dinghy or miserably straddling the front* of the boat until someone took pity on me (or got annoyed) and brought me back to shore.

I did like taking the rowboat, which didn't tip, out to the tiny, uninhabited sheep islands just off the coast of their beach. Local farmers took their sheep out to the islands at the beginning of summer and let them pasture there undisturbed until fall (access being granted to them by the king or perhaps the early colonial government too long ago to remember). Owen, Rachel's eldest brother, asked Rachel and me if we'd like to camp out with him overnight on one of the sheep islands. Boy, would we! Any chance to be near the handsome, gentle Owen, included in his plans, was my idea of heaven. I'd had a crush on him for ages. I think I even let him take me around the harbor once in a sailboat. He was the only boy I knew, or adult for that matter, who was so careful with other people's feelings. I trusted him; I knew instinctively that if I got scared, he'd stop and bring me back to shore right away, and without making a big deal about it either. A nice, nice boy.

That evening, we rowed across to the island with our sleeping bags, water, and all the things we'd need for a cookout supper on the beach. Rachel and I went to track the sheep while Owen did the useful stuff like building a fire and putting the water on to boil. We were unsuccessful—all we spotted before the underbrush grew too thick were some sheep droppings. So we went back to the beach to help Owen gather mussels for our dinner.

After dinner, we laid our sleeping bags out in a row on the beach. It was getting a little chilly so we climbed in and lay on our backs looking up at the stars. Stars everywhere. As we watched the sky and talked, we

---

*Yes, I know: *bow, stern, starboard,* blah, blah, blah. The only word I wanted to hear was *port.* What is it about amateur sailors that they feel this evangelical mission to inflict their pleasure on the unconverted? If being damp, cramped, and threatened with drowning or decapitation from that swinging boom is your cup of tea, fine. Make mine Michelin's five stars, thank you very much—I get *very* ill-tempered just thinking about sailing.

noticed one star behaving peculiarly. It seemed to be meandering around the sky. How comp*letel*y cool, our own UFO. We fell asleep talking happily about UFOs we'd seen or heard about.

I awoke in the middle of the night, leapt up, and just barely made it behind a big rock down the beach before my bowels let go. Then the other end started. Oh, I was so ashamed. I knew Owen would hear me going to the bathroom and throwing up, and he'd think I was the most disgusting person on the planet. When I was finished erupting, I called Rachel, and as soon as she got close enough, I whispered to her to bring me the roll of toilet paper. I got myself cleaned up while she went back for a toothbrush, toothpaste, and some water to rinse with.

I couldn't even look at Owen when I walked back and climbed into my sleeping bag. He asked me if I was all right. I nodded. "You know," he said, "you must never eat mussels again. When you're allergic, the next time can kill you. Promise me you'll remember." I nodded. And then he put his arm over my sleeping bag and hugged me! I was stunned. He picked up my outside arm, as you might a paralytic's, and put it around him. Romance resided in my imagination, as a prelude to a kiss, and not yet in my body. The hormones that move one's arms automatically toward embrace had not awakened.

Then he kissed me. On the mouth. It was the most exciting thing that had ever happened to me, but only in hindsight, in the telling and the remembering. During the actual moment, I was in way over my head so I sat up quickly and nudged Rachel, who was asleep on my other side. I said I had to go again and asked her to come with me. We walked closer to the water and I told her the best secret I had: Owen *kissed* me. That was the best part, telling my best friend about my first kiss. She wasn't sure she believed me; for both of us a real kiss belonged to that liminal region somewhere between a dream and the light of day, like a womb before the quickening, wherein dwelt such things as UFOs and fairies and meeting the Beatles in person. When we got back to our sleeping bags, I made her switch places with me and sleep next to Owen.

Back in Hanover, that fall, Rachel asked Owen if he "liked" me. When I arrived for a weekend visit, she said, "Oh my God, you were telling the truth about kissing Owen! I asked him if you were the one he liked and he said yes."

I lived for the nearness of Owen. He was away at boarding school so I only got to see him on vacations. Skiing, I prayed I'd sit next to him in the van or the ski lift or at the lunch table. Nothing ever "happened" again, which was perfect, too. He confirmed he still "liked" me when Rachel asked. And I got to long for him, achingly, comfortably, from afar.

16

The Birds and the Bees: Hitchcock's

✥

However inexhaustible the passions are, I vow to extinguish them.

—The second of the Four Great Vows
recited by Zooey in *Franny and Zooey*

BACK IN THE CLASSROOM THAT FALL, we fifth graders were suddenly disturbed by an unearthly howling coming from the playground. The whole class jumped up and looked out the window. Two dogs were out on the playground, and they were stuck together. The farm kids were the first to laugh because they knew what they were witnessing. The rest of us soon caught on. Mrs. Spaulding rapped sharply on the window. She turned to us, glaring, and said, "Simmer down, people. People! I said simmer down." But the slow simmer had begun, bubble by bubble, toward the full heat of puberty, and nothing, not even our principal, Mrs. Spaulding, could stop it.

Our mothers sensed it, the upward-thrusting energy, the great tangle of roots and swollen bulbs pushing beneath the flat white blanket of winter, and they tried to stop it. They pruned us back hard, to keep us tidy and under control. My mother began to braid my hair back so severely it lifted my eyebrows up. At least four bobby pins were jammed into my bangs to keep them off my face. I was swathed in shapeless woolen dresses so ugly and plain that even I noticed and hated them. Viola's mother had a different strategy toward the same end. Tomboy Viola was sent to school looking like a baby doll in flounces and petticoats and curls her straight hair was subjected to from the cursed Toni home permanents her mother gave her.

Each morning, after our mothers dropped us off at school, Viola and I headed straight for the basement to perform our morning ritual. Viola held her head under the sink to dampen down the terrible curls while I pulled on her hair and blotted it between paper towels. Then she helped me break through the fifty-odd yards of rubber band wound round my braids, pulled them out, and checked for stray bobby pins.

Each afternoon, there was hell to pay when our mothers saw we'd done it again. "Honest, Ma, it just came out. On the playground, at recess. What do you want me to do, *sit* all recess? Jeesum Crow!" They must have worn their hands out spanking us, but it didn't stop us. Each morning, curls "revived" by rollers went down the drain, braids and bangs liberated from bondage.

When spring came, the changes that were going on beneath the surface began to reveal themselves in our play and behavior. We girls stopped playing in the woods on our own at recess and began, instead, dancing to 45s we played on the blue, portable record player I brought to school. We practiced the new dances we saw on *American Bandstand;* the Pony and the Swim were added to the Twist. Although we danced in pairs of girls, and the boys played marbles in pairs of boys, here and there a boy and a girl would split off from the group and walk around the playground together, sometimes arm in arm for a few minutes, and then go back to their marbles or dancing. The intermingling of boy and girl was limited to this chaste promenade with your partner two by two, but the point wasn't *what* you did together, it was the fact that somebody "liked" you. Now, when we played house, girls would show off the little key chain or cereal-box prize, more precious than diamonds, that their "steady" had given them. The girls who had older sisters knew they wouldn't be allowed to go steady until high school, most of them, so that made it even more exciting. I had always been chosen early as a valuable player for teams of tag and red rover and jump rope, but in this new game, as sides were chosen, no one picked me.

I was in the J. J. Newberry five-and-dime in Windsor with my father when, like a skinny boy sending away for Super Weight-On drink, I spotted my miracle. There, in the jewelry bin, was a pendant with a big gold initial in the center of a plastic wood-tone circle, suspended from a foot-long golden chain. It was gorgeous. Daddy didn't ask me why I bought one with an *R* on it, thank goodness. Perhaps he didn't notice.

On Monday, I wore it to school hidden under my blouse. When recess came, I told the other girls that I had met the cutest guy over the weekend. He's from Claremont and his name is Ritchie Davis. It wasn't long before I was surrounded by girls asking for news of Ritchie who lived all the way over to Claremont that had a movie theater and everything. Ritchie took me to see movies that hadn't been shown in theaters for some thirty years. I told the girls and even some boys all about *The 39 Steps* and how Ritchie had held hands with me during the scary parts. Then, as I slowly pulled the pendant out from under my blouse, which, given the length of the chain, provided ample, even Hitchcockian, dramatic time, I announced, "We're going steady."

A FEW OF THE GIRLS SKIRTED THE ISSUE for another year or two by moving blithely from dolls to horses. They drew horses, talked about horses, rode horses, curried and stroked and fed and watered horses, and on the playground, pretended to be horses. For the rest of us girls, as well as all of the boys, it seemed, the progression was from a preoccupation with the animal kingdom of toads and caterpillars to the birds and bees of the human world, without the mediating stop at horses.

Our sexual education was confined to observations of animals, unavoidable in the country. Naturally, the farm kids were exposed to the more veterinary specifics of procreation. But for all of us, what humans "did" together when they "did it" was a vast screen of projections, observational misinformation, and the lore passed down as a legacy from the older kids. The chaste, sedate promenade of relations between the sexes on the playground met its doppelgänger in the dirty jokes and stories we told and heard in our efforts to gain entrance to the grown-ups' big secret.

Oh, what we filled the vacuum of information with! A sump pump of necrophilia, cannibalism, and excreta spewed forth like an uncapped oil well across the playground. One dirty joke was about a guy who is lost and asks to spend the night at a farmer's house. Sure, says the farmer, but you have to share a bed with my daughter. Okay, says the weary traveler. At breakfast the next morning the farmer offers the traveler breakfast, but he refuses, saying he's too full to eat. The following morning the same thing happens. The third morning, the traveler finally admits to the farmer that a curious thing was happening: "I tried to kiss your daughter but I got a mouthful of rice." The farmer says, "Rice? That's not rice, those were maggots; my daughter's been dead for a year."

Another joke involved a guy eating out a woman. I guess somebody heard the phrase and took it literally—who wouldn't? This guy is eating out a woman, the joke goes, and he keeps coming across various foods, the more vividly described the better. The punch line is that it somehow turns out that, like an archaeologist, what he was coming across were layers from guys the previous evenings who had had dinner, eaten her out, and vomited into her hole. Nice, huh?

Holden spoke for all of us when he said, "Sex is something I just don't understand. I swear to God I don't." But Holden, published in 1951, was long gone from my father's world by the time I was old enough to wonder. He had moved on from Holden's human confusion to Teddy and the young Seymour's world of preternatural, omniscient knowledge. Seven-year-old Seymour, for example, writes to his parents about the camp director and his wife, explaining that their marital problems stem from their not having "become one flesh to perfection." With the help of Desiree Green, an eight-year-old who possesses, he says, an admirably open mind, he could demonstrate the proper technique to them "in a comparative jiffy."

VIOLA AND I HAD just finished undoing our hair and she said, hang on a sec, I have to pee. After a minute or so she called out to me from behind the stall door, "Peggy, can you go and get me a Band-Aid from Mrs. Spaulding? There's blood on my underpants. I think I sat on a piece of glass in the bathtub last night." She was terrified when it didn't stop for several days and seemed to keep happening every month or so.

I, too, made a horrifying discovery. I was in the bathtub, and suddenly I saw them. Overnight, two dark hairs had sprouted on my thing-I-had-no-name-for.* It was like when the snow first melts in the spring and reveals not lush green grass, but mud and a tangled mat of yellowish exposed roots; petrified, white, powdery dog poop from last year; and all manner of things that look as though they crawled out from under a rock. My girlfriends and I watched in fascination and in horror as otherworldly shapes began to push through the surface, like little hairy fiddlehead ferns and mushrooms that, when they first poke through the ground, bear no resemblance to the grand unfurled forms that show themselves to the open air. Damp, earthy, peculiar-smelling things too red and shiny and rounded. One nipple grows inverted, the other one sticks out; no one explains you won't go through life a freak. We would have died before we let anyone but our best girlfriends see, showing ourselves in secret sessions in haylofts and tree houses, examining each other like lepers for more signs of it spreading.

I was up in a classmate's attic when we discovered, under an old trunk, a secret book of knowledge. We were hoping to find old dressup clothes. What we found was her older brother's secret stash of *Playboy* magazines. We gazed, glazed with desire, at the perfect mounds of breasts and buttocks. The Playmates in the early sixties were like Barbie, no sprouting pubic hairs; in fact, no pubis at all, and big, luscious ice-cream-sundae boobs. The gap between those girls and us was unspannable. Even in our wildest, bravest imaginations we couldn't make the leap; we felt ourselves a separate species. We decided we must be lezzies. We weren't quite sure what they were or did, but we knew they were girls who were sexually attracted to girls instead of boys, and I, at least, was *very* worried about this. I surely desired and thought about Miss March's boobs and couldn't imagine thinking

---

*Boys had dinks, wizzers, things, dongs, and so on. Girls' parts "down there" were a mystery too dark to mention beyond babyhood when they had pee-pees or wee-wees—inseparable from the only function "it" appeared to possess. Another dark thought—now in middle age, I still haven't escaped those black hairs that mysteriously appear, full grown, in ones and twos, on chin or cheek or nipple's areola, without warning. A friend of mine, going through a painful separation from her husband, once sat crying on my couch. "Who will tell me when those witchy hairs sprout on my face? I'll be in an old-age home somewhere, with no husband to ferret them out and pluck them. I'll be one of those hairy old ladies," she sobbed.

Herbie's or Henry's "thing" I'd seen in third grade was anything other than completely gross, and the idea of their actually sticking one in me and peeing like the stuck dogs on the playground was beyond the outer limits of gross. Plus the way animals screamed and my mother bled on Kotexes she kept in a bucket under the sink, and how she had to have stitches after my brother was born and sit on a rubber doughnut, I knew it was not only totally gross but hurt and tore you up. A lezzie in the first degree.

Another source of unclothed secrets was the *National Geographic* magazine. But the breasts we saw in those pictures were pendulous and neutral as cows' udders. I didn't mind having those issues around the house until one day I found an issue *right on our own coffee table* that had a photograph of a bare-breasted, barely pubescent native girl. One of us! I could barely stand I was so dizzy thinking my parents might have seen the magazine before I got to it and had seen what she, I, we, looked like. Keep it our secret, don't let them see or they'll know what's hidden under my shirt and in my underpants. I was paralyzed with panic, my face so hot with shame I couldn't think. I grabbed the magazine and ran for the door. Outside I didn't stop running until I was deep in the woods. I dug a hole and buried the evidence.

At the same time that I was desperately trying to duck and cover up, my mother's sexuality was beginning to emerge from beneath a long winter of convent schools, ignorance, and abuse. That's not how I would have described it then, though; for me, that spring, she became an animal. The sex I saw or heard in nature was a teeming swirl of madness and violence. During mating season, horrid sounds and screechings emerged from the woods. I'd seen my dog Joey have a madness come over him, and he disappeared for several days, returning to sit on the couch and lick his sore, swollen "red thing," as my brother and I called it. Blood lust and lust were inseparable in my mind.*

---

*Mr. Antolini, Holden's teacher, promised him that if he applied himself to his studies, he'd find that he wasn't the only person who was ever "confused and frightened and even sickened by human behavior." I was tremendously relieved to find out, when as a graduate student I started going to the theater for the first

MY MOTHER, BROTHER, AND I came down with a vomiting flu and fever in the January thaw. My father came over to give us some homeopathic medicine. My mother was in bed. I was in the doorway when she sat up and pointed a finger dramatically at my father and yelled, "You're *poisoning* the children. . . . I cannot stand it a minute longer. I am going to my mother's." My brother and I—"poisoned" or not—were not invited to join her.

I found out later that year that she hadn't gone to her mother's, but instead had had a romantic rendezvous with a boyfriend in California. An ex-boyfriend of hers just happened to spy them at some restaurant there. The little sneak told my father, who, in turn, told me. I kept it to myself for about a year and then sprang it on my mother, a little act of false "glimpse" terrorism, at an opportune time: "Oh, by the way, I know where you were last year when you said you were at your mother's in New York." I told her where she was, and with whom, but refused to say how I knew.

I could pretend to be all-seeing and all-knowing, but when my mother's eyes clouded with passion, hatred, anger, fear, and desire, what was truly terrifying was the realization that she couldn't see me at all. I looked in her eyes and saw no person, no solid ground beneath the blue. She was like some force of nature let loose, a dam breaking, a fire in the wind, a twister. She struck close to home that spring, tearing a rent, a wide swath, in the social fabric of Cornish.

My father pulled into the driveway and strode over to the house. "Where's your mother? I have to talk to her. Claire?" he called in the strained voice he always used with her. His throat literally closed up and he got hoarse, it was such a huge strain for him to speak to her. He went into the house and met her on the landing. My brother and I took our first-row, front-balcony seats on the stairs. "Claire, Mary Jones just called me in tears. She said that Joe is leaving her and wants to marry you. Is that true?"

---

time (student rush tickets were less than five pounds at the National Theatre Complex in London), that I wasn't alone. Several Mediterranean writers captured the heated, swirling madness of mating just as I had felt it as a child: Pirandello's *Chaos*, Kazantzakis's *Freedom or Death*, Lorca's *The House of Bernarda Alba*, in which a mother (played by Glenda Jackson) watches over her five daughters in a house, shuttered against the terrible Spanish sun, and they prowl like cats in heat trying to escape and find relief in the cool of the night with a passing soldier.

My parents never once sent us out of the room nor said to us that they had to discuss something in private. My father—far more than my mother, who took great pains at times to tell us that Daddy was a good father—aired every accusation, ugly feeling, name-calling, every bit of his and my mother's dirty linen, in broad daylight. For a person so devoted to a cult of privacy surrounding himself and his work, he had less of an appropriate sense of privacy, what one should and should not say before an audience of children, than any other adult I've ever met. Behind the curtain of virtue is a private table reserved for a party of one.

As my father demanded to know whether what Mary had said was true, I watched my mother's face intently. What I saw shocked me. I assumed she was guilty but I expected a defense, an outraged denial, a protested innocence. Instead, what I saw was a frightening, silly little smile. She was flushed, but it didn't look as if from shame or embarrassment; she looked like an excited little girl. My father may as well have asked her, on her way home from school, "So what's this I hear about little Joey Jones dipping your braids in the inkwell, is it true?" When she spoke, I could tell she was lying, but it was the way a child under five lies, looking at the cookies on her lap and telling you the doggie must have dropped them there. In a child, it can be naively sweet; in an adult, it is almost indescribably enraging. It made me want to beat her head in just to wipe that creepy, silly giggle off her goddam face, and to smash her teeth down her throat if she didn't start talking like a grown woman instead of in that little voicy-poo. I sat on my hands, as I often did throughout my childhood and teens, scared they'd go for her throat and never stop. I really mean that: the self-control involved in not strangling her often left me limp with exhaustion. She told my father that she just couldn't understand *what* could have made Joe fall in love with her, silly man, and *of course* she would never think of marrying him.

I knew that part was true, that she wouldn't think of marrying him. The huge unfairness of it all nearly crushed me. Joe was a guy with short legs and a tight little behind that scooted around the bases really fast when we played softball together. He was no match for my mother at all, and I sat there on the stairs thinking, Pick on someone your own size, you bully. Of course she "did it" with him, I thought, but the silly man fell in love with her, and she was only playing with him, the way our cat Pearly toyed with a chipmunk stupid enough to get into her clutches. It wasn't fair. Most of all it wasn't fair to Mary or the kids.

Joe moved to California. I was certain that Mary would never let us play with her kids at their house again. But Mary went out of her way to show us it wasn't our fault, and that what had happened was something that concerned grown-ups. I don't think she said it exactly, but I felt it. It made me crazy though to see how much the kids missed their father, how disrupted their lives were, and how little it registered with my mother. She seemed almost retarded in her total lack of a sense of responsibility or even basic understanding of the consequences of her actions. Like a child who hides her head under the blanket and thinks no one can see her, my mother began to tell us in a giggly voice that she had a "meeting" to go to. I knew; I saw the sex look that erased the personal landscape of her face.

My father called her a "pathological liar." He put it in moral terms, so now I had a word for "it," at least. I could express moral outrage at her sins. He gave me a language to vent my rage so I didn't have to sit on my hands quite so often. One evening, I confronted her in the kitchen and lectured her about her behavior, which by now included having some of her boyfriends stay the night. I didn't care for myself so much, I told her, it was my brother I was concerned about. It wasn't good for a young boy to see her being a "slut." She tried to slap me across the face, but I ducked and left the room.

My father's main concern wasn't its effect on us, he never mentioned that, it was the $5,000 a year he had to pay her for child support. He was outraged that he was paying to "feed her boyfriends." "You don't eat and shit in the same place," he'd often tell me at age ten or so as we drove by the house, referring to my mother having boyfriends there. He complained about the support money constantly. He, too, I realized later in life when I tried to get him to pay for my college education, as it was stipulated in their divorce agreement, had no more sense of being responsible for his actions in the real world than my mother did, except as it concerned his work. Child support, pet food, clothing, tuition—all were part of the great conspiracy to "sponge" off him.

When I was a child, though, he was faultless in my eyes, a bit difficult and downright peculiar sometimes, but morally faultless. My father and I sat judge and jury and found my mother guilty of moral crimes. It's easier to feel moral outrage than terror. Even though I focused my attention on the things she did that were wrong, what terrified me was the unidentifiable, unspeakable thing I had no words for, that something was deeply wrong with her. I had a horror of her bodily functions; even her clothing I didn't want to touch for fear something unclean was catching. My mom had serious cooties.

I had no explanation for the fact that Claire, at one moment, could be my mother who loved me and, in the next instant, as with a sandstorm in the desert, all traces, all recognizable features of her humanity were erased. Sometimes I thought she was possessed; then I decided she was just plain wicked. It wasn't until I was in my twenties and working in a home for abused and abandoned children that I again saw that "not there" frenzied look in someone's eyes, and that flushed, silly, spooky little smile. I was coaching the girls' basketball team and doing individual gross motor evaluations of the younger kids. I'd have a child playing, eyes focused, anchored, and present, and the second anything sexy, or bodily, happened—someone mentioned going to the bathroom, or a male teacher that a little girl liked came into the room—it was as if the integrity of that child's being fell apart; the eyes had a smeared, clouded look, face flushed, and that spooky smile appeared.

The second time I saw that transformation was in my thirties. I was living on the first block of Marlborough Street, one of the "best" blocks of Boston, in a building owned by a retired hooker who still ran a few girls out of the basement apartments off the back alley. I lived there for twelve years and spent many a summer afternoon on the front steps hanging out with the working girls. They were, like our landlady, nearing the end of their careers. One had bought a little house in Tennessee and was planning to move back near her family when she retired. She told me she got into the business because she had fallen in love, when she was young, with the wrong guy, who "turned her out," and she added, because of these, pointing to her huge bosom. She used to do freebies for a blind guy who came around with his dog. He was sweet and nervous and came in the front entrance, like a gentleman caller, instead of slinking through the back alley like a john. We always greeted him as though he were there to pick her up for a date. The other woman, Vickie, had a father who had started her.

One afternoon I was on the stoop with Marcelle and Vickie. The conversation turned to the woman who lived on the first floor, a society girl who worked for the Fine Arts Museum. Apparently she had had her new investment-banker boyfriend over the previous night and they were rather noisy in their lovemaking. Marcelle and Vickie were in fits of giggles like two schoolgirls gossiping about it. I would have thought that screwing was about as interesting to an off-duty hooker as nuts and bolts to an assembly-line worker. Over the years, I saw it time and again: they went from forty-something-year-old women chatting about roses (we had a pretty rose garden in front) to fifth graders the minute anything sexual came up. Little girls seemed to coexist with middle-aged women with no integration, no blending of the ages. Now you see her, now you don't. The Lady Vanishes.

17

A Perfect Ten

❧❦❧

I WOULDN'T BE NEEDING MY "*R*" PENDANT when I started sixth grade at a new school that fall. I bid a grateful adieu to my make-believe boyfriend Ritchie, who had stepped in so gallantly and served me so well—taking me to movies and giving me gifts when no one else would. Vast, empty tracts of the real world were coming under cultivation. It was 1966 and my mother decided to send my brother and me to Norwich Elementary School in Vermont. Norwich is a town directly across the river from Hanover, home of Dartmouth College. The school went up to sixth grade, after which all the Norwich kids went to Hanover for grades seven to twelve. It was a good school with a wealth of resources, and a good choice for all parties concerned, except for Viola and me, who wouldn't really get to spend much time together again until we'd grown up.

We sixth graders were the big kids of the school, and having my brother in first grade made me take my leadership responsibilities to heart. We were assigned in pairs to safety patrol, where, after training, we were expected to serve as crossing guards on the streets around the school to make sure all the kids who walked to school crossed safely. When we were on duty, we each wore a white safety-patrol belt of heavy canvas with a shoulder strap that went diagonally across the body. Off duty, you had to fold it a certain way, ceremonially like the flag, before storing it for the next day.

We took our responsibilities soberly; there was no horsing around, but even more surprising, there was no throwing our weight around and being unnecessarily bossy. The teachers managed to hit just the right tone of service and responsibility. I wish I knew how; I'd bottle it. The best thing about safety patrol, I found out as the year went on, was that you were assigned your partner, you didn't get to choose. Each season I was teamed up with someone who wasn't part of my group of friends, and whom I would not otherwise have gotten to know. Away from the cliques of "best friends"—town versus gown and so on—we got to know our partner quietly, privately, over time, one-on-one. I spent the fall on safety patrol with the quiet, shy Linda Montrose, who turned out to have a lovely sense of humor. Spring duty was shared with Pauline Whalen, the only girl who was able to befriend Ethel, the poorest kid in our class, judging by B.O., breast size, and number of years held back. Ethel was fifteen or sixteen, fully developed, and year-round wore terrible, shabby cotton summer dresses that must have belonged to her mother. Through the long winter, she wore boys' ankle socks or bare legs instead of warm stockings like the rest of us. One day on crossing duty, Pauline told me that Ethel's father had whipped her real bad this time. She had shown Pauline the terrible stripes on her back in the girls' room.

The next year, in seventh grade, there was Ethel, walking the halls wearing her perpetual blush and faded old cotton dress, pregnant as a barnyard cat. She did *not* have a boyfriend. Everyone knew, but nobody did anything about it. That was my world. Telling a grown-up anything was tattling; you did it to get somebody in trouble. Never, ever, did I think of grown-ups as resources for getting somebody *out* of trouble.*

It had been the same at Plainfield. Everyone knew about RuthAnn, a girl a year ahead of me in school, that her father was also her grandfa-

---

*My father wrote a story years ago called "Elaine" about a stunningly beautiful girl who is mildly retarded. Elaine is sixteen and in the eighth grade. She was, he wrote, the only girl wearing lipstick at her eighth-grade graduation except Theresa Torrini, the eighteen-year-old "mother of an illegitimate child by a taxi driver named Hugo Munster." Elaine lives with her mother and grandmother in the Bronx. She is a lamb among wolves and is later raped by her first date, a movie usher. My father describes the three of them, mother, daughter, and grandmother, walking up the street together to the movies, Elaine "looking like centuries of Juliets and Ophelias and Helens. . . . There were thousands of Bronx people who saw them on their way. There was never one to cry out, to wonder, to intercept. . . ."

ther. That's how it was put. When the original mother died, the father took up relations with his eldest daughter and produced an entire new generation of kids, including RuthAnn. What a man did on his own property was his business—you could disapprove, but it wasn't your business. Pauline gave me a darn good look at the dark side of privacy, where parents' unbridled freedom to do as they pleased could create a private hell for their kids.

I also discovered that breaking down the walls of privacy and sharing your problems with a friend made you not feel so weird and alone. It was at Norwich School, I found out, much to my relief, that I wasn't the only one who thought her mother was a "slut." My classmate Nikki and I got to talking about our little brothers one day, and it turned out that we had both tried to intervene on their behalf to keep the boyfriends out of the house. Nikki's mother was pretty, smart, and divorced just like mine; and just like mine, Nikki's lecture to her did no good at all. It drove us crazy. Since they were "doing it," these guys should have slunk out the back door like foxes, tails between their legs, and flown the coop before dawn. But there the boyfriend would be, sitting at the breakfast table, bold as a rooster. We couldn't believe it. We were *fu*rious, impotently furious.

Nikki dropped out of school in ninth grade. This was unheard of in Hanover, but quite legal in New Hampshire. You had to finish eighth grade, then what you did was your own business. This usually resulted in a lot of guys who shaved in the eighth grade in some school districts, rather than a lot of thirteen-year-olds on the loose. Nikki used to hang out in Hopkins Center, the Dartmouth College arts building. I'd see her in the student café smoking cigarettes, drinking coffee, and reading. She never looked at loose ends; even at thirteen she looked as if she were supposed to be there, working on her Ph.D. or something.

My father spotted her in Hanover from time to time, in later years, while I was away at school and would write and tell me the news. In one letter he mentioned that he had run into Nikki's mother in the checkout line at the supermarket. He acknowledged she was probably disreputable as hell, but admitted that "your stupid father" liked looking at her face. Back then he was, like Holden, honest about his attraction to a pretty face, and about the discrepancy between what the hormones desired and what the mind knew was best. It never concerned me though, because I trusted him completely to control himself, unlike my mother. I thought he might remarry someday, but the mortifying prospect of one's father "dating" never crossed my mind, so outraged was he on the subject of my mother's loose behavior.

❦

YOU MIGHT THINK IT WAS COOL, back then, that my dad was J. D. Salinger "the author," but in sixth grade and junior high, that fact wasn't even a blip on the screen of any of my friends' awareness. Among my group of friends, there was nothing an *old* guy could do, worse yet, a *par*ent, that was anything but the polar opposite of cool. Younger kids and parents and teachers were unbearably dumb; we were somewhere on the slope between dumb and cool moving upward with a rock climber's determination and tenacity, while the seniors lounged at the top, the apogee of cool, master of all they surveyed.

My little brother, Matthew, had achieved a certain dominion over his world right in the first grade. He was the marble king. He started with a small bag of marbles like every other boy, but his kept getting bigger and bigger as he won the other guys' marbles each recess. By midfall, he had to store some of them at home in shoe boxes, he had so many. Daddy had taught him to play marbles a couple of years earlier, and by now he was deadly. I don't know if Daddy taught him Seymour's technique*; I wasn't privy to the secrets of boys, and playing marbles was one of the mysteries, right up there with peeing in a urinal. My brother's life and mine didn't cross paths very often. At school, we were separated by a chasm of grade level and gender. At home, as well as during the long commute to and from school, we coexisted with widely varying degrees of tolerance. The only thing I remember us doing together, with any regularity at this point in our lives, was going out to eat with Daddy. Although he still played with my brother, marbles and cars and stuff, he didn't seem to know what to do with me anymore.

---

*Seymour's secret can be found in one of my favorite passages. It begins, "One late afternoon, at that faintly soupy quarter of an hour in New York when the street lights have just been turned on and the parking lights of cars are just getting turned on—some on, some still off—I was playing curb marbles with a boy named Ira Yankauer . . ." (*Seymour: An Introduction,* pp. 201–2).

Going out to a restaurant—the ones at home at least—couldn't hold a candle to picking mushrooms, on our long-ago walks together, and making an omelette with them when we got home. Restaurants in our area were nothing like the exotic Wolfie's in Florida or the Russian Tea Room in New York. Ours came in three basic sizes. First there were the "fancy" places where you could get a shrimp cocktail. These consisted of a single cavernous room filled with a sea of tables with tablecloths and dim lighting for "atmosphere." When we went to the Montshire House or Lander's or the Windsor House, Daddy complained loudly about the lighting. Every time. He'd tell the waiter that next time he'd have to bring his flashlight to read the menu. Every time. The next size were the Howard Johnson's, home of the deliciously clamless clam roll, and peppermint ice cream cones with real candies in them.

The third type of restaurant was the small place with maybe ten Formica tables and booths or just a big lunch counter. These places served ice cream in a raised, pewter-colored, scratched metal dessert dish that sat on a plate with a paper doily on it. I always got chocolate ice cream with butterscotch sauce; my brother, vanilla with chocolate sauce. We eyed each other's ice creams with a surveyor's expertise, to see who had gotten luckiest with the collar. The collar, before the days of gargantuan serving portions, was the little ruffle of ice cream that surrounded the round scoop. If you were lucky and the ice cream (or its server) was a little warm, you might get half again as much ice cream in the collar. If cold, you got just the perfectly round scoop. My father never failed to let us order ice cream, nor did he ever fail to tell us that "frozen protein is *poi*son for the liver, almost *impossible* to digest."*

The only restaurant I really liked going to, and where I felt happy when I was there, was Tony's Pizza on the road to Claremont. Tony made the pizza, and his beautiful little girl, Maria, who was just

---

*Daddy later developed a way of purging himself of such delectable "poison." He told me, quite proud of his newly discovered technique, that he'd stick his fingers down his throat and vomit it up. As one who struggled with bulimia for too many years, I find, in retrospect, his naivete less than appealing. Years later, he would teach Joyce Maynard this same technique of eliminating such impurities from her body.

Matthew's age, sometimes came over to the table to bring us something. We always had the same thing: pizza with extra cheese, ginger ale for me, orange soda for Matthew, and a martini with an olive for Daddy to start, followed by a glass of Chianti. One day, soon after Tony's opened, Daddy told Tony that his was the best pizza he had ever eaten . . . except for *one* place in New York's Little Italy—Rosa something or other. Tony's eyes narrowed; he took his cigar out of his mouth and said an address, street, and cross street, in Little Italy. "Yes, yes, that's the one!" my father exclaimed. "Don't tell me you've been there?" my father was in the middle of asking when all of a sudden Tony had his arms around him, embracing him, slapping him on the back, tears in his eyes. "That's my mother! That's my mother's place!" If you made that up in a story, no one would believe you.

The other thing my brother and I shared on these occasions was the sermon du jour. Our father recited the same litany, in a desperate, passionate tone, ever since I can remember. I cannot begin to count the number of times I heard it growing up, at least once every month or two from the time I was seven or eight until I left home and was beyond redemption. I'm not exaggerating. It reached a crescendo that year when I was ten. Whether this was in response to my mother's emerging sexuality, or to the prelude of mine, or to neither, I don't know. It began: "Make sure you marry someone who laughs at the same things you do." Sometimes he'd add a cautionary tale such as the one about a date who, in the middle of a movie theater, actually laughed at a bit of slapstick, the pain it caused him and so on. Where other parents might lecture you, ad nauseam, about not making the same mistake they did, "stay in school, get an education, make something of yourself so you don't have to sweep floors for a living like me," my father's litany of warning told his children not to make the same terrible mistake he did in marrying someone like our mother. The litmus test of compatibility was laughing at the same things at the movies. "Opposites may attract, but not for long." Then he'd stare off with his I'm-about-to-impart-wisdom expression (oh, boy, *lec*ture time), as if it were the first time we'd heard it. "Treat like with like," he'd say. "Like with like"—the main tenet of his beloved homeopathy.

But who is alike, who is a landsman, who is an appropriate mate? If we take his criterion—laughing at the same movies—then Holden and Phoebe are a perfect fit, as are Babe and Mattie, and my father and the ideal readers he imagines and addresses in *The Catcher in the Rye* and woos outright, unabashedly, with a "bouquet of very early-blooming parentheses: (((()))))" in the opening of *Seymour: An Introduction.*

Unlike me, his ten-year-old characters, my fictional siblings, were perfect, flawless, reflections of what my father likes. Holden's beloved sister, Phoebe, got it just right, every time:

> You never saw a little kid so pretty and smart in your whole life. . . . She's only ten. . . . You'd like her. I mean if you tell old Phoebe something, she knows exactly what the hell you're talking about. I mean . . . you take her to a lousy movie, for instance, she knows it's a lousy movie. If you take her to a pretty good movie, she knows it's a pretty good movie. . . . Her favorite is *The 39 Steps,* though, with Robert Donat. She knows the whole goddam movie by heart. (*Catcher,* p. 67)

Babe's ten-year-old sister, Mattie, gets it right, too. In one scene he is waiting for her outside her school where she has stayed late, with a few other girls, to hear her teacher read from *Wuthering Heights.* Babe saw the girls coming out of the building:

> Maybe they didn't like *Wuthering Heights.* Maybe they were just bucking for rank, polishing apples. Not Mattie though. I'll bet she's nuts about it, Babe thought. I'll bet she wants Cathy to marry Heathcliff instead of Linton. . . .
> "Babe!" she said. "Gee!" . . .
> "How was the book?" Babe asked.
> "Good! Did you read it?"
> "Yep."
> "I want Cathy to marry Heathcliff. Not that other droop, Linton. He gives me a royal pain," Mattie said.
> ("Last Day of the Last Furlough")

My father's ideal reader gets it right, too. A few pages on, Holden described a nightclub crowd's reaction to a showy pianist. Holden speaks directly to the reader:

You would've puked. They went mad. They were exactly the same morons that laugh like hyenas in the movies at stuff that isn't funny. . . . People always clap for the wrong things. . . . Anyway, it made me feel depressed and lousy again.   (*Catcher*, p. 84)

I once told my father, I think I was about eight at the time, that he only liked people in homeopathic* doses. He thought that my observation was so true and so insightful that he used to repeat it to everyone he knew, the way some parents go on about your first words or first trophies and blue ribbons. What I meant at the time, and I think he understood, was that he liked people only in minute doses, but I realize now that it's true on yet another level. He only likes people who are like him, *homeopathically* like him, identical entities with identical properties, varying only in size and shape. Like with like.

Being a girl with extremely sensitive antennae, I managed to keep in his good graces most of the time, to be the swell girl, the girl in the shaving mirror. In so doing, I dwelt in his magical world of stories and wild mushrooms and hotel breakfasts where no grown-ups, with their phony rules and conceits, were allowed. But the price of admission was steep. To enter his world, a girl had to become, in a sense, fictional and split off from the depth, complexity, and imperfection of a real, three-dimensional person. The mental gymnastics required to reflect his view and avoid rejection involved more than selectively expressing, or accentuating, one aspect of myself. My mind didn't bend; it split in such a way that I became almost two people: the part of me that played with my friends and thought my own secret thoughts, and the part of me that was his voice in my head and enabled me to be a person he loved. This was something I learned to do without much reflection. It became

---

*From the Greek *homoiopatheia,* from *homoiopathes,* having like feelings or affections; *homoios,* like, similar, and *pathos,* feeling, suffering. The theory or system of curing diseases with very minute doses of medicine that in a healthy person and in large doses would produce a condition like that of the disease treated (*Webster's*).

automatic, the fractured glass a part of the structure of my being.*

In my father's story *Zooey*, I was surprised to see some self-aware-ness of this trait. At least, his mother seems to have his number. Bessie Glass tells her son Zooey, "you make people nervous, young man. . . . If you don't like somebody in two minutes, you're done with them for-ever." What Bessie says about Zooey was certainly true of my father in relation to me. When I fell out of sync with him, the consequences were sharp and swift. After one disagreement my father and I had in the car on the way home from school, he called me on the phone to discuss it, which, as a ten-year-old, I thought was a very grown-up thing to do. I remember the conversation exactly. He said we'd better find a way to make up because "when I'm through with a person, I'm *through* with them." Then, as if I needed convincing, he told me a story about a close friend he'd had a falling-out with and never spoken to again. I'd seen this happen with not one but most of his few remaining friends. He ended by saying, "I'll always love you, but when I lose respect for a per-son, I'm done with them. Finished."

Even though his words made my stomach churn, I thought it was cool that he treated me as if I were an adult. Now that I am an adult, I think, Are you nuts? This is a ten-year-old child, *your* ten-year-old child you are talking to like this! But as Zooey tells his sister Franny:

> "And don't tell me again that you were ten years old. Your age has nothing to do with what I'm talking about. There are no big *changes* between ten and twenty—or ten and eighty, for that matter."

Young Seymour (age seven) writing home from summer camp, in "Hapworth 16, 1924," tells his three-year-old twin brothers that their age is no excuse for estranging themselves from their "chosen career,"

---

*In the book *Destructive Cult Conversion: Theory, Research and Treatment* (American Family Foundation, 1981), Dr. John Clark of Harvard Medical School's Department of Psychiatry writes: "In effect, the convert's mind seems to split. A factitious second personality (the cult personality) begins episodically to achieve a certain autonomy as it struggles with the old one for position in the forefront of consciousness. The stress on the individual here is, of course, very great."

tap dancing, for more than a few hours at a time. "I laugh hollowly down the years at the trite reports and customs firmly connected with the tender age of three!" Seymour continues with similar age-inappropriate messages for his sisters as well. In this, my father's last published story, the confluence of adult and child has reached the point where the resulting offspring, the characters created by this Alice in Wonderland–like admixture ("Drink this") of small child and old man, results in a creation that strikes me as more a product of taxidermy than of real, flesh-and-blood intercourse. No blood, phlegm, filth, and excreta here. These little Indians are preserved, unchanging, under glass, as in Holden's beloved museum.

When I was ten, the thing I was most conscious of hiding, under glass as it were, from my father was that I had any interest in boys. (Now I'd put it a little differently and call it "my sexuality" that I felt a pressing need to hide from him.) When a couple would kiss in a movie we were watching, I distinctly remember saying, "Eeew!" and feeling like a liar. I was like his character Raymond Ford's poem: an unchanging, "perfect ten" on the surface; beneath, not a wasteland but an inverted forest with all the budding foliage underground.*

The flip side of perpetual childhood, in this conflation of child and adult, is the adult child, the "wise child." From the moment, somewhere around the age of four and a half, when I realized that I was far more in tune with my baby brother's needs than were my parents, I believed myself to be more grown-up than the grown-ups. This had both life-sustaining and life-threatening results. I often relied on my soldier's sixth sense to keep me out of harm's way. Being a little adult, however,

---

*Joyce Maynard writes in her memoir: "Jerry says nothing, ever, about me as a physical person. . . . No words are spoken about either of our physical bodies. . . . He virtually never mentions sex." He does not mention, or perhaps notice at all, that Joyce, in her self-starvation, stops menstruating. In an article on "post–mind control" syndrome (*Social Work*, March 1982), Lorna Goldberg and William Goldberg, co-leaders of a therapeutic group for former members of religious cults, found that "almost all the ex-cultists appear to be much younger than their chronological age and display an asexual innocence. They act childlike although they may be well into their twenties. Indeed, during their time in the cult women often stop menstruating and men's beards grow more slowly. During the initial postdeprogramming stage the ex-cultists regain their secondary sexual characteristics."

made me a poor judge of safe and appropriate places for a *child* to play. It now makes perfect sense to me why, at ten, I thought my baby-sitter was my boyfriend instead of the child molester that he was. In this "inverted forest," I was neither shocked nor did I feel any of the other things one might expect a ten-year-old girl to feel about a twenty-two-year-old man climbing into her bed. Like Franny Glass, I had been taught that there were no important differences between eight and eighty.

Mac, my baby-sitter, was a senior at Dartmouth and a deejay at the college radio station. He picked me up from school in his sports car, held hands with me on the gearshift, and drove me home to Cornish. After Matthew went to bed, Mac helped me with my homework, rewarding correct answers with long French kisses. The kissing itself felt like fish wiggling in my mouth, but I figured it was like starting to smoke: with practice the coolness of doing it outweighs the gross taste and feel. Tucking me in, he'd say he really shouldn't touch me like this, but I wasn't sure *why* he shouldn't.* I thought it was totally cool to be going out with a college student, though of course, in hindsight, we never actually went out anywhere.

When I found out from my friend Beth at a sleep-over that Mac had been "tucking in" a number of girls he baby-sat for, and one of the girls had told her mom, it hit me all of a sudden that he wasn't my boyfriend at all; he was a perv. I felt so gross.

And, of course, I told no one.

---

*I'm not implying that my father *caused* the molestations, any more than my mother did in hiring the man. The perpetrator, Mac, is the only one who caused it. But this confusion of boundaries, which my parents and I certainly had, as to who's a grown-up and who's a child, creates conditions ripe for such exploitation.

18

Notes from the Underground

❧❧

IN 1967 THE WHOLE WORLD BURST INTO FLOWER. An eleven-year-old girl, even a tall one, was easily camouflaged in a sea of sunflowers. Big Day-Glo daisy stickers bloomed on countless bedroom walls, paisley swirled across bedspreads and dresses, dashikis enrobed black and white alike in colors of the sun, girls' long legs sprouted up through the pavement overnight. The trail of my own scent was undetectable amidst great wafts of Yardley's English Lavender, Jean Naté lemons, incense and peppermints.

Before the beginning of school—oh, manna from heaven!—my mother let me go shopping for clothes. I don't know why she finally stopped insisting on my wearing drab, English-schoolgirl, itchy-caterpillar-like tweeds and felts and woolens. I emerged from a store in Hanover that day with a beautiful, soft, blue, fluffy, acrylic knit mini-dress that I wore with white windowpane stockings* and a garter belt that wasn't from the store where we always bought my sensible white Carter's Spanky Pants, a name that always caused me to cringe, as if underwear shopping wasn't devastating enough.†

---

*Sort of like fishnet stockings, only with half-inch squares instead of tiny triangles.

†For young ladies, garter belts weren't kinky back then, they were standard. You wore socks or stockings. Undergarments were more like trusses: white, tight, and lots of metal fasteners. Even thin moms like mine wore long-line girdles with built-in garters for the stockings. "It's new! Made with Lycra, too! With holding power that won't wash out, introducing the new Playtex eighteen-hour

I also bought a paisley mini-dress with orange patterns on a yellow background, colors previously illegal in my closet, and a navy blue dress that had horizontal stripes of yellow and red. The coolest thing about the latter dress, other than the colors, was that, at the bottom where the hem was, some extra material was rolled up and stitched, forming a slightly padded inch-and-a-half-thick ring around the bottom of the dress. Sort of like a Hula-Hoop sewn into a dress. *Very* "mod."

I was allowed to buy a pair of normal shoes, shoes like the other girls wore, for the first time in my life. My mother was sure they would *ruin* my feet. There is nothing wrong with my feet, but I had had to wear orthopedic-looking lace-up oxfords, "sensible shoes," every day since I learned to walk, even to birthday parties where the other little girls wore patent leather Mary Janes. We bought a pair of size 9 (I was a size 8½, but the extra half size was so my toes wouldn't be ruined the very *mo*ment I put them on), navy leather Mary Janes that were blessed with a heel of about an eighteenth of an inch. That made them *real* pumps! Heaven on earth! Heels. I also had a blue raincoat, a "slicker" to Beatles fans in the know, with a big zipper up the front and a bold yellow band about a foot wide around the middle. What a marvelous thing, for once in your life, to feel you look great instead of dreadful. I know most of the world has to worry about having enough clothes to cover body parts and keep warm. But, oh, what a lovely thing to feel pretty; it was the first time in my life.* "I could have danced all night"—and not ruined my toes.

When we got home, my mother let me take my old dresses from the closet and put them in a bag for "the poor children." This time, however, "the poor children" were no longer siblings of classmates with real faces and real embarrassment at the situation; they were a distant concept. Into the giveaway bag went my three old dresses, like evil, ugly stepsisters. In went the tight maroon-and-cream-plaid wool jumper worn for two years over a choice of cream or maroon turtleneck, with

---

bra with cross-your-heart protection. It lifts and separates. Even for full-figured gals like me, Jane Russell."

*I remember crying, even though the days of my mother choosing my clothing were far behind me, when I read that lovely scene in *The Accidental Tourist,* where a painfully shy, homely little boy whose mother dresses him terribly was taken by a nice man to a store to get his first pair of blue jeans. He looked at himself in the mirror amazed: "Wow, I look great!"

white bobby socks, and sensible shoes. In went the navy wool jumper with the contrasting navy-and-white-plaid skirt that always hung at a queer angle and itched; and in went the most hated of all, a dog-doody-brown jumper, made of hatting felt so stiff that it bent into me like cardboard when I sat down. Boy, did I hate that dress. I could have hung it in effigy and burned it as they did the stuffed "enemy" at the Dartmouth College bonfires the night before a game. Or dumped it into the harbor like the Boston Tea Party we'd been reading about in our history book at school, "no taxation without representation." Freedom.

Once again, a dollar surreptitiously spent at the Newberry five-and-dime in Windsor, home of my gold-tone "R" pendant, provided me with contraband accessories and solid cachet among classmates: a pair of screw-back earrings that had great big "pearl" balls that dangled deliciously from two-inch gold chains, and a tube of white lipstick. I smuggled these beauties into school. Where once it was just Viola and me who went straight to the girls' room to do our forbidden uncurling and unbraiding, now there were legions of us in the girls' room before school applying make-up, rolling up miles of skirts at the waist to the desired mini length, some even having a smoke in the stall. The air was thick with excitement.

Each seventh grader was assigned his or her own private locker on the first day of school. I loved this, that the first order of business was to give you a secret place to put things. The little slip of paper with my combination written on it was as magical to me as my secret, moonlit worlds of fairies and wood sprites had been years ago. It was a key to my own world, away from my parents. Inside the locker, there was a hook for my coat, a bottom shelf for boots, and top shelves for books, notebooks, brush and comb, lunch bag, or purse of money for lunch in the cafeteria. It also served as a mailbox for friends who might wish to leave a note on your locker or push it in via the vent slats. Once in a while there were locker inspections, but I never took them personally; they were more for one's own protection against some gross guys who left their gym socks or ham sandwich in there, stinking up the hall for weeks on end. Drugs had not made it into the junior high school at that time, so it wasn't like a police search. We heard rumors of "hippies" smoking pot, but it was smoke curling on the far horizon, distant, scenic and cozy, not near and threatening.

We switched classes every period, sharing the halls with the entire junior and senior high school. I made my way down corridors, surfing the wave of moving students, on that thrilling edge between mastery and danger. We passed seniors, on the top floor where the halls were carpeted, sitting on the floor by their lockers, taking up space with confidence, hanging out, stitching up a hem, talking till the bell rang over the intercom and the corridors became deserted and only those with hall passes, stopped and inspected at roving checkpoints by hall monitors, could proceed. Having been raised on a wholesome diet of World War II espionage movies, this system of passes and checkpoints and forbidden territory did not escape my eye. On lone forays to the girls' room, hall pass in hand, I gathered intelligence regarding patterns of enemy movement. I was scarcely aware I was doing it. By the third week of school, I had the system down. My chance came at the end of the month when I needed to be absent for a whole day, for a reason I forget, probably dental, and in order to be excused, I had to collect all of my teachers' signatures on a form. I copied each signature before turning in the form to the office. Now I just had to get a pass someone was dumb enough to fill out in pencil. Having spent my entire life picking my way through a veritable minefield at home, between my mother's explosions and my father's narrow path, school was a field day to negotiate. With my dad I pretended I was still the girl who doesn't "understand the Parisians, thinking love's so miraculous and grand, oh, they speak about it, won't live without it, oh, I don't understand the Parisians" *(Gigi)*. At school, however, *je suis une boulevardière.*

The few places where school and home rubbed up against each other were the hardest to negotiate. I'm sure I'm not the only girl on the edge of adolescence whose father "went mental" about something every couple of weeks. My wearing mod stockings made him nuts. He wouldn't say it to me directly, but when he'd pick me up from school as he did on occasion, he'd survey my schoolmates waiting for buses or rides and decry the "joiners, followers, and sheep" all wearing "the uniform of fashionable nonconformity." One afternoon he lost it completely. I had drawn a small peace symbol on my leg with a pen in study hall. "Oh, my God!" he cried out, and put his hands over his eyes as if he had seen something so awful he couldn't bear to look. Then he stuck out his finger, jabbing in the general direction of my leg. "What . . . the hell . . . is *that?*" he said slowly, flatly, spitting out the words with contempt. Man, my stomach went crazy. "Nothing. I don't know. What?" I thought he was going to hit me. *"Christ* almighty. Do you have any idea what would happen if we pulled out of Vietnam? A bloodbath," he yelled. "That's what would happen, the Communists would come in and there'd be a bloodbath. You don't know them, you don't know what they're capable of." I licked my finger and tried to rub it off. Duck and cover.

I didn't disagree with him; I knew next to nothing about the war in Vietnam except the flat way Chet Huntley or David Brinkley read the daily body count on the evening news. There was something much scarier, much more real and ominous, about those cold statistics, for me anyway, than seeing the Gulf War "up close and personal" on CNN. Sort of the way black-and-white photographs often seem more lifelike than color ones. I get the shivers writing about it. I kind of understand, now, why seeing your daughter wearing a peace symbol could feel like seeing a swastika, an attack on everything you and your army buddies had fought and died for. But then it just scared the hell out of me. I had *no idea* what I'd done.

It seemed that everything I did in terms of dress or style (which is all the peace symbol meant to me at the time; it was my mother who was starting to get involved seriously in the antiwar movement) that celebrated my fitting in at school provoked outbursts of rage from my father. Traitor: I was becoming *like* other people, people other than him. Sometimes these scenes would then be followed by his profuse, desperate pleading for forgiveness, as if I were his wife or something, which was even worse than the yelling somehow, it made me feel *really* icky and uncomfortable.

It was becoming increasingly tricky for me to stay in his good graces. Once in a fight I was having with my dad, he accused me of not caring about him or my brother or anyone in the family, just my friends. I countered, "Well, *you* don't even *have* any friends." He replied, as he has done on several occasions, that he didn't have the same *need* for friends as I seemed to have, implying, of course, that it was a weakness on my part.

What I didn't have the words for at the time, but only felt somewhere in my bones, was that to fit into my father's family, to be his per-

fect Phoebe, would have meant turning, like Daphne, into a tree.* I realize now why I saved all the notes my friends and I passed to each other
in school that year and recall the "underground foliage"—the secrets of
who likes whom, the hidden kisses, bodies meeting bodies beneath
crepe-paper decorations at dances—with such affection, when so many
other mementos fell by the wayside as time went by in move after move.
To my dad, I'm sure our concerns, if I'd been so foolish as to let him
know, would have seemed contemptibly shallow. I, however, treasure
this time when I joined the dance of life, splashed and cavorted in the
shallows, albeit hidden from my family, rather than sitting on the island
cliff contemplating my navel. Just as I believe his Glass characters are
cheated out of the joys of childhood reading by their focus on adult
books and concerns, so, too, I feel they are cheated out of the joys and
sorrows of inhabiting the mind and body and world of an eleven-year-
old. To everything there is a season, and my turn had finally come to act
my own age.

※

AT HANOVER JUNIOR HIGH, for the first time ever, I fit in. I don't remember how I got to know everybody. It seemed to just happen. I
was placed in the 7–1A track where the most popular kids were.
Cliques are probably easier to write about if you're on the outside.
When you're in one, at that age, you don't really know what everyone else is doing; you're just not aware. We were the cool group, the
boulevardiers, the A-minus underachievers who wrote secret notes
to each other about who liked whom and planned parties in study
hall.

The smartest kids were in 7–1 and they were different; they actually
studied. They even *talked* about schoolwork. Tracking is a tricky thing,
attempting to group together kids who are alike. I'm sure it reinforced
and perpetuated the established economic order—the kids with B.O.

---

*According to the legend of the nymph Daphne, she rejects Apollo's advances
and is turned into a laurel tree by her father, the river god Ladon. She chose to remain "an unmoving tree rather than the bride of Apollo" (*D'Aulaires' Book of
Greek Myths,* p. 95).

were in 7–4 and took home ec and industrial arts, and so on; but at the time, it reflected the order so well that it didn't seem like an agent of it, it seemed objective and true. Like with like.

For a couple of kids, the tracks were a less than perfect fit. Gail, for instance, was part of our group socially, but took some classes with the dumb kids. I remember in sixth grade she couldn't hear syllables the way the rest of us could. Was *girl* one syllable or *gir-ul,* two syllables? She was really smart and beautifully expressive, but just didn't get certain things; her papers had lots of red *x*'s all over them. Now there's a term for her difficulty, learning disabilities, but then it was a mystery. Gail actually knew Joan Baez. She called her Joanie and knew the correct pronunciation of her name—"Bize" rather than "Bye-ez," as the rest of us mistakenly did. So cool.

The other friend I had who didn't quite fit the track was Anna, who took some 7–1 classes. She was far more mature, both physically and mentally, than the rest of us were. She actually needed a bra, a garment we all wore but most of us only aspired to filling. She seemed to be able to handle homework and hormones simultaneously with humor and grace. Anna seemed to float comfortably between boundaries; she was smart and fun and cool at the same time. I'd be fascinated to know how life went for her. She used to report in on the 7–1 kids and give me a glimpse at how the tribe on the other side of the island lived:

Dear Peggy,

What goes on at your house, I've called 4 times but all I get is a busy signal zzzt-zzzt-zzzt. Does Rachel want us to feel sorry for her or something.

Man that kid (Van Orden?) that was outside of the classroom (Miss Berks) well, when everyone was talking to us about that detention he kept on rubbing shoulders with me. GROSS!!!!!! He is supposed to be a real sex maniac.

You know Martha and Judy and their group? [7–1] Well, they don't 'dare' say the word sex. They treat it like it was a swear word, you know they say (when they do) S-E-X. Shhhh!! Oh dear me.

Love,
Anna

The blending of the Norwich kids with the Hanover kids was a bit bumpy. Loyalties were strained as sixth-grade alliances were regrouped. My best friend Rachel McAndrew, with whom I spent summers in Maine and many a weekend overnight, was now my classmate in 7–1A. Rachel's two best friends in sixth grade (*in* school that is; we were best friends outside school) went on to 7–1. I was jealous of her attention to them; she was jealous of my new friendship with Anna, and of my Norwich friends. As the year progressed, though, our group in 7–1A was seriously occupied in working out the question of "who likes whom" between boys and girls, while simultaneously still working out questions of "like with like" between friends of the same sex.

Most of our work, and by that I mean the business of sorting out who likes whom, was accomplished in study hall where secret communiqués were passed back and forth. Study hall was held in a huge room on the new, carpeted second floor, with desks divided into three blocks of neat rows. Off to the side of the room by the windows was a big dictionary on a stand. It had the strategic advantage of being the farthest point from the study hall proctor's desk, and it served as our mailbox. You and a friend would decide on a password and place the note you'd written at that page in the dictionary, and then your friend would go up and get the note instead of risking passing it and getting caught. No one ever stole a note meant for someone else, that just wasn't the system. On Mondays, Rachel and I would pick a new word for the week:

Peggy,

I just went to the dictionary and looked under *unisexual*—having to do with one sex.

    Castrate—to remove male glands.

    Luv—they didn't have anything. <u>Cheap</u>.

    That's my favorite word.

Bye Rachel!!!

P.S. Is your knee getting better? It looks like it. Bye.

I would grow nearly six inches that year, and my knees were having trouble keeping up. It was great for the hemlines though! What was decent at the beginning of the year became *decent*—our slang for cool/great—by January. I found myself "in with the in crowd," the Dave Stone group, quite early on in the year. I had heard about Dave before meeting him because his father, Dr. Stone, delivered me and had been my pediatrician ever since. On my last checkup, to enter seventh grade, he'd told me I'd be in the same class as his son David. I wasn't impressed so much as curious: Who was that nice Dr. Stone's boy, and would I be able to ask him what happened to his dad's leg? (He had a wooden one, my mom told me when I asked her why he walked that way.) The first weeks were a bit confusing:

> Dear Rachel,
>   I think I am going to get out of the group. Dave and the others were friends with me yesterday and now they don't even know I'm alive.

Then I started getting to know Will, one of the boys in the group, and we helped each other solve a number of mysteries. First we had to figure out whether we "liked" each other. That solved, we went on to form a real partnership. What a treasure to have a member of the opposite sex you can talk to and trade secrets with. Otherwise it's like Holden, all trial and error and mystery. By the way, an historical note is necessary here I think—when we talk about "sex" in notes, we meant making out, K.I.S.S.I.N.G. as the jump rope chant goes. "First comes love, then comes marriage, then comes junior in the baby carriage."

> Dear Will,
>   I am not "thick" I just can't read your handwriting. You have dropped a million girls on the grounds that they didn't play with you enough. That means you think more of sex than Love. If you really loved someone you wouldn't care if they constantly gave you sex. I'll be good friends with you now. Later it might be different. Much different. But that is the future.—   from Peggy

> Peggy—
>   You are completely right. I never thought of it that way.
>   Thank you
>   Will

Dear Peggy

Who is around? I am lost. I want to just be good freinds with you *[OK]* and Joan. I much rather just like you as a freind than a girlfreind. *[I feel the same way]* Cause you are better that way. I don't like to go places in the school because I would rather be in a study hall. *[You like study hall?]*

Bye
Will

P.S. Who should I like?

Will,

You like Joan don't you? *[Just as a freind she is better that way]* If not there is nobody who wants to go with you. When I asked you over I did because it would be fun <u>that's all</u>. *[I know]* When we made-out I did just because I like you a lot. Not because I love you. *[Same.]*

Hi Peggy

I agree with you. Lets do it. I like you a lot too! But not someone to love aussi.

I do know most boys better than you. And you probably know most girls better. I like Linda N. but I am afraid its hopeless. Who do you think I should like. Or who needs and likes me. Please tell me.

Write
Will

Will,

Try Rachel. I asked her what she thought of you and if she wants to go with you. She said, "I don't know him anymore. But I don't know mabey." That's what she said.

Write back Peggy

The notes I saved record that the first school dance of the year was the occasion of much excitement, intrigue, and blundering. Can you believe this guy?

Peggy this is poor (ron) speaking if someone you liked asked you to go to the dance before DAVE might you go?

ronnie

Peggy

    I'm sorry about saying "When was the last time you washed your hair?" Don't tell rachel that I said I'm sorry. She would just make fun. If I asked you to go to the dance [might] you go? I couldn't ask rachel because of what I said to her in study hall.

ronnie

Luckily for me, Dave came through with flying colors.

    Peggy, after lunch or sometime else, not in class I have to ask and tell you something.

O.K.—D.S.

Peggy,

    The thing I wanted to tell you was . . . If someone asks you to the student council dance say you've already been invited by someone else <u>me</u>.

O.K.?
D.S.

Even more fun than the school dances were the weekend parties each of us, in turn, gave. Rachel had the best house for a party of all of us (except one girl who had an indoor swimming pool, but that was so out of this world it almost didn't count). The McAndrews had a huge playroom in the finished basement beneath their living room and dining room. It had a TV and a fireplace and a big couch with cushions that you could toss all over the floor and lounge around on and eat popcorn and nobody cared. Rachel had three older brothers and sisters, so by the time it was her turn to have parties, all the battles had been fought. Her parents retired to another part of the house, and the playroom was strictly off-limits to younger brothers and sisters for the evening. The door to the upstairs remained shut, the music loud, and as the evening wore on, the lights virtually off.

    Rachel's party itself is eclipsed in my memory by one of the loveliest moments of my life. It was one of those few moments when time stands still and everything is perfect. Simon and Garfunkel were singing "Sounds of Silence"—"Hello darkness my old friend, I've come to talk

My mother doesn't remember many details about the first year of my life. It's mostly lost in a dark haze of depression. What she does remember is that, in general, as my father became enchanted with me—by the time I was four months old and smiling he told his friends the Hands, "We grow more overjoyed every day"—my mother continued to lose ground.

Cornish, where we lived, was wild and woody.

Peggy pulling Daddy's nose. "It was most exceedingly pullable-looking hair, and pulled it surely got; the babies in the family always automatically reached for it, even before the nose, which, God wot, was also Outstanding." ("Seymour: An Introduction," 1959)

This lovely woven slat fence, which as young as age four I climbed with ease, was referred to by reporters and biographers as an "eight-foot-tall impenetrable fence with a sort of guard tower overlooking the house."

The "guard tower," courtesy of FAO Schwarz.

My view of creation as a sort of miraculous immaculate conception was supported by my father's mythic stories about me, such as how I went to the keyboard before I could barely stand unassisted, and picked out a tune perfectly, the first time.

My father told me stories about a naughty little girl, Lucia Ferenzi, and her lion, Samba, that bore a remarkable resemblance to things good little Peggy and her lion, Simba, might have done.

My aunt Doris told me strange and wonderful things.... She called the skin on my face "your complexion."

Peggy and Matthew, 1960.

Princess Margaret (*front, right*) has two small boys in her class, Mark Hawkings and John Eccles. Margaret swam before Elizabeth, went to gallery, applauded her sister.

Claire Douglas, age five, is the first little girl on the left. Photo from *Life* magazine, July 17, 1939.

Peggy on vacation in Florida. I have the same bathing suit as the Mayfair Bath Club girls, but oh, that face!

The author, at age ten going on twenty, in 1966.

to you again, 'neath a halo of a streetlamp I turned my collar from the cold and damp"——and Dave and I were slow-dancing, the moon shining through the basement window; his cheek touched mine, and we didn't move apart. I'd never felt anything so soft in my whole life, nor did I again until I held my son for the first time and touched his face as he nursed, just him and me and the quiet of the night.

And the vision that was planted in my brain still remains
and echoes in the well of silence.

❦

WHEN THANKSGIVING CAME ROUND THAT YEAR, I had a lot for which to be thankful. For a short time, all my stars were lined up in the heavens. Even my mom had done something right in the male department for once. Most of the guys she brought home were young dopes. Like Alex, a college student she dated, who once came into my room all puffed up to give me a charming "father knows best" lecture about being nicer to my poor sweet mother——this from a guy whose voice had barely changed. "You *asshole*," I said, tired, contemptuous, despairing. "Get the fuck out of my room."*

I told my dad what Alex had said and that I told him he was an asshole. Daddy laughed and said, "You said that to him, really?" "Yup." "I'll bet he was shocked." I just shrugged my shoulders; I didn't say it for effect, I was just calling a spade a spade. What I *really* felt was none of Alex's charming business. What I felt was, who the hell are you to talk to me about anything, especially my mother, you little boy. How *dare* you.

Around Thanksgiving my mother started seeing a man. A real, genuine grown-up, one of only two real, grown-up men I remember her dating. The other, Alan T., is still an important part of my brother's life and mine. Aside from being a pleasure to know, both when I was a kid and as I grew up, I don't know what I would have done without Alan at several

---

*Once again, truth is stranger than fiction: Alex was a college housemate of the man who would become my therapist. When I started therapy, in my late teens, I certainly didn't have to prove to him that things were crazy around my house. He remembers telling Alex to leave the kids alone and get out of there.

crucial junctures of my life where he ran interference for me with the real world, such as the time my divorce lawyer started making passes at me and threatening to raise his bill if I didn't comply. Alan put me in touch with the "big boys," an old buddy of his who is a divorce lawyer to the "stars," who set things right for this small fry in short order. Alan has been there for me in a way my parents never were, bringing to mind the saying "When God closes a door, he opens a window."

Although Alan has been far more a part of my life, I've written about Ray here, because Alan wove in and out of our lives over such a long period of time, it feels as though I've always known him. I can't remember when Alan and my mom started seeing each other; I think they may have met even before she knew my dad, although I do remember being devastated one particular time they broke up because it was just before a promised visit to see my hero, Steve McQueen, the handsomest man in the world as he sat on that motorcycle in *The Great Escape,* on the set of Alan's movie *The Thomas Crown Affair,* or maybe it was *Bullitt,* I forget. Alan would have taken me along regardless, but my mother nixed it, something about Faye Dunaway and how could he.*

When I met Ray, I could tell instantly that he, like Alan, wasn't trying to be nice to me to get in good with my mom. Kids can smell that a mile away. And it stinks, let me tell you. Ray was widowed, I think, though I'm not sure, and his son lived with him. He loved his son, and even though Skip was a senior in high school—a time when boys don't tend to be exactly demonstrative about their attachment to their parents—you could tell Skip loved his dad, too. Ray told me that Skip wasn't always called Skip. Up until sixth grade he was called Billy. One day he came home from school and said, "Dad, I want to be called Skip," and that was that. Ray didn't seem to notice the fierce armor I wore. He'd give me a bear hug just as if I were a kid or something. And he *never* spent the night at our house. If he ever did, it would be because they were married, not shacking up and all that gross stuff. Even when he took us all camping together, I never once had to worry about what

---

*Apparently, he was seeing Ms. Dunaway at the time, or at least my mother thought he was, I don't know, I only remember her name being hissed.

my brother might be exposed to or worry about them "doing it." I never even gave it a thought. He took such nice care of my brother, I felt as if I could almost relax and take a vacation myself.

My brother and I talked about that camping trip recently. We both were surprised how strongly the images of that weekend stuck in our mind. "The red ball," he said, "do you remember I lost my red ball on the lake in the wind and Skip rowed across the lake to get it for me?" I don't just remember, it's etched indelibly in my mind. The sky is a surreal gray, the lake gray and choppy, the trees gray before snowfall, the only bit of color a red, red ball blowing across the top of the water. My brother is crying, and Skip, without a word, pulls the boat down to the water. We jump in and Matthew stops crying. Skip rows across the lake like the wind, and I reach out my hand into the tossing reeds by the shore at the other side of the lake and catch hold of the ball. When we get back to shore, Ray has built a fire in the cabin and it's cozy and warm and almost time for supper.

The only time we stayed over at Ray's house was after one camping trip when a freak snowstorm hit. He insisted, quite sensibly, that we stay rather than drive the extra twenty miles from Hanover to Cornish. In the morning Skip drove me to school in his MGB. Skip, I might mention, was, in addition to being kind and thoughtful, the most handsome boy in the entire senior class. I was not alone in that opinion either. His hair was fairly short on the sides, but the bangs were *Meet the Beatles* long in front, and he had to toss his head a lot to keep it out of his eyes. "Oh, my God, Rachel, I might be Skip's stepsister. [Massive giggles and "oh my Gods" and amazement.] Rachel, he has the coolest living room with big windows, and everything is light and new. [It was one of the early "contemporary" houses.] Maybe next Christmas we'll have a tree in the living room and open presents and Skip will be in his pajamas." "Oh, my God, Peggy, that would be soooo cool. You are so lucky." ". . . Well, let's hope she doesn't blow it."

❦

RAY TOOK US TO EXPO '67 IN MONTREAL. They had loudspeakers everywhere that were playing the Beatles' new song, "All You Need Is Love." We waited in long lines, on perfect sidewalks like the ones in Fort Lauderdale, to enter pavilions, each sponsored by a different country. *Pavilion.* Isn't that a beautiful word? We each got to pick a country. I picked Spain, I think, for the bright colors. My mom picked France. At a restaurant in the French pavilion, they ordered something called steak *tartare,* which I found out means raw. I almost barfed.

I couldn't wait to tell my boyfriend Dave about it when we got back.

Dear [crossed out] is too personal. To David,

Do you like art class? I think it is O.K.—but really weird. I am drawing pictures of odd people. I hope I can go to the party. Will is a pill. Rachel hates him.

BOY, I HATE YOU TOO. AH, HA, HA,

that was an oppisite statement. Ah, ha, ha

Over thanksgiving we went to Expo and my parents tricked me into eating a bite of steak tar-tar. Do you know what that is? RAW meat!!! Mr. Bromley caught me writing and I am in English now.

Rachel and I are enemies because she is jeolous that I like Anna and Rachel hates Anna.

L (almost—too bad) rom
Peggy Barf Belch head

Who could resist my charms? Fortunately, he liked me anyway. Art class was weird, in large part because the teacher, Mr. Bromley, was going out with the sister of a boy in my class. She was a senior, and her yearbook picture even mentions it: "Likes Bob Dylan and Bromley immensely . . . skillfully slips cigarettes up her sleeve as she leaves class on the way to——?" Anna once overheard Mr. Bromley talking to Mr. Lavell, our math teacher, saying he worried if we really *understood* him. Barf. I found out in art class that if you spilled rubber cement on the table and let it dry a little, you could make your own superballs by rolling it up layer after layer during art period. When Gail had a party on the weekend of my birthday, a couple of kids brought me small presents including my own jar of rubber cement as a joke, because that's all I did in art. Her parents accused me of sniffing glue and stopped the party. All the kids knew it wasn't true, but her parents didn't believe us. I don't really blame them for thinking that, but the whole thing just seemed so dumb*—if they'd really known us, the idea that anyone in our group would actually sniff glue would have been so completely off base as to be inconceivable.

It was almost Christmas, and for some kids it was time to pay the piper. Grades were coming out. My father let me know in no uncertain terms that he thought grades were bullshit. That was a great relief for the next few years when mine were lousy; not so nice when I finally started getting good ones and got the same reaction.

Peggy,
 . . . I am going to get creamed about my marks. They said
that if I didn't get a good report card, I would get grounded.
I'm getting maybe 3 D's. What really bothers them is that I
have the capacity to be in the top 10% of the class. I agree, but I
am bored to death and will be cremated.

Write, Gail

I don't remember vacation. I probably skied a lot, by myself, at Mt. Ascutney, which is what I usually did on vacations. Back at school in January, Dave and I were working things out, note by note. I'm sorry to say that it was usually I who was the problem, getting mad over little things. Let me say clearly that I was just plain difficult. Part of the trouble, however, was that my dad's lectures had seeped under my skin to such a depth I couldn't get at them. Every time there was a gap, a break, in the "like with like" and a boyfriend liked something I didn't, or vice versa, it threw me into a panic. It is only within my current marriage that I've been able to get this under control, albeit imperfectly. My brother once told me that he, too, had a hell of a time working that one out of his system. Dave was unbelievably sweet and patient.

---

*I'm so dumb that at a memorial service for Rachel's mother last year, I saw Gail's mother and urgently, passionately, wanted to convince her I didn't do it. I refrained, but barely.

Peggy,

Please tell me what is the matter? You are mad! Please tell me if its at me. Also I want to know if you still like me? I do still like you. Please write back <u>soon</u>!

D. Stone

Peggy,

I am sorry that I have been the way I have but now I know what you want, it is better (I hope.) It has been really hard because I didn't know what you wanted. Now I can do what you want and can be the way you want. Its so much harder to be the boy because you don't know weather the girl wants you to put on her coat or something. Therefore when they don't the girl gets mader and mader. Please don't give up yet.

David Stone

p.s. <u>LOVE</u>?

Valentine's Day was just around the corner. I wanted to get David something nice, but not too nice or I'd be embarrassed. I wandered around Hanover for a while trying to decide what to get him. I told Mom I had some shopping to do and she didn't bug me about it, which was great. I finally came across a bin of psychedelic posters with all sorts of Day-Glo optical illusions on them. I couldn't choose between two of them so I got them both. I knew he'd like them. I planned to put them on his locker first thing in the morning so that he could still make me a Valentine if he forgot. I was pretty nervous, though. What I found on my locker the next day when I went to school was one of the nicest surprises of my whole life. Not one person that I knew, not even high school kids, gave flowers. But there, on my locker, was a single red rose. David's mom had helped him put it in one of those little green florist's stem tubes with water in it so it wouldn't wilt. Twice-blessed flowers.

HERE IS WHERE FICTION IS MORE FUN. The girl should grow up, marry her sweet prince, and live happily ever after. Here's what happened. March. Mud season. Mom and Ray stopped seeing each other, and her boys were back. I decided to have a party and thought it would be cool to invite some older "men." Anna had been going out for a little while with an eighth grader. She broke up with him, but I invited him anyway. None of us seventh graders had invited eighth graders to a party. I changed all the lightbulbs downstairs in the living room to blue ones and put my posters up on the walls. Because my house was so much smaller than everyone else's in our group, it was hard to create the illusion of privacy—a kids-only lair. It still felt like my parents' living room, but the lights did help some. The other thing that made creating a cool, independent illusion of our own world hard was that my house was so far away, parents couldn't just drop you off and magically turn back into pumpkins and mice. There was a whole parental rigmarole about carpooling and directions and country roads and mud. It was decided that at 10 P.M., the boys would all go home in a couple of station wagons and the girls would have a sleep-over.

My party sucked beyond belief. Several couples broke up, I danced half the evening with Tim, the eighth grader, not even noticing that Dave was sitting by himself looking miserable until Rachel got mad at me for it, and by then it was time for the boys to go home. Thanks to me, and my big idea to invite older kids, the entire junior high school, seventh and eighth graders both, would know I had had a really bad party. Dave wouldn't look at me in school on Monday, and I didn't blame him. I guess I was going with Tim now. That weekend I wrote Dave a letter:

Sunday blah Afternoon
1968

Dear David,

I realize now what an ass I made out of myself and how I hurt lots of people. Tim is not the first person I've fallen for without much reason, but usually I don't go as far as to really get involved with them because I know it will pass in a day or two so I keep my head. I found out about Tim and he isn't at all what I thought he was, he's nice and everything but he isn't for me at all. I just wanted to tell you this but I don't expect much because if I were you I wouldn't take anyone back if they treated you the way I did. We both got it in a way, my party was a flop—not as bad as Gail's or Brian's party—but it was bad.

From me

I still have the letter because I never gave it to him. I was too ashamed.

And echoed in a well of silence.

19

"To Sir with Love"*

❧❀❧

Nothing in the voice of the cicada intimates how soon it will die.
　　　　　　　　　—quoted by Teddy in *Nine Stories*

SPRING VACATION WAS AROUND THE CORNER and my dad was taking
Matthew and me to England and Scotland for two weeks. I couldn't
wait. I had no idea, at the time, that it would be the last time we'd take a
real vacation together as a family. Writing about our last travels together, the twilight of an era, is bittersweet, like an Indian summer, a
temporary reprieve, a stay of winter. And like most tales of leaving
home, or the end of an era, something is lost, something is gained.

Daddy, Matthew, and I were off to London. Mom drove us to the
airport, fifteen minutes away, in Lebanon. The driveway to the airport
is easily missed. It's just past the dump, now called "sanitary" something
or other, and the crushed-stone pit. Back then, besides the dump and the
gravel pit, there were just miles of open fields growing cattle corn. Now
it's all shopping malls and fast food. I saw my first McDonald's a few
years later, on that stretch of Route 12-A, and watched the sign outside
with a kind of hypnotic fascination and disgust—like looking at a car
accident—as the numbers mounted: over 7 million sold, over 11 million
sold. I imagined all those carcasses stacked in great heaps in the parking
lot around the West Lebanon McDonald's.

---

*Lulu top hit for 1967, from the movie of the same title.

The airport was little more than a shack and a runway. Inside the shack was a small, five-stool lunch counter where guys sat and had a sandwich and coffee and watched the plane come in. On the lunch counter, by the cash register, was a wire rack of Wrigley's spearmint gum and yellow packets of Juicy Fruit gum. Next to that, another wire rack with rolls of Life Savers in two flavors: grown-up toothpaste-tasting peppermint, which my mom, in her never-ending battle against bad breath, bought when she forgot her green, "this-is-*not*-candy" Clorets with real chlorophyl, and the rainbow-colored rolls that kids bought. My system for eating the roll was red, yum; green, yuck, give it to Matthew; orange, so-so; yellow, so-so; and the white mystery flavor I thought was slightly sophisticated, like an acquired taste, not for babies. Matthew made it even better by saying "yuck" and trading the white ones to me for green ones. I liked seeing the packs of gum and the rolls of Life Savers neatly displayed, each in its own rack, a sight that predates another inroad into the disorder of the universe: the alarming confusion of the two, gum and Life Savers, in "yipes, stripes, fruit-striped gum." When that product made its way to Barto's store in Plainfield, it smelled good and Life Savery, but once you put it in your mouth, the stick got mushy and almost instantly lost its flavor. You wound up cramming the whole pack in your mouth within minutes and were left with a handful of empty wrappers and a big tasteless glob the color of paintbrush water.

We had a couple of hours to kill before the plane to New York was scheduled to take off. Travel was an event that not only required a ritual rising at dawn but until about 1965, white gloves. I have clear memories of riding in New York taxicabs looking down at my gloved hands. All those ritual designations that one is entering a different place—grandmother's, the city, church, a ship—were disappearing. When I was young, my experience of place had much more texture to it than now; the world was more like a pieced quilt—here a bit of a favorite summer dress, there my brother's overalls—than a factory-made blanket, uniform and alike. Although I dislike intensely the distinction clothes and habits make between people—old-money rich, nouveau riche; popular, untouchable; virtuous and slutty; and so on—I do miss the distinction clothes and habits can make between kinds of place. I can't quite put my finger on it, but there is a difference in tone between a special event or place providing a person with an excuse to wear something nice, and the idea that something nice requires a reciprocal formality on your part, like a thank-you note, or covering your head with a scarf when entering an Italian church.

It was a world where clothing could signify not what time it is, but rather, what *kind* of time it is. Gazing down at my white-gloved hands in a New York taxi, I slipped into a quiet reverie; someone knew where and when the cab would arrive, but for now, the packing, the hurrying, the carrying, the "doing" time was over and there was a respite, a "being" time to sit and just be, a little girl gazing at white gloves in a taxicab. In middle age, my white liturgist's robe usually signifies *what* time it is: it's time for church. I busily serve people wine and bread at the Communion rail, half-consciously worrying if the bread will run out, or if the music will finish before everyone is served and you're left with an awkward silence in which all the personal bodily sounds of swallowing and creaking are projected publicly in the splendid acoustics of our fine church, or whether I'll spill the wine on one of the tiny old ladies kneeling—it's a bit tricky to offer the cup so close to the rail, and God forbid they should wear a wide-brimmed hat and you can't even see where their mouth is, which doubles the leap of faith in the offering. But once in a while, there comes a time when the work of the Mass ceases, the priest or guest speaker is giving a sermon or delivering a long liturgy, and I sit on the liturgist's bench and gaze down at my robed hands, not quite mine, smelling the hempy smell of cloth and dust. I'm a child lying on my back in a barn among the roped bales of hay, looking up at the dust dancing in shafts of sunlight streaming in through knotholes and eaves. Barn swallows darting like miracles in the air. A cloud passes between the sun and the stained-glass windows that slowly blink like the eyes of a cat in the sunshine. Sounds of language wash over me, sounds that fall on my soul like a gentle rain on dry roots. It is not time to react to language, to agree or disagree. It's a different kind of time, a time to lay me down in green pastures and beside still waters, a time to restore my soul.

A MAN IN A UNIFORM announced that the plane was ready for boarding. We went out the door of the shack onto the tarmac. A waist-high chain-link fence stood between us and the runway. We watched the men push a great staircase on wheels up to the plane's door, high off the ground, and then someone opened the little gate in the fence, which most of us could have stepped over, and welcomed us aboard. I climbed the stairs and went inside the airplane. The aisle sloped sharply upward and I automatically reached for the seat-backs to help me propel myself up to the front. My brother and I looked into the open cockpit. The captain chatted with my brother and showed him stuff. Once we were all seated, the captain started to rev up the propellers, which seemed to come on one by one, at least that's what it sounded like. The stewardess talked to us in a friendly way and checked our seat belts and we were off. Later she gave us soda with roundish ice cubes in it and a "snack"—a word not permitted in our house. Daddy was disgusted that my brother and I had each eaten our whole roll of Life Savers. He said, "Can't you just eat one or two and put the rest in your pocket to save for later?" "No" remained unsaid.

Someone told me that the pink blanket we could see over the island of Manhattan was smog. I still find it frightening. I told myself to try not to breathe too much when we landed. La Guardia was a blur as we disembarked (the bastard word *deplane* was not yet invented), collected our luggage, and made our way to the taxi that took us into the city for an overnight stay. My father had something to do in the city before we went to England I guess, I don't remember.

I was twelve, my brother eight, my father forty-nine. The Plaza had fallen out of favor with my father, and carrousel horses had fallen out of favor with me. We stayed across Fifth Avenue at the Sherry Netherland. I was nearly beside myself when the maid, all aflutter, told me the Beatles had just vacated our room. I was madly in love with Paul McCartney. (Oh, middle age, I just had to look up how to spell McCartney!) I spent *hours* looking for strands of hair or other such treasures—alas, to no avail. My little brother humored me and looked, too; that is, when he could tear himself away from the window where he was counting taxicabs. He kept coming up to me, helpfully, with lint.

I was soon to have a second chance to be near my beloved Paul in England, center of the universe. We took a Checker cab to JFK International Airport. It "cost a fortune," my father said.

I would see St. Mark's in Venice a few years later and hear Monteverdi vespers sung by a four-part choir from its balconies, north, south, east, and west, but my first cathedral, and, to date, unsurpassed in heights of wonder and awesome vastness, was the new Trans World Airlines Terminal. What is it about hugeness, vastness that is enclosed and encompassed, that feels the way it does? Here were polished walkways suspended in the air like two arms stretching upward to the heavens. It was like *The Jetsons,* only better. Trees were growing *inside* in containers; I'd never in my wildest imagination thought of an indoor glade. The trees had smooth, jet-black pebbles covering their feet. My father picked one up and caressed the surface with his thumb. He said how marvelous it would be to have some beautiful stones like that at home. He put it back carefully.

We went upstairs to a restaurant where we could look out a floor-to-ceiling window and see planes taking off and landing. Lights began to come on. Spotlights in blues and whites lit up the stage drama before us. We were up past our bedtime, and we knew it, which added to the excitement.

When we boarded the transatlantic jet, I was in for another big surprise. Daddy had booked us in first class. The seats were enormous. He complained unquietly about the cost; it was fabulously expensive, something he'd never do for himself, but he thought it was worth it when traveling with children, "so you guys can stretch out and sleep," he explained, justifying himself to I'm not sure whom.

Matthew collected things. Some small boys are like little crows. He collected the little salt and pepper containers, the wet-wash, the small, individual-size wrapped bars of soap, and our flight-pack cologne. By the end of our vacation, he had more tiny bottles of cologne and little soaps than any other eight-year-old boy on the planet. As if any eight-year-old boy would ever "freshen up" as invited on the packet. These went right into his shoe boxes and dresser drawers alongside his marbles and Matchbox cars. Matthew wasn't just a casual collector who tossed his specimens into a drawer and forgot about them. He reveled in his collections. He took them out again and again, and not just to look; he patted them, sorted them, ran his fingers through them. His was a truly sensual pleasure in accumulation. He told me once, when he was in second grade, that he wished he were Richie Rich (a wealthy comic-book character) so that he could have a room full of gold coins and just roll around in them.

I, on the other hand, wished to feel Paul's lips on mine as he sang, "Close your eyes and I'll kiss you." In sixth grade, I cut out of a magazine a large picture of Paul's face and taped it to a pillow so I could practice kissing him. How far to open my lips troubled me, to find the right distance between the Scylla of closed-mouth child's kissing and the Charybdis of *gross* tongues. The pillow fell far too short of reality; it was maddeningly frustrating, like when I was little and my friend Rachel and I lay in a field staring up at the stars, willing ourselves to fly. We almost did, we felt ourselves lifting, but just couldn't quite make it off the ground. So close and yet so far. But every mile our jet traveled across the Atlantic was bringing me closer to that sweet object of my desire. My father had said it might be possible to meet John Lennon through his publisher but he didn't make any promises. Where there is John, there is Paul . . .

After supper, I put on the eyeshades and slippers that were in my TWA toiletry kit and tried to go to sleep. I'd never slept except in a bed lying down and I tried to lie down in my chair. My brother fit perfectly and was asleep amid the comforting glow from the rows of night-lights, and cozy pools of light shining on private readers. I kept trying to crumple up my legs like those bendy wire tricks that, I'm told, if you fold them just the right way, unlocks the puzzle. Finally, I draped my legs over the armrest into my brother's seat, which, had he been awake, would have elicited howls of protest and probably a border war. It was safe for now and I fell asleep.

We awoke to washcloths and orange juice and too-bright lighting. The captain said we'd be landing at Heathrow in twenty minutes, where the local time was 7:25 A.M. My brother collected more things off his breakfast tray. We took off our TWA slippers and put on our shoes again, brushed our teeth with these cool toothbrushes that came in two pieces inside a plastic case, and looked out the window for land. England.

At Heathrow, we walked through miles of corridors. Daddy had a rule that you had to carry your own luggage—not the big stuff that was checked, but whatever you had brought with you—toys, handbags, overnight cases—you were responsible for. It seemed fair and sensible to me and nipped in the bud all that whining about carry me, carry this, etc. It also made me feel proud to carry my own weight, as it were. At customs, a man with an English accent asked if my father was traveling for business or pleasure, and Daddy answered him succinctly and politely. He often horsed around with people, but having been in the army, he always knew when not to horse around. I never saw him joke around with a stranger—a waitress, someone in line at a checkout counter—who didn't truly laugh and enjoy the familiarity and the humor. He was a terrific judge about that sort of thing. He never made strangers feel as though the joke were on them, but rather, that they were in on a joke. And you never had to cringe the way most kids do if their father starts to joke around in public. The customs officer stamped our passports, and we were on our way.

We waited in a queue for a taxi to take us to our hotel. We got into one of the large, identical black London taxis waiting patiently, no honking or hollering—"C'mon, Mac, let's move it, pedal's on the right"—as in New York. My father reached his hand up and touched the roof of the cab, a gesture of benediction. He loves anything with headroom—London cabs, rooms with high ceilings—and takes anything less as a personal affront. He used to reach his hand up and touch the ceiling in the addition to the Red house my mother had planned, cursing it and scowling darkly nearly every time he entered the room. I believe he remarked how marvelous London taxis are, touching the roof, every single time we entered one the entire trip. I'll eat my hat if he didn't do the exact same thing, gesture and words, last year, some thirty years later, when he and his new wife traveled to London.

The cab let us off in front of the Cadogan Hotel in Sloane Square. It was across the street from a beautiful little park that shone in the bright morning sun. The hotel wasn't like the big ones I was used to in New York; it seemed more like a friendly old brownstone on the Upper East Side, all gleaming brass and Oriental rugs rather than the Plaza's large chandeliers and fields of plush carpeting. I liked both varieties very, very much. What I didn't like was the birdcage elevator that was to bring us up to our rooms on the third floor. I'd never seen one before, and when the operator opened the screen to let us in, I balked. I knew instantly, and with total certainty, that there was absolutely no chance I could make my body step inside. Wild horses, Nazis, it was just not going to happen. I stood there, blocking the way, I imagine, for enough time that the porter began looking impatient in that tight, superior way the British can do when they want to. I said simply, "I can't." My father didn't say a word to me; he informed the porter we preferred to walk, and upstairs we went, suitcases and all, as if it were the most normal thing in the world not to be able to get into an elevator all of a sudden. Sometimes my father's topsy-turvy, Alice-like inversions of what's normal can be pretty wonderful. He is the only person I know who would not have at least tried, with varying degrees of patience, to suggest, "Oh, honey, don't be silly, there's nothing to be afraid of."

At the top of the stairs, the porter opened our rooms and my brother and I walked into the twin-bedded one. Daddy followed us in and motioned me to keep walking. Mine was the single room. Unbeknownst to me, he had booked me into a single, and he and my brother were to share a room. He said, matter-of-factly, that I was getting to an age where I should have my own room. The boys would bunk in together. Somehow both my brother and I felt special.

My room was lovely. It had tiny blue flowers on the wallpaper and a sink, right in the room, with stiff white linen hand towels. It was probably the first time in my life I washed up voluntarily. I sat on the bed and looked out the window at the park. It was green, green, green. I'd never seen anything like it. It didn't have that dusty look of parks in New York, nor the wildness of the outdoors in New Hampshire, nor the marigold artificiality of gardens planted in front of banks or courthouses or traffic islands. Lush, verdant, vibrant, you could feel the energy of the plants and flowers tumbling and laughing in great masses, like children at recess, rather than sitting in stiff rows like soldiers. Yet somehow there was a pleasing order to it all; each plant had room to express the shape it held within its roots, without crowding out its neighbor. Lovely green lawns flowed around islands and banks of flowers creating calm, open places to rest the eyes and mind and soul.

We went to St. James's Park and fed the ducks, marveling at the variety, and successfully identified them by name with the help of a poster of English waterfowl that the park service had so sensibly and thoughtfully posted for the benefit of those interested in such things. Matthew fed peanuts to the chubby little black squirrels, distant cousins of our big American gray ones.

We went to Buckingham Palace to see the changing of the guard.

Matthew watched for about ten seconds and then turned around to re-sume taking pictures of cars. He took rolls and rolls of film, with my fa-ther's blessing, of exactly what interested him and nothing else. We have almost a whole album full of pictures of nothing but cars and the occa-sional stranger's behind who happened to get in the way of his camera as he focused on yet another car or lorry or taxi.

My father, again, was terrific about not forcing museums or other things one "should" see on children. We took a ride up the Thames on a tour boat, and the guy kept talking about Greenwich mean time, and let us off, presumably in Greenwich, for a few minutes to see absolutely nothing. Someone, I forget who, got snotty with my father. He was in-censed, not so much at the snottiness itself, but at the injustice of it, of the British looking down their noses at Americans. "They forget *we* bailed them out in the war," he said to me. It's a touchy thing with Yankee Anglophiles, being snubbed that is. I saw a lot of it during my three years at Oxford. Some Yanks reacted by becoming more British than the British. I honest to God met a first-year graduate student who, at a drinks party, when I asked him where he was from, thinking Sussex or Surrey, proclaimed in Shakespearean *alto voce,* "Gaddy, Indi-onna." (Yes, that's Gary, Indiana, folks.)

Other Yanks, such as myself, who had been raised saying *trousers* and *tomahtos,* had a heretofore unexperienced surge of patriotism; I was tempted to go out and buy a "jogging costume," that is to say, track suit, emblazoned with the American flag on one shoulder and PEGGY #1 on the other. (Wearing your workout clothes outside the sporting arena is, for the British, akin to wearing one's pajamas in public; it's just not *done,* dear, except, of course, by those dreadful Frisbee-playing Americans noising up the college gardens.)

My father was most comfortable in the company of the not-quite-English Brits from the former colonies. We ate Indian food at every op-portunity and listened to Daddy talk about how marvelous the Indians were as a people. He admired their delicate hands and wrists, gentle manners, and their religion, which he called the jewel of the East. Like all his love affairs, it was successful from afar. Had he experienced the diverse humanity of the continent, the sometimes officious, tangled bu-reaucracy, and the daily reality of pecking orders at the post office or on trains, instead of waiters in London restaurants, or holy men in his books, I think his ardor would have soured as quickly as it did with any loved one in the flesh.

We spent the next morning at Harrods. My father marveled at the great Food Hall; we could hardly tear him away. He finally went upstairs and bought my brother a beautiful Harris Tweed suit. I chose a blue mini-skirt with suede buttons up the front and a suede-fringed belt. It cost ten pounds, and my father was absolutely appalled by the price. He almost ruined it for me, but not quite. I took the tags off and wore it on the spot, for we were headed for Carnaby Street. He calmed down during the walk, and by the time we got to Carnaby Street, he discreetly stepped back and let me walk a little bit ahead of him so it wasn't totally obvious to all those cool kids that I was with the old guy behind me. I didn't dare buy any of the cool stuff like dangly plastic daisy earrings while he was around, though I vowed to sneak off somehow and come back later in the week.

I got my chance when we went to visit a family we knew from Maine, in London on sabbatical. Their son, Keith, object of Rachel's long-distance desire, was my age and had been in a movie. He had a blond Beatle haircut and offered to show me around. My father told me later that he watched us walk across the park together from the MacNamaras' window. "You guys looked good together," he said.

Keith's mother approached me at a funeral last year. I hadn't seen her in nearly thirty years, and she asked me if I remembered visiting them in London. "Your father was quite upset that you'd rather go off with Keith than with him, do you remember?" No, I hadn't noticed in my rush for the door. Keith took me to Madame Tussaud's and back to Carnaby Street and we held hands walking. He wore a button that said "If you had sex last night smile!" When we met up with my father and brother in a Wimpy's for hamburgers later on, Daddy laughed just as hard as we did at the grown-ups' reactions to the button. Our young waitress blushed deeply and giggled as if we had found her out somehow.

The following day we took a trip to Hampton Court to go through the maze and to see one of Daddy's oldest friends, Bet Mitchell. She and her former husband Mike were my father's closest friends and also his neighbors when he'd lived in Westport, Connecticut. Matthew enjoyed racing around the paths through the hedge maze at Hampton Court. I panicked and, I'm sorry to say, bolted *through* the six-foot-tall hedges in the direction of the sun and got the hell out. Bet took us to lunch and I ordered duck *à l'orange,* which sounded fancy and grown-up, and I tried not to struggle with the cutlery. Bet was like *The New Yorker* people in that she included me fully in the conversation, listened to me with great interest and quiet respect when I felt like saying something, but left me just as respectfully alone when I didn't. Somehow I felt included even when I wasn't talking and "joining in" in the conventional sense.

After lunch, Daddy, Bet, my brother, and I went to visit Edna O'Brien for the afternoon. He told me with a conspiratorial wink that Edna was a good writer and a hell of a nice girl, but she wrote some *really* dirty stuff. (Not crummy, bad dirty, but sexy, naughty dirty.) Like a kid talking about a naughty and daring classmate, he clearly was really rather shocked and giggly about what she chose to write about. I wonder how many other writers of banned books are, in fact, rather prudish.

After tea, Edna took us out to a park where something was going on that was supposed to be of interest to children. The park was packed with people, and I had an attack of claustrophobia. I had trouble breathing and told my father quietly so the others wouldn't hear. He picked me up and put me on his shoulders, high above the crowd. He said to the others that it was too crowded here to see anything and strode off across the park as if it were the most natural thing in the world to carry a five-foot-seven-inch twelve-year-old on one's shoulders, which perhaps he thought it was.

The only not so fun part of the trip was the main reason he had come over in the first place. He had been corresponding with a teenage girl, and things had blossomed into a pen pal romance. He was to meet her for the first time in person. We planned to drive through Scotland with her in search of where my father's beloved *39 Steps* was filmed.

We flew to Edinburgh, where the girl met our plane. I could tell something was wrong the instant they greeted each other. I didn't know what was wrong until he told me, later in the trip, how terribly embarrassed he was when he saw her. Embarrassed and guilty. I asked him why, and he looked at me as if I were puzzlingly obtuse, when it was as plain as the nose on her face. "She's terribly homely, poor girl, I had no idea." Now this girl did not have two heads, nor was she ugly; she was plain. And that was that for my father. At the time I accepted it as law: boys don't make passes at girls who wear glasses, requiring no further question on my part. Who knows, maybe she didn't think he was such a bargain either. I rather doubt it though.

She was quite nice, but rather shy and awkward, and I had to share a room with her for the duration of the trip. They would not have shared a room, regardless of attraction, since, unlike my mother, my father was not of a generation or a mind-set in which a gentleman was remotely open about his sexual activities, if indeed there were any. This made all the difference in the world to me; the lack of overt sexuality on his part made things decent in my own mind, unlike my mother's behavior, which so mortified and disgusted me. I wish, for this girl's sake, though, that she had had a room of her own, rather than having to share one with me. I felt so sorry for her and I thought she probably wanted to cry but couldn't because I was around. She sniffled a lot at night, but I was afraid to say anything, to try to offer a kind word, because she was the type to have allergies and adenoids, and I didn't want to make her feel any more homely if she was just sniffling and not crying. My memory gets a bit cloudy at this point because I saw Hitchcock's *Psycho* at a local Scottish movie theater, which unhinged me so that the next couple of days are a blurry mess, as if seen through a shower curtain.

What I saw of Scotland, as we drove from Edinburgh to the west coast, I thought was spectacularly beautiful, but most of the time I was horribly carsick and either throwing up or lying still in the backseat with my eyes squeezed shut trying not to throw up. Most of the scenery I saw was at the all too few and far between spots in the road where it was possible to pull over and let me vomit outside. The respite from the nauseating motion, the cool air in my face, and the relief of having just vomited made the already beautiful countryside look like God's finest on the day of creation. Damp heather and heath smelled heavenly, lakes sparkled like Pearly Gates.

My father was absolutely delighted when we were delayed by a flock of sheep in the road. That was how, in *The 39 Steps,* the hero and heroine were able to escape, handcuffed to each other, from their captor's car. The sheep blocked the road, and while the driver was shooing them, our heroes snuck out the back door and hid under a little stone bridge over a stream. We looked for signs to Alt-na Shelloch, but came up empty.

Years later, when I was home from Oxford, I was dating a British investment banker whose family had a house and farm in Scotland. My dad asked him, when they were playing golf over in Windsor, about *The 39 Steps,* if he knew where it was filmed. My friend's mother not only knew, she remembered the filming, and when I visited, she pointed out the very house, still with its lovely diamond windowpanes, where Robert Donat was "led up the garden path, or is it down, I'm never sure." I sent my father some photographs I took of the house and of the little stone bridge where they hid by the stream.

We drove westward across Scotland from Edinburgh to Oban. At Oban, or perhaps it was north a bit at Mallaig, we caught a ferry to the Isle of Skye. A big seagull bit my brother on the finger as he held out bread to them at the railing. All I remember is him crying a lot—it was a nasty bite that broke the skin—and my father was consumed in remorse that he had let Matthew feed them by hand. My father was *furious* with the seagulls.

Things picked up again as we dropped off his not-to-be girlfriend, boarded the *Queen Elizabeth II* at Southampton, and set sail for home. Thank God it's just cars and sailboats, and not ocean liners, that make me vomit. Once I figured out where everything was, including all exits and lifeboats, I relaxed and enjoyed myself. I met up with a group of teenagers the second day and really started to have fun. That night, I stayed out later than my bedtime hanging out with them. Daddy came looking for me. I was holding hands with a young man as we walked down a corridor with a bunch of high school juniors and seniors headed for the dance area. When we turned the corner, I spotted my father coming from the other direction. I ducked into a side room, dragging my date by the hand. Daddy didn't come after me. He allowed me to pretend I didn't see him and to return on my own, a few minutes later, so as to let me keep my dignity. At an age when the mere existence of a parent was mortifying in public, Daddy was about as unmortifying as a parent could be.

❦

I ARRIVED BACK AT SCHOOL TO A SLEW OF NOTES, asking after the Beatles, planning new dances, and with fast-breaking fashion bulletins. I'm sad to say, I had no news to report of the Beatles. Crazy as it might sound, I hold but one regret from my childhood—by regret, I mean sorrow for things that could have been, rather than sorrow for things that I wish were possible, such as my parents' mental health, for example. I really, really regret that I didn't meet Paul. Then. Although my father promised me that if I still felt the same way in a couple of years, he'd do his best to arrange it, I didn't know it at the time, but, of course, the magic was not timeless. It did not belong to the realm where there is no difference between ten and twenty, or ten and eighty. It belonged to a time when the whole world was bursting into flower, and a twelve-year-old girl, even a tall one, was easily camouflaged in a sea of sunflowers; a time when big Day-Glo daisy stickers bloomed on countless bedroom walls, paisley swirled across bedspreads and dresses, dashikis enrobed black and white alike in colors of the sun, the trail of her scent undetectable amidst great wafts of Yardley's English Lavender, Jean Naté lemons, incense and peppermints.

20

Safe Harbor:
A Brief Interlude Between Islands

❧❦❧

THE SUMMER OF '68, BETWEEN SEVENTH AND EIGHTH GRADE, I was off to a ski camp on a glacier in June somewhere in Montana. What I wound up learning was not how to be a better slalom racer, but something far more important to me. I learned what life was like in an extended family who made room in their lives for an islander. My technique in both areas, family living and skiing, needed a lot of improvement. I had won medals in a couple of races, but only in downhill events where, at that age anyway, the person who could live on that thin edge between movement and disaster, and keep a clear head, won. I did okay at giant slalom, too, where the gates were set far apart, and again, it was more speed than finesse. My nemesis, however, was the slalom event with its zillions of poles set so closely together it was almost like ballet to get through; you had to be so quick and nimble and graceful. I was a nervy, powerful skier, but with all the finesse of a cannonball. I just didn't have the chops to go all out and do all those tiny turns at the same time. I almost always skipped a gate or caught an edge and fell.

The camp bus met us at the airport to take us from Billings, Montana, to Cook City and base camp. I don't remember how long the journey was, several hours at least, but I do remember thinking we were all going to die. I'd never been on such steep mountains and such narrow roads. The girl next to me took a look out the window on one curve and promptly vomited all over the seat. I'm sorry for the girl, but it turned out to be one of the best pieces of luck I've run into. If God works in mysterious ways, this surely was one of them; I landed in the arms of a family who, to this day, remain some of the most important people in my life. A girl named Liza invited me to sit with her rather than in the vomit. Liza's mother and two younger brothers were on the bus, and by the time we got to Cook City, her mom had arranged it so Liza and I could be roommates.

The town was spooky. It looked like a stage set for the Clint Eastwood movie where, in the opening scene, some guy gets bullwhipped for about forever. (I can't tell you the rest because I ran out of the movie theater.) It was all dusty with unfinished splintery-wood buildings; the sort of place that might still have outhouses, I thought with dread. But when I saw a big sign on the general store that read "We sell fireworks," I knew everything would be okay. Contraband was the coolest. On a trip to Venice with my grandmother and mother, I had sailed through New York customs with one red and one black Venetian stiletto knife, scored on a stroll through the back streets near St. Mark's, tucked in my sweet little navy blue purse along with my beautiful Murano glass egg and a millefiori broach. Anything to declare?

The first night Liza and I had a scare. We caught some creepy boy peering in our cabin window. Her mom, Mrs. R., immediately had us moved into the main hotel. The next morning, after breakfast, we were trucked up to the snow line in the back of some sort of convoy of dump trucks. There, we were met by a Sno-Cat with ropes hanging from the back that we were to hold on to while it pulled us up to the glacier. It was a sunny day in June, the snow sparkled, and I felt confident because I was one of the few kids who knew how to fashion a makeshift Poma lift with my ski poles on the rope tow, freeing my hands, and because I had the pleasure of my new friend's company. Liza's mom, an instructor at their local ski area, had covered our ears and noses with zinc oxide so we wouldn't get sunburned. All the cool instructors were wearing zinc oxide the same way, I was relieved to discover. I couldn't wait to get started.

As the Sno-Cat towed us higher and higher, I tried to take a breath and suddenly found there was no air. I started blacking out, or "redding" out really; the zigzags that blanketed my vision from the outside in were red not black. I'm fuzzy on how I got back down to breathable air. They said it was altitude sickness and it would pass in a few days, but try as I might, it never did. Liza's youngest brother, Joel, was having a ball, but the rest of the family was less than thrilled about the skiing, and so Mrs. R., never one to let an opportunity go to waste, arranged to borrow a station wagon, and we spent the next few days touring nearby Yellowstone National Park. What a blast that was, like walking around in one of my science fiction books, great mud pits burping sulfurous bubbles, otherworldly blue-green, jewel-like craters of liquid, and geysers of warm water that carried smells from faraway places, journey from the center of the earth.

Stranger still was being a member of such a closely knit family in which parents and children did not, for the most part, lead separate lives. I had no template for that, not even in books, where, at that age, most of the characters were orphans or living with a strange aunt or running with a pack of friends away from home on holiday. Foreign "adventures" I understood; daily life with a family was entering terra incognita. After camp, I spent most of the rest of the summer with them at their home in Pennsylvania. Liza's brothers, Sig and Joel, shared a room plastered with ski and racing-car posters, while she and I bunked in together in the "princess suite," the small room of a beloved only daughter, done to the nines in "girl" thanks to Nana's sewing machine, and Kurtz Brothers' Department Store downtown, where Mr. R. was a partner. I had a great summer, riding Joel's go-cart around their cul-de-sac, riding around in cars with boys Liza knew because she was sixteen. I tried my best, at the time, to ignore her middle brother's existence because at thirteen, he was, technically, a year older than I and, as such, was a walking threat to my inflated opinion of my own maturity. No way am I *that* young, I'd think, looking at him, rolling my eyes.

When God was doling out patience and good cheer, Mrs. R. got a triple portion. I had no idea how to behave in a family that wasn't at war, or whose parents hadn't, basically, recused themselves from active duty. Mrs. R. still teases me to this day, saying, "Remember how mad you got when we said, no, you couldn't do [such and such]?" I was, indeed, ready to put up my dukes and fight to the death over every little thing. "You used to say your dad would have let you." (I kept it to myself that I would have told my mother to f—— off.) I don't remember my reaction so much as their saying, firmly and gently, "Well, dear, you're in our house now and we say no." *Big* sulks hurled at Mrs. R., which didn't seem to trouble her in the least. She was the grown-up and I was the kid, and if I wanted to sulk, fine; it wasn't going to rain on her parade. I stopped sulking.

Stripped of my bluster, though, I felt downright uncouth, like a bull in a china shop. I kept trying to plow through things that required civilized stepping. I don't mean things like using the right fork or pinkie spoon; it was all this weird stuff like operating under the assumption that, come what may, you're going to work things out, because you're family and you're going to be family until death do you part. Even after.

Through the years, I'd go with their family to my first wedding, first funeral, first bar mitzvah; thanksgiving and mourning, celebrations and days of atonement. And the same cousins, aunts, uncles, grandparents, and children showed up, rain or shine, at family gatherings year after year. If some couldn't make it or were sick or had passed away, they still remained a presence, their stories were told. Even the ex-wife (for the longest time there was only one in the extended family) didn't just vanish into oblivion; all someone had to do was mention her horrible poodles, Beaujolais and Bubbles (BoBo and Bubbie), and the names alone were known to provoke untold glasses of ginger ale or milk laughed up through the nose at the kids' table.

What a singular thing of beauty to have had the experience of moving from the kids' table at large family gatherings, to the teenagers' group, to the young-adults-who-ought-to-be-getting-married-soon, to the blessed producers of GRANDCHILDREN (oy, do we have pictures!), who now sit at the kids' table together. What a ballast as the planet hurtles through the universe, a way to check in and regain perspective and a sense of where you fit in, or more importantly, *that* you fit into a pattern of life regardless of how strong or how tenuous your grip on life may be at a given time. Nor is this some perfect fiction like the Waltons. There is luggage teetering off the overhead rack a-plenty, but no one goes unclaimed. And there is always a place set for Elijah.

TOWARD THE END OF THE SUMMER, the whole family—Mr. and Mrs. R., Liza, Sig, Joel, and I—piled into the station wagon to drive me back to

Cornish. Mrs. R. asked me recently if I remembered the big argument my parents had had after we arrived. "You had a strep throat and Claire wanted to get you on antibiotics. Jerry wanted to treat it homeopathically. I think your mother won." She smiled, shaking her head. *Plus ça change* . . .

I don't remember that particular argument; why should I when I'd heard variations on that wretched theme my whole life. Even if it had been a real doozy, it would have been eclipsed anyway by emerging events. Shortly after the R.s went home, Daddy called to take us swimming in the Coxes' pond in Windsor. This is something we often did each summer—we had a standing invitation. I put on my new two-piece bathing suit that I'd bought at Mr. R.'s store, threw on a T-shirt and shorts, and waited outside for my father to pick up my brother and me.

I'm sitting in the front seat of the Jeep. Daddy all of a sudden looks at me as though he's never seen me before. Oh, God, he's looking right at my chest. "Is that really you under there?" he asks. There is no right answer. Either way I'm a phony.

They weren't falsies exactly; all bathing suits had shaped cups in them back then. Which isn't to say, however, that I didn't like the effect, but *not* on him. The boobs were real enough . . . well, almost, but immediately I noticed a change in his behavior. I'd come under watch, suspected of being one of *them,* the enemy, a phony. I started to become the object of his suspicion and attacks, previously reserved for my mother, athletic men, and college professors.

At the same time that my sexual development was catapulting me out of my father's world, life at my mother's was increasingly sexually charged and unsafe. She was sleeping with younger and younger guys, college students in fact, and as I grew taller and prettier, they were looking at me in that predatory way. It was mortifying having my mother behaving like a wild, rebellious sister. I had heard from several different sources, usually kids with much older brothers, that my mother's nickname around Dartmouth's campus was Mrs. Robinson. I didn't understand the full implications of that until I saw *The Graduate,* where, to my horror, both the mother, Mrs. Robinson, and her daughter were objects of Dustin Hoffman's character's sexual attention. This added an additional layer of humiliation and revoltingness to the Mac "baby-sitting" affair, to think that he might have been playing the "Graduate." I also took it to be a portent and knew I had to get out of that house before I got any more developed, or it was just a matter of time before one of those boys woke me in the middle of the night and might not take no for an answer. I slept with my fists balled in readiness and my baseball bat under the bed.

I wanted to move in with my dad and continue on at Hanover Junior High where I had had my first happy school year ever. Next fall, in eighth grade, maybe I'd get the nerve to write to Dave and see if he could ever like me again, and maybe Mom would get back together with Ray and settle down. No maybes, it was *out* of the question. It would have interfered too much with my father's work. With that door slammed, it may surprise some fans of Holden Caulfield, hater of prep schools, but at age twelve I was packed off to boarding school for the remainder of my "childhood." There was no room at either of my parents' for me to grow up any more.

PART THREE

BEYOND CORNISH

❧❦

And moving thro' a mirror clear
That hangs before her all the year,
Shadows of the world appear.
There she sees the highway near
Winding down to Camelot.

—"The Lady of Shalott," Alfred, Lord Tennyson

21

Island Redux

❧❦❧

While this is often a very stimulating and touching place, I person-
ally suspect that certain children in this world, like your magnifi-
cent son Buddy as well as myself, are perhaps best suited to
enjoying this privilege only in a dire emergency or when they know
great discord in their family life.

—Seymour Glass, "Hapworth 16, 1924"

THE BROCHURE FOR CROSS MOUNTAIN SCHOOL had arrived. It was
a foregone conclusion that, were I to go to boarding school, it
would be Cross Mountain, since my grandmother had offered to pay for
my tuition as she'd done for my cousin, Gavin's child, to attend. All the
"best" people sent their children there, dear. The Rockefellers, the Bid-
dles, the Aga Khan's daughter, heads of foreign dictatorships with messy
wars in Central America, heiresses with messy divorces, people in the
arts, writers, producers, movie stars. I looked at the pictures. The school
was in the midst of the Adirondack Mountains. About eighty children,
age seven or eight to thirteen, fourth through the eighth grade, had the
privilege of living there September through May. Parents had the option
of sending their children to camp there, too, June through August. Like
Holden Caulfield's Pencey Prep, Cross Mountain appeared to be bullish
on "molding character." Holden, reading from Pencey's brochure, said:

"Since 1888 we have been molding boys into splendid, clear-
thinking young men." Strictly for the birds. They don't do any
damn more *mold*ing at Pencey than they do at any other school.

And I didn't know anybody there that was splendid and clear-thinking and all. Maybe two guys. If that many. And they probably *came* to Pencey that way. (*Catcher,* p. 2)

Cross Mountain School promised to teach children what they called the three Rs: to mold them into persons "Rugged, Resourceful, and Resilient." (I recall Winston Churchill referring to the B.S.s of his British boarding school. We were, he said, "Beaten, Buggered, and Starved.") The brochure was full of photographs of smiling, pink-cheeked children harvesting vegetables on the school farm, doing barn chores—very *Little Red Book*. No paisley dresses with pumps and stockings here. Their list of required clothing was specific and Spartan: work boots, black buckle galoshes, denim barn jacket, long underwear, and thick socks, jeans, and work shirts. Dresses were permitted on Sunday evenings at dinner.

If I'd known how the school's creators, Herbert and Kit Watson, had been occupied before they had students, how they came to teaching, that icy apprehension that I was entering someone else's dream that was to become my nightmare would have been a certainty. Recently I read the Watsons' biographies in the alumni brochure. Herbert Watson's story is entitled, in bold letters:

All Things That Go On At The School Come Right Out Of My Childhood

As a child, I might have thought, how cool, the same way countless people have said to me, "It must be so cool to have J. D. Salinger for your father." When *young* persons, for whom my father has said he writes, read Holden's response to his little sister when she asked him what he wants to be when he grows up, I think they have a very different reaction from that of a real grown-up, one for whom all things do *not* come right out of one's childhood, unmediated by maturation. Holden said:

> . . . I keep picturing all these little kids playing some game in this big field of rye and all. Thousands of little kids, and nobody's around—nobody big, I mean—except me. And I'm standing on the edge of some crazy cliff. What I have to do, I have to catch everybody if they start to go over the cliff—I mean

if they're running and they don't look where they're going I have to come out from somewhere and *catch* them. That's all I do all day. I'd just be the catcher in the rye and all. I know it's crazy, but that's the only thing I'd really like to be.

(*Catcher,* p. 173)

When I read this passage as an adult with a child of my own, my first reaction was outrage. Not at Holden, it's a nice dream for a boy to have. But outrage at the fact that I once was one of those kids. Where are the grown-ups? Why are those kids allowed to play so close to the edge of a cliff? Where are the responsible adults who should build a secure place for those kids to play, or a fence at least so that some young boy like Holden or some young girl like me doesn't have to engage in perpetual rescue?

My grown-up reaction to the title of Herbert Watson's biography is to wonder: Have you learned nothing as an adult? On reflection, my experience at this school is a story about what can *really* happen when people—"nobody big"—get together and decide to play school at the edge of some crazy cliff. In Kit's bio she said, "After college I came to New York City. . . . I didn't know what I wanted to do, or what I *could* do. Mamma said that as a child I collected younger children and played school, made markets, and ran shows. I loved children. I applied at several of the progressive schools—no luck. Eventually I got a job as a playground supervisor to tide me over that first winter." She applied for a job with Harriet Johnson at the Bureau of Educational Experiments. She was accepted, and in her interview she said she was asked, " 'Miss Cavendish, do you know why we gave you the job?' 'No, I don't.' 'Because you don't know a *thing* about education.' I didn't have a lot of preconceived ideas!"

Her husband Herbert's story begins with his family's farm on the edge of failure. After high school, he won a scholarship to Cornell's School of Agriculture to take a twelve-week course on farm management. He worked at the liberal arts part of the college to make ends meet, he said, "waiting table for the rich college boys wearing raccoon coats" (the very same rich boys and girls whose children would be waiting table and mucking out stalls at Herbert's Cross Mountain). He took courses in farm machinery repair, veterinary medicine, feeds, and feeding. "I came home an educated farmer after my twelve-week winter course at Cornell. I started out big guns—next summer I was going to make the farm break even. Then one hot summer's day I was cultivating corn in a field with a horse and a cultivator, and a man came down the road and wanted to know what I'd be doing in the fall. I said I'd be tending the cows and putting out the cowshit—that's how farmers talk. So he said, 'I'm looking for a schoolteacher,' and I said I didn't know of any in the neighborhood, and he said, 'I'm looking at you. I've been talking to the principal of your old high school, and he thought you could do the job.' " That was how Herbert Watson became a teacher at the age of eighteen. He liked teaching and enrolled in a tuition-free teachers college, but was not satisfied with it. He knew he could never afford the tuition at Cornell—about the equivalent of Cross Mountain tuition—but eventually went to Antioch, where the students could work their way through. There, he supported himself working as an assembly-line worker at Ford, a magazine salesman, and a teacher at the New Jersey State Institution for Feeble-Minded Males . . .

Herbert, in his speech to the Cross Mountain School graduating class of 1950, said, "Generally speaking, I think life is too easy, too soft, too undemanding, at least so far as natural, basic primitive experiences are concerned. It is fortunate that you have lived here close to the wilderness and that you have traveled in the forest enough to be sometimes hungry, thirsty, fatigued, wet, cold, lost, fighting black flies, or surrounded by darkness and strange noises. I wish there had been time for more experiences of this nature."

"Fanatics have their dreams," wrote Keats, "wherewith they weave a paradise for a sect."* But fanaticism also converts paradise into private prisons.

⊰⊱

IN SEPTEMBER, my mother and I set off for school. I stared out the car window forgetting to blink. Hours passed, and the mountains just got higher and higher, the villages fewer and farther between. All I felt was a leaden dread. My bridges were burnt, even my house in Cornish was closed up for the year. While I was away at ski camp, my mother had packed up the essentials from the Red house and moved

---

*Anders and Lane, *Cults and Consequences*.

to a partially furnished, rented house in Norwich. Matthew would now be within walking distance of his school, and she could easily commute to attend classes at Dartmouth to finish the degree she had broken off years ago to marry my father. It all made sense, but I felt really strange about it. Mom's stuff was in her bedroom, Matthew's stuff was in his room next to hers, and I recognized some of the living room furniture. They would be living there. My stuff—desk, bed, toys, posters, all colors of Dannon yogurt tops glued to my bedroom door next to the Keep Out sign, Day-Glo daisies; everything but my clothes and skis—remained in our house in Cornish, where my mother, brother, and I would return for summers only. On other vacations from school, I was to stay in the guest room on the ground floor of the house in Norwich. I could choose which of the two double beds down there to sleep in. The good thing was that I had my own bathroom and phone extension downstairs. The not-so-good thing was that it felt like a motel.

As we drove, I thought of a story I'd read about young women in the eighteenth century, transported by ship to Australia, who packed whatever belongings they were able and said good-bye to home, family, and country forever. The map of the world I held in my own mind was, perhaps not unlike theirs, quite flat. You fell off the edge if you sailed too far, but not before encountering strange and terrible serpents and sea monsters. Life, for me, lay east of Cornish, in London or Venice, or in warm southern places like Florida and Barbados. We were heading in the wrong direction. Toward desolate places. Toward Lions and Tigers and Bears, Oh My! It was deeply, deeply humiliating to me that the words I formed in my mind were "I want my mommy."

We lurched along the narrow highway that threads between massive, towering cliffs that plunge down into bottomless, black glacial lakes. This landscape was a favorite subject among the school of American Romantic painters who wanted to evoke the feeling of sublime awe, verging on vertigo, in the face of the dramatic forces of nature. I am aware it is supposed to be staggeringly beautiful.

My mother broke the silence of hours and said, with the best British schoolgirl good cheer that she could muster, "Well, *here* we are." A small sign on the highway was all that marked the school's presence. We turned off the highway and drove down a dirt road past the school barn and vast manure pile, past fields of "organically grown" vegetables the brochure had promised—or threatened—depending on one's point of view. We arrived finally at a dead end where stood the school's main building, which housed several dormitory wings, classrooms, dining room, basement art studio, and offices. We were greeted through our car window by kids with maps who directed us to the proper dormitory, or "houses" as they were called.

I had been assigned to Glass House, which was about a three-minute walk from the main building. Some of the older "Rugged, Resourceful, and Resilient" boys were in dormitories as much as a mile away, which made for quite a hike on winter mornings before dawn when, if you spit, it froze before it hit the ground—technically at about forty degrees below zero Fahrenheit—and made a cracking noise as it shattered. I learned that the beautiful dorms I'd seen in the brochures were the new Hill Houses. These had been well designed for housing institutionalized groups of children, not families, and had nice large bathrooms with multiple small sinks, and a living room rather like a ski lodge in layout with many couches and chairs around a big fireplace. Upstairs, off a wide, sunny, skylighted corridor, were rows of carpeted double bedrooms in bright colors with cozy built-ins and a picture window between the beds.

My dormitory was an old house built for a family, now being used to board eight children in four small rooms at the top of a narrow staircase. Being called Glass House, it was, in this place down the rabbit hole, quite the reverse—dark and gloomy. Herbert and Kit, the headmaster and headmistress, lived in an apartment on the ground floor of Glass House. I never saw it. A large, unmarried woman who taught riding and math had a plain room at the top of the stairs. She helped my mother and me bring my trunk and bedding up to the room. I carried my precious portable record player, which I had refused to leave home without; *The White Album* had just been released, *need* we say more? My roommate had not arrived yet, so I chose the bed nearest the window, a mistake I would not have made had I known that the policy in Glass House, as in Cornish I might add, was to turn off the heat at night. A pox upon several thousand years of Stoic thought from ancient Greece to Gordonston that equates cold and moral fiber!

My mother hung up my two dresses, knowing I might not get

around to it for months, and said something encouraging about the closets. That done, we walked back to the car. She waved good-bye, or at least she must have. I just remember standing there, immobile, staring dumbly at the rear of our car as it drove away, the dust rising from the road. Some timeless time passed, and I turned and walked down a path past the root-cellar shed beside the main building.

It was then that the world lurched terribly and I became unmoored. I tried to move my body toward an opening, a doorway into the main building. The sliding, flowing water I was becoming roared in my ears as I neared the edge of the falls. Into the long corridor, I flowed and tumbled past dozens of little open lockers, cubbyholes with no doors, no safe places to hide. I had heard that one had my name on it for my galoshes with name tapes inside, barn jacket with name in the collar, standard issue caught and exposed on a hook. Undulating unlockable lockers; I was sliding down the wall, blinding sunlight streaming in the corridor windows, the air thick bands of swirling haze.

A Cheshire cat's teeth appeared, smiling in the long corridor. My size. It said, "Hi, I'm Holly. What's your name?"

Peggy. Peggy. Peggy. The word made the leaden trek up from my lungs across my tongue, and finally, finding an opening in my mouth, it escaped: "Peggy. I . . . I hate this."

The smile grew wider and said, "Yeah, this place *really* sucks. I should know, I've been here since I was ten." And she rolled her eyes. Then, perhaps reading my mind, or perhaps because those Cheshire eyes spotted the movement of my body seeping out from under my clothes and running down the edge of the hall toward the drain, she said, "Come on, I'll show you a good place to hide."

My Cheshire friend has adopted strays of all sorts over the years. I've seen her befriend cats abandoned in Manhattan alleys, feral and filthy, who suddenly find themselves on her kitchen floor, lolling belly up for her to scratch, and answering to names like Mayhem, Chaos, and Fiorucci. She would spend her teens prowling backstages and backseats of limos in search of rock-and-roll tomcats. At twenty, she was the only person to show up for the first day of class at Columbia Law School dressed in a leopard-print spandex bodysuit and thigh boots. At thirty, as her law practice with a major record company skyrocketed, members of heavy metal bands with names like Faster Pussycat and the Scorpions shed their spikes and sat around her kitchen table raving about her lasagna.

When Holly befriends you, it's for life. You know you'll always have a place you can show up and call home. We recently toasted our fortieth birthdays with champagne and chocolate in her *warm* Jacuzzi in Beverly Hills. She swore, upon leaving Cross Mountain, that she'd never again be cold, hungry, or forced to play dodgeball. And I can testify that she hasn't a single pair of sensible shoes darkening her many closets. "This sure beats the chimney," she said with her big grin as we clinked champagne glasses.

The chimney was our sanctuary that long year at Cross Mountain. She shared her treasured secret hiding place with me not five minutes after we met, leading me down the corridor and into the library. Around the corner was an old fireplace, not in use, with cushions beckoning where logs had been. It was supposed to be a cozy place to read. What she had discovered was that if you crawled in and shinnied up the chimney, some sainted bricklayer in his mercy had left a ridge about three feet up where, if you leaned your back against the opposite wall, you could just about stand. On cold days, Holly and I would spend two illegal hours perched inside that chimney when we were supposed to be participating in "out-time" activities, which neither hail nor snow nor sleet nor rain excused.*

As we talked, there in the chimney, my body gradually started to flow back into its form. By the time we heard the dinner bell, it had set firmly enough to survive the jiggling and jostling corridor full of kids headed for the dining hall. Holly showed me how to read the assigned seating chart posted there. We ate in "families" of six. One teacher sat at the head of the table, one child server at the other end, whose job it was that week to bring the dishes served family-style from the kitchen to the table, and then to clear. In between were four other children, two on each side. At the table, as in most of the dormitories, the children were mixed in age and sex, again to mirror a family. Families rotated weekly.

My roommate spotted me after dinner. This wasn't hard, as I was

---

*My school report confirms this: "A bit reluctant to plunge fully into out-time, Peggy has nevertheless come to enjoy sports like volleyball. —Paul"

I think that's how I'd like to see my obituary begin: "A bit reluctant to plunge fully into out-time, Ms. Salinger . . ."

the only new girl in the graduating class that year. We walked back to Glass House together. I could tell right away that she wasn't one of the "cool" kids; she had some wacky album called *The Shacklefords Sing,* but she was tremendously warm and kind, and I knew, even then, that I was lucky to have her as a roommate.

After a few weeks, I was learning the ropes and fitting in nicely. I figured out what chores to sign up for that kept me inside: table setting, hall sweeping, and various other main-building janitorial tasks that did not involve a dawn hike to the barn. Classes went smoothly and I was making friends easily. The friendliness and generosity of the children there still astounds me. We "little women" of the eighth grade spent part of each day, informally, as surrogate mommies to the little girls, the eight- and nine-year-olds who needed hugs so badly that we forgot we did, too. We'd sit up at night patting the head of a crying, homesick little child who had awakened with nightmares, or hug a proud little one in the hallway who had just learned how to ride and wanted to tell someone. The most amazing thing, to me, was the almost total absence of the usual teasing and petty meanness among my classmates that one often sees with children of that age. In an entire year, I witnessed only three instances of unkindness on the part of my classmates. Each involved name-calling about a physical characteristic of a person. Some boy called my roommate "Scabby," a cruel reference to a mild skin disorder she had, perhaps eczema of some sort. I threatened to put his head through the wall if he ever said that to her again. The second instance involved a girl from Africa who had a large bosom, immense to we silly white children, who was called on occasion by her last name "Wagner-Boobs"; and lastly, a mean name, "Chaz the Spaz," referring to one boy's jerky gait—I don't know if it was a neurological twitch or a nervous one. I don't mean to minimize the pain caused these children in any way; nevertheless, it's extraordinary that in living with about eighty fourth through eighth graders twenty-four hours a day for a year that there was so little teasing among the children. They were, I think, a remarkably nice bunch of kids. Certainly they were to me anyway, without exception.

The other odd thing, very much in contrast to my earlier schooling, is that Cross Mountain was a remarkably unsexy place. Perhaps it was the incest taboo created by both co-ed housing and the fact of being thrown together as a substitute family, I don't know. The few kids who paired off were more like the middle-age WASP couples in Orvis catalogues: linking arms and walking sedately down the path, perhaps a peck on the cheek good-night if they'd been going together for a year or two, tossing the occasional snowball as the only sign of flirting. Unlike Hanover Junior High, where most couples formed and dissolved monthly, and there was lots of dancing and making out, and talking about dances and making out, at Cross Mountain, the closest that my friends and I (the fast kids who snuck out of our windows on moonlit nights to go night walking) came to making out was what we called swapping smoke. The kid who had the cigarette would offer the person he or she "liked" a sort of mouth-to-mouth exchange of smoke: as the smoker breathed out into your mouth, lips touching, you breathed in. It was pretty great. But if anyone had gotten on base that year, I would have known about it, trust me.

And the way we talked about whom we liked was very, very different from the previous year's talk or indeed from the following teenage years of talk. It wasn't about how far you went or wanted to go, or who was rumored to have gone with whom. It was much more like the social chat about husbands and children I engage in, at forty, with play-group moms. "How's Will, I hear he scored two goals in soccer today. Do you think you'll be able to go to the same school next year?" And so on. Odd.*

Things were going pretty smoothly until one evening, I returned to my room and something just didn't feel right. Something was wrong, I smelled it in the air. My eyes scanned the room taking light-speed inventory. I looked over at my bedside table and my eyes came to rest on a small Swiss wooden box, about the size of my hand, that my father had given me. It was light blue with pretty hand-painted flowers on it. It had

*I'm not sure the kind of hypermaturity we showed was evidence of good health, but I do know that given the general level of neediness and abandonment we embodied, it's a darn good thing kids didn't get in over their head sexually. The following year, in high school, breakups often engendered full crack-ups and a stay in McLean's. When your boyfriend or girlfriend is your whole family wrapped up into one person, the one who kisses you good-night and has breakfast with you in the morning, attachments can become symbiotic in the extreme. At Cross Mountain, twelve- and thirteen-year-old passion was nipped in the bud and proceeded directly to sedate middle age.

a tiny key that fit a keyhole to open the lid. It had been closed when I left in the morning. Now the lid was slightly askew, and upon closer inspection, I saw that the hinges were broken and the tiny keyhole looked as though some ham-fisted person had taken a large screwdriver to it. The paint was even scraped off in several places. Nothing was missing because nothing had been in it. I turned toward the closet and found our clothes disheveled, some half off their hooks, and my sleeping bag was out of its case and unrolled. I sat down on my bed and picked up my pillow I'd brought from home, to hug it to me. Not only had the liner been unzipped, but the foam rubber had been ripped open, leaving little shreds of torn foam scattered across my sheet. The roll of Life Savers I'd hidden inside the pillow was gone.

My roommate came in and saw the look on my face. She froze. "Peggy, what's wrong?"

"We've been robbed," I said in a flat voice. I rose and showed her our closet and things.

"We've been searched," she said, correcting me matter-of-factly. "They come in and search your room to make sure you haven't hidden any candy. You can usually expect one after each holiday, but you never know exactly when they'll come."

"But they *broke* my stuff."

She lifted her hands, shrugged sadly, and let them drop at her sides. There was nothing else to say.

The following day I was summoned to the first of many "sessions" with the headmistress, Kit Watson, who as a child "collected younger children and played school, made markets, and ran shows." Boy was she ever still running the show with the children she'd "collected." Holly accompanied me as far as the corridor leading to Kit's office in the main building. "Good luck. I'll wait for you in the chimney." The next part of the story is extremely hard to write. My fingers feel like lead as I try to type. I have a hot-water bottle on my stomach. Yesterday I shut down, gave up trying to write about this and took two Ativan (a sedative in the benzodiazepine "family"), and walked slowly around the pond near my condo. Today my body smells like poison as I sweat out the Ativan and fear and toxins. I wonder if you can take a laptop computer into a sweat lodge.

I walked down the corridor and knocked on her door. A voice said,

"Come in." She pointed to a chair in front of her desk and said, "*Sit* down." Kit didn't need to say much to be frightening. She had a large, leonine head, no-nonsense, short gray hair swept off her square forehead, small eyes, and a strong jaw that, when she spoke, revealed extraordinarily massive teeth, which she tended to bite together, resoundingly, in an unconscious twitch, almost as if she had to clamp them together to keep them from leaping out of her mouth and tearing into her victim. She had the roll of Life Savers that I'd hidden in my pillow sitting on her desk. She never once mentioned them.

Holly had told me what her opening parry would be. Kit, as if on cue, said, "I could tell right away, Peggy, that you were going to be one of our problem children." Long silence. "You don't fit in here, do you." Silence. "You know, Peggy, none of the other children really like you. They *want* to like you, they really do, but your behavior and your attitude must change before they can."

I foolishly mumbled, "I have plenty of friends."

"No . . . no . . . they're just in*tim*idated by you. They don't really like you. I know, because they've come to me and told me so." I shut up, but she could tell I wasn't falling for it. I wasn't shaking and sobbing and half out of my mind; "melting" was what she and her daughter Katherine called it when they "broke through a child's defenses."

"We want to *help* you but you have to *let* us. You have to tell us what you've done."

I sat there stone-faced staring over her left ear. Something about the intonation of her patter did not allow the usual escape: split off and wait till it's over. Even now I can sleep through construction going on outside my window, jackhammers and all, but if a television or radio is on just softly enough to hear bits and pieces of sentences, enough to arouse the mind's automatic problem-solving curiosity, I'm sunk. My mom came at me like a jackhammer. My father like a guillotine. This woman whispered, crooned her fury like the pillow talk of a rapist. She fingered the telephone cord slowly as I sat there immobile, then *slam!* she brought the big black phone crashing down on her desktop. She held me in her gaze, leaned across her desk so I could feel the heat of her breath, and spat out ever so quietly, "You *viper.* You snake in the grass." She snapped her teeth together spasmodically, in loud punctuation. "You know why your parents sent you to me. Don't you? . . . I said, *don't you.*" Teeth snap shut. "*They* failed to flush you out, you snake, but I will."

These are not words you forget. Mind you, this was a time before drugs entered grammar schools, at least this one: we're talking about a few pieces of candy for personal use, not pushing heroin to children. What shocked and terrified me was not that she said weird and mean things, nor even the intensity of her fury; I was sort of used to that from home. What was so deeply disturbing and creepy is that she could express such fury and seemingly remain calm and in control of herself. Truth be told, she scared the absolute hell out of me.

Tears began to roll silently down my cheeks. She stared at me for a while and then said, "I can't stand the sight of you any longer. You may go." As I stood up, she said, teeth smiling, "We'll have another little chat soon, I promise you."

I was shaking all over, so much so that my legs didn't hold me against the chimney wall very well. After these sessions, Holly and I joked to save our lives, to reweave the shreds of pride that Kit had ripped apart. No one had made me cry since I was five years old. I was one tough cookie and took pride in it. But each and every session, some tears, no matter how hard I tried to hold on to them, tumbled out. Holly would wait for me outside Kit's office and stitch me up with jokes and laughter. "Hey, good job, you really gave her a run for her money that time. Level-one record, two hours and fifteen minutes!" And she'd do an imitation of Kit's opening incision: "You 'prob' kids. We know you have a problem and we'd *really* like to help [chomp], but you have to tell us [chomp] what you've done."

Over time, Kit went through her repertoire. She tried to use the technique that worked so well on Holly and a lot of the other kids. Telling me that the kids secretly disliked me, and that I had no friend but Kit and so on. But I was solidly put-together on that subject. I knew who my friends were. She always won tears, she wouldn't let you out of her office until she did, but she hadn't "melted" me. You knew the longer you held out, though, the longer you'd be in her presence, the longer it would go on. She never let you go until you confessed to something, sobbing and shaking. You could see the victory in her eyes and you were turned loose. For now.

It took months of her "sessions," as she called them, to find my Achilles' heel. It was the first time I saw her eyes smiling. I know now that if you accuse a child on the cusp of adolescence of being a sexual pervert and of harboring homosexuality in her heart of hearts, chances are pretty darn good you'll hit paydirt. Back then, though, I thought she must have some evil psychic ability to read my mind. It must have shown somewhere, somehow, that in fifth and sixth grades I gazed at Miss March. I'd even played "lezzies" with other girls my age, at the pond; we'd go under the raft and lift up our bathing suit tops and "show" what we had. One time a really fast girl, who was up visiting friends for the summer between fifth and sixth grade, suggested we all strip naked, and she pretended one of the others was a slave and pretended to cut off her breast and shake salt on the "wound," and she even bit her lightly on the vagina. I was entranced and repulsed and couldn't stop thinking about it for a long time afterward. Especially at night. Many boyfriends and much heterosexual "making out" later, I still secretly worried that I might be a lezzie.

Once Kit narrowed in on that one, I was writhing. She forced me to type a letter to my mother on her typewriter in her office, that she had written out in longhand. It took several hours since I didn't know how to type, and every time I made a mistake, I had to start over again. In the letter, I had to confess that I was a pervert and a lesbian as well as being crazy and paranoid. No one was out to get me, she often said: "We just wanted to *help* you, but you won't let us."

I'm surprised that my mother didn't immediately recognize the letter for what it was, a forced confession composed by someone else. I had *never* willingly told my mother the time of day. Claire was about the last person on earth to whom I'd volunteer such hugely personal information involving secret fears and sexuality. My guess is that she was so starved for any communication from my monosyllabic and generally sullen thirteen-year-old lips that she was invested in believing it was a confidence voluntarily given. Who knows. But to her great credit, she responded clearly and effectively to the absurdity of the letter.

[1969]

Dear Peggy,

Thanks for your beautifully type written letter.

I was very upset to hear that you & Dougal & Brion [boys]

were lesbians—I'm not sure that I am logically quite up to working it out, though, but, I am sure you *all* should be deeply concerned—(especially Dougal & Brion—do *their* mother's know? Should we all get together to discuss it? Can you demonstrate?)

As for the rest EVERYONE appears weird to someone else somewhere and through a breakdown in, or lack of possibility for, communication and understanding between them, appears to be doing very strange things. Don't let it get to you.

Craziness arises from things being blocked not from self-expression. It comes from not being able to face reality nor express one's worries. If there is a pressure or pain too deep to bear then a necessity rises, in some people, to short circuit experience so that it doesn't—as is feared—destroy them. Craziness is really an appropriate reaction to what is too intolerable for a certain nervous system to bear. It occurs in weak egos not in strong ones, so I don't think you have any need to worry about it.

Just don't block and close up.

But, also, on the other side, take into consideration other's weak egos and tendencies toward self-protective hypocrisy or fantasy and BE KIND. If this is not possible keep out of their way. If this isn't possible because they have you in some sort of authority bind, try not to let them get you down and listen, if you are able, to any valuable or pertinent advice; for the rest be tolerant of their weakness knowing that it is *their weakness*. If they weren't fallible they'd be reaching you.

You are, and it seems ridiculous to have to write it to you, but I was worried by your letter—

Not paranoid

Not crazy

Not perverted

Unsettling to some adults—YES—Definitely!

If you have deep resentments just try to think them through clearly and cooly—you may be right.

Please be sensible. Please don't get kicked out of school. It isn't worth it. There are too many good things, really good things happening there.

Guess that's all.

I love my daughter very, very much: perverted or unperverted, lesbian or fairy, crazy or sane, weird or square, undersexed or oversexed—(they are all only definitions in somebody else's mind anyway.) Just try to think and know what you are doing and why and if it is right for you, try not to hurt anyone else or yourself.

> Your loving and moralistic,
> Mom

I could have died with embarrassment when she said the part about "demonstrating," but I was glad that she at least knew how dumb it was to call boys "lesbians." Everyone knows boys are "homos" and girls are "lezzies." If only I had known at the time who had the dirty mind and who didn't.

I begged my father to take me home. I called him weekly, collect of course, with the one phone call we were allowed to make each Sunday. I could always hear someone listening in on another extension. Older people often breathe loudly and don't know it. What I didn't catch on to, until Holly pointed out the obvious, was that the letters home that we were required to write once a week, sitting, as a school, in the dining hall, were open to inspection before being mailed. "Why do you think we have to turn them in with the envelope unsealed?" she said, rolling her eyes. In a session with Holly, Kit made the mistake of quoting too closely from a letter Holly had written, and she figured out that Kit was likely to have been mail-reading rather than mind-reading. These items aren't mentioned in those chirpy "How to find a good boarding school for your kids" guides. Questions to ask: Do you tamper with the mail? Do you listen in on phone calls? Do you search rooms? Do you allow children access to food when hungry? Do you keep the rooms above freezing in the winter? What are your disciplinary procedures? I'd want to know about the state of basic human rights sorts of things before inspecting the beautiful riding stables or the state-of-the-art science lab.

Regardless of the suspected surveillance, I told my father what was happening to me, though not the mortifying details of being accused of harboring the wrong sexual orientation, and that Kit was out to get me. He believed me. He said he'd met several "Kits" in his lifetime. Mostly in schools or in the army, he said. He told a few stories that hit the nail on the head; he definitely had her number. But he didn't come to get me.

At Thanksgiving, he drove up for a visit. Parents were allowed to visit for the day but not to take their children home. Or so I thought until, years later, my father drove up to Cross Mountain to take my brother home for Dartmouth football games several times during the fall of his first and second years there. Maybe the policy changed after Kit retired.

Kit was all smiley-smiley to him when he came to visit at Thanksgiving and put her arm around me. He said she didn't fool him in the least. "She wants people to believe she's a *won*derful woman, a pio*neer*ing educator, but you see right through her. She'll never forgive you for that, Peggy, never." He said I was "cursed with a readable face" just like him and I couldn't hide how I felt about people. I saw her self-image in the mirror and must have let it show that I thought, You don't really look like that, you're *not* the fairest of them all.

My father also had some interesting things to say about the school program. We put on a big show for the parents with music and skits and all sorts of wonderful artistic stuff we were being exposed to. Don, the music teacher, composed the songs and the school play in a great flurry just three days before the performance. We were so impressed (though less so when I visited fifteen years later on Thanksgiving, heard the same buzz about the show being composed in just a week or so, and I recognized half the tunes), I expressed my enthusiasm to my father about the amazing amount of work Don was able to produce in such a short time. Daddy said, "He knew all fall that the show had to be ready by Thanksgiving, didn't he?" I nodded. "I don't find it so admirable that he waited until the last minute to begin work on it, do you?" Hmmmm. I never thought about it that way.

Daddy called a spade a spade, but he neglected to give me a few pointers that his "rugged, resourceful, and resilient characters," Seymour and Buddy Glass, had mastered when faced with bullying directors of camps or schools. Seymour, already a three-R savant at age seven, writes of an encounter between the camp director, Mr. Happy, and Buddy. During Mr. Happy's weekly inspection of the boys' bungalows, he starts giving Buddy, age five, holy hell about not making his bed the way Mr. Happy did in the army. My father often told us that at military school there was always someone coming around inspecting your bunk—regulations stated that a quarter must bounce a certain height on your bed to pass inspection. Seymour said he didn't "step in or interfere with these bullying insults. I have complete confidence in this young lad's ability to fend for himself at all times." Sure enough, the ever-resourceful Buddy, in the midst of Mr. Happy's tirade, suddenly turned his eyes upward so that only the whites showed, a trick he'd mastered, scaring the bejesus out of Mr. Happy, who left in a hurry, "forgetting to give your self-reliant son any fresh demerits!"

Perhaps my father overestimated his daughter's powers of resilience and resourcefulness. Nevertheless, Daddy did arrange, during his Thanksgiving Day visit, to speak man to man, I suppose, with Herbert about Kit's behavior toward me. The results were not heartening. My father told me over turkey dinner at the Mirror Lake Inn that Herbert was genuinely embarrassed and dismayed by the strength and unseemliness of his wife's feelings toward me. But, Daddy said, "Herbert is a weak man. I don't think he'll be able to stand up to her at all." And that was the end of that. "Have some chocolate cake. It won't be as good as Wolfie's I'll bet, but it looks pretty good."

After dinner, my brother and I went downstairs to where the inn had a game room. In the corner of the room stood two gorgeous candy machines, sacred objects, risen idols awaiting our silver offerings. Celestial gifts of Sky Bars and Milky Ways and rainbow-colored Life Savers rained down from above into our waiting hands. Food, food, food. I was *always* hungry. At school they maintained total, absolute control of food. Personal snacks of any sort were strictly forbidden. Even saving an apple from the table to eat later was punished. We were to eat what was in front of us at mealtimes and nothing in between. If you were in the vicinity of the main building during the late afternoon, two of the kitchen staff, both named Gladys, were allowed to dispense a measured spoonful of snack: shoe-leather-hard bits of dried date that you warmed in your mouth and reconstituted with your saliva for about ten minutes before they were chewable. Even British boarding schools regarded a child's personal "tuck box" from home as close to sacred. Here it was strictly verboten. Holly and I whispered "Health Nazis" under our breath while bent over in the bitter cold, harvesting the winter root crop. We mimed bludgeoning each other to death with an organic turnip.

As requested, my brother had brought from home a plastic container with a tight-fitting lid. In my letter, I had asked him for an airtight container to collect leaf specimens. We stuffed it full of soft white dinner rolls and candy, and when I returned to school that evening, I headed straight for the woods and buried it a foot deep in the ground. Barring hounds, I figured I was safe.

❧❦❧

IT INFURIATED KIT that she was in the minority, of one really, to truly hate me. And these were teachers who were not shy about sharing their dislike, if not loathing, for students. Witness the bluntness of the progress reports as to our character molding that were sent home at the end of term:

> [My midyear report from the headmaster]
> Peggy's fall term here has been filled more with searching, experimenting, questioning, and to a limited extent complaining rather than well-organized, productive effort. She is eager to find direction and values but still too uncertain of herself to make strong commitments. . . .
> It is more than likely that a girl with her sensitivity, talent and projective power will mature into a well-organized, happy person. Our regret is that in her particular case her time at Cross Mountain is too short for the establishment of solid self-confidence and competence. I am hopeful that she and we together can accomplish much in the few remaining months. She is making notable progress.
>
> —Herbert

[Holly's initial year-end report from the headmaster]
As Holly approaches the end of her first turbulent year at

Cross Mountain School, there are many signs that she has grown to a better understanding of herself and her relationships and responsibilities to other people. She still exhibits the characteristics of a self-centered, self-pitying, immature youngster [don't hold back now, Herbert, tell us what you *really* think] who is struggling valiantly to assert and establish herself in a world that both challenges and frightens her. . . .

On standard achievement tests given this spring she had a median score of 11.6 which is a very high score for a girl ending 7th grade. Actually, this score is about the same as it was last fall and suggests that her energies have been used more in coping with the demands of group living than advancing herself scholastically. [Or perhaps it suggests that we haven't taught her a goddam thing since she's been here?]

I think Holly's second and last year here will be far more affective [*sic*] and productive in all respects; although like all of us, she has some rather strong personal characteristics to contend with and manage. —Herbert

[My house report from the other house parent, Sue]

Peggy has, on the whole, made an excellent adjustment to the very difficult situation of arriving here from somewhere else for only the senior year. She is quite socially adept and has developed many friendships and much influence among her peers already. She and her roommate have a good time together and with the other girls in the house. A certain laxness in regard to possessions, efforts, and obligations has been her greatest difficulty, but she is showing good signs of progress in most of these areas even though you might not suspect it from looking at her room! Much of Peggy's time has been spent in experimentation with what we have to offer, and her whole review was punctuated with remarks about what she wanted to try next, and what to pursue further. She has done a little free time art work, much work in music, read several books, went to Montreal after surviving a day when she could speak only French, worked in the laundry and on the ski hill, served on the bicycle committee and two dance committees, and did

some exploring around the place. She is already a girl of considerable maturity and strength, and it is a pleasure to watch her moving ahead so vigorously. We are glad that she is with us.
—Sue

[Holly's house report by Katherine—Kit's daughter—and her husband, John]

Holly went through a quite turbulent beginning at Cross Mountain. Her concern only with herself, her babyish protests, complaints, and down right rude behavior soon made her a target for teasing and unkind attitudes on the part of the children. It took many sessions both with us and with Kit to help her see what she was doing and her defense of such behavior began to melt. . . . The social demands of a community such as ours are great and Holly has found the adjustment difficult. . . . In other areas, two examples being skiing and softball, Holly protested loudly about the encrouchment [sic] on her "rights" and refused to participate. Because of our conviction that we can do no child a favor by letting such behavior succeed, we insisted on Holly's participation, and she soon discovered the pleasure that these activities had to offer. I think that the only area where this was not the case was our out-door camping program, for she still claims to "hate" trips. . . . I told her that unless she could develop a less self-centered attitude toward other people that she was not really ready to assume the responsibility of being a member of the senior Class. This seems to really have had an effect on Holly. [No joke! Threatened with yet another year in that place.] . . . Her major interest continues to be reading, but her selection is moving away from shock value books such as *The Valley of the Dolls* and *Hell's Angels* and her most recent reading includes *I Never Promised You a Rose Garden* and *The Wayward Bus* . . . she reads the *New York Times* daily and most of the magazines in the library. [Another house report said Holly reads at least three books a week—no mean feat with activities scheduled every waking hour—including, they listed, *Autobiography of Malcolm X, Tales of the South Pacific, Call It Sleep, Catcher in the Rye, Return to Paradise, Tortilla Flat, 1984,*

Jane Eyre, Wuthering Heights, To Kill a Mockingbird, Tess of the d'Urbervilles, Airs Above the Ground, Black Like Me, The Stranger. "To name a few," it said.]

My favorite line from this house report, one that Holly should have had framed on her office wall as lawyer and vice president of business affairs for a major record company, or perhaps in her current job as a member of the management team for such rock bands as Motley Crüe and Duran Duran; or maybe on the wall, in the home she shares with her husband of twenty years, a successful producer and songwriter for heavy metal bands, right next to the forty or so gold and platinum records they've earned:

> At this point, Holly's favorite activities do not involve interaction with other children. *Her major attempt to make contact is an apparently contrived interest in rock and roll.* It is our hope to help her acquire the skills that will enable her to gain the pleasure that comes from group activities.
>
> —Katherine and John [my emphasis]

A mutual friend of Holly's and mine recently read the above house report that talked about Holly's "contrived interest in rock and roll" and suggested she send a copy of it to the school on her record-company letterhead. He was stunned by her response. He told me that instead of the Holly he knows—one of the toughest dealmakers in the business, no-bullshit, take-no-prisoners negotiator and lawyer—she looked like a deer caught in the headlights. "No way!" she told him. "They'd know where I am."

Holly had gotten off to a great start her first morning at school when she found out, to her eloquently and loudly expressed horror, that she was not going to be allowed a cup of coffee—good or otherwise—and no, she could not bring the *New York Times* to the breakfast table. Newspaper reading beyond the farm and tool section was highly suspect; coffee, sugar, and Satan were synonymous. While I had arrived at school poorly educated—I really had to keep on my toes to keep up and I knew it—Holly arrived in seventh grade working near the level (11.6) of a senior in high school. She was bored out of her mind. Clearly, this occurred to no one. In this temple built to honor the gods of Muscular Christianity, being a smart, well-read urban Jew meant big trouble.

[French] Holly can be reading something completely unrelated during class, and yet score well under "cross-examination" despite the heaps of complaining that seem to go into any efforts she makes. —Barry

[English] Holly writes beautifully and has no mechanical problems with English. Her assignments are always done well and turned in on time. . . . Holly has improved in her class habits somewhat, but is still quite loudly negative in her comments. She has learned, I believe, that it does not accomplish anything to blatantly refuse to do an assignment. She will do very well on a spelling test, and write "This is a crummy test!" at the top of the page. —James

I'm rather surprised and disappointed that James, a clandestine friend of mine (Kit, he said, would make his life hell if she knew we were friends) whose family visited me in Cornish on summer vacations, seemed so bullish on attitude and character-molding in his report on Holly. For me, he and his wife were a lifeline of warmth and affection and support in an otherwise very cold place on the part of the adults. In fact, he would write to me at Cambridge School the following year complaining:

You are a topic that Herbert and I cannot discuss, which I am reluctant to discuss because of the strong emotional basis of my feelings, but which Herbert chose to discuss with me the day after I talked with you on the phone at your mother's house. The old argument was taken off the shelf, dusted off, and discovered to be completely unresolved. (The basic issue, from my point of view is this, which will perhaps explain its inherent "unarguability." You stand accused, by much of the school, of certain crimes. Of most of the crimes of which you have been accused you are guilty. It is not my function to defend you, and I have no intention of "defending" you, because

I question the very assumptions upon which their whole definition of a "crime" is based. . . . I hate to say it, but the way the world is set up now, much of your energies will be devoted to disguising your true feelings, and at the same time doing your own thing to the greatest extent possible without bringing down the wrath of someone you depend upon. It's a game but one that we're all locked into. We can't quit because we don't like the rules, because at present there is no place else to go. It's a real bringdown, one which will bug you a lot in the future. It bugs me—CMS is the place where the rules are most agreeable to me, but also the place where they require the most strict compliance to the GAMES I have ever seen. There are two people here out of the entire faculty that I feel I can be totally open with, and those are D.&B. The rest—even P.—make me feel as if somehow, somewhere, Big Brother is watching. At times I feel as if I may as well be a junior exec in an advertising agency, so strong are the rules of protocol and "attitude." Makes me wonder. . . .   Love, James.

Makes *me* want to wonder, "throw up both my hands."* It also makes me think about Holden's exchange with his teacher, where he is told that life is a game and he needs to learn to play it by the rules. Holden agrees with the teacher out loud, but to himself, he thinks:

Game, my ass. Some game. If you get on the side where all the hot-shots are, then it's a game, all right—I'll admit that. But if you get on the *other* side, where there aren't any hot-shots, then what's a game about it? Nothing. No game.   (*Catcher*, p. 8)

I took Holly out to lunch recently to pick her brains for this chapter. I asked her what she remembered of Kit. In profound contrast to Viola and me reminiscing about Miss Chapman, our fourth-grade teacher, and giggling about how she once shook Vi so hard she wet her pants, Holly and I had no giggles. Holly told me that she has tried to put the whole thing as far out of her mind as she possibly can, with multiple

---

*Marvin Gaye

drugs when necessary. She said she's been pretty successful at doing so, yet every once in a while she'll be walking down the street or riding on a subway car, and suddenly she'll shudder as if death itself had brushed her sleeve. Then she'll realize that the old woman across from her looks something like Kit.

22

Christmas

❦❦❦

DADDY WAS COMING TO PICK ME UP and take me back to Cornish for Christmas. Looking back, it occurs to me that my mother always got the hard job, of dropping me off, whereas my father got to be the good guy who picked me up at vacation time. I packed my suitcase, mostly ski stuff, because I'd spend most of the vacation on the slopes at Mt. Ascutney. I also packed a few mandatory craft projects we were to bring home as gifts and evidence of our enriched education. Some of the children, such as Holly, worked for weeks, weaving truly splendid pieces on looms, experimenting with color and texture, learning to love the sensual feel of drawing wool through thread, fingers flying. Years later, there were times I experienced something perhaps similar at the piano. A place beyond technique and practice, where creation in the mind's eye flows seamlessly through body and instrument. Beyond I and thou. Other children worked in clay, making pots on great stone wheels turned by foot, or by shaping large coils of it into vessels. Carefully, they chose their glaze and painted the raw clay. Then, in that leap of faith beyond one's control, they placed their unfinished work where, in the womb of the kiln, the alchemy of creation takes place. A percentage of the pots, no matter how well made, abort, crack and char. It's not so much due to inherent flaws, but to the luck of placement inside the kiln. The vicissitudes of flame kiss some and burn others. The shelves of the pottery studio held their quotient of kids' lumpy ashtrays, but here and there were pieces worthy of the life corner in a Japanese house.*

As for me, the art teacher's terse two-line report speaks volumes: "Peggy has been generally uninterested and unproductive. She has made some drawings, paintings, and clay work." Unproductive, yes. But I watched in awe. My own creations were aborted in their conception. They never even received a spark of life; instead I produced scraggy, sterile, unloved pieces of cloth as small as I could get away with and not cause trouble. Like Penelope, I tore apart in secret what I wove during the day. I never dared to love a lump of clay enough to succeed in erecting smooth, shapely mounds from the spinning wheel that magically, at the touch of a deft finger, opened themselves into perfectly shaped vessels. Mine rose up from the wheel, off center and misbegotten, only to collapse back into a flaccid heap.

I could, with effort, do an average job, academically, in the classroom, but it was written in stone that I could never create anything beautiful. My failure was further proof of all that was said, yelled, slapped, and hissed in my ears: something was terribly wrong with me. I had learned from my mother, early on, that there was something deeply shameful about me. I had learned from my father that there was something deeply shameful about *any* imperfection. He hid the process of his creation as if it were his most carefully guarded secret. He hid whatever he worked on, as well as himself I might add, until it was deemed perfect. I cannot tell you the raving lectures I heard up to this point about "second-rate" artists. Winning, being first-rate, a true creative genius, wasn't everything, it was the *only* thing. God help the poor shnook who tried and was not, in my father's view, a true Master. It was perfectly honorable to go into business or take up a trade of some sort; it was the artist who was pilloried with his rancor and contempt, as if he or she were a heretic blaspheming against all that was pure and holy. I'm not talking just about serious attempts at literature. I'd seen him go purple denouncing some hippie maker of macramé plant-holders at a crafts fair

---

*The "life corner," or *tokonoma,* is the place of highest honor in the house, a small alcove in which the family places a beautiful scroll or piece of pottery, maybe some flowers—but only the best is saved for this place of quiet meditation. Guests are seated with their backs to the alcove so that they become part of the place of highest honor and are (spiritually) protected by it.

who had the nerve to call himself an artist. Folk art by housewives at the Cornish fair was okay, it just depressed him. But just let someone fancy him- or herself to be a real artist, and I'd receive an enraged outpouring that lasted the entire car ride if I was unlucky enough to be a captive audience.

The only things I could do well, in eighth grade, were things I had learned so long ago that I couldn't remember a time when I didn't know how to do them well. I learned to ski when I was three or four, play piano at three, read before kindergarten. My view of creation as a sort of miraculous immaculate conception was supported by my father's mythic stories about me, like the time I went to the keyboard before I could barely stand unassisted and picked out a tune perfectly, the first time. I was surprised to learn at Cross Mountain that I wasn't wonderful at the piano. I had a lot of natural talent, but there were kids who actually practiced, and practiced in an organized, disciplined fashion. My piano teacher that year wrote:

> Peggy's piano work is characterized by a desire to skim the fundamentals in order to achieve a momentary "splash." Her ability to concentrate on work that is not of immediate and obvious appeal is curiously lacking. She has a talent and could probably easily achieve a considerable competence if she were more willing to work a little.

While I certainly understand this teacher's interpretation of my behavior as a sort of laziness, the fact is that the concept of creation as a process, rather than as a product that magically appeared if you had the genius, eluded me totally and completely. Salingers do things perfectly or they keep quiet about it. Again, I'm not talking about poetry here, I mean every aspect of life you can imagine. I never even followed a recipe, for example, until I was married; I truly thought food just happened or flopped. Mine flopped, so why bother. I ate out of the box or carton. As for keeping a room clean, controlling and manipulating the stuff of life in actuality, rather than the stuff of the mind in daydreams, I waited in a panic until I was neck deep in mess and somehow hurled a drowning battle scream and attacked it. My closest and most eloquent friend, David, once stood at the transom to my Marlborough Street

apartment and said, "Peggy, that's not a kitchen, that's a cry for help."
My college thesis adviser used to ask me, nearly every time he saw me,
"Peggy, how do you eat an elephant?" The right answer: you cut it up
into very small pieces. The Salinger answer: you drag it into a dark cave,
alone, and swallow it whole or die trying to vomit it up. Or you declare
that anyone who eats elephant is beneath contempt and stalk off in the
other direction.

There was an even more pressing reason than shame and ignorance
to hide away any interest or desire. Had I loved, it would be a small matter of time before the scent of my pleasure drifted upstairs to Kit's den. It
slipped out, that fall, probably via one of my teachers' activity reports,
that I passionately wanted to go on an overnight riding trip to Clifford's
Falls. Each time a trip came up, I would sign up, and each time Kit
erased my name and informed me that I'd have to wait until next time.
Finally, on the last trip before graduation, she let me plan and anticipate,
rather than removing my name from the sign-up sheet as she had done
before, right up until the evening before we were to leave. She caught
me in the hall on the way upstairs to bed and said, "I'm sorry, Peggy, but
I just don't think you've earned the privilege of going on the riding trip
tomorrow." Had I had a horse phobia, you can bet I'd have been saddled
up faster than Annie Oakley.

⋆⋆⋆

I PUT MY UNLOVELY CHRISTMAS PRESENTS into my suitcase along with
my teddy bear, and a pile of clothes no one would know were mine
without the name tags.* As I closed my bag, Jenny called up the stairs to
see if my father had arrived. She was going to catch a ride home with us.
Her family lived in Woodstock, Vermont, which was directly on our
way.

She left her suitcase at the door, but carried her precious violin upstairs. By seventh grade, Jenny was already an accomplished musician. I
had accompanied her several times in concert, playing the simple basso

---

*One of my chores that fall was laundry. With name tags, nothing is hidden. I
had an intimate knowledge of who had been naughty or nice—bed wetters, first-
time bleeders, all the privacy of medieval wedding sheets held aloft for all to in-
spect and proclaim the deed done.

continuo while she soared above. That week Jenny, Jason—another violinist—and I had played a Vivaldi concerto for two violins and harpsichord/piano as we had done earlier for the Thanksgiving "showcase" for the parents. This time we were taken in a van to an old-age home to play. I was a little frightened to be around old people. Frightened of the smells and the infirmity. Some of the old people did sit in their wheelchairs in the day room and drool, their minds a million miles away. But the joy that lit up many of the faces as they listened to us play was something to behold. I couldn't believe that playing music could make someone's eyes come to life like that. It was the most valuable piece of education I could possibly have been given. It is natural, I think, to feel small and helpless in the face of great suffering and need. I felt I had so little to offer. I still feel that way. Yet somehow, miraculously, our meager offering of a few loaves and fishes was transformed into a feast for the multitudes. This first Christmas concert gave me the courage, year after year, to visit the sick, the aged, the lonely, often with empty hands but trusting that somehow in touching the hands of a stranger a gift would appear.

I asked Jenny not to mention the concert to my father. I just said he was weird about that stuff. I knew exactly what his reaction would be, but it was too hard to explain. Charity was a highly combustible subject at our house. If my mother was foolish enough to let him get wind of any charitable act she might have undertaken, he'd say, "Oh, Christ, it's the Lady Bountiful. Ego, ego, ego," or, "The Lady Bountiful, thinking how good and kind and generous she is being—Phooey!" Twenty years later when I finally read his books, again and again I came across the same haranguing suspicion and denunciation of any unveiled female act of charity. Holden, reflecting on the nuns he met collecting for charity, thought how his aunt, or Sally Hayes's mother, both of whom did a lot of charitable work, would never do it without lipstick and fancy dresses "and all that crap," and people around to "kiss their asses." Or again, in "A Perfect Day for Bananafish," a four-year-old girl asks Seymour about his wife:

"Where's the lady?" Sybil said.

"The lady?" the young man brushed some sand out of his thin hair. "That's hard to say, Sybil. She may be in any one of a thousand places. At the hairdresser's. Having her hair dyed mink. Or making dolls for poor children, in her room."

My father would, in all seriousness, rather step over a hungry man and do nothing to help him than help him and feel as though he were a swell guy to help. If you do a charitable act you have to do it perfectly, the left hand not knowing what the right hand does. Otherwise it's all ego and not worth doing.

If you're standing outside a theater and some old gal comes up selling gum, give her a buck if you've got a buck—but only if you can do it without patronizing her.

For *whom* is it not worth anything? one might ask. The recipient is not even in the picture. Only the reflection of the one attempting to make a mitzvah is beheld. Missing is the vast area between Mrs. Hayes and the nuns, between being such a jerk that you make the person you are giving to feel like dirt, and being the perfection of God incarnate. For my father there is nothing in between, no sense of God or "goodness" being able to use imperfect vessels. No sense of being good enough. No middle ground between perfection and damnation. No big round earth to walk on between heaven and hell.

Luckily, kids don't need an explanation when you ask them not to talk about something in front of your parents. All parents are kind of weird anyway. Jenny said not to worry, she wouldn't mention the concert.

My father arrived and we piled into the car. On the way home, Jenny and I sang to amuse ourselves. We had learned lots of rounds at school that fall. Daddy was enchanted. He made us promise to send him a tape, from school, of us singing. We never got around to it, though, I'm afraid to say. Partly because I didn't bother, which isn't nice, and partly because I had this weird feeling that he had mistaken me for someone else. Our singing in the car wasn't just beautiful or pretty, to him it was *perfect,* it was poetry. He had made such a big deal of our singing that I felt like an impostor; if I taped it, he'd realize how ordinary and just plain pretty—not magnificent—it was. It's a weird feeling to be given powers you know you don't possess, to be put on a pedestal, albeit temporarily.

Four hours later, we arrived in Woodstock. The stage set was in place and there were white Christmas lights, with bits of greenery and holly, on all the bridges and houses in the square. We said good-bye to Jenny and headed over the river to Cornish.

When you're a kid, to know what your house really looks like, you have to go away for a while and come back again. This time I noticed things. You approach my father's by making a sharp turn off the dirt road into his driveway. You can't slow down in the wintertime to make the turn without the risk of not making it up the steep driveway. Unlike the road, which is packed dirt, the driveway has a layer of chipped stones, horrid stones to walk on with bare feet because they're all pointy. They make a treacherous scree in the winter as well.

The driveway leads directly into the mouth of his garage. Between the garage and the house on the hill above it is an underground passageway of cement with dozens of small steps. The builder made a three-inch rise instead of the standard one for some reason, and it feels as though one is taking baby steps. We long-legged Salingers find this particularly annoying. At the top of the passage is a door leading into the cellar of the house. It's more like a cave than a basement. This is because the land my father chose for a building site wasn't meant to accommodate a house. The builders dynamited through a steep slope of thick granite, just enough to allow a house to perch on the edge, rather like mountaineers setting up camp with slings on a narrow ledge. The cellar is not built of concrete blocks; it's just blasted-out rock with some cement poured on the floor to make it flat enough for the freezer and washer-dryer to sit. You come to another door and enter the house. Sort of. You have to climb up one more flight of stairs to reach the living room of this modest, chalet-style, one-level ranch.

The living room has what in modern parlance is called a cathedral ceiling, meaning it is higher than the regulation eight feet and set at an angle rather than flat. A wall of windows opens onto the view of Mt. Ascutney and beyond into New York State. Unlike the house in which I grew up in Cornish, where one had the comfortable feeling of being grounded somehow despite the immensity of the view, Daddy's house is perched on the side of a steep hill with no cozy enfolding of trees and no feeling of being on the ground. It's like the view out an airplane window or a skyscraper, a little less human, a little less real. A cliff wall.

I don't know if it ever struck my father that way. It's not the sort of thing I'd bring up with him. He might have gotten touchy about it. The view is rarely visible, however. My father keeps the curtains drawn, or mostly drawn, day and night. Light comes through where the curtains stumble and fall across backs of chairs or little tables. The view is revealed a bit like the "good furniture" in a lower-middle-class living room—on special occasions and for visitors. My brother's house, I noticed last time I visited, stands in a similar odd relation to the vast beauty of the view. He built his house on a steep slope in Malibu, gotten at a bargain price because developers had considered the land unusable to accommodate a house. A great wall of windows gives you a 180-degree panoramic view of the Pacific Ocean. All the expense and design of a modern house to take advantage of the spectacular view, and the blinds, made of lovely transparent rice-paper-looking manmade material, are drawn 95 percent of the time, day and night. They're lifted for the occasional sunset, or when I visit and like to sit and stare.

Perhaps the view becomes too familiar to notice over time, indistinguishable from a brick wall outside the window of a cheap apartment that you think you won't be able to bear but in time becomes nearly invisible, part of the woodwork as it were. I have moved apartments probably twenty-five times in my life, most of the moves as a teenager and in my twenties. I learned that if you don't make a change, paint the wall, fix an eyesore, replace an ugly tile within two weeks of moving in, you'll never do it. The eye, in time, is a frighteningly good editor and smoother of flaws. It takes a guest coming to visit to remind one of the dwelling's eyesores.

Eyesores. That brings me to my father's deck. It was made cheaply and badly. The railings were rickety even when first built and offered little real security and much false. Over the years the boards rotted out in several places, leaving one with the precarious feeling of a rope bridge spanning a jungle river, the hero's leg falling through a gap in the planks as the bad guys come nearer and nearer. I would *never* let my son out on it. The deck extends about four feet from the living room on two sides, chalet-style. It should be a glorious place to savor the wilderness from the safety of home, like a snowstorm watched from beside the hearth, or rain from shelter. It is nice to have drinks out there, but it would have been nicer if it had been done right—providing that sense of security so necessary to porch pleasure. Instead, it's like looking over the edge of a cliff. My father, as if seeing the deck through my eyes, and hating me a little for it, would wiggle the railings with a look of disgust and no little irritation. It was the same expression he wore when reaching his hand upward in a house with low ceilings and found he could touch them, or when entering a cab that was neither his beloved London cab nor a New York Checker cab, with their raised roof. He seemed ashamed of the broken stairs leading up to the deck, but he never had them repaired.* He just sort of hated you for witnessing it and thereby, as in the Zen tree falling in the forest, or Teddy's orange peels, making it real.

My visiting, even as a child, but more so the older I got, made him aware, because of my otherness, my presence, not because I mentioned it, that the house was not perfect. Nor was it clean. It was neat and orderly, but not cared for beyond the surface tidying. The Oriental rugs in the living room were some beauties he had bought over the years at nearby auctions, along with an assortment of lamps and end tables. If you looked up, however, the air of tasteful country gentility ended abruptly at the wainscoting. The ceiling in the living room was a rather horrid, nubbly, sprayed-on, textured stuff that he cursed the builders for talking him into. Mind you, he *is* a tightwad about nearly everything, and the house is a prime example of the adage "you get what you pay for." Cobwebs and soot from his fireplace clung to the nubbly ceiling, which, in a few years, went beyond "bachelor dirty" to eccentric. The toilet bowl in the bathroom my brother and I used, the "guest" bathroom, became stained and brown in only a year or two from minerals and lack of routine swishing. There were always clean towels for us, but I never liked to put my toothbrush down on the sink. Without putting it into words, I was aware that cleaning it myself would have been an embarrassment to him, an insult, a commentary on his lack of attention. He so disliked anything squalid and unclean that to acknowledge it would have been an unthinkably rude awakening. The water that came out of the faucets was from an artesian well, but unlike the water in the Red house, this smelled badly of sulfur.

---

*Sometime in the nineties, his third wife, Colleen, had them repaired.

He used to have a cleaning lady come in to help out, but she was so talkative that it drove him crazy to have her around. Had she been unpleasant or mean, he could have cut her off and retreated to his study guiltlessly. The problem was that he knew her to be a kind woman, and he therefore felt terribly guilty about not being able to bear her chattering presence. In the end, the human encounter proved too much for him and he eased her out.

Behind the living room, going into the hillside as it were, is a galley kitchen and a parallel narrow, long bathroom, each ending in the door to my brother's and my room. It was not really ours, but it was the one that was called ours when we visited. When Daddy had the house built, we were allowed to choose the colors for the paint and trim for the room. Being kids, we chose our favorite Crayola-crayon colors, aqua (pronounced a resounding New Hampshire *ack-wa* not *ah-kwa*) and magenta. We wound up with a subdued pastel pink, not magenta, and the trim was forest green, not aqua, but it was close enough; we weren't too disappointed. The closet mostly held Daddy's good suits and jackets, the top shelf, one or two hats and some bags of things that we never looked into. We made room in the closet for our stuff when we visited. I think a drawer or two in "our" dresser was made available as well. Mostly though, our things just stayed in our suitcases under the twin beds.

I don't know why his suits didn't fit into his own bedroom closet. Though I've visited his house for more than thirty years now, I've never seen his closet or his bathroom. His bedroom, bath, and study are in an L off the kitchen. The door is kept locked. I've been invited inside maybe two or three times in my life when he wanted to show me something in his study. Once it was some new bookshelves he was thrilled with. Another time to show me a new filing system he had thought up for the material in one of his safes. A red mark meant, if I die before I finish my work, publish this "as is," blue meant publish but edit first, and so on.

Several big, floor-to-ceiling safes were housed in the room that was his study/bedroom before he built the L. My memory is a bit hazy about this room, but I remember clearly that at one time he slept in it, because he showed me how he had rigged up the bed so that his feet would be higher than his head, for some yoga reason. Beds had to point due north as well, for electromagnetic health. Above the safes in the old bedroom/study were reels and reels of movies collected over the years before video. The top edges of the room, where a picture rail might be, were papered with my old drawings from his Green house.

The dogs, Joey and Nice Doggie, barked like madmen as always when we arrived. Joey was the dachshund we got after Malinka, a large white husky, began snacking on our neighbor's pigs. Apparently she didn't even bother to kill them first: she just bit chunks out of them on the hoof. I was about seven at the time. My mother told me what Malinka had done and said that we had to give her away to an Alaskan sled-dog team. When I was fifteen, my boyfriend Dan, who loved Nice Doggie, asked me about other dogs I'd grown up with. I told him about Malinka and how we had had to give her away to an Alaskan sled-dog team. He looked at me in silence and then with an eyebrow raised said, "Pegs, Alaska?" "Ooh!" I remembered hearing at the Windsor diner that someone had shot a white wolf, but I hadn't put two and two together. Funny how certain things from one's youth get buried in a time capsule. Just as well.

After the great white Malinka, my parents bought Joey, a dachshund puppy whose tail had been slammed in a door by accident. When he wagged, it looked a bit like a propeller. Looking at silly city dachshunds in their sweaters and bootees, you'd never guess that they were bred for badger hunting. Real badgers, not the cute ones in stories, have a set of nasty teeth and a temperament to match and are about the last creature you'd want to go down a hole and drag out. That's just what dachshunds do. Joey turned out to be a far more avid and bloodthirsty hunter than Malinka had ever dreamed of being; she was just too lazy to come home for lunch, I think, and stopped for a bite to eat. Joey *lived* for hunting. But his chosen prey were wild, not domestic, animals, so he was not deported to an Austrian badger team. He would disappear for days at a time, and you could hear his blood-crazed howl coming from somewhere deep in the forest. He was either a little crazy or a little stupid or probably both in his single-minded pursuit; I cannot tell you how many times he came home with a face full of porcupine quills that my parents had to pull out one by one with pliers. And the number of tomato-juice baths after being sprayed by a skunk—countless.

Joey was also allergic to bees. When stung, he went into convulsions and became rigid and had to go to the vet for shots. Daddy tried to treat him homeopathically with no luck. He lived nearly fifteen years before Daddy accidentally ran over him with his tractor while mowing the field. It was sort of a relief. Never a terribly savory dog—my brother and I used to watch in horror and fascination when he licked his "red thing" as we called it—he grew quite arthritic and wheezy in his old age and spent most of his time asleep, twitching and grunting on the rug in dream pursuit of his nemesis.

Nice Doggie was a prince among dogs. He was a mutt with lovely brown eyes, blondish fur, and a body that looked like that of a well-fed fox. He showed up on my father's deck one day and simply would not leave. Nice Doggie had chosen him and that was that. My father relented after several days and took him in. He named him Nice Doggie because he said he liked the idea of a little child patting the dog and saying "nice doggie" and then Daddy could say, "That's his name, how did you know?"

❦

MY FATHER IS A SUPERB DOG WHISTLER. He can put two fingers, pointer and ring man, in his mouth and call the dogs miles away. I tried and tried to learn to whistle like that. All I got was dizzy. My brother can't do it either. I think an oboe reed is probably easier to master. The whole family finds highland sheepdog trials with their subtle and nuanced language of whistles and gestures one of the most thrilling things on the planet. My father especially.

Nice Doggie was happy to see me. He was so intelligent that you knew when he was happy to see you, he meant it. Joey was happy to see anybody who fed him. After nearly four months at Cross Mountain, I felt about like Joey. Food. I stood in front of the refrigerator and hardly knew where to begin, a whole den full of badgers. At my father's house, though, you sort of had to sneak food. He didn't so much mind your eating, it just drove him crazy to have somebody else poking around his kitchen. I used his pans wrong or put things back in the wrong place or didn't put things in the dishwasher the way he did. He grumped about the mess and having to do dishes, but he couldn't stand it when you did them either. He let me fix myself something to eat once in a while, but you could tell he forced himself to. And he just couldn't stop himself from hovering nervously. Most of his kitchen stuff was from Sears, not fine china, but it didn't matter. He always had weird drinking glasses that he was excited to have discovered. That year he had these hourglass-shaped glasses that looked like miniature drip coffeemakers. The ice would stick in the bottom half for a while and then, without warning, slip over the middle ridge and plummet into your teeth or nose. Boy was I glad when the last of those glasses broke. A lot of the stuff he had back then that I thought was weird was, like his interest in alternative medicine, just twenty years ahead of its time. Chinese rice bowls, chopsticks, tamari, sesame seeds, steamers—all standard items nowadays in an urban middle-class kitchen. Those glasses haven't made it yet though, thank goodness.

It is a tall person's kitchen. The shelves are built up high, and useful things such as cereal and rice are on top shelves where people of average height tend to store odd parts of food processors and pimentos. He has big, glass honey jars filled with gingersnaps, hard candies, and treats, which he digs into guiltily and hungrily. "Poison," he'd say. They look beautiful. His freezers upstairs and down are packed, post-Depression/post-rationing style; if you like something, buy dozens and hoard them. Packed away are the latest Sara Lee cakes he's discovered, vegetables from last summer's garden, sticky buns from the Hanover Co-op, boxes of pure frozen horse meat (don't ask, I have *no* idea why) for the dogs.

He hates to cook and complains and grumps and generally creates a tense atmosphere when he does. Nevertheless, he takes no shortcuts. He makes beautiful soups from scratch with vegetables from the garden and beans and rice. He's always on the lookout for good recipes and, when he finds one he likes, often sends it to those he thinks might be worthy of such a good soup. The list grows smaller.

Breakfast at his house is always delicious. He cooks eggs perfectly, never runny or overdone, a buttered toasted bagel, green (cooked) little peas or perhaps some wild greens he's picked on one of his walks, and wild mushrooms broiled in butter. He squeezes oranges on a hand juicer and mixes in just a bit of fresh lime. My tastebuds prickle just thinking of it. I think I appreciated it so much, even at that unappreciative age, because of the striking contrast to the daily fare at my mother's. Hers was straight from the English nursery: milky, runny scrambled eggs that we called mucous eggs or snot-on-toast, and Special K, which, in its dry meagerness, made me feel anything but special.

At my mother's house we ate breakfast at the table, often with cereal boxes stacked a foot high between my brother and me in such a way as to create a demilitarized zone; we fought less when we couldn't see each other. My mother grimly chewed her food over the din, while enforcing the rule that you had to eat half of whatever you had on your plate. At my father's, we ate at a table only when my brother was quite small; after that we ate on trays in front of the television. This was a treat when I was young, but the older I got, the more the constant presence of the television at mealtimes bothered me, especially as my father grew increasingly deaf and the volume got louder and louder.

The next morning, with the predictability of Old Faithful, the comments would begin indicating he had enjoyed my presence long enough. I'd seen it every overnight visit for years. First, the pacing would start. Up and down the living room like a caged cat. This was followed by the general observation, directed at the air, and to no one present of course, "I can never get any work done when *people* are around."

He'd set us up in front of the TV while he went back to his study to attempt a few hours of work, but it was clear he was not successful in doing more than a few bills or necessary letters. So, too, his irritation at my "constant *fressing*"* grew. There was nothing to do at his house in the middle of winter beyond eating and movies and TV anyway. Reading was done surreptitiously because God help you if you were reading a book he didn't think was a *good* one. Talking to my friends on the phone was tricky because it pissed him off and there wasn't any privacy in the living room.

It's hard to relax when you know you're an irritant, that your mere existence is an irritation, regardless of your behavior. The following day, forty-eight hours after I had arrived, my brother and I went back to my mother's house in Norwich, where I spent the rest of my vacation.

On the way back to school, Mom passed the Farleighs' car on the

---

*Yiddish for animals eating: people *ess,* animals *fress.*

highway. They had three children at Cross Mountain. We pulled over and it was decided that I would ride back with them. It was perfectly sensible, but I couldn't bear it. I wanted to cry out, but I couldn't. I was four years old again, trapped under the sheets, tears silently running down my face, and all the fireflies were dead or in hibernation.

23

Midwinter

❦❦❦

In the bleak mid-winter,
frosty wind made moan,
the earth as hard as iron,
water turned to stone.

Snow lay falling, snow on snow,
snow on snow on snow;
in the deep mid-winter,
long, long ago.

—Anonymous

ONE DARK DAY IN JANUARY, Kit noticed an oversight in my character molding. I had not yet "volunteered" to take advantage of the
opportunity to participate in any of the overnight camping trips.* She
informed me that if I didn't participate in the very next trip, I would not
graduate. It was a three-day hike, midwinter, up Mt. Marcy, the highest
peak in the Adirondacks, wearing regular stiff, heavy, 1969, downhill
ski boots and regular heavy, downhill skis that had sealskins strapped to
the bottom of them for traction, which of course broke or slipped loose
every half hour or so, necessitating bare-fingered adjustments that
would have tested the patience of a watchmaker.

I was deeply scared because, past a certain altitude, I can't breathe. I

---

*"We want our students to be lost and be able to find themselves, to be cold
and know they can find warmth, to be hungry and know they won't starve," said
Kit in an interview in 1968.

had discovered this at Camp Billings and had been reminded of it again the summer before Cross Mountain at the ski camp on a glacier. The van dropped us off beside the road at the entrance to a trail. We set off, rugged, resilient, and resourceful, wearing our downhill skis (not light, cross-country ones), carrying full packs of food, clothing, and sleeping bags. Eight children and one, count 'em, *one* teacher. "If a body catch a body comin' through the rye . . ." It didn't take a genius to figure out that there was no turning back. If somebody were to break a leg, the teacher would have to carry the child a full day's hike to the road and leave the rest of us on the mountain alone. We had no radio communication, and for the entire three days, we passed no one. It was irresponsible, idiotic, and insane.

Here's my "risible tale" of injury and mishap on a mandatory outing, which, as Seymour said about strawberrying in the mud, no thirty-year-old man nor sixty-year-old woman had any business inflicting on a child:

At first the trail was fairly level and manageable. We skied all morning. By lunch, I was exhausted but not collapsing. By the afternoon, the trail began to climb, and by evening we reached the shelter where we would spend the first night. Our camp was an open-faced lean-to, the shape of a triangle on its side but somebody forgot to draw in one of the lines. Food is supposed to taste good cooked out of doors, but this was no Eddie Bauer commercial. It was freeze-dried slop that stuck in the throat on the way down. We ate quickly and almost silently, too worn-out even to joke around. I peeled off my damp jeans, climbed into my sleeping bag in a line of other children side by side like peas. The only bit of luck was that my bag was next to a boy I had a crush on. I enjoyed knowing he was near for the few seconds I remained conscious.

The next morning, I realized the stupidity of taking off damp jeans. They were frozen stiff. The sky was an ominous gray and a light snow began to fall. We ate breakfast and set off, leaving our sleeping bags there and carrying only food. The trail was steep from here on in, and I followed endless herringbone ski marks of the kids in front of me as they ascended. I became keenly aware of my pulse beginning to drown out all other sound in my ears. Several hours into it, I saw fear in my teacher's face when he looked at mine. I asked him what was wrong, and he told me my face had suddenly gone from bright red to ashen. He took my pack, but there was nothing to do but go on. There was no hint whatsoever of my being a slacker; it was clear that my best was not good enough. Dangerously so. I think it dawned on him, at that moment, just how out on a limb we really were.

It was a task not of his own making. He was quite happy, I think, to take kids who were up to it and wanted to go, but it was another thing coaxing a child he knew was forced into it. He, like many of the other teachers who found their way to Cross Mountain, was a bit of a misfit. He was an extraordinarily peculiar-looking, ears-akimbo, awkward kind of guy. I was never quite sure whether he had been in a terrible accident that had rearranged his face sort of all over the place, or whether he had been born that way. Paul would have been quite ugly-looking but for the fact that he didn't have a mean bone in his body. Instead, his gentleness modulated his features into an odd, quizzical expression.

I learned a terrible law of the forced march: the person who needs the most rest gets the least. Every time the teacher and I caught up to the other kids, they had been waiting some fifteen to thirty minutes. So after five minutes of rest, it was time to push on. I felt like the biggest failure on earth. I didn't understand the rosy glow I saw in the other kids' faces. It became clear to the teacher and to me that I was on the verge of collapse. I was ashen, dry; I had no more sweat or tears; I couldn't think straight. I heard myself moaning as I climbed. I hadn't enough strength to cry. The other kids can do it. And I may die. Weak, weak, weak. Kit's words struck home. I must be a coward. I have no moral fiber, I don't have what it takes. Failure.

Late in the afternoon we hit the tree line. The kids were waiting, having a snack. Breathing was nearly impossible. I inhaled in harsh doglike cries and whimpers that utterly humiliated me to have all the kids hear, but it was beyond my control. Paul told me to look up at the mountain because we could see the top for the first time. It was the *worst* thing I could have done. I can't judge distances, and though, in reality, it was about an hour further, it looked to me as though we still had to go the distance we had come, and I knew that was out of the question, beyond any glimmer of a possibility. I looked down at the snow and barren rocks of that scrubby elevation in utter despair and lay facedown in the snow to die.

I began to leave my body. I didn't know then that I have an autonomic response that causes rapid and life-threatening dehydration. At forty, failure and collapse can occur within a half hour or so of adrenal stress or vomiting and I'm in the hospital for a day or two before I'm properly rehydrated and stable. At thirteen, I thought it was some shameful weakness. What I knew then and know today beyond a shadow of a doubt is that a boy named Charles Romney saved my life.

To this day I think of him as an angel entertained unawares.* I didn't know him very well. I'm not sure anyone did. He was the boy I mentioned that some kids teased because of his slight twitching and odd gait. Lying facedown in the snow, I think the other kids were probably afraid to come near me, the way an injured animal or a sick person can be sort of sickening or creepy to witness. Charles had left the group, unbeknownst to me—I was out of it—and sat down beside me in the snow where I lay. He said, "I just want you to know I think you're really brave."

It was like being shocked with paddles back from death. I turned my face in the snow a little and looked at him with one eye and said, "Why?"

Charles said, "I know Kit made you do this, and I think you're really brave, that's all." We didn't say any more. He gave me some water and I slowly drank. After a time I took a piece of bread, the first my body would accept that day, and then another. Communion. I didn't pee until we arrived back at school a full day later. I only noticed because, back at the lean-to, I thought myself lucky not to have to bare my bottom to the dull, cold wind.

When I plunged my face into the icy river by the campsite, it was a sharp pain, like cutting oneself, pain that said you're still alive, away from the dull place beyond pain, the sluggish, sucking vortex where death comes slowly, like the thick, dark molasses that I finally urinated.

---

*Hebrews 13:2—"Be not forgetful to entertain strangers, whereby some have entertained angels unawares."

24

Springtime in Paradise: *The Producers*

❧❧

THE BIG PURGE CAME IN THE SPRING. My friend Jamie and my
boyfriend Dougal were expelled; Dougal's best friend, Brion, and I
were placed on probation till the end of the year. It had something to do
with a pack of cigarettes, I think, but I honestly can't remember the details. They got lost in the awfulness of the aftermath. I'm sure it was
something dumb, equally sure it was not wicked or life-threatening. It
was nothing like giving little kids cigarettes, I'd never ever do something like that, nor, may I say, like sending eight kids up a mountain in
midwinter with only one adult.

In recounting this tale, I'm conscious of setting a bad example: I
haven't forgiven myself, as I'd urge another to do, for the betrayal I was
coerced into committing. Even saying "They made me do it" sounds
lame. No one had a gun to my head. I violated one of my most deeply
held principles of loyalty to my friends. I didn't tell on someone, that
would have taken many, many more "sessions" with Kit. But after I
wrote the hugely embarrassing letter to my mother in which I confessed
to being a sick sexual pervert, a lesbian, and a crazy, paranoid person
who imagined that people were out to get me, Kit had one last thing she
required. (Bring me the broomstick of the Wicked Witch of the West.)
If I was to graduate and get the hell out of that place, I had to write to
my friend Jamie, who had just been expelled, a letter that Kit had composed, but in my own hand, confessing how wrong we all were and
what loathsome creatures we were, etc. She told me I had an hour to

think about it and come back with my decision. Write the letter and graduate, or not.

I went up the hill alone to decide what to do. I asked myself, How can I bear another year in this place? If I run away, where do I have to go? I reasoned that Jamie knows Kit and won't believe a word of it. She'll know I'd never say anything crappy like that. I decided to copy Kit's letter and send it. And that's what I did. Jamie's guardian, a great supporter of the school, wrote me a *really* nasty letter in return, which I received back at home in Cornish that summer. She said, quite rightly, that what Jamie needed now was support from her friends, not shaming, and that I should be ashamed of myself for writing such a letter. I was. Totally. "I betray you, you betray me underneath the chestnut tree," as it says in Orwell's *1984*. Do it to her, not me, to her.

Why I couldn't organize myself to write back and tell her guardian what had happened I don't know, and I sorely regret it. But Kit would probably have lied her way out of it in any case. I felt like a piece of shit for agreeing to sign the letter and copy it in my own handwriting. I really thought Jamie wouldn't pay a bit of attention, but of course I'm sure Kit didn't let her go without setting her up to believe she, too, was a worthless piece of shit. Jamie had been a dues-paying member of the Prob Kids Club for years and a recipient of Kit's "help" for too long not to be thoroughly convinced that she was an orphan because no one, except Kit of course, could want such a defective kid in the first place. How could Jamie ever expect to be attractive and lose all that blubber if she persisted in sneaking in candy—as if a clandestine candy bar every month or so would cause the perhaps fifteen pounds extra she carried, perfectly natural for a twelve-year-old. Kit, whether bluntly or by intimation, let Jamie know that her guardian entrusted her to Kit to make a young lady out of her. Everyone else had given up on her, and it was Kit's duty to help.

That was the deep mind-"melting" message: we're the last stop before nobody takes care of you. I was convinced it was CMS or the streets. I had no idea of any other options. None. No shark-infested waters were needed around this Alcatraz. We "prob kids" were convinced that we had no place else to go, and worse, that no one else would take us in.

One kid, and only one, saw through the big lie. He was a seventh-grade scholarship boy from Harlem. After he figured out the bus schedule, he stole out of the dorm one night, about a month into the term, walked the seven miles to the bus station under cover of darkness, and was halfway to Harlem before he was discovered missing. He was the only kid we had ever heard of who ran away. You can bet his mama didn't send him back to those crazy white folks either. From deep within the library chimney, we cheered and cheered.

❦

THE SENIORS, AS WE EIGHTH GRADERS WERE CALLED, had to apply to schools for next year. A few of us had no choice in the matter: these were legacy kids running back several generations at certain schools. For most of us, though, the matter was decided during library time where we pored over the large guide to independent secondary schools. Camilla, who lived for horses, chose a school that didn't even bother to show the school buildings—they went right to the thoroughbred stables, Foxy Croft or something. I hope it was a lovely choice. Five of us, including Holly, chose the Cambridge School of Weston on the basis of one outstanding feature: it was the closest co-ed boarding school to a major city. The description in the book said students often took the train into Boston on weekends to take advantage of the rich cultural attractions the area has to offer. Bliss! Coffee, sidewalks, public transportation, freedom.

The girls all wore new white dresses for graduation. Mom and I found a beautiful one in Hanover with cutout lace flowers on the sleeves. Jason, who would also attend the Cambridge School in the fall, and I performed a concerto for violin and piano. I played Robespierre in the senior play. Both my parents came. I rode home in Dad's car. My brother rode with my mother.

❦

HERBERT AND KIT RETIRED several years after I was graduated. They were gone by the time my brother went to Cross Mountain. He loved it. He might have loved it even if they were still in charge, who knows? He even held a fund-raiser for the school at his home in Malibu and is currently on the board of directors. A brief perusal of the alumni magazine makes clear that some people, looking back, remember Cross Mountain as the best years of their lives. None of us is wrong about the place. Like most places it can be heaven or hell depending on the company. The point I tried to impress upon my brother is that any total environment like that—a boarding school, a prison, a mental institution, the family, the army—needs far more checks and balances built in to ensure that vulnerable populations are treated appropriately by those charged with their welfare.

This did not happen for my friends. When I left Cross Mountain for Cambridge School, I kept in touch with eight classmates out of a total graduating class of about twenty. By the end of *ninth* grade, within the year following graduation from Cross Mountain, Jason, my concertmate who had had the privilege of four years at Cross Mountain, was in a mental hospital—I watched him start having to count everything in the universe or it would blow up; Dougal was in a mental hospital and later took his own life; Jamie was in a mental hospital; Charles, the boy who saved my life, was in a mental hospital the following year and is now dead; Holly was drinking herself into a benumbed stupor; Brion was dead, Dougal told me, from an overdose of heroin; and as for me, I was not a girl who had come through with all her f-a-c-u-l-t-i-e-s intact. When I was finally scared into seeking psychiatric help at age sixteen, I was diagnosed as a "borderline," a designation that could not have described more accurately a young person at the edge of a crazy cliff.

Domine Jesu Christe, Rex gloriae, libera animas omnium fidelium de poenis inferni et de profundo lacu: libera eas de ore leonis, ne absorbeat eas tartarus, ne cadant in obscurum: sed signifer sanctus Michael repraesentet eas in lucem sanctam. Quam olim Abrahae promisisti et semini ejus.*

---

*"Lord Jesus Christ, King of Glory, deliver all faithful souls from pain infernal and from the bottomless abyss: deliver us from the jaws of the Lion, let not her teeth devour us and swallow us down into dark oblivion: let St. Michael lead us into holy light. As Thou promised of old to Abraham and to his seed." From the Latin Mass for the Dead.

Or, please say the Mourners' Kaddish, which concludes:

O'seh shalom beem-romav, hoo ya'ah-seh shalom aleynu v'al kol Yisrael, ve'imru amen. (Let He who makes peace in the heavens, grant peace to all of us and to all Israel. Let us say Amen.)

25

Woodstock

❧❧❧

On either side the river lie
Long fields of barley and of rye,
That clothe the wold and meet the sky;
And thro' the field the road runs by
*   To many-tower'd Camelot.*

LIZA, MY FRIEND FROM SKI CAMP, called to tell me the big news: there was going to be a music festival not too far from her house, on Yasgur's farm. Could I come? Wild horses . . . There was only one problem; when I told my father about the festival, he said it sounded like fun and wanted to come along. Okay, forget for a moment that you think Holden's creator is the coolest guy in the universe. Imagine it was *your* dad who wanted to join the fun. Oh, boy! Later that week, he decided he had too much work piled up on his desk to take a break and go with us. Gee, Dad, that's too bad, really. I called Liza and told her the bad news: WE'RE SAVED!!!

I arrived at their house with a small bag containing what would be my uniform for the next three years: blue jeans and my dad's button-down oxford shirts worn untucked. A few days before the festival, Liza and I were devastated to learn that her parents had no intention of letting us stay the night at Woodstock—notwithstanding my howls of "But my dad would have let me." Mrs. R. knew the back way to the farm and dropped us off each morning within about a mile or so of the concert field and picked us up each evening at the same meeting spot. Liza and I slipped right into the gentle crowd and were gone. "We are stardust, we are golden, and we've got to get ourselves back to the garden."

I don't care how impossible it is to believe, Woodstock really was a momentary glimpse of paradise on earth. I find it hard to write about, because so many of the things I want to say that were beautiful are things that in any other context make me squirm, such as being all brothers and sisters, sharing food, sharing hugs; even the word *sharing* now sets off my cult-alert button. Then, however, it was as though the entire natural world declared a three-day cease-fire on carnivorous activity. I have never before or since felt so able to "let my hair down" and be myself in public. Boundaries could come down because there was such an extraordinary absence of predatory trespassing. And I'm not talking about those gatherings and workshops where people are coerced into "open" behavior, mandated "sharing time," like being caught passing notes in school and the teacher asks you if you'd like to come up front and *share* it with the rest of the class. At Woodstock, for a few moments, there was no pressure to conform and no pressure to nonconform. If you wanted to take your clothes off and go swimming, that was cool; if you weren't comfortable with that, you could wear your underwear or go in dressed, whatever. I could smile at a stranger and not feel like, Oh, shit, now I'll never get rid of him. So strong was the ethic of live and let live, do your thing but don't step on someone else's toes, I felt free to say no. You could say stuff like "Okay, I'm done talking now, I'm going to go for a walk," and the person would just say, "That's cool," wish you well, and move on. I remember the public service announcements that would come over the sound system: "Hey, we hear there's some brown acid out there that's not great. It isn't poison, so don't trip out, it just isn't made so clean, so you might want to avoid it. I mean it's your trip so you do what you want, but if you're going to do it, we suggest you just do half. . . . Joe Griggs, come to the medic's tent to the left of the speakers, your old lady is having a baby. . . . Sharon Schwartz, call your father."

Doing your own thing usually seems to amount to some jerk smoking a stinky cigar upwind from you or pissing upstream, but not here. People were so incredibly polite at Woodstock. That's what the townspeople kept saying in amazement, those kids with all the long hair and stuff, they're so polite. The chief of police even said, Don't get caught up in what they look like—that's just on the outside—inside I've never seen such a bunch of real good American citizens. Another old guy in the documentary *Woodstock* said, Can you imagine if you got five hundred of us adults together with booze? You'd have a nightmare on your hands, and here there are five hundred thousand of these kids and not one fight, not one incident.

Why sometimes an absence of normal rules brings out a rampaging hell of looting, rapine, and murder, and other times a green pasture where the lamb lies down with the lion, and the scorpion has no sting, is a mystery to me. I surely need a piece of Woodstock to get me through the evening news sometimes. Remembrance of sweet apple blossoms and bees, and dancing in the rye.

❦

HIGH SCHOOL STARTED OUT sort of like a continuation of Woodstock, but it went on too long. In the beginning of the year, we had our distinctly 1960s version of the Fresher teas and mixers my mother had told me about. A whole bunch of us would get together, someone would bring wine, someone the cheese or other munchies, another some joints, and we'd all troop off into the woods, find a nice open spot on the pine needles, and sit in a big circle and pass stuff around. These were afternoon forays, garden parties, a time for conversation and laughter, not opportunities to get blitzed—that was for nighttime.

I wasn't the only one, I found out years later, who didn't inhale. My dad had told me that marijuana does some kind of damage to the kundalini, a spiritual passage in the spine that opens naturally with meditation but is forced open unnaturally with drugs. My brother said once, when we were in our thirties, that he, too, stayed away from drugs throughout high school because of what Dad had said. It's just the kind of thing that speaks to an adolescent. None of that corny "killer weed" crap (I'd been smoking Marlboros since I was eight years old, when I figured out that anyone with change for a dollar could get them from the machine at the ski lodge); here was something that could cripple one's journey toward enlightenment. That spoke to me. But it sure was fun to sit in a circle and pass it around. The spell woven by the scent of the pine trees and spruce, burning hemp and patchouli, friendship and laughter; I left a little ring of pine needles.

My father's metaphysical warnings were not the only cause of my avoidance of many things dangerous; I had inherited, for better or for worse, his soldier's sixth sense for trouble brewing, as well as his interrogator's fundamental distrust. And for some reason, I never developed the adolescent sense of invulnerability or "not me." I figured if a piano were to drop out of the sky, I had a great big *X* somewhere on my back. I couldn't see it, but I knew it was there. My attitude toward others' disasters ranged from "there but for the grace of God go I," to my number must be up next.

Several weeks into ninth grade, a friend took a tab of acid (LSD) that he thought was a one-way tab but turned out to be at least triple strength. He stared at the sun and permanently damaged his eyes, not terribly—he became a lawyer I heard—but he will always see spots. After the hospital, he was locked up at McLean's, a mental institution. I took two buses and a cab to visit him each week. Holy shit, what a terrifying place. He was in a beautiful old mansion with a grand staircase that I had to have a badge to ascend and an escort as well to lock and unlock doors as I made my way through the labyrinth of corridors to where my friend was being kept. He had a room to himself, fit for a grand hotel, but the maids and janitors were running the place and had control of all the keys with access to food and water and toilets and fresh air. My friend told me they were playing mind games with him. He wasn't stupid and he figured out that it was to increase his resistance to frustration or some damn thing, but it stank. They'd say he could have a certain number of cigarettes and then give him a different number, fewer, and tell him they never promised the original number. The games he told me were dead-on; I'd seen similar myself, as a victim of Kit's psychological "treatment." I could tell he needed to rest and get his head together, that was for sure, but I could also tell he wasn't the kind of crazy where you imagine those things. We wrote up a plan to get him out of there, back and forth on a piece of paper, in case anyone was listening in, and talked out loud about poetry, pretending that's what we were writing, in case anyone was observing. He was to cooperate and give them exactly what they wanted, methodically, until he gained campus privileges. As soon as he could walk to certain places unescorted, somebody would meet him in a car by the trees and take him to an apartment where it was safe to crash. He must have slept for three weeks straight on a couch in a room with the curtains drawn, waking only to eat what the people who were living there, or staying there, made for him.

I wonder if teens today have such places where they try to take better care of each other than they've ever been taken care of by adults. I can't tell you how many safe places there were to crash in the sixties and early seventies, how many hippies, friends, both known and unknown, would take you in. It was like that. More food and hugs with no strings attached, nothing expected in payment; I can scarcely imagine it now, it seems like such a different world. Not heaven by any means, lots of deep, dark depression and troubles and loneliness and emptiness, but there sure were a lot of kids taking turn being catchers, a generosity that could make your head stop spinning.

❈❈❈

SHORTLY AFTER MY FRIEND landed in McLean's, I received a letter from my dad telling me he found it hard to imagine what my life was like at school. He had heard from my mom that I liked school better than I did at first, which he said probably meant that I was enjoying my friends' company a lot, which, in turn, made him wonder if their company was worth enjoying. Great, like I have another option? Moving in with the Brontë sisters perhaps? Then followed a major lecture on it's not who you are with your friends that counts, that's all an illusion anyway, it's who you are when you're alone, what goes through your mind in those moments of aloneness that really counts. All this stuff about some Zen question, "who you were before you were born," and what is your Original Face. All I could think of was another friend who told me he had had a bad trip one time and saw everyone's faces melting off their bones as he walked past them. He wanted to put his eyes out but, thank God, didn't. If that's the kind of stuff you think about when you're having one of these moments of aloneness, that or promising the universe for the tenth time this week that you really will eat just cottage cheese and lettuce for lunch every day until those pounds come off, or that if a certain boy doesn't like you back, you're really going to die, or that you'll really read the important books on religion that you asked your dad to recommend, after you write that note to a certain boy and rip it up a hundred times, then you can have aloneness. Dad talked on and on about Zen and translations, bad and worse, of the Bhagavad Gita, but how can you be mad at someone who takes the time to write you a three-page single-spaced letter that ends I love you, dear old Poogoss (an old nickname of mine).

We had roommates, not just for the reason that the school could make more money that way, but also to save us from drowning in our adolescent aloneness. Holly and I wound up roommates after her assigned roommate refused to continue rooming with her, and my assigned dorm parents refused to continue to have me under their roof, after they accused me of stealing a bottle of wine from their quarters. (It was a stupid incident, stupid on my part, where I was kidding around and pretended to take it to freak out a fellow student and total goody-goody, who was baby-sitting. I returned it to the shelf a few moments later. She told on me, and the dorm parents thought that I only put it back because I was "caught" by the baby-sitter.)

I moved into Holly's room in another dormitory. It was known as being the worst room in the school. It was too small to walk around in, you climbed from bunk bed to desk, the ceiling was so low that you couldn't sit up in bed on the top bunk, and naked pipes were suspended from the ceiling. It was a true pit. Oh, yes, and there was almost no daylight since a seven-foot-high fence ran between the side of the dorm and the street. The fence was less than a foot away from our window. It was put there because the previous year some guy had pulled his car over and was caught looking in the window. Ah! But does anyone smell a strategic advantage? It was an excellent room from which to sneak out at night, undetected, between the fence and the wall, and off into the woods. I'm going to have to drive by there to make sure I'm not dropping a dime on the current occupant. Who knows, these days, maybe everyone is up studying on their personal computers half the night to get into a good college. I doubt it, though.

Holly had a problem that her other roommate couldn't deal with. It seemed simple enough to me. Come home dead drunk and make a nuisance of yourself, I stick you under a nasty cold shower until you sober up. Simple. Ditto for whining. She still tells people proudly that I cured her of whining. I slugged her and promised I'd do it again till she stopped. Not the sort of thing a grown parent could or should do to a child, but *in loco parentis,* we did our best with those we loved, and I sure as hell didn't see any parents stepping up to the plate.

My father told me that it was hard for him to imagine what my life was like for my friends and me. He would soon get a three-dimensional look, albeit a brief one, when a bunch of us, about a dozen or more, took the bus up to New Hampshire for the weekend to see Sly and the Family Stone in concert at Dartmouth. We stayed overnight at someone's parents' house in Belmont—they weren't around—and took the bus up to White River Junction the next morning. I can't reconstruct the logistics of how we all wound up on my father's living room floor; maybe we went in separate groups in both my mom's and my dad's car, I just don't know. It was a pleasant afternoon hanging out on the rug, drinking soda, eating whatever, my dad being a nice host. He liked us. And we weren't staying long, which was even better. He told me he thought it was strange but nice that we all hung out together in a group, boys and girls together, as friends. When he was growing up, he said, girls were like a separate species. He really liked how natural we all seemed with each other.

I was a little thrown off when I took everybody on a walk over to the Red house where I'd grown up. I had told them how beautiful it was, but when we got there, I suddenly saw for the first time what a small, modest place it really was. It wasn't a status thing, it was the reality check that was so strange. I felt a little like Gulliver waking up.

Somehow we got to my mother's house in Norwich, where we were going to crash on the floor that night, and again, somehow, when darkness began to fall, we were holding our tickets and finding our seats to see Sly and the Family Stone. "Dance to the Music." It wasn't something for grown-ups, it belonged to the pleasures of another season, our time, the way one's fragile adolescent boundaries, just taking form, loosen and blend with the music and the night and the moment. After a few years, access to that magical world seems to close over, like a baby's fontanel. On to pleasures of a different season. Possessing fragile boundaries, where past and future slip away and you're totally in the moment, while magical in times of joy, sucks beyond belief when you're depressed or sad or miserable and can't remember a time when you weren't sad and can't imagine a time when you'll ever be happy again. But this weekend we were together with friends, at one with our music, our time, our world.

Breakfast at Mom's house in Norwich, lots and lots of eggs and toast, people rolling out of sleeping bags and smiling. At some point my mother and a professor she was seeing tried to be one of the gang and said something "cool" about smoking "pot." *So gross,* don't these people know they're o.l.d.? I did something sort of mean, certainly mean-spirited. I took some oregano out of Mom's spice rack and dumped it along with a few other cooking herbs into a baggie. I rolled it up and put it under a towel in the downstairs linen closet. I kid you not, she called a few weeks later to let me know she found "something" we'd left behind. Oh, yeah, what'd ja do with it? She and her professor friend, she said with a girlish giggle, smoked it. Just as I thought, rolling my eyes, so queer. Please, somebody, remind me when my son is a teenager that "cool" parents are *so* uncool.

To everything there is a season, turn turn turn, and it's not *your* turn, if you're thirty or forty or seventy, to be wholly ten or fourteen or sixteen again; because if you are, then your kids or your students are forced to be old before their time. There were two old guys at school, one was a "dorm parent" and the other a *really* old teacher, both English teachers for what it's worth, who were having sexual intercourse with students. In both cases that I knew of, it was the girl's first time. It's not so much statutory rape that occurs to me as an appropriate charge, but rather Theft of Youth, or a kind of Vampirism these men should be charged with. The Greek and Italian country people have it right: allow your daughters out of your sight only with garlic and henbane woven into their hair and tucked into the hem of their dresses to ward off all things unnatural and out of season.

In my father's frequent letters, one thing he never asked about was "how's school," meaning classes. He had lost touch with Holden's days of earthly pain—friends drinking, a kid jumping out a window, his friend Jane's stepfather "getting wise with her"—and had departed for esoteric realms that left me behind entirely, but at least he hadn't left the galaxy to the extent that he thought classes might be a great topic for conversation. Class time was, for me, at best a distraction. It was not un-like the myriad commercial interruptions of an engrossing movie on television: an annoying reminder that my life was "brought to you by" the Cambridge School of Weston.

Some students actually learned something. I'm not saying the education there was totally irrelevant, just that it was to me at the time. Every once in a while, around report time, it intruded in the form of having let down my adviser, Mr. Castillo, yet again. He was such a nice, sincere man who, to my real sorrow, believed in me and in my ability to use my mind. Like Holden, I kept promising to apply myself, meaning it, and I kept letting him down. I finally had to change advisers, I couldn't stand it anymore, disappointing him that is. After that I "underachieved" with a clear conscience. I should probably have sent him my awards from Brandeis or Oxford with a thank-you note to let him know he needn't worry about me anymore, that I really did discover the pleasure of using my mind and "applying" myself for the sheer joy of it. But for me, high school was neither the time nor the place.

I paid attention sometimes, but not to the things that helped on tests. In the classroom where we met for English, for example, a beautiful glass mobile hung above us in a skylighted alcove. I remember the sunlight catching pieces of broken glass, in dozens of colors, each separate piece wrapped in a thread of silver, like a present tied with ribbon, the threads dangling from a single silver circle at the top. I do not remember a single solitary thing I read all year. I've come away from high school with exactly two books remembered: *Nicholas and Alexandra,* chiefly because it was so unbelievably huge, even in paperback, that I couldn't believe we'd ever get through it. I recall a certain pride in sheer volume when I finished it. The other book was *Les Chaises* by Ionesco, because I loved my French teacher, Suzanne. She took us to see the play in Cambridge, at night, like real people, on her own time.

It was not just the internal and social business of adolescence that made classwork so peripheral; society at large was in turmoil. America was at war in Vietnam. Around the beginning of November we heard there was going to be a march on Washington to protest the war. Many parents agreed to write permission slips to a phony destination so we could go. Perhaps the school needed such permission slips to cover themselves legally, but with the charter buses to Washington from the Weston area stopping off in the school parking lot, I don't exactly know who was fooling whom. It was nighttime and I slept in the overhead luggage rack the whole way down, feeling very clever to have found a place to stretch out on the crowded bus. We were to spend the day and return home on the bus the next evening, so no one had brought luggage. I was excited to find that the author of one of my favorite children's stories, *The Diamond in the Window,* in which kids really do get caught in dreams, was on board. I didn't speak to her, of course, assuming she'd hate the invasion of her privacy. One of my favorite "children's" books, I thought; this person wrote books for the eight-to-twelve-year-old group. I was thirteen years old on that bus to Washington.

The letters I received, in conjunction with this trip, one from my mother and one from my father, are from two rather interesting planets, but not the one I lived on. My mom was so into the antiwar movement that I nearly didn't go. P.S., I had no idea who "Green Phantom" was then or now. It's a weird feeling to be called someone else's nickname, a "familiarity" from a dimension you don't happen to inhabit.

Nov. 10th 1969

To whom it may concern:
Peggy Salinger has my permission to spend the weekend of November 14–16th with Adrienne F. and her family.

Yours truly,
Claire Salinger

Dear Green Phantom,
Enclosed are a few good things on Vietnam. Excellent book *Peace in Vietnam* put out by Quakers—good on theory and background. The others are the best of the things I have on hand. Please read them. If you object to the war, wish to go to Washington and demonstrate then I think you should know what you are demonstrating both for and against. Please return the *Peace in Vietnam* book when you are through. Please circulate others after you've finished them.
I am having a hectic time. School is busy and requires much traveling. I am also getting deeper and deeper into protest work, so seem to be leading 3 full lives (other as mother and housewife—private type things) worthwhile but tiring!

Now for the dates:

1. I put off your orthodontist 'til Fri. Nov. 20 at 2 P.M., will write school for permission. Dr. Beebe said you had missed no appointments, didn't sound a bit mad about one you were late for. *NO* apt. this Friday.

2. Enclosed permission slip for Washington.

3. If you don't go let me know as soon as possible. If you do go: think *Peacefully.*

4. I will be away all day Sat. (from about 4 A.M. to 11 P.M.) am going to Canada with some members of American Friends Service Committee to give medical supplies to NLF and North Vietnam as part of stop the war day.

If you want to be at home that weekend its fine with me as long as you know I'll be away Saturday. Daddy and Matthew will be going to a Dartmouth football game Sat. afternoon otherwise you could be with them or in Hanover or whatever you feel like. *I would love it if you came with me,* for I think you would like the people but the car trip is long and I don't know what we will face at the border.

Anyway let me know. I could drive you on Friday if I knew well enough before hand.

It rained for a week here. Aretha [my cat] brought home a young fish. Still don't know where she found it. Maybe from one of our rich neighbors' outdoor fish ponds. Maybe the sky dropped it. Maybe it thought our swollen brook a river. I think Aretha is pregnant again!

No more news—

Much love,
Mom
XXXX

p.s. Keep an account of how you spend your money!
p.p.s. Fill in Adrienne's last name please.

Oh, the drama! But she was probably quite right in saying I should know something about the war if I was to go to the protest. I read the book cover to cover . . . right! I was never a pacifist, nor did I think I was at the time. I was partly just being a follower, a "sheep" as my father put it, and partly protesting against the lies I thought we were being told. I'd heard stories of guys over there fragging their superiors who were following insane orders, such as having to stop pursuing the enemy when they crossed a certain geographical line on a map and just sit there like ducks while the enemy regrouped and attacked again. But I was even sicker about this business of my mother and her friends giving money for "medical supplies" (not to mention a North Vietnamese orphanage) to the NLF. Did you just fall off the back of a turnip truck? There is a war on. If you don't think that money will find its way to the war, you're a complete *idiot*. Or so I put it, with my usual tact, to my mother. That seemed like a bigger lie than even the stuff that came out of Washington.

My father's letter arrived a few days after I got back. He was writing in answer to some questions I had about macrobiotics. A friend of mine went macrobiotic and I was seriously worried that he was going to starve himself to death. He looked just terrible. I asked my dad for some help in this matter, knowing he used to adhere to the diet. He wrote back a long, detailed diatribe against the founder of macrobiotics, George Ohsawa. It must have taken him hours. I was glad to have it, even more so that my father had suggested meeting with the boy over lunch sometime to let the conversation flow naturally, since it might turn him off in a letter. How many kids in the sixties could write home to their parents with questions about new stuff like macrobiotics and get a multi-page single-spaced letter in return? Sometimes strange is not so bad. But strange barely begins to cover it.

The basic argument was that George Ohsawa could not have been a good scientist or discoverer of worthwhile, valid principles of diet and health because he was, himself, an impure person. He was a name dropper and an opportunist, according to my father. This was the first and foremost argument, that the source of the diet was not a pure person, and therefore, his purported discoveries could not be pure. Then my father documented some basic lies and cover-ups, such as that Ohsawa himself died of cancer when he promised perfect health to those who followed him. Fair enough. And a whole bunch of stuff about crystalline properties of salt and blues and violets and the subtlety of yin and yang classifications that escaped Ohsawa, to say nothing of Miss Salinger. The letter was interrupted at one point, I remember, because my brother had awakened from a bad dream and walked into my father's study crying, so he had to take a break from writing to me to put Matthew to sleep in his (Daddy's) bed with the lights on. This was both astonishing and inconceivable to me, or I should say, were it me. I'd have no more dared knock on either of my parents' door at night—well, it wouldn't even have occurred to me as a possibility. It's amazing how siblings can experience totally different families, how life can be so much different for one than the other, and they're both telling the truth. At the very end of the letter he mentions that I should take good care of myself if I go to Washington. "Please do. You're the best of girls and I love you."

I guess he missed the news that night; the letter was written the evening of the fifteenth, and the march had been that day. I did take care of myself though. Most people seemed to be trying to crowd as close as they could to the speakers near the Monument. There was no way I was going to get caught in the middle of a large crowd if things got ugly. I hung around the outskirts of the Mall lawn, keeping one eye on the speakers, one eye on possible escape routes up the streets and into large stores or hotels. The day was pretty peaceful, and back on the bus, I sort of regretted not finding some people to eat my lunch with on the Mall, but this was *not* Woodstock. If you've ever seen riot police in full gear—space helmets, gas masks, shields and weapons—any notion of a street party you might have entertained vanishes *in*stantly.

What brought the war home to me, during my freshman year, was the draft lottery. (Each birth date was assigned, randomly, a number from 1 to 365, 1 being your ass is on the next plane over; 365, party time.) My boyfriend, Michael, was a senior and his number came up 73. I did not want him to go: not to Canada or Vietnam—not anywhere without me. Michael. Although several nice boys had approached me during the fall of my freshman year, I basically ran and hid like a spooked animal. One day I noticed a young man, a senior, shining golden in the sunlight that fell across the campus green. He smiled softly and turned away. There was something magical about him, like my woodland friends who preferred to do their dancing on moonlit nights deep within the pine forest. I would not have been surprised to have discovered telltale fairy dust on the grass where he had been standing just a moment before. I don't remember how we started talking or what we talked about. I mostly remember how, as infrequently and mysteriously as a rainbow, joy would break through the dark clouds of his eyes. I'd have walked through fire if that was what it took to reach him, to take his hand and lead him out of the aloneness that seemed to grip him with tendrils strong as flesh and blood. There was a Neil Young song out at the time called "The Loner," which said, "If you see him on the subway . . . step aside, open wide, it's the loner." I took this to be a battle flag thrown down in front of me.

I'm not sure when it was that Michael fell in love with me, but I knew he loved me long before it was said. Somehow, while we were talking about something else, we met. I have the feeling that the part of us that still had the courage to love snuck out of our respective fortresses, to meet the other, body to body, in the moonlight, while the other part of us stayed back in the darkness of our rooms talking, like two disembodied voices, or prisoners in solitary scratching and tapping to another unseen behind thick stone walls. I'm only now beginning to understand the "curse whispered in my ear" should I look down from the Salinger tower but thro' the mirror blue, let alone leave my room and go down into the field of barley and rye. At first, when I tried to write an embodied account of our relationship, one that might offer a hint, like a fragrance in the air or a poem or perhaps a certain change in the light, to awaken the reader's own remembrance or dream of first love, I ran up against a stone wall.

I can tell you about the damp blond curls, like a baby's, that formed at the nape of his neck as he slept. I can tell you I was as startled as if I had seen a ghost when I unexpectedly came across Michelangelo's *David* from the back, as I wandered happily around Florence by myself in my mid-twenties. But the silent soldier in me is too strong to be overridden by force of will. What worked so well to avoid pain and invasions as a child, the retreat deep beneath the surface of my skin, became a hard, hard wall to crack. My strategic withdrawal worked so efficiently that it wasn't until my early twenties when I began to notice hints—like an accent that appears when drinking or an unaccounted-for scar discovered where one doesn't usually look in mirrors—that there was something unknown to me, hidden from me about myself.

This revelation, when it first came to me, nearly knocked me off my feet. I was in an airport hugging my friend Jacobo Timerman good-bye. He had just been released, a few months before, from a clandestine jail in Argentina where he had been tortured, and was, like me, attending The Aspen Institute. I saw the scars as we sat in a Jacuzzi looking up at the stars, smelled the oranges and grapefruits he hoarded in his closet because he had craved them so on the scurvy starvation diet of the cell, jumped out of my skin with him at sudden noises, rejoiced at the miraculous normality of being able to pick up the phone and talk to his beloved wife and sons. As we were hugging each other good-bye—and Latin American friends are generous huggers, none of this Anglo kiss kiss in the air and you're off—it suddenly struck me that I couldn't feel myself hugging him, my hands on his back, at the same time I felt him hugging me, his hands on my back. I tried and it was like a movie camera that jumps from one perspective, from behind one person, to another angle, behind the other person. I could not simultaneously integrate being hugged and hugging, I couldn't get the camera angle that includes both persons. Islands.

What I was aware of, even in my teens, is the Achilles' heel of lone island dwellers, of those too long in reclusion. For us, when a body meets a body, the result is not two people dancing in the rye; but rather, it is like the embrace of twins conjoined in the womb (formerly called Siamese twins), who may share a single heart, a liver, a leg, and so on, and attempting separation is, more often than not, hazardous to the life of one or both under the best of care and circumstances. Yet the closeness, the merging and becoming as one, after being so long alone, is indescribably wonderful, rain on desert wasteland bringing forth a miraculous resurrection of hidden, dormant life. I can honestly say I do not regret a single reckless, beloved moment.

※

WHEN MICHAEL'S DRAFT NUMBER CAME UP, I had just spent a great vacation with him and his family. At their house, I held my own in touch football in the field with the three brothers. With me there, they could play two on two instead of round-robin when their dad was at work. I couldn't throw the ball too well, but I could run like hell to make up for it. I think all the boys, being older than I, and gentlemen, probably let me think I was more useful than I really was, but never mind, I'm not adjusting the memory: I was Gale Sayers in motion.*

---

*Chicago Bears running back, *poetry* in motion.

A few weeks after spring vacation, I received a letter from my father informing me that my grandfather had died. No, that's not right; he informed me that *his* father had died. Doris and he had managed things with a "minimum of crap and ceremony," he told me. No mention, no thought, that I might have wanted to participate in some "crap and ceremony" for my grandfather. I hadn't even known he was ill, and had been for months, when I might have visited him. Granny was, he told me, being difficult about the whole thing because, he said, she had a bad conscience. Lecture on rotten marriages. There was no inkling on his part that she might, for better or for worse, actually miss her husband after some sixty years of marriage. Aunt Doris told me later that Granny said she missed seeing that hair (he had striking, thick, lemony white hair) on the pillow in the morning.

I sent Granny a plant and a card in sympathy. It was the least I could do, the most I was allowed to do. My father told me that Granny was pleased and touched by the note and the plant, but her eyesight was getting so bad that she couldn't write to tell me. He thanked me as well, as though I'd done something really out of the way, above and beyond the call of duty. What sadly low expectations of, and for, family.

The same thing happened, only worse, when Granny died the following year. Once again, he never even told me she was sick. Nor did he tell me about her death before my mother read about it in the newspaper. (This was the same way I learned of my brother's engagement. They had forgotten to tell me. It sure is weird being in a family where you often learn more in the press than from each other.) When I asked my father about it, he again said he had wanted to "spare me all that crap." He was, I thought, referring to hospital visits and funerals. Knowing him as I do now, I think he also meant sparing me from such "crap" as family and connection. Doris recently told me that when Granny was ill, she often asked for me. Doris said, "Mother missed you so."

⚘

AT THE END OF THE SCHOOL YEAR, I dropped my stuff off at my mother's, said hi to my brother, and took off for my boyfriend's house for a two-week visit, which, like the seven stranded castaways on a three-hour tour, extended indefinitely. After fielding some wild and stormy phone calls from my mother, Mrs. S., my boyfriend's mother and my hero, politely but firmly decided that she would not send me home under any circumstances unless it was my decision. That was the first time in my life that any adult had ever stood up to my parents and said directly, "This must stop, I won't allow it." Someone finally said to my mother, I will take care of your daughter until you are able, and it will be my pleasure. That's how she made me feel, as if I were a pleasure to have around. Can you imagine that? She still hasn't sent me home. (Nearly thirty years later, I still have the pleasure of her company, and her grown boys' and their wives' and their kids' company.)

My father met Mrs. S. several times and paid her his highest compliment: he said to me that she is a real lady, and that she reminded him of Mrs. Hand, the only other woman I'd heard him refer to as a lady. When Mrs. S. became widowed, I harbored hopes that they might get together; she is also, I might add, a beautiful, elegant, intelligent woman. He hadn't been seeing anyone since his divorce from my mother, as far as I was aware, and Mrs. S. embodied all that he praised in a woman. A year or two later, when my father's teenage lover moved in with him, I would learn a big lesson about the vast difference between what my father espoused verbally and whom he espoused in real life. However, the summer I lived with Mrs. S., my boyfriend Michael, and his brothers, she was, in my hopes and thoughts and dreams, my eminently suitable stepmother, mother-in-law, and mother of choice. Still is.

Because Michael had a summer job, I had a lot of time to write in my diary, which would serve, throughout my teenage years, as a tattered "Chart" in the absence of a "Heart in port." I also had time to write letters, and my roommate Holly and I kept in close touch. I offer my vote for best letter from summer camp, and it is *not* Seymour's from Hapworth, but Holly's from Brentwood. A real person's letter from camp. It was addressed in bold letters—I'm sure *much* appreciated by the camp staff who collected the mail—Holly Tobias, "Brentwood Concentration Camp, Angelica, New York," postmarked 1970.

Dear Peggy,
　　Oooh, am I ever furious! Tonight we had that marvelous

all-purpose of evening activities: the Brentwood campfire. The
cabins are each supposed to dig up a song, which we sing.
(there isn't actually any campfire—I guess they're afraid we'll
hurt ourselves.) So, as a suggestion to our cabin, I mentioned
that Country Joe and the Fish song, "Feel like I'm Fixin to Die
Rag." ["Don't ask me I don't give a damn, Next stop is
VietNam"] Of course, we had to write it down and submit it to
a counselor panel for censoring—they must, of course, weed
out anything corrupting; i.e. anything that is against war
(un-American!) or anything that is not cheery. (unsuitable)
They were *shocked,* and told us we couldn't sing it. I asked why
not, and they got all offended and self-righteous, and
proceeded to give a few feeble protestations. (Well it just isn't
nice, that's all . . . you know, it just isn't the *attitude* you should
have.) Well, I was sick of the "approved" songs, (each campfire,
we sing such goodies as "The ants go marching" and most of
the soundtrack to "Sound of Music"—off key, of course.) Also
everybody sings as if they are ill, and all the counselors go
flapping through the swarms of kids, shrieking "sing, *sing!*
Come on, kids, let's hear it! I wanna hear a little *camp spirit!*
LOUDER!" And so on and so forth. Until we run out of
approved songs, at which point it is about 8:30 and they send us
to bed, or they try to make us all sing "100 bottles of beer on
the wall" (We have to say "Coke" though—no kidding—
instead of "beer") all the way down to the end. (Two bottles of
Coke on the wall, two bottles of Coke, if one of those bottles
should happen to fall . . .) Anyway, I didn't exactly feel like
staying, so I left, which is a no-no, because you are never
allowed to be in the cabin by yourself. You are also forbidden
ever to take a walk by yourself. (They are afraid you might
smoke *a cigarette!*) *(Shock!)* Not only is nightwalking a no-no
but one of our counselors sleeps with her bed in front of the
door, to make sure that no one passes through the portals—
going *in* or *out.* Don also stays up—no joke—'till one in the
morning, patrolling with a flashlight and his dog. Christ!
Speaking of which, half the camp goes to church every Sunday.
Pious. Nice.

There is no such thing as a private phone call.

We periodically have trunk inspection.

As for me, a week ago I flatly refused to go to activities I didn't want to go to. There was no way they could *make* me play dodgeball, so Don just leaves me in peace, and steers the visitors *around* me.

I hope that you and Michael are seeing each other more and that your nerves have settled. And as for my coming and visiting you next year in Mclean's, I'll probably be sharing a room with you there! Why don't we start another Prob Child Club? Sort of like A.A. (which I may join by next year! No, actually I haven't been drinking too awfully much lately.) You know, where all the members play shrink to each other.

Well, that's about all. *Nothing* is going on here. All the boys look like Kevin A. with a crew cut, they have all the sex appeal of Jon. B, and the winning personality of Dan R. Yeccch! Also, they are all under 13.

The food is inedible. One time we had pizza, (awful) bread and cake for lunch. Nothing else. No fruit or vegetables or (god forbid!) vitamins. I got sick from lack of vitamins and I got tonsilitis and ran a fever and was packed into the infirmary for 6 days.

WRITE!(I love mail too!)

Love ya,
holly

ps. I HATE IT HERE!

pps. I bought both James Taylor albums . . . sort of as a monument to R. (But I have sworn that I will never talk to him again!) Now, in memory of S. and R., I have 2 James Taylor albums and 3 Creedence Clearwater albums. I'm completely insane! But I really like the albums anyway, especially the James Taylor.

pps. Say hi to everybody I know.

26

Lost Moorings

❧❧❧

Ooooh storm is threatenin' . . .
——Rolling Stones

IN SEPTEMBER, HOLLY AND I WERE BACK AT SCHOOL AGAIN to start tenth grade, but all was not well. Michael, having been graduated the previous spring, was now overseas, studying in Paris. I lived for our weekly phone calls and held on to his blue, *Par avion* letters as tightly as de Daumier-Smith held Sister Irma's letters or the boy in France held on to Mattie's. I, too, was in a real panic that I might not make it, I might not be able to hold on until I received the next letter. I slept with Michael's woolly sheepskin jacket at night, praying that his scent wouldn't fade from the coat before I could bear it. I was waiting, basically in hibernation, for Christmas when I was to fly to France and spend the holiday with him.

He called on December 10 to wish me a happy fifteenth birthday and to discuss our plans for my arrival a week or so later. He didn't sound quite right. He said everything was fine, but the minute I stepped off the plane and into his arms, I knew it wasn't. I have to tell you, I *hate* Paris. It was cold and gray and icy and damp and everyone was speaking in French. The friends of his parents, with whom we were to stay for a few days before leaving for the south of France, were lovely. Their apartment was beautiful and they had all sorts of pretty things to eat that I'd never seen before, such as marrons glacés and whole preserved apricots and kumquats, like orange jewels.

Our hosts' little boys were just learning to speak, and their French and English were delightfully mixed up. One showed me proudly how he could "put the wrapper *dans la poubelle.*" After the children were put to bed, the parents discreetly retired and left Michael and me the living room to ourselves. I pressed and pressed and he finally told me, in sheer misery, that he had met a thirty-year-old French divorcée who had two children, and he wasn't sure he was still in love with me. I remember that part perfectly—where he sat on the couch, the marrons glacés on the coffee table, even the sheet music on the piano. Then suddenly it went dark. I remember another flash photograph, an image that lasts a single frame. I am on an examination table of some sort, in our host's home office. His wife has her arm outstretched reaching for some medication on a high shelf. She is going to give me something to make me sleep. Michael told me the next day that I hadn't fainted, I'd been crying and breathing hysterically; our hosts couldn't help but hear, and they gave me a sedative. I was absolutely mortified. I'd never disgraced myself like that, lost control with no memory and become so completely unmoored.

I went about the business of seeing Paris with a grim determination, sleet inside and out. I emerged briefly in a garden with statues by Rodin tucked into corners, *The Kiss,* and something with a group of people in a circle groping and in chains—I can see it but I don't remember the name. Maybe *Les Aveugles.* The blind. We decided there was nothing to do but go on with the holiday as planned, and we took the train to the south of France where another friend of the family, an artist, had an apartment he was not using over the holiday. There was no mistaking the occupation of the absent owner: large canvases of his work were everywhere, some hung on walls, some leaning up against them. This artist went down to the sea, all over France, and collected bits of dolls, baby dolls, that washed up in the tide, and he glued these akimbo—an arm here, an eyeless head, a torso there—as if they had washed up dead on various parts of his canvas.

Each day I walk down to a beautiful open-air market, full of fresh vegetables and fruit and cheese and flowers. I was so far behind my eyes it was like looking through a movie camera at everything. I pointed to things, afraid to speak after the waffle seller on the street in Paris was so nasty about my French, mimicking me with a sour face as if he'd stepped in dog doo, but soon I was trying to speak and was being met with farmers' smiles. A man at a flower stall handed me a small bunch of wild-flowers to smell, making large sniffing gestures. So sweet I nearly disap-peared again, but the sun caught me and I handed him the coins and walked back to the apartment. I put the flowers in a glass of water and emptied my shopping on the table. I sat at the little kitchen table in the bright sunshine and watched, quite detached, as entire wheels of Brie and loaves of bread disappeared. I was not thinking, not reflecting, just chewing and gazing blindly, taking in ballast.

I walked along the boardwalk by the sea; the fresh breeze and salt air was clearing my head a bit. Out in the harbor there were three huge U.S. Navy ships. Two sailors behind me thought the tall, thin, pretty girl walking just ahead of them was French, and they said something really dirty in American, laughing, thinking she wouldn't get the joke or un-derstand. I was so scared I made myself walk a measured pace and listen for footsteps all the way back, shaking, key in the lock, shut the door. I had to sit still, in the bathroom, for a long time and stare at the pattern on the wall, like some fixed point on the horizon, so I didn't vomit. After that, I no longer walked by the sea alone. Michael offered me his arm as we walked, sea breeze in our hair. Did he know I might blow away?

I bought Michael's mother a bottle of Cabochard, the perfume she wears, in the duty-free at Orly and one for myself. I have absolutely no idea at all where I went after I got off the plane back in the United States.

⬥⬥⬥

I WAS NOT A PERSON with her faculties intact. When I went to spend a weekend away from school at a friend's family house in Connecticut, my doppelgänger appeared again. As in Paris, "I" disappeared and another "I" disgraced myself in my absence. We had a few drinks, and I mean a few, not many, at a cocktail party my friend's parents were having, and the next thing I knew, I woke up in the morning. His parents, he told me, were out for a walk and had asked me to leave. Apparently I had taken off my clothes, stood on the balcony over their living room stark naked, and I'm not even going to say what I yelled to the assembled guests below, I'm still too mortified nearly thirty years later. He grabbed a blanket, wrapped me up in it, and put me gently to bed. He wasn't mad or anything, and he said it didn't surprise him that I had no memory of it because he had this strange feeling that I was somebody else, I didn't even talk like me.

I knew there wasn't that much drink in the world to do that to me, but I kept the secret horror I might be schizo pretty tightly under wraps. I neither reached out a hand for help nor bolted the door. I did what had worked at Cross Mountain: I took care of others who were a lot worse off than I. I became a "catcher" to save myself from, as Holden said, "sinking down, down, down" and drowning in my own blood and misery. Other kids sought me out as a good person to talk to about their problems, and I got a reputation for being the person to call if someone was in crisis, tripping out, cutting themselves, suicidal, or whatever. I had and still have a gift of being a good soldier in a crisis and calming everybody down.

I started doing after-school tutoring at Centro Latino in Waltham and being a mentor to a young Hispanic girl who needed help with her homework. I also volunteered one afternoon a week at the Fernald State School for the Retarded. The first time I went there I was taken to a huge room, the size of a gym, that had naked, moaning men in it. Some playing in their feces, some being hosed down. The stench, the other-creaturely noises, the sight of adult male nudity, bludgeoned me, and after about five minutes, I excused myself to the supervisor, ran outside into a field, and threw up. When I went back the following week, they placed me in a higher-level ward where the young men wore clothes mostly, and you could do puzzles and games and talk to them. One of the guys I remember called himself Jughead. He seemed quite fluent and intelligent until one realized that his entire conversational repertory consisted of repeating phrases he'd memorized from an *Archie and Jughead* comic book. Another absolutely beautiful, perfect-looking little boy used to take my silver ring off my finger and roll it back and forth delicately, slowly, on the table in front of him. I think, had he been left to his own devices, he would happily have starved to death rolling that ring back and forth gazing at it in a reverie until he was released from this nightmare incarnation.

※

WHEN MICHAEL CAME BACK from France that spring, he seemed wrapped in an impenetrable fog of depression. So thick, so dense, was the gray, I really wasn't sure he could see my hand in front of his face. I felt, like my mother before me, adrift at sea. The only thing that was clear was that when school let out for the summer, I would find neither "Wild Nights" nor "mooring in thee."

That summer, between tenth and eleventh grade, I was fifteen, and I alternated between staying at my dear friend Amy's house and the street. Amy was a day student at Cambridge School and we became like sisters. Neither of us was capable of shouldering the burden of being family—mother, father, sister, brother—to the other, but I never saw two kids try more valiantly to do so. The first week or so of the summer, I awoke one morning in the sunshine of Amy's bedroom, and as I opened my eyes, I saw I was lying on top of the sheets and wearing a dress. What caught my attention was the mud all over the front of my dress. I let it register for a little while, rather like the time when I was eight years old and I noticed and observed, totally detached, that my pink-and-white seersucker dress had turned red as I carried my broken arm across the field. Terror struck with the dawning realization that I had no idea where I had been since the previous afternoon. I got up and ran down the hall to find Amy. She was in her sister's room and I woke her up. "Amy, Amy, wake up. What happened to me?" I'll never ever forget this as long as I live: she said wide-eyed and slowly, "You don't know?" Oh, shit. This time I think I had more than a few drinks, but a lot less than I consumed on the average weekend at school. We were at an outdoor drinks party in her uncle's backyard. The adults were drinking heavily; her father and his brother were psychiatrists, but they were obliviously, aggressively, off duty. We were invisible, as usual, leading our own lives and watching the sunset, which is the last thing I remember as a narrative. I recall, Polaroid snapshot fashion, a moment in the dark in the back of a car: Amy's boyfriend had slapped my face. That's all. Amy told me that shortly after sunset, I started speaking French to the gathering. She thought I was joking for a second or two, but it struck her very quickly that I didn't look or sound like me, the way I would sound speaking French, that is. She said it was very spooky because my mannerisms were not my own. When "I" started weeping and shouting and thrashing about on the lawn, her parents told Amy and her boyfriend, Willie, to call a cab and take me home to sleep it off. In the cab, "I" expanded, becoming a large, black, Southern woman, speaking what Amy could only think was some sort of patois, something like Gullah with English. She could understand bits of it, but not all. I started crying hysterically again and her boyfriend tried slapping me in the face to snap me out of it. I reportedly went through a few more iterations, or personalities, on the way home, but fell asleep almost instantly as Willie carried me upstairs and laid me down on Amy's bed. Her parents were angry that I'd disturbed the neighbors, but drunken scenes were pretty de rigueur around there at the time, and mine was forgotten. But not by me.

Amy's house, not unlike mine, was a world through the looking glass where everything was inverted, or the reverse of what one might expect it to be. What got me thrown out was not my outrageous behavior at the party, but my accidentally burning a cooking pot with peas in it on the stove. I was so scared when I did it that I hid the pot. Her mother found it, threw me out of the house, and I spent the next while homeless. (Neither of my parents was a viable option.) It was already dark when she kicked me out, so first things first, I broke into a cellar in a nearby apartment building because I saw a couch through the window grate. I tried to sleep but was so worried that someone—the building super or another shelter seeker—might notice the broken window, catch me there, and attack me, I couldn't do more than catnap. All the comforts of home.

I have to say, though, that given my circumstances, I was incredibly lucky. I hung out a lot in the South End, way before gentrification brought whites to the area; it was just the plain old ghetto back then. I was out on the street all kinds of crazy hours, staying with Amy's boyfriend sometimes, his cousin's neighbor another night, sometimes at old Marva's house. I'd met her at a bar and she liked me. She was shot dead one afternoon in front of her granddaughter. It's a miracle I had a pretty cozy summer: fish fries on the barbecue, sitting out on the stoop in the warm evening air, drinking blackberry brandy on the basketball court, and nothing bad ever happened to me. Partly because I was smart enough to hang out with the old folks and not get mixed up with trouble, partly due to the extraordinary generosity of people I met, largely because of blind dumb luck.

When I did get into trouble, it was my own stupid fault, nobody else's. My French teacher, my pretty guardian angel, bailed me out of jail. I had stolen an $11 pair of black satin hot pants from Jordan Marsh. Amy met me at the store to hang out and to try on clothes. She had some really cool clothes, mostly from swiping stuff. She said it was really fun, she did it all the time and showed me how, cramming half a wardrobe into her massive handbag. Guess which one of us got caught? No sooner had I slipped one tiny pair of hot pants into my pocketbook, than a store guard slipped a tight grip around my arm and it was all over. I had $40 in my pocketbook and offered to pay for them, but no dice, I was going downtown. The store had a policy of prosecuting everyone, and the police cooperated to the hilt. I rode in the back of a police car, tears streaming down my face. Each officer took an arm and escorted me like a criminal on TV into the station, where they put me into a holding cell by myself and locked the door.

Different officers walked by every twenty minutes or so and just shook their heads or clicked their tongues in disapproval or said things like "A young girl like you, a thief, imagine that." The scariest part, one that they hadn't planned on I think, was that I had no guardian who could come and claim me. My parents were out of state, and I was looking at an overnight in the D.S.S.* juvenile lockup where a girl I knew once told me there were big lezzies who beat you up and stuff. I called Suzanne, my French teacher, and she came and got me. Oh, man, jail was one place I never, *ever* wanted to see again.

Later, I used to get out of a car and walk if I found out there were drugs in it—I knew if someone was going to get caught, it would be me. Same with taxes and so on. I'm a big fan of nipping that sort of thing in the bud. I had to go to court twice over those darn hot pants and even see a probation officer. I remember having to go in front of the judge, and the court-appointed lawyer told me to "lose the jeans" and get a "damn skirt." I borrowed one from another girl who looked as if she knew the ropes and was waiting to see the same judge. We traded clothes quickly in the girls' room, hardly speaking, and flashed the thumbs-up sign.

Cops and court personnel kept looking at me as if to say, What the hell are *you* doing here? They sort of made you feel as if you'd let your favorite uncle down. Boy, am I ever grateful I got slammed before I re-

---

*Department of Social Services, for those fortunate enough not to be familiar with the acronym.

ally got into trouble. Even at the time, I wasn't used to people taking an interest like that, as if you were part of the community and they expected better. "And don't let me see you down here again, young lady."

My probation officer was the only one who seemed cynical. She dismissed all that "I've learned my lesson" talk as though she'd heard it a hundred times before. She was pragmatic, and her parting words were that it would be a good idea to stay out of downtown department stores for the next six months.

❦

SOMEWHERE INTO THE FALL TERM of my junior year, I was in trouble with the powers that be once again. In fact, my entire dorm was suspended, en masse, for alleged drinking. One of the teachers was visiting my dorm parents when he observed a bunch of us girls all rowdy and giggling and, he claimed, acting drunk. No bottle was found, no evidence of liquor on the breath was mentioned, just the way we were acting. Now, to tell you the truth, I have no idea whether or not some of us were, in fact, drinking at the time. This is because some of us, most especially me, were drinking with such regularity, it is impossible to remember if this was or was not one of those occasions. I couldn't get too self-righteous about the whole thing on my own behalf, but one of the girls in the dorm, a tiny thing named Phoebe who played the violin and studied, got so scared that her parents would kill her for being suspended that she couldn't stop shaking. It's a particularly terrible thing to see someone very underweight, skeletal almost, shaking with fright.

We protested the suspension as a travesty of justice. My mother called and asked my permission to stage a "sit-in" protest in the headmaster's office. The idea embarrassed me hugely, but she did ask, and I said it was okay, so I don't have a leg to stand on. She arrived with her sleeping bag and some food and locked herself in the headmaster's office, issuing a written statement of exactly what she was objecting to, and her list of demands. The outcome, if I remember correctly, was a compromise. We were still suspended for two weeks, but it would not go on our permanent record. One of my dormmate's parents invited me to come along with them and spend the suspension weeks at the Cheeca Lodge in Islamorada, Florida. My friend and I decided to treat the holiday as a chance to lose weight. I had been in a constant struggle with food since I lost Michael, trying to fill the empty place inside. She and I skipped most of our meals, bingeing, instead, on untold numbers of heads of iceberg lettuce sprinkled with saccharin from little pink packets back at the room.

My father wrote me a letter thanking me for my postcard from Islamorada, which he said sounded rather like Fort Lauderdale but without Wolfie's. He said he hoped I'd been able to watch the whole suspension proceedings with some "detachment" and to note how justice becomes distorted when each side uses the truth for its own purposes. Love to you, old kid.

27

Kindred Spirits

❧❦❧

Credo in unum Deum, factotem caeli et terrae,
visibilium omnium, et invisibilium. *

W E ARRIVED BACK FROM OUR SUSPENSION from school, my friend
and I provokingly tan, to find that we had been split up and assigned to different dormitories. I'm not quite sure what the thinking
was, if any, behind the move, but it turned out to be a life-altering piece
of luck for me. I was transferred to a private house on school property
whose elderly owners rented out two large, upstairs rooms to schoolgirls. The girls in the smaller room were Minnie-Lu, a Choctaw Indian
from Oklahoma, and Sheila, an African American from Miami. I
shared a room with a Jewish girl, Debby, and Tracy, a Gros Ventre Indian from Montana. Later, Pat, a Seneca from upstate New York, would
replace Debby. The Native Americans at school were there through the
federal ABC program—A Better Chance. I don't know what, if any,
"better chance" this program in general or Cambridge School in particular offered any of them. Perhaps it has changed, but back then it took
smart, poor kids right off the reservation or out of city projects or back-
woods Maine and dumped them off at lily-white boarding schools with
no cultural support system whatsoever; not surprisingly, the graduation
rate for the Native Americans I knew was pretty abysmal. I, however,

---

*I believe in one God, Creator of heaven and earth, and of all things visible
and invisible.

without doubt, was given "A Better Chance" at life through our friendships. As I write this, I'm wearing the beaded bracelet my roommate Tracy sent me in celebration of my fortieth birthday. In the night-table drawer, next to my bed, are the beaded, deerskin, medicine medallions to wrap my braids that Tracy's grandmother made for me for my sixteenth birthday. I believe she knew how much her grandchild's friend needed some good medicine. Now Tracy writes and tells me that her daughter, Carleen, whom I remember rocking in her baby swing, just had a baby girl of her own. Our kids haven't met yet, but I can't wait. Maybe this summer at Crow Fair, we'll see.

On school vacations, I often went with Pat to stay with her family on the Seneca reservation, outside of Buffalo, New York. She has seven brothers and sisters. The boys, twins then fourteen, had one room, and Pat, being the eldest at fifteen, had a room to herself; the other girls, ages twelve, eight, four, and three, slept on bare mattresses piled in one room; and the baby slept in a room with Pat's mom and stepfather. Her mom had a pretty good job at the hospital, except she had to work a lot of nights, and her stepfather was a really important man in the tribe. Pat's real father had died before I met her. I almost met him, though.

Once in the middle of the night at school, Pat sat up in her sleep, moved to the end of her bed, and stretched out her hand. Since I sleep with one eye open and have since I was a kid, I sensed danger and grabbed her arm and didn't let her touch what she later told me was her dead father's hand. She said that if she had touched his hand, she would have gone with him. After that, we slept with our beds together.

I loved Pat's family and felt more at home on the rez than I had since I was a little girl in the forest, and things visible and invisible were accorded the same respect. With my Native American friends, I felt as though my life had come full circle: the fragile balance between dream worlds, forest worlds, spiritual realms, and what most middle-class white people would call reality—cars and jobs and bills—that was part of my life was also part of theirs. We tried, with differing degrees of success, to navigate among these worlds. I recall, for example, my Hopi friend from Second Mesa, Arizona, telling me about trying to explain to her air force captain why she had to go on leave to complete her corn-grinding ceremony or the consequences for her would be dire. Like my friends, I believed in my bones, in a place beyond reason, in the reality of things that go bump in the night. Like many Native Americans of our generation, I, too, lacked the cultural roots, the teachings of previous generations, to be able to handle that kind of boundary-crossing with equanimity. We saw and felt things we didn't know what to do with and then got drunk in order to provide an explanation for the disorientation and dislocation caused by knowledge not understood, dreams without context.

The experience of "glimpses," things you know before they happen, but can't explain how you know them, was something that on the rez was taken in stride, as part of life rather than a freakish thing. I felt right at home the day Pat and I decided to drive out to visit her grandmother, whom I hadn't met. She lived way out and had no phone. When we arrived, her grandmother was waiting by the door. She took my arm, with no introduction, and said she'd just finished making up a batch of corn soup for me. Pat told me later it was a special soup you made for someone, with ceremonial ashes of some sort. I'm sure it was just what the doctor ordered.

Pat's mom said that since Pat and I were sisters anyway, we should make it official and give me a tribal adoption. I didn't tell anyone about my fears, but I just didn't feel ready to inherit all those ancestor spirits as new relations. I sensed that my roots were not deep enough to weather well the influx of all those presences.*

---

*I was at the Museum of Fine Arts last year and stopped in to listen to a presentation by an ethnomusicologist who studied the ritual music and chant of Tibetan monks. Toward the end of the lecture he turned on his tape recorder, as he had been doing, to play segments of chant. All of a sudden I was overwhelmed by a great swirling, whirling amassing of foreign presences. I gripped my seat, scared as a young child on a roller coaster, and hung on, frozen till it stopped, as the lecturer continued babbling about form and structure. Afterward I asked him the nature of that last piece of chant he had played. He said it was a chant to invoke the spirits of the dead. He told me, slightly sheepishly, that he had taped it surreptitiously—it wasn't one of the ones the monks had given him permission to record. I wanted to hit him. I was so mad I didn't even think about what he might think of me, and calmly (on the outside, that is) I told him what had happened when he did that. Do you have any idea whom you invited, or whether they were expecting tea or if they might be angry at their non-reception?

My questions were not entertained by him either, except perhaps in the form of an enhanced attention to the intricacies of packing up his gear. Quickly! As my dad once wrote of such academics, deaf to their own subject matter: "a peerage of tin ears."

In hindsight, I don't think the elders would have let me go through the adoption ceremony without preparing me, teaching me, taking good care of me, but at the time, I was so used to looking out for myself that it didn't even occur to me. I just thought I'd be up the proverbial shit creek without a paddle.

◈

BACK AT SCHOOL, Pat, Tracy, and I began to go on road trips up to Dartmouth on weekends. There were a lot of Native Americans at Dartmouth, and weekends were one long party. One snowy day, I met Dan, who would see me through my teenage years as my boyfriend, and through the rest of my life as my beloved friend and brother. He was on the sidewalk outside of Chase Hall, where most of our friends lived until the college built Indian House. I can still remember seeing him and feeling my braces with my tongue, wishing they weren't there. What I don't remember is whether he was on crutches or I was. I guess you could call it merging at first sight.

Dan swears to this day that I lied about my age. (As his own daughter approached her teens, he got even more adamant!) I say I just never happened to mention it until my sixteenth birthday came around and his jaw hit the ground. He was eighteen or so (depending on which birth certificate you choose; his mother has two of them about six months apart) and a sophomore. His dad was a Mohawk high-steel worker, like many Mohawks from the rez outside Montreal who drive down to New York to work on skyscraper construction all week—they're famous for walking along steel girders, forty stories up, as if they were on the ground—and drive back home on weekends. His mom, we discovered recently, was several people—multiple personalities sharing one frail body that lived on cigarettes, coffee, and the kind of dry assorted cookies that come in cardboard boxes with a cellophane window that only old people seem to buy in small, neighborhood markets. She was, but for the grace of God, and a lot of help from my friends, the very thing I was terrified I might become. But I never again had a blackout or "schizo" episode after Dan and I met. We were both loosely moored indeed, but somehow managed to keep each other afloat until adolescence subsided, and I got some psychotherapy—no, *a lot* of psychotherapy—and he

transferred from Dartmouth to Oberlin, for him a much more support-
ive environment where he finally allowed his brilliance to shine all the
way through Yale Law School.

To this day I have no idea how, in 1972, a New York tabloid got
wind of our relationship; I was not exactly what you might call a social
butterfly. They referred to Dan as "that Red-Indian that Salinger's
daughter is dating," which, according to said tabloid, should "bring the
recluse out of the forest!" I think Lillian Ross, our friend from *The New
Yorker,* spotted it and told my father, who in turn told me about it so I'd
hear it from him and not someone else. Contrary to tabloid predictions,
however, when I brought Dan home for inspection and interrogation,
Daddy took to him so well that he brought out old tapes of me singing
my war songs at age four. Dan is the only person I know of who has seen
some of the goodies in my father's arsenal. *I* wasn't even allowed to see
most of them.

Daddy had taught me to shoot the way Seymour taught marbles—
no aiming. You just think of the gun as an extension of your arm and
point. If you think about it, you miss. I liked to choose a daisy far away
and nip off just the flower; if you got the stem, it didn't count. Daddy
was impressed with Dan's marksmanship, and it takes a lot to do that,
but I wasn't crazy about the "not there" look Dan got on his face when
he shot. Even less crazy about it two years later when I walked into my
college dorm room to find him naked, sitting in the dark, with a .38
pointed at his face, ready to blow, and I had to talk him back. Or the
time I woke up to find him sitting bolt upright, shotgun pointing at the
end of the bed. When I carefully asked what was up, he said, "Don't
you see them, don't you see the bastards?" I crossed myself. Thank
God, this time, I could not. I'm spooked by the unseen worse than anything else, the kind of thing a gun can't touch. Silver bullets and henbane maybe.

Dan would never have survived his childhood had he not been
very, very smart. Lots of people, aside from family members, had tried
to kill him: living on the South Side of Chicago in the middle of Black-
stone Ranger territory and being the wrong color didn't help. Given
the expertise he developed in strategies for survival, it wasn't all that
surprising that he had a natural talent for chess. Over Thanksgiving of
'71 he was in a chess tournament in New York City, so when my dad

On my first day of boarding school, a Cheshire cat's teeth appeared, smiling in the long corridor. It said, "Hi, I'm Holly. What's your name?"

Peggy, age twelve, near the first day of boarding school.

Peggy, number 22. Joyce Maynard wrote: "I like Jerry's children, but I have little in common with this cheerful, friendly twelve-year-old boy and his basketball-loving sixteen-year-old sister."

Hanging out at the
Cambridge School.

I was a Grade D auto and truck mechanic for the Boston Edison Co. and member of
the United Utility Workers Union of America, A.F.L.-C.I.O., from 1975 to 1980—
unaware at the time that Holden Caulfield had dreamed of dropping out of school and
working in a garage somewhere, pumping gas.

Graduation day, 1982, Brandeis University. Phi Beta Kappa, summa cum laude, with high honors in history and legal studies. Above, left to right: My mother, brother, me, and my father. Left and below: My brother, off camera, made my father laugh.

Number 5, captain of Oxford University Ladies' Basketball Team.

Celebrating the end of examinations.

Graduation day, 1984, Oxford University. M.Phil. in Management Studies. To the left is my mentor and dear friend, the late Geoffrey Barraclough, with me and my brother, Matthew.

Chaplain Peggy Salinger, with Mia Klumpenhouwer, age nine, after performing a marriage ceremony for friends, September 1, 1990.

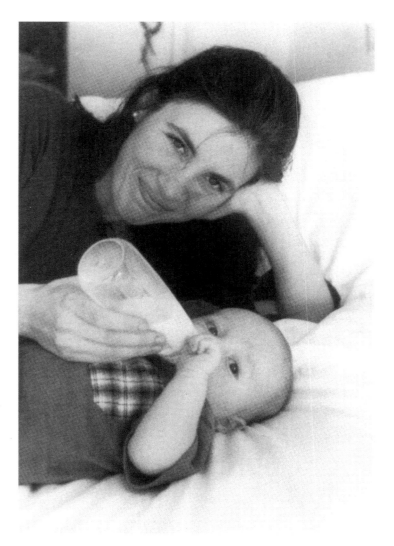

The author and her son.

A friend helps.
A friend laughs with you.
A friend helps you up when you are hurt.
        (—the author's son, age five)

wrote to tell me he was going to be in New York for Thanksgiving, I thought I'd hitch a ride with him. I also wanted to visit a school friend, Trisha, who had been hospitalized in New York for at least a year with a strange paralyzing disease. My dad spoke to her and convinced her to try sitting, or being sat actually, in an orgone box.* No miracle cure to report.

My diary, which I kept from ninth grade throughout high school, records the holiday pretty succinctly. I caught up with my writing during down time, like in class. The Thanksgiving holiday entry begins, "Here I am paying attention in math class as usual." I wrote that my dad and I checked into the Drake Hotel and had a few meals together on the day before Thanksgiving. On Thursday, "he was going to go out somewhere and I was going to stay at the hotel and order a feast from room service." I didn't think much about it, but when I called Holly, who was in town for the holiday, too, she was horrified at the idea. She called back and we went over to her grandmother's for Thanksgiving dinner. After dinner, "we went looking for a movie and booze, found neither, and went back to the hotel, watched a Bogart movie, and sacked out. Friday I kept trying to call Dan but he wasn't in. Daddy left and dropped me off at Holly's father's house."

I finally worked up the nerve to stop by the hotel where the chess tournament was being held. When I saw Dan, he was really happy to see me, but he was staying in a room with three other chess players from the Dartmouth team, so it would not have worked out to stay there, to put it mildly. Have you ever been near chess players during a tournament? It's not pretty.

I flew back to Boston that night. I remember looking down at the city from the plane window and feeling frightened that Dan was somewhere down there amidst all those millions of lights and I was up here in the night, separated from my mooring by miles of black sky.

❦

---

*Wilhelm Reich's invention to capture purported energy rays that he called orgones.

CHRISTMAS WAS A WINNER, TOO. Dan was in Chicago and I was in New Hampshire. I wrote in my diary:

Dec. 24th '71
I HATE Christmas. I can't wait until the whole business is over with. What the fuck am I doing with my life? I'm fat as hell, and completely hung up over Dan . . .

Monday 27 Dec.
Christmas sucked beyond belief. Dad and I had a fight. I miss Dan. I got new pens.

That's all I wrote that day. I packed up and left and spent the rest of the vacation staying with Amy's boyfriend in the South End. While I was there, I wrote about the fight I'd had with my father. It had started, as usual, over seemingly nothing. For some reason he got angry that I didn't return a phone call from someone I hadn't seen since fifth grade, but whom my father liked and chatted with each week as he paid her for the groceries she'd rung up. He had suggested she call when I was home, I guess. I wrote (cover your ears, gentle reader!):

The following day Daddy blew his cool. He went on about how I didn't give a damn about anyone but myself and my friends in Boston; not him, Matthew, or anyone else. I was turning into a crass and vulgar person and was hanging around with vulgar and coarse people. He said, in partial reference to my Langston Hughes book, whom he said was a trashy poet, that I was being absorbed head and foot into that culture. "You'll always have my love and affection but don't make me lose my respect for you. I change a great deal once that's lost." Suck my ass, J. D. I cut out the next day.

❧❧❧

THE NEXT VACATION, Dan was back from Chicago (I don't know why he was away for a term), and we went to stay at Pat's for the break. Winter was ending and it was time for spring cleaning, Indian style. Pat told

28

The Baby Vanishes

❦

THE SUMMER BEFORE MY SENIOR YEAR I stayed in my father's old apartment over the garage in Cornish. Dan had a job teaching for the summer with the ABC program at Dartmouth. I might have moved in with him, but my little brother was home in Cornish for the summer, too. I didn't want to set a bad example, so each and every morning before he woke up, I made sure Dad's old Saab, which he gave me (couldn't hold a candle to the Jeep!), was back in the driveway. Dan was great about that, too; he took my brother around and played basketball with him, but he did not show up at the breakfast table.

One day that summer something quite out of the ordinary happened. I went into town for the mail with my dad. I waited in the car while he went into the post office, no sign of either Mr. Custe or Mr. Curzon. Daddy got back in the car and was looking at the front of an envelope. He stared at it for a few moments, then calmly tore it, unopened, into several pieces and put it in the side-pocket trash. When he looked up, he said it was from Sylvia, his first wife. It was the first he had heard from her since they'd split up after the war. "Weren't you even curious what she might have to say?" I asked. I couldn't believe it. He said no, when he was finished with a person, he was through with them. At the time, I was impressed by his self-discipline and ashamed at the knowledge that I would have had to at least peek at the letter were our positions reversed. I wondered, silently, if I had a half sister or brother somewhere.

When I was a very little girl, I used to sit by the side of the road and wait, looking up the road. When my parents asked about it, I told them I was waiting for my older brother to come home. I wasn't playing, either; I can remember it clearly, waiting for him, certain he was out there, somewhere.

Shortly after the letter, I was in for another surprise when I woke up at my father's house and went into the living room only to find this girl enveloped in a flannel nightgown, sitting on my father's couch. He may have mentioned her, but I don't remember anything but the strangeness of meeting Joyce Maynard. Forgive a fellow teenager's thought, Joyce, but *this* is what Daddy had been waiting for all this time? This is the first "woman," to my knowledge anyway, he invites to stay? I mean she was perfectly nice and everything, but who expects to find someone looking like a twelve-year-old girl? In the place of a potential stepmother, here was this bizarre little sister of sorts. It was so *weird*. When she got dressed, she was wearing these little Mary Jane–style sneakers, straps and everything, and Daddy said, "Aren't those great, Peggy, you can get them at Woolworth's, you know. Joyce has them in several colors." I grunted noncommittally and thought to myself, Yeah, Dad, they're grrrrreat. Gonna run right out and get me some *real* soon. Right after I turn into a *total* geek, okay? Converse All Star high-tops were the only thing to be wearing that year, those and my beloved pair of killer black suede, over-the-knee boots with three-inch heels and a contrasting orange suede platform on the bottom. And any self-respecting teenager slept in her boyfriend's basketball T-shirt, size XX-large, not a kid's flannel nightie. In my book, if you were a grown woman, you wore a wedding ring, a bathrobe, and were dressed before breakfast with the exception of the flu, Mother's Day, or nuclear war. In my book, in my fiction.

Joyce, too, wrote about meeting me. I'd nearly finished the first draft of my own memoir when hers came out, so it was interesting to compare two views of the same event.

> Sometime in the night Peggy comes in and lies down in the single bed beside mine. It's late. She's been with her Dartmouth boyfriend. When I wake up, she's still asleep. . . .
>
> It's close to noon when Peggy emerges from the bedroom. . . . She's not unfriendly, but neither does she exude enthusiasm.

"I want you to meet Joyce," Jerry says. "She's the one I told you about. She wrote that magazine article."

"Hi," she says. Then she picks up a magazine and flips through it. No small talk.   (*At Home,* pp. 111–12)

. . . I like Jerry's children, but I have little in common with this cheerful, friendly twelve-year-old boy and his basketball-loving sixteen-year-old sister . . .

Where my way of operating in the world has always called for large amounts of conciliatory behavior—cuteness and charm, dissembling for the purpose of pleasing adults—Peggy's demeanor speaks of uncompromising honesty. Peggy, though she's two years younger, seems far more self-possessed than I. Whatever insecurities she may harbor, or secretly competitive feelings she may have toward me, I watch her with a kind of awe and fear, viewing her as someone who seems far more sure of herself in the world than I am. In Peggy's presence, I feel naked and oddly silly.   (p. 143)

To tell the truth, I didn't give her too much thought. It was, indeed, like having someone naked and oddly silly in the room; I instinctively looked the other way, to avoid embarrassment. Dan and I seemed so normal, which was both comforting to me and a source of discomfort in comparison to the "whatever" (that's how I would have put it then—I just didn't "go there" in my mind) of Dad and Joyce. She wrote:

Sometimes they [Peggy and Dan] hang out together in Jerry's living room. They come over on Sunday afternoons to watch sports. They bring their basketballs. Peggy carries hers in a case. They do not abide by Jerry's dietary rules, that I can see. [Dan] even drinks Coke.   (p. 169)

When Dad and Joyce broke up, I had the misfortune of being around. We were in Daytona Beach and my dad took me aside and told me that Joyce would be returning home tomorrow. I didn't ask why, but he uncharacteristically volunteered that she wanted to have children and he was "too old to hear the pitter-patter of little feet again," so he thought it only fair to cut things off quickly and cleanly. There was no rancor in his voice, none of the usual diatribes against women. He thought she had a perfect right to want to have children of her own and, like de Daumier-Smith said of Sister Irma, though not in so many words, thought that he should set her free to find her own destiny. I couldn't help but feel, at the time, that the realities of even a brief vacation with his own children had convinced him that he had no desire to do it over again. I knew he loved us, but the prospect of having children around for more than a few days had a chilling effect on whatever fantasies he and Joyce may have entertained about having a child together.

Joyce confirms my suspicions as to the sobering draught of reality that a week with real children can present to those who deal primarily with fictional children, dream children: "Bint."

> He stares out at the water, the children, the hungover college students on spring break, the cars racing up and down across the sand. He looks very old. His shoulders are hunched. He rests his forehead in his hands.
>
> "You know," he says, "I can never have any more children. I'm finished with all this." (p. 206)

Joyce says he told her she should go back early to Cornish and pack up her things so as not to upset the children. Just as I had imagined my father's English girl wishing, on our trip to Scotland so many years ago, Joyce writes that "lying there in the darkness while she [Peggy] sleeps, all I want is to be able to cry freely. But I know I mustn't wake Peggy. So I go into the bathroom." Apparently the sound of her crying awakened my father in the next room, and he joined her in the bathroom, briefly, whispering to quiet her down. I must say, I find it hard to believe that I slept through all this; I'd have been up in the blink of an eye if my brother had been so much as sniffling. Perhaps I just tuned her out, I don't know. She vanished the next day. It was as if she had never been there at all.

❦

I WAS THE ONE WHO, in reality, got pregnant that year, though I didn't suspect anything until I started vomiting every morning before school. I came across a slip of paper in an old box of mementos recently. I had no idea I'd kept it. It was from a clinic in Lexington and said simply: "pregnancy test positive." I was living in Lexington, a suburb of Boston, at the time, in an apartment I'd rented with Janis, a classmate from Cambridge School who had decided that she, too, could not stand another year of boarding school. We looked at a few schools, including Lexington Christian Academy, where the Celtics used to practice and Jo-Jo White would let us sneak into the balcony to watch if we were quiet. The best was one day listening to their coach prep them for the next day's game with the Knicks. He went through New York's roster and discussed strategy man by man until he got to Walt Frazier. He just shook his head and said, "And Frazier is Frazier." Nobody laughed, nobody needed to say anything more, the man was untouchable that year. Our other choice was the public high school in Lexington. We chose the latter, for reasons I no longer remember, rented an apartment, made up a guardian, and enrolled at Lexington High.

In hindsight, I would have been better off at an inner-city school than suburban Lexington High. At least I wouldn't have felt like such an oddball. My classmates seemed worried about things like getting grounded and prom dresses. I was worried about waitressing, pregnancy, and paying my rent. My father grudgingly sent a sum of money for the year that would have kept a roof over one's head in the 1930s. I told him he was saving all that tuition money, but he still had a fit about sending any at all. He had no problem with my living wherever; it was the money that, as usual, sent him into a rage about everyone wanting something from him—they were all "parasites," one of his most common expressions, usually reserved for women and college professors. Was I ever pissed when I found out from a biography that he lived with (and lived off) his parents until his mid-twenties. Oh, sorry, he's a true artist, that's different. I wouldn't have minded working a lunch counter and being broke, lots of kids are; what stuck in my craw was that so much of my anxiety was so damned unnecessary—he wasn't exactly without means. Luckily I had the foresight to invent a guardian with a low income, so at least I got free lunches at school.

A fictional guardian turned out to be a handy thing, too, for responding to notes about absenteeism. I attended school Tuesday, Wednesday, and Thursday, and spent the long weekends with Dan up at Dartmouth, except during basketball season, when I had daily practice. I'd write notes about how I was deeply concerned about Peggy's absences, but managed to slip in that if she was getting A's in three days, what could I do?

When I told Dan I was pregnant, it was early in the morning. He rolled over, half-asleep, and managed a really quite elegant proposal of marriage, which I accepted. A month later he told me he'd be spending next semester on an exchange program in Africa, but would be back by the time the baby was due.

Leaning over my toilet puking one morning before school, I freaked. All I could think was, I can't do this alone. At nearly four months pregnant, I bailed out. I took, without asking, $150 from my brother's passbook for an abortion and bus fare to New York. It was the saddest episode of my whole life. I wanted the baby, I was just too scared and too alone, and I had no idea that any help, welfare, AFDC, etc., might be available. They don't teach you those kinds of life skills in prep school.

My friend Amy's father, a psychiatrist, wrote a letter for me to a New York clinic, saying that in his opinion it would cause irreparable harm or whatever if I carried the baby to term. You had to have a letter from a doctor in those days. I sure wish I had known about group homes for young mothers or other kinds of support, but it didn't even occur to me that there might be anyone to help, anyone to take me in. Perhaps, in hindsight, I could have stayed with some of my old friends' parents, but the way I felt at the time, I couldn't even imagine a safe place. In my mind, I was entirely on my own. Friends could help me out, but I didn't need a friend now, I needed a grown-up to take care of me and help me learn how to take care of a baby. I wish I'd had someone like me, the person I am now in middle age, to turn to. Dan has often said the same thing to me, how he wishes we had had someone like him, at middle age, around to help us out the way he now talks with his son and daughter about relationships and problems that they're having.

I wanted the baby, I just didn't want to be a mother because I knew I didn't know how. I knew I'd do a lousy job, and that scared me to death. Scared into death. I take full responsibility for the decision, mind you, I just wish I had known how to take full responsibility for the child instead. Pat and Tracy both got pregnant that year as well, but they went home and had their babies. Even without the photographs they periodically send me of their daughters, I always know just how old my child would have been. At the moment, she would have been the exact same age as my son's baby-sitter. I find myself giving her silk scarves and good sweaters I've had forever. And pearls for her college graduation.

❧

I DON'T REALLY FEEL like going over it again; I said it all in my diary anyway, just how unromantic teenage pregnancy can be in reality:

[1972]

I'm trying to calm down to keep from going mad. I'm left alone again. I'm so afraid of being left alone again with my baby. Puking over the toilet all alone wishing I could die. All alone waking up and thinking my God I'm going to be a mother all alone. Watching my stomach growing all by myself. No plans for frilly white curtains and pretty Fisher-Price toys for the baby in a bright new room that *we* set up. No body to tell me, "Don't lift that, its too heavy. Here let me get it for you." No one to say, "Oh its kicking just think there's a little me in there." No, not for me. For me its hiding it for as long as possible, feeling my thoughts all ALONE. Left alone all alone and so confused my god I'm a mother. Looking out the window of the bathroom all alone and puking. Eating shitty lasagna in the school cafeteria with nobody to tell me to eat good food.

I'll probably be going through labor all alone with Doctors all in white staring at my body helpless with my feet tied up in stirrups out of some Marquis de Sade horror movie while people poke and rip out my guts all alone nobody waiting for me in the waiting room. No nobody paces the floor for me. Oh yes he's in Africa and he'll visit us sometime. He really wants to be a father to the baby. Yes on Sundays when the diapers have been changed and the 4:00 AM feedings all alone and the questions asked "Am I going to be able to be a good mother—Why doesn't this blasted baby ever shut up and get to sleep"—all asked all alone. Oh yes he'll be the father allright like a wound that never heals. . . . Maybe I'll be in Alaska or Hawaii he says. I've been looking forward to this trip to Africa for a long time. I'll be back before the baby is born.

But here I am all alone in an empty apartment. I'm pregnant and all alone. I swear to God sometimes I feel like I'll be all alone for the rest of my life. Christmas at somebody's house where you're a stranger or worse yet Christmas in a hotel room with a lover who's a stranger in a foreign land with sailors all around all alone. Walking by the sea almost happy again when you realize someone's following you so you run back to an empty lover and apartment only to be all alone while he's there. . . . It aches so much. It aches and aches you want to be loved and held but you know the feelings aren't mutual, alone in your feelings. The world drops out from underneath you every time you let yourself need somebody and your left emptier than before because you made more room in your heart and now there's more to fill. Just like my uterus it's emptier than empty. Worse much worse than just empty—there's more room now its been stretched out dilated vacuumed scraped had foot long pieces of metal coming out with bloody gauzes on it and life gets sucked up into a big machine with a motor the sound of a thousand vacuums. And Pain. The horrible agony of something being ripped and torn and scraped out of your most fragile parts like your guts themselves will be the next to follow. Looking up at the white ceiling with no pain killers or anesthesia with pop music playing out of the radio which is piped into every room including the death rooms, excuse me, the operating rooms. Stab of pain—"Oh dear, that's only your cervix dilating." Huge needle jabbed into me—"Oh dear, its only a shot to numb your uterus." And when its all over there's no soft sensitive wide eyed boy who looks like he's barely old enough to get the cab over by himself to look scared and like he wants to cry but lovingly at me. He can't say anything, but two by two the young kids in blue jeans leave together holding each other like in the Donovan song, "we stood in the windy city, the rain dropping tears in our eyes."

Me and the fat girl who came all the way from Pennsylvania and a few others leave alone. There's nobody in the waiting room for us. I get the girl from Penn. a cab, and myself go back to the projects where I rely on another baby to help me. Bad idea. Amy can't handle it. She wants to party. I need somebody so bad so I run out of the apt. all alone into the dark streets of New York at midnight. Gangs of Boys on the street corners shouting obscenities. I'm scared. I forget how to get to the bus station and even if I did get to the bus station where the hell would I go. I have no one. I am alone and frightened. I go back to the apartment which is better than sleeping in the subway especially since I'm bleeding a whole lot and am supposed to be taking it easy incase I hemorrhage. How the hell can I lose more than I've lost all ready. Think I care if I hemorrhage and infect—Hell No. I already have an open wound that will never heal. So I go back and cry myself to sleep on a couch in the livingroom alone as usual. So many nights spent crying myself to sleep all alone.

IF MY LIFE IS GOING TO BE LIKE THIS FOREVER I JUST CAN'T STAND IT. Will I always be in some shitty apartment all alone with nobody when I need somebody the most? Will I always be pregnant and alone? Will I? If staying with Dan says that the answer is yes then I don't want to be with him. I don't trust him with my guts.

All I want is a *home*. Someplace nice and cheery where its MY home and I belong and I'm loved. Somewhere where I can always depend on the person who loves me not to leave me lonely. Someplace I belong. Someplace peaceful and safe. Sometimes I feel like I'll never ever find a home where I'm wanted loved and TREATED RIGHT. I feel like I'll never be not alone in some dump with bare light bulbs and no lampshades. . . .

Well I successfully stopped my hysteria. No more rocking and crying and talking to myself out loud. I suppose thumb sucking goes next but why take away all life's little pleasures at once! Actually, seriously, I'm really glad I can stop myself when I get hysterical. I can tell when I start shaking and rocking and feeling super lightheaded that it is time to STOP. And I still can. When you have no one it's imperative that you can control yourself and shrink yourself or else your up shit creek without a paddle canoe life saver etc. etc. I still feel kinda pregnant and alone.

Shit it's a good thing I'm not or I'd really be SUPER CRAZY right now. Well, I'm off to find a friend in Jesus cause boy do I ever need one!

I sure hope and pray that Dan is OK and not alone. I know he knows what it means to be alone up in that shitty hotel room with lead paint chipping off the walls Big Bad Hard Tough 13 year old boy scared shitless so shitless he doesn't even know it and all alone. That kills me. I hate to think of him like that. That little guy in the photograph in pajamas, barely four, nearly beaten to death by his old man in a drunken rage. The little boy spilled his last can of beer. Fractured chest, one eye blown out, face rearranged monthly 'till the old fucker died. I always wish I could have been there to make things better. When he needed me I wasn't even born yet! . . . It must be pure living agony and hell to be a parent and not be able to provide for your kids. Pure living hell.

I may be getting an ulcer. I hope not but my stomach sure hasn't felt too hot lately. Now its throbbing like its been throbbing and burning for the past few days. Actually, I almost hope I do have one and I don't know why.

***

SHORTLY AFTER RETURNING from New York, I applied to Dartmouth early decision and was rejected outright. My father was furious at Dartmouth—my daughter's not good enough for them? I now had to decide which of my secondary choices I wanted to attend. The selection criterion was proximity to Dan, who stuck around, after all, at Dartmouth. This is the crisis, the "sizable decision," my father referred to in the letter he sent me when I didn't get in. He said he was glad I always kept my head in a crisis. He enclosed some homeopathic medicine for the head cold he thought he heard in my voice over the phone.

***

I GRABBED ON TO JESUS like the drowning young woman I was. My daily diary entries of boys and babies and booze were interrupted in bold letters: "MAY 5th I GOT SAVED." I had never set foot in a church in my whole life until now. The closest I'd come to any formal religion was when, at Cross Mountain School, Holly had brought me to synagogue with her once during the High Holy Days so we could escape school for the day and sit someplace warm.

I was talking to a classmate, Earl St. James (today the Reverend Earl St. James, I hear), feeling deeply miserable and adrift. He and his sister invited me to come to church with the family. I thanked him, but said that it was a real stumbling block to me that anyone should go to hell just because they weren't Christians. When, years later, I brought this question up in divinity school, a Jesuit classmate of mine said, "The pope says we have to believe in hell, but no one says we have to believe that there is anyone in it." Earl was such a kind and gentle person, he didn't need Jesuit reasoning as his witness. When I said I didn't believe in hell for non-Christians and wasn't sure that a good God would even think up such a place, he said simply and thoughtfully that he didn't know how it all worked, but he, too, believed in a merciful God and maybe there were chances for others, ways of getting to heaven that we don't know about.

I decided to take him up on his offer and spend the next Sunday with his family. The St. Jameses lived on the top floors of a four-family that they owned in a predominantly black and West Indian section of the city. They belonged to a tiny church right around the corner from their house. The parishioners were all Barbadian; well, all but that tall, stray, white girl the St. James family brought along with them. Sunday morning we ate a big breakfast, and Mrs. St. James hurried to put Sunday lunch in the oven to bake. Red-eye peas and rice, couscous with sour fish sauce (which for years I thought was called "coo-coo with sah-fish sauce"), and roasted chicken. It was like Thanksgiving. It *was* thanksgiving.

We walked to church together. Large brown women in flower print dresses and white straw hats greeted each other: "Good morning, sister." Children passed by neat as a pin in little suits or dresses. A sprinkling of men. The pastor was more than ninety years old. His skin was deep black, not blue-black like some Africans', but rather so brown and furrowed it had turned black over time like rich Barbadian earth. He had such a strong accent that I could not understand a lot of what he had to say. But when the man asked if anyone wanted to come forward and lay their burdens on Jesus, I heard the call to come forward loud and clear. "Does anybody want to receive Jesus Christ as Savior and Lord?" I wasn't sure about the "Lord" part, but a savior sounded pretty wonderful. This Jesus and his family seemed to have strong medicine.

As the pastor invited those not yet saved to come up to the altar rail, people got down on their knees and prayed or almost chanted, "Thank you, Jesus. Thank you, Lord." Some got moved by the Spirit and looked as if they were having convulsive fits, yet it wasn't the kind of fear-filled bedlam I was used to when boundaries broke down. The swirl of sounds and smells and movement, the women's Ice Blue Secret deodorant and flowered dresses, songs and prayer, wove together a different kind of time and space. As the boundaries of this reality faded a bit, there was not the kind of annihilation or unbeing that I'd witnessed in madness; but rather, a kind of re-being or re-creation that happens in those rare epiphanies in art, music, theater, religious ritual, and lovemaking. I am over the edge, but flying, soaring on the updrafts above the cliff, not falling down the dark abyss. I'm not swept along to the altar, I'm gliding. I kneel and people lay hands on me and pray over me, asking if I wish to accept Jesus as my personal Savior. Yes. Yes, I do.

I walked home feeling light and happy. I wasn't made to feel self-conscious or special, they didn't like me any more or any less, nor did they treat me as any more or less welcome in their home. Espousal of their belief wasn't a prerequisite for love and affection and respect. They were just happy for me and available if I wanted to talk or had any questions—of which I had lots. I was not used to people listening to me, really listening. I learned the difference between cult, where one is required to leave large pieces of who one is at the door, split off, as the price of entry, and community.

❦

I SKIPPED MY HIGH SCHOOL GRADUATION. Class of 1973. Daddy called and said, "You don't want me to come to graduation and all that crap, do you?" How could I admit that I wasn't too sophisticated to want any of that pomp and circumstance crap. He almost certainly would have come if I had had the courage to appear stupid. And perhaps he wanted to but said it that way so he wouldn't feel stupid. Anyway, I didn't go because I really *would* have felt stupid when all those kids were hugging their parents and taking pictures and being taken out for dinner.

THE NEAREST COLLEGE TO DARTMOUTH, as I looked on the map, seemed to be New England College in Henniker, New Hampshire. It was about forty-five minutes down Route 114 from Dartmouth and offered, as a bonus, a season's lift ticket to the local ski area as part of the activities fee. I met some good friends there and had a couple of really good teachers—especially my genetics professor, who took us all on a field trip to Boston to see the Spring Flower Show, where he wore his usual dark cape and swooped amongst the orchids. Aside from my introduction to drosophila and plant biology, the best thing about my year and a half of college, given my state of mind, was meeting my foster parents. They hosted a teen Bible-study group in their home, which is how I met them.

I like to think that I was of some help, being the eldest of about ten foster kids and four adopted ones at any given time. But the biggest help by far was to me, that's for sure. They took in kids no one else would take. Deaf kids, kids with seizures and cigarette burns on their genitals, seven-year-olds with drug addictions (black beauties from their biker parents to keep them quiet), three sisters who wanted to be placed together, mentally retarded twins. I finally had a place to come home to that was as much mine as it was any of the other kids' in the house. I didn't feel like a guest, as I did everywhere else, including my father's, perpetually worried about wearing out my welcome.

DAN AND I BROKE UP when I was nineteen. We were living together that summer in Cambridge and fighting so badly we couldn't stand it anymore and couldn't figure out how to make it stop. I'm not kidding. When we decided we had to call it quits, we sat there in the apartment we'd rented for the summer sobbing so hard we had to soak towels in a bathtub of cold water and put them over our faces. Who'd believe you could love each other so much and not get along. Several months later, in a panic, I did my own version of Dan's bolting off to Africa or Alaska, only I went through with it. I dropped out of school, asked my karate instructor to marry me, and he did. I thought it was God's will.

I had wanted to have the wedding in Cornish at Saint-Gaudens in the summertime, but my mother and I fought so much over initial plans,

I said to forget about it. Actually the plans were the least of it. I went up to check out the facilities at Saint-Gaudens. Just before we were to go down the road to visit, I had to use the bathroom at the Red house. I came back outside and called out I was ready to go. Mom ran out of the house wild-eyed, dangling a wet, used tampon. She was screaming at me, "How could you have flushed it? How could you, this is country plumbing, how could you be so . . ." While her boyfriend tried to calm her down, I backed out of the driveway and was gone. My foster parents hosted the wedding.

My bridesmaid, Amy, had some serious misgivings about what I was doing since I had only known the guy a few months. My dad called Amy and told her he was sick about the whole thing and was sure that I was making a terrible mistake. She agreed and asked him to come to Boston and talk to me about it. He refused, saying, "I have so much piled up on my desk right now, it's impossible." She called me right after he hung up, shocked, so I know I have the quote exactly. I found out, years later, that he'd also called Dan to intervene. Dan agreed I was a mess, and that he, too, was a mess about our breakup, but that if he'd known what to do about it, we'd still be together, and told my dad he was on his own on this one.

The evening before the wedding, my wedding party—six brides-maids and six grooms—all squeezed into my foster parents' tiny four-bedroom ranch house along with all the family's many kids who had come home for the wedding. My dear old friend Viola drove down to be one of my bridesmaids. She was put in charge of looking after my dad and keeping him on good behavior, especially since my mother would be there. That night, a thunderstorm hit so badly that the roads from the highway to the ski area, where I was to have my reception, were washed out. In the morning, we slithered down the road to the trailer park where the mother of my Big Brother/Big Sister program kid had kindly offered to set my hair. Big hair.

The ceremony itself was delayed for two hours because my fiancé's parents were late. We drove up and down the highway in the family van, looking for them for an hour or so, me in my Qiana wedding dress, getting stickier by the minute. Then we thought we'd just better get the show on the road, or off the road, as it were. We had hired a preacher to do the ceremony and provide the music; he was one of those traveling evangelists who do a whole package with a sort of proto-karaoke tape recorder set up with a microphone for gospel songs. He never showed up. My foster father ran out of the church, down the road, and grabbed the town's justice of the peace, who came into the church, no lie, wearing a fishing hat with fishing thingies stuck all around the brim. He kept the hat on during the ceremony. My husband's parents and cousins turned up just as we were leaving the church for the reception. I felt awful about them just missing it, but we didn't know what else to do.

At the reception, which Dad for some reason paid for, he was easy to spot. My dad was the one standing up with a pained look on his face, Viola trying to intervene, as his finger gesticulated, furiously counting heads, with body language subtle as Marcel Marceau's, certain he'd been taken advantage of. "I paid for eighty people, where the hell are they!" The storm prevented a number of people—though not the tough guys from the karate school, of course—from making it there, including the caterers with the Chinese food, who finally showed up with cold lo mein about an hour late. My mother came, but after the pictures were taken, she told me she had to leave; she was meeting some friends for a canoe trip. I said, "But this is my wedding. Can't it wait?" She said, "But I've been planning this for *weeks,* dear," and left. It could have been worse. At my brother's wedding she met the bride's widowed father and, a few months later, announced that she was moving back East to live with him.

❀

ALTHOUGH MY MARRIAGE didn't work out in the long run, I have to say that it was pretty restful till it blew up. He was cheerful, pleasant, helped around the house, and left my insides alone. No scary merging, just pleasant cohabitation. For most of our marriage, I worked a swing shift, 4 P.M. to 12 A.M., at Boston Edison, and he, I thought, was working nights, so we didn't see much of each other, which was also okay.

Best of all, for the first and last time, thus far anyway, I *loved* my job. Right after we got married, I had gone to work as an airport security guard, but had to quit after I threw this weird little "sergeant" who was harassing me up against the cement wall of her office cubicle. Then I got a job waitressing, and one of the girls told me that the Edison (Boston's electric utility company), headquartered across the street, was hiring clerks, and that it was a great company to get into. After my shift was done, I walked over and applied. It was sort of embarrassing because the human resources guy asked me if I could type, which I couldn't. But he asked me to put down all the education I had, and for some reason, probably because I felt dumb about applying for a clerk job when I couldn't type, I included a night-school class I'd taken in auto mechanics after the last car repair bill I'd received and couldn't afford. He asked me how I'd like to come to work in their Mass. Avenue garage. I looked at him as though he had two heads, and he did something really cool. He pushed the printed details of the starting salary for clerks across the table toward me. Then he pushed across the starting salary for Grade D auto and truck mechanics. Wow! That's how I became a mechanic for the Boston Edison Company from 1975 to 1980.

I was scared to death my first week or so. I thought the guys would resent a girl in the shop, but luckily a co-worker, Cathy, had preceded me and was such a wonderful person and good worker that my way was very smooth. Cathy, in contrast, didn't even have a shower installed for her in the ladies' room for about six months, they were so sure she wouldn't make it. At first, I got the business from a few of the guys, but somehow I wound up having a garage full of about ten grandfathers, a dozen fathers, and a whole bunch of brothers. They'd been ribbing me for months, saying that the old leather hippie bag I had was big enough to steal car batteries, and so beat-up and stained it looked as if I *had* been sneaking them out at night. They pooled together some money for my birthday and bought me a nice handbag and a cake—a gorgeous thing from Linda Mae's bakery—for a surprise party at coffee break.

I was a member of the United Utility Workers Union of America, A.F.L.-C.I.O., wrote for the union paper, and helped organize a chief stewards' conference on health issues, such as asbestosis. What a great feeling to have worked hard writing an article and the next day have guys hanging off trucks cheering when they came up to the gas pumps. It was our union secretary, Don Wightman (shortly to become union president), who gave me the encouragement and confidence to give college a second chance. I was working that summer, in lieu of a layoff, at Edison's Pilgrim nuclear plant at a time when it had the dubious distinction of being the dirtiest (most radioactive) plant in the nation. Don and I got to talking over a grievance we were filing down at the nuclear plant, and he asked me if I'd given any thought to my future. He told me he knew it was none of his business, of course, but that I was a smart kid and could probably go pretty far, even in the union maybe, if I went to college. I said I hadn't exactly done too well in school, and he said, So what, I know you're smart. Why don't you just take a day course or something and test it out. I worked four to midnight so it would be easy enough to arrange. I said I'd think about it, especially with the layoffs yet to come when they shut down the old coal-burning station near town.

Brandeis University's admission officer said that if I "aced" the two courses I was taking, one at Harvard Extension, one at B.U.'s Metropolitan program, both taught by full professors for working people in the community, they'd consider my application. When I told my father the good news, he had a fit, first with me, then with my mother. He said he'd warned me when I got married that he wouldn't pay for anything. To my mother, he said, "What does she need college for? What's *she* going to do with her life that she needs college?" Mom threatened to go to the press if he didn't pay for my college education as stipulated in their divorce agreement. Well, that insured compliance all right, but not without a nasty letter in which he informed me that if, indeed, I should be accepted anywhere, to have them send the bill directly to him, but he sure wasn't happy about it. He said that some of the most unpleasant exchanges of his life had been with me and he hoped we'd do better in the future. He enclosed some homeopathic medicine to counter the radioactivity I was exposed to at the nuclear plant.

※

WHEN MY APPLICATION to Brandeis was accepted, I applied for a nine-month leave of absence from the Edison and it was granted. My replacement didn't come through for about a month, so I began my first term working full-time 4 P.M. to 12 A.M. and going to school full-time days. Actually, that made the transition easier on me, because I was really scared I'd fall flat on my face at college, and I sure didn't want to lose the good job I had. Brandeis went out of its way to ease the transition, too. They had a special orientation program for older students who were starting school in their mid-twenties. We got to meet each other the first day, and I can't tell you how much that helped me not feel like a total oddball. The first person I met was Steve, a Hispanic guy from the Southwest who had just gotten out of the army. He asked me what I did for a living, and I said I was a mechanic. He said, "Yeah, right. Let's see those hands." With quite the street "attitude," as if I had nothing to prove to him, I lazily put out a hand. One look, and his tight face broke into a grin and he said, "Hey, all right, girl!" A high five, and that was the beginning of that friendship.

A few weeks into the term, just about the time my replacement at work showed up, life fell out from underneath me. I pulled into the driveway after my shift at about 12:30 A.M., got out of my car, and some guy appeared out of nowhere. I thought he was going to try to kill me, but, thank God, it turned out that he was just there to repossess my car. After he realized I wasn't going to give him any crap, he apologized for scaring me, handed me some papers, and drove off with my car. I'd bought that damn car with the down payment I'd earned working round the clock for nearly a week during the blizzard of '78. My husband sent in the car payments and the mortgage payments on the house that I had bought with a down payment through the credit union. I just gave him my paycheck to deposit. I hated fussing with bills, so I was happy for him to handle it. The mail came after I left for work in the afternoon, so I never suspected a thing. Well, girls, you know what comes next. Several weeks into college, I have no car, the bank is repossessing my house in three weeks, all my savings for college are gone, and so is my husband. No arguments, no fights, no scenes, just gone. A call to a lawyer told me to get everything I still owned out of that house ASAP or it's joint property, to say nothing of the fact that he might come back for it.

The creepiest thing was not knowing who the hell I'd spent the last few years with. No one who knew him could believe it, he was such a nice guy, always cheerful, always smiling. Seriously spooky. My guess, in hindsight, is that he got into some bad debt with guys who don't play games about collecting. Something about big black cars pulling up to the curb, and him telling me how to throw bleach in somebody's face if they break through the door. Living in a war zone and not asking questions were second nature to me, though, and I just took it basically in stride. Part of life. Like the reporters or kidnappers or bogeymen who climbed trees outside the Red house when I was a kid.

I'm not quite sure how it all came about, but Saturday morning bright and early my new friend Steve from Brandeis, fresh out of the army, and my old friend Lou, not so fresh out of the marines in Vietnam, showed up with a truck and began moving out matériel on the double. We were out of there by noon. I was in shock, physically and every other way, and I really don't know much about what happened the next few weeks—just that my friend Lou took care of it. Took care of me. I stayed with him for a few months I think. The girl he was dating, who is now his wife, wasn't thrilled, but she was both understanding and levelheaded, which is the way she is, one of the most thoroughly decent people I've had the privilege of knowing. Lou drove me to school and literally fed me food, with a spoon, in front of the TV until I came out of shock a few weeks later. He had done time in an orphanage as a kid. God bless friends—kinsmen—you don't have to *explain* things to.

Thanks to friends, and maybe to the fact that as a kid I'd learned to read as if my life depended on it, I didn't miss a single day of class and got straight A's that semester. Later that fall, I found a beautiful, sunny apartment on the top floor of an old Victorian parish house behind a church in Concord center. It was flooded with light no matter the time of day from the tall, thin pairs of arched windows, north, south, east, and west, constructed to mirror the church's arched windows. Morning and evening carillon from the church bells next door was like the cowbells to and from green pastures I listened to as a little girl in Cornish. The apartment cost too much money but my mom had called and said, "Take it, there are times in your life having a beautiful place to live is more important than being sensible," and she sent me the extra money. She also didn't make me feel like an idiot for being blindsided by a man.

When the shock wore off and I had a little time to think, I realized that, given the kinds of terrible things people do to each other, I had gotten off easy. All my ex-husband took was money; he never hurt my feelings. By disappearing, he also gave me a chance to start over.

29

A Mind in Port

❦

GOING TO BRANDEIS was one of the best decisions I've made, or perhaps I should more modestly and accurately say, one of the best pieces of luck that has come my way. It was, in hindsight, as important to my sanity and growth and life as choosing, albeit unsaid, in seventh grade, to live in my body rather than to renounce it and stay a two-dimensional ten forever. As seventh grade was a discovery and a celebration of life in the body, Brandeis was a discovery and celebration of the life of the mind. My *own* mind, not somebody else's. It was clear from the moment I set foot in the classroom and looked at the requirements of each class, each major, each degree, that Brandeis was totally committed to graduating *educated* students, people who knew how to think for themselves, and not simply regurgitate a reflection of the teacher's point of view on an exam. I always had the feeling that students were there to learn, and that learning was a valued, respected activity. An education was something intrinsically valued rather than looked at merely as a means to an end, or in terms of what "product" they or we produced. Although we were well prepared to go on to jobs or further education when we graduated, we weren't narrowly "pre" anything—pre-med, pre-law, and so on.

The extraordinary thing to me at the time, which I must say makes a lot of sense to me now that I'm twenty years older and a mother, is that this was not accomplished by letting students act like little pre-adults and do their own thing. There were (and I hope still are) requirements that made even an older student such as me chafe at the bit: Why did I need to take an art class, a biology class, an English class, distributives across the spectrum of learning? And not one of these required distributives was a "rocks for jocks" class. They were the real thing. The "name" professors, the big guys and gals with the big salaries and reputations and books, were the ones teaching the freshman classes. The best was not saved for an elite of graduate seminars and senior concentrators. You got their best whether you wanted it or not. The big professors graded their own papers and exams, were available for conference hours whenever you or they thought you needed it. They helped their graduate students learn to be good teachers rather than treating them as cost-effective substitutions for themselves so they could get on with the business of publishing. I am, of course, particularly sensitive to feeling as though I am interrupting somebody's work. There, I felt as though I *was* their work. And, boy, were we expected to work in return. I think that when teachers invest their time and energy in you, they have higher expectations of excellence, and a higher right to demand it. The "phony" quotient on the Salinger scale, in my experience at least, was subzero.

I can't help but think that the roots of Brandeis University influence the way it regards the cultivation of the mind. It was founded by people of the Diaspora, people fleeing Hitler, people deeply aware that the things of true value are those that can be carried with you in your mind. The ups and downs of life can take away everything else in an instant. Being broadly educated leaves you less vulnerable to the changes life throws your way in bad times, and open to a hell of a lot more fun in good times. Take my friend and former basketball and softball teammate Margie, for example. She is a biochemist and can tell you some fascinating things about her research work, but she can also tell you some equally fascinating things about her vacation trips to Rome and Greece where she pursues an interest in ancient art and ruins that she was introduced to in an art class she was "forced" to take freshman year. My friend Wayne, one of the youngest recipients of a Ph.D. in economics and politics, currently a senior member of the World Bank, writes plays and teaches ancient Greek theater and philosophy in his "spare" time. These are professionals you don't dread having your best friend marry or being seated next to at a dinner.

I don't mean to say that Brandeis has never graduated what my father calls "a narrow-minded bore, a mindless follower," or someone who'd jump out the window at the first layoff, but it sure didn't encourage it. This was brought home to me perhaps most poignantly at the time in a history seminar in which two of my classmates were graduate students from the People's Republic of China. The culture clash was astonishing, and a priceless education to the entire class. Each of us would, at some point, read out loud to the class a paper we'd written. When it was their turn to present their papers, the Chinese scholars reported to the class what everyone and his grandmother had said about a particular question. But when asked what do *you* think, they showed blank or confused stares, even after a year of being encouraged to do so. Some of the Americans' papers were short on roots—what others had thought before them—and, with the hubris of youth, proudly reinvented the wheel. We were sent back to the books, of course, but the excitement, the growth, the life of the mind, though pruned, was vigorous.

At the end of the school year my leave of absence from work was up, and I went back to work at the garage for the summer. It was good to be back, but sad, too, as I suspected it would be for the last time. I decided at the end of the summer to cut the cord and risk college full-time. That December, it was my basketball teammates, rather than my workmates this time, who threw me a birthday party. My friend and favorite sender of rude birthday cards, Margie, was in charge of decorating the cake. The frosting was green and in big bold neon letters it said Happy Quarter of a Century! (I guess twenty-five seems old when you're nineteen or so.) It was pretty great. I'm looking forward to what she comes up with for my fiftieth.

DURING THE SUMMER between my sophomore and junior years, I had a once-in-a-lifetime opportunity to spend some time alone with my maternal grandmother. She invited me to come with her to Aspen to attend a round-table seminar chaired by Mortimer Adler at The Aspen Institute. The reading list was right up my alley, a continuation of my Brandeis introduction to what Adler calls Great Ideas, from Aristotle to Zoroaster. (Well, I made up the *Z* part; Zoroaster wasn't on the list, but I liked the sound of it; I think the list ended with *T* for de Tocqueville on *Democracy in America*.) These seminars provided senior members of management—heads of Fortune 500 companies, as well as labor leaders and a mix of people from the arts and government (plus two students, myself and a local high school student)—the opportunity to examine rigorously their assumptions and beliefs about the proper conduct of men and nations. I truly can't think of a few weeks better spent. It was particularly moving to see how much the experience meant to some very successful heads of companies who had come up through the engineering route and had never had the opportunity to do this kind of work and reading and thinking. But this was no touchy-feely group; Adler was more like a drill sergeant in his rigor and intolerance of sloppy thinking, and like an old judge in his fairness in hearing different points of view. I shall never forget sitting up at night with my grandmother, each of us in a twin bed, preparing the next day's reading. It is an especially precious memory as she was diagnosed with inoperable cancer a month later and died shortly after Christmas that year.

One morning after I had been arguing a labor point of view on a subject, with some success, in seminar, one of the observers, an older man with broad shoulders and big hands, walked up to me, shook my hand, and said, "Well, now, who are you, and how do you know anything about trade unions?" and invited me to lunch with him and his wife. He said he was Jim Callaghan, and when someone called him Mr. Prime Minister, I suddenly realized that the nice chap to his right was also a bodyguard. We corresponded off and on for some years, and he and his wife invited me to tea at the House of Commons and asked if I might like to come to England and work for him as an intern after I graduated. I declined with regrets, because I'd been accepted to a master's program in management studies at Oxford University and had decided to do that instead.

What impressed me the most, however, was not the excitement of the House of Commons, but what I observed in a quiet moment during a dinner at Aspen. Someone was giving an after-dinner talk, and Mr. Callaghan and his wife, Audrey, were seated across the table from me, dutifully listening, as I'm sure they've done many thousands of times. Their chairs were turned slightly toward the speaker so Mrs. Callaghan's back was toward her husband. I watched as he gently traced with his forefinger a little pattern on her back, almost absentmindedly, the way you reach for someone you love in your sleep. I'll never forget it.

And the way he spoke of her volunteer work at a London hospital with the respect of a statesman, putting her first. What a marvelous thing it is to meet someone who truly loves and respects his wife and in old age still reaches for her quietly, a sanctuary in the midst of a madding crowd.

❦

WHEN MY GRANDMOTHER DIED, she was kind enough to leave me sufficient funds that I didn't have to worry about making a living for several years, and I was able to attend to my studies at Brandeis and, later, at Oxford with some peace of mind. It also permitted me during my junior year to do an unpaid internship with a labor lawyer with whom I'd worked on asbestosis prevention back at the Edison. I loved studying the law, but being a lawyer was another thing, seeing what they actually did most of their working hours. What a gift to find out what you *don't* want to do before you commit yourself.

Another thing my grandmother's generosity enabled me to do was to afford to go to therapy more often. I sat my mother down after my grandmother's funeral and basically bullied her, shamelessly I might add, into seeking psychotherapy for herself. Good move on both parts. She has gone on to write books, earn her Ph.D., and make a real career for herself. She has also learned to be a good grandmother to her grandchildren. My aunt said of my mother, "I don't know how she lived with Sonny all those years. He never should have married. She should be very proud of herself, making a successful career as she's done, it can't have been easy."

❦

MY SENIOR YEAR OF COLLEGE was a struggle. I had won a scholarship to support my senior thesis research, on the history of the passage of the first Workman's Compensation Act in 1897. It enabled me to spend the summer in London, working at the British Museum Library and the archives of the Trades Union Congress. I had come back with some pretty thrilling stuff (to me, anyway, and to my advisers) and wanted to do justice to the material. I also had a full load of classes. My intellect stayed intact, I could still study, but I was in big trouble. I did not blank out as of old; this was trouble of a different color. I had begun to suffer from perceptual hallucinations. I was fully conscious that the physical sensations I was experiencing were not real—the library floor would feel as if it were pitching and roiling, and I felt as if I were trying to stand and walk in a wave-tossed canoe, or the stairs would suddenly appear to be two inches from my face and then ten feet below me—but as in a nightmare where you know you are dreaming but can't make it stop, I was helpless. Often when I went to the library to study, I was hallucinating so badly I had to have a friend help me to my desk. It wasn't pink elephants and that sort of thing, what happened were major perceptual distortions such that I couldn't figure out where I was in relation to anything else. It was rather like walking along a sidewalk in the dusk and suddenly stepping off a curb when you don't expect it and your body isn't prepared to make the automatic adjustments it makes based on signals telling it where it is in relation to the environment. Chartless.

It wasn't just at school that this happened. My friends took me out to the movies for a little rest and relaxation. I enjoyed the movie, but when the lights came on, I realized that I had absolutely no idea how to maneuver my body out of the theater. I knew I was in my seat, I could see the exit sign, but I simply could not put the two together and spatially orient myself. I sat in my seat sobbing, "I don't know where I am. I don't know how to get out of here or where to go." They led me out by the hand and got me in the car. The ride back to my apartment was terrible. I looked out the window at once-familiar streets, totally disoriented, scared, crying. All I could say was I don't know where I am, but what I meant was I didn't know where I was in relation to anything else. I knew full well I was in the car with my friends, the approximate time, date and year, who is the president of the United States—all those other questions they ask you at the admitting desk. It was I who was out of plumb with the world.

I don't know why this started happening, whether it was the pressure, or perhaps the fear that the end was in sight, and I didn't, as yet, know where I would go or what I would do after college. Breakups are always hell on me. Toward the end of the year, at crunch time when I was trying to finish my senior thesis and take five other classes at the same time, it got so bad that I couldn't drive at all. The road and my car just wouldn't line up in my mind. My friends Ted, Mitchell, Margie, Wayne, and Rachel took turns driving me home to my apartment each night and often stayed the night curled up next to me on my bed, then drove me back the next day. I loved my classes and my work and wept thinking it all might be taken away from me by mental illness or breakdown. But everyone around me—my teachers, especially Professor Touster and Professor Barraclough, my friends, my doctor—was fighting as hard as I was for me to hang in there. I'm so, so grateful.

When I went up to the podium several times during graduation ceremonies to receive various awards I'd won, I knew exactly whom to thank. They were sitting in a row clapping and cheering, separating my parents at either end, my peacekeeping troops, to whom I owed my survival and success, Phi Beta Kappa, summa cum laude.

30

"Rowing in Eden"

❦❦

Ah, the Sea!
Might I but moor—Tonight—
In Thee!

—Emily Dickinson

DREAMING SPIRES. In the fall of 1982, I went up to Oxford. I was a graduate student at Trinity College, Oxford, and had a beautiful bed-sitting room above Blackwell's Bookstore overlooking the Sheldonian Theatre. From my desk or my bed alcove I looked out onto the dome of the Sheldonian and its wonderful gargoyles standing guard. Church bells from every college rang out across the city each evening calling students home for supper. Mornings, I walked past horses in a green and dewy pasture, a shortcut on the way to the Centre for Management Studies just outside the city proper. Afternoons, I studied, had tea with friends, played lawn tennis, went punting on the river (once), and took long walks through college meadows and gardens safely enclosed behind medieval stone gates.

Unfortunately, I was also throwing away precious amounts of time with my old false friend bulimia again. This problem, however, vanished into thin air the moment my body met a body in a green English meadow. He was a tall, dark, and very handsome New Yorker (half-Jewish, half-Spaniard) who was studying economics at Magdalen College. He had a reputation, well earned I believe, for being rather a Don Juan—going from pretty señorita to señorita in rapid succession. Girls didn't seem to mind his reputation; in fact, they pursued him. Not this girl. Our first month of "dating" consisted of study dates in the college library, after which I'd walk him to the Trinity gate, in full view of the porters' lodge (the guardians of the gate and protectors of the students inside), and bid him good-night. He invited me to a black-tie dinner held at his college, and I was surprised at the looks of curiosity, and occasionally outright hostility, I received from his group of male friends who hung out together in the M.C.R. (graduate student lounge) encouraging one another's avoidance of work. (To be fair, it is quite hard for many students to handle the amount of independence one is given with regard to one's work at Oxford. There is almost nothing in the way of external pressure and accountability to help you get your thesis written.) One of his friends even asked me, quite bluntly, what I had done to him! It was a bit of a betrayal to the boys to get started on one's work, and, I think, they quite missed the vicarious pleasure of the exploits of their handsome companion.

For the next two years we were inseparable. Even when I went to San Francisco for spring break to see the city and stay with my mother, who was living there at the time, I received letters from Marc every day, sometimes twice a day. No one had ever reached out to me that way before, held my hand in his across oceans. I began to trust in the solidity of his presence, that he wouldn't, like de Daumier-Smith's fickle joy, seep through my fingers in the morning and be gone. Often, this solidity could take on a mule-like obstinance that drove me crazy, which, in turn, drove him crazy. "You're so *picky,*" he'd say like a solid plow-horse to an obnoxiously skittish, neurotic thoroughbred. Traveling together was a source of constant friction and passionate, stupid arguments over accommodations, driving, radio volume, temperature controls, where to eat, and what to do. But at Oxford, "Rowing in Eden," the lion lay down with the lamb, and most of the time, it was lovely. His college rooms were in an old mill house where C. S. Lewis once lived, behind Magdalen College, down a lane in a field of flowers by a stream. His bedroom was directly over a small waterfall where, on occasion that spring, I was awakened in the morning by the sound of a pair of swans and their eight little cygnets who made their home beneath the old mill.

I wrote to my father "a day in the life" sort of letter, and he wrote back thanking me for my good news and said it made good sense that I was savoring it. He suggested I read a book—which as usual I filed in my overflowing bin of books I "should" read but didn't—by Joanna Field called *A Life of One's Own,* in which she tried, on paper, he said, to take a close look at her life to discern the underlying reasons for what she called the "fat moments," moments of contentment close to bliss. He said it might be both fun and instructive for me to undertake a similar look at the real whys and wherefores of why Oxford seemed to suit me to a T. What there is about a certain Oxford street or land or hall or room that excites pleasure or well-being in me. Or makes me feel tranquil or wonderfully independent or full of goodwill.

I had also mentioned in a letter, rather delicately and obliquely, that I was happy in a love affair that was not his prescribed "like with like." He said it was duly noted that I have a big, good-looking boyfriend who doesn't take long walks by himself or do or say anything particularly sensitive, but nonetheless suits me. The business of pairing off, he said, of alleviating solitariness, is a problem that can't be solved satisfactorily short of nirvana.

In my thoughts I underestimated Marc's sensitivity, but my body didn't; it knew this was someone it could trust. My skin began to thaw after a lifetime of numbness and retreat. He noticed it first and put it into words, *sensitively,* I might add in belated admission. In fact, I think he understood something about me that I wouldn't know for years to come. In one of his letters to me in San Francisco, he told me that he had felt a momentous change in me. He said simply that on a certain night, just before I'd left for vacation, we were making love as usual when suddenly, without warning, he felt me open up to him. I guess he met my body for the first time. I know I did.*

I wrote to Holly telling her about Marc. Always on the lookout for my well-being, and having reached that certain age, most especially my financial well-being, she was not pleased with me. "You go all the way to Oxford, England, where guys have titles and *castles* for God's sake and

---

*I am *not* discreetly referring to orgasms here. Press the right buttons, and that can be accomplished and I'm not even present—I'm a million miles away in my tower. I'm talking about something much harder; that is, actually inhabiting my body long enough to invite someone in. If you have survived childhood trauma, you'll know just what I'm talking about. If you don't understand, consider yourself fortunate—I mean that.

you fall for a New Yorker!" I, however, had had enough of reclusion in four gray walls and four gray towers.

> Or when the moon was overhead,
> Came two lovers lately wed:
> "I am half sick of shadows," said
> The Lady of Shalott

❦

DADDY CAME TO VISIT ME once while I was at Oxford, but he didn't *tell* me he was coming, so Marc and I were in Portugal for term break. I arrived back to numerous phone messages, and when I rang, his flight home was the next day. I met him in London for a quick lunch, and I never did get to show him my beautiful college, or some of the other places I'd written about. He had stayed for days in a terrible hotel room where the air conditioner was broken. I asked him why he didn't insist on moving to a better room or a different hotel. (I wouldn't have put up with it for even a night, if there was an alternative.) He shook his head in a way that made me sad; he seemed so much less powerful than the Daddy I knew. So much less powerful in the world, dare I say it, than I. I thought about the golf games my brother and he used to play over in Windsor. Daddy always won, until one day my brother found he was beating him, rather easily. Matthew came home and told me he threw the game. I don't think he's played my father since. Like the pencil markings on the bathroom wall that record our heights. Somehow they stopped when my brother, now six feet five inches tall, was within about a quarter of an inch of my father's mark at six feet two inches. Seeing him inept, in comparison to me, I think I finally understood how my brother had felt. "But I thought you wanted to win," I had said to my sporting, competitive brother. Sometimes you do want to win, sometimes it's just too sad.

❦

MY GROUP OF FRIENDS AT OXFORD were decidedly unsporty. A bit of tennis maybe, a brisk walk through the countryside to a pub. I led a second, separate life from them. I was captain of the basketball team in my second year, and at the University ski race held in Wengen, Switzerland,

I placed second in giant slalom, and third in slalom—the first-place winner in both categories was a young Scotswoman from Cambridge University, who had been on the British Olympic ski team, and her time score was in a different universe from those of the rest of us mortals. She was such a terrific sport, setting up courses, gate-keeping, cheering us on, that no one had anything but respect for her. My beloved uncle Terrence (my mother's youngest half brother and a professor of economics) was thrilled at the news. Two half-Blues* in the family! He dutifully tried to introduce me to the pleasures of cricket, taking me to his club matches with him. I liked him so much, I gave it my best effort, but I guess I just don't have it in my blood. God, it goes on for so long! I hope he wasn't too disappointed when he saw that "I'm locked in an elevator and I'm never going to get out" look of panic on my face after a few (hundred!) hours in the stands. He just said cheerfully, "Well, then, I think we've had enough, wouldn't you say? Shall we go home to tea?"

❧

MARC WAS IN NEW YORK my last year at Oxford. We spent the long holidays together, ran up terrible phone bills, and wrote to each other. He surprised me with a visit on Valentine's Day, calling me from Gatwick at about six in the morning to say he'd just landed. He arrived carrying an overnight case in one hand and a lovely blue hydrangea plant in the other, mumbling shyly something about he would have brought a bouquet of flowers or roses, but they wouldn't have lasted as long. Bliss.

Like many of my father's characters, I, too, wondered, "in a real panic," how I would survive until Marc's next visit. I quite literally would feel my stability and energy draining out of me after a few days of not having him near. My well-being was very much "a liquid, slipping through my fingers," without my hand in his. Fortunately, I was excited about my thesis project so I was able to throw myself into my work between visits and hang on—barely.

I wrote a letter to my father to tell him about the work I was doing. I still have the letter because I never mailed it. I'd never written such a

---

*Rather like being a letterman in America. At Oxford and Cambridge one is awarded a "Blue" for excellence in some sports, such as rugby and cricket, "half-Blue" in others that aren't quite as "British."

lengthy, spontaneous letter to him, and I didn't feel confident enough to send it. The envelope says "Wrote this ages ago. Well sat on!"

Dear Daddy,

(Long but *nothing* serious—just talkative this evening)

I've been thinking of you a lot lately. Maybe because a dear old friend of mine is dying of cancer and it reminds me of feelings I picked up when I was little about (not really about but from being around) your nice friendships with Dammy Littel and with Mrs. Hand. Professor Barraclough, who insists I call him "Geoffrey" so I do, but I don't think of him that way, is 75 and we've spent the last two Christmases together—once with Mom and Matthew in New York and once here in England with his 2nd wife (he's had 3 or so). He went trudging around Oxford with me the year before I decided to come and it was during a record snowfall—cold wet and stupidly English—they don't clear the sidewalks just walk right through the sludge miserably. He has been genuinely sweet and kind to me at Brandeis and on 'till now. It makes him happy to see me eating and enjoying chocolates if that makes any sense. Anyway he's in remission now so the first thing I asked him, at the risk of being too blunt about talking about death but not that much of a risk, was whether or not he had his work in order since I remembered how relieved I was when you showed me one time how you had everything labeled and organized so it wouldn't either be thrown out by stupid people or make things hellish for smart ones. He had done about half of it but had been putting off the rest.

Some work I'm doing for my thesis has been so interesting lately. I've been interviewing some people at a newspaper printing plant. It's an old plant, 80 or so years out of date in some of its technology and the biggest one (except for one new thing in Japan) in the world. An old dinosaur in interesting ways. They still set lines of type manually on huge old linotype machines and one of the setters showed me how it worked and gave me a slug with my name in raised letters. I was actually dying to have one but I felt too embarrassed to ask.

I went in around 10:30 at night and started at one end—
where they receive some of the pages through facsimile
transfer (sort of a xerox by phone lines—not really but good
enough) from London, then on to a room that was like being
on the inside of a camera where they change the size of
photographs, then to the artists room where 5 men sit on stools
with grey and black paint pots and touch up photographs by
hand. Miss World was on that night so they were doing photos
of the girls and T.V.s were on all over the plant in various "tea"
corners.

Then I went up to the linotype area filled with machines
and clicking noises and people running up and down to get bits
of copy to set in type. Next to the linotype room was a room
with low, suspended ceilings and greenish florescant (?) light
and about six or seven guys were sitting at computer terminals
setting the pages by computer (the advance on the old lino
method) and feeding computer punchout tape into a machine.
They looked tired, bored and were wearing ties which
wouldn't have seemed sad if they were young but they had
rough old hands and drinker's complexions just like the guys
out on the floors. Outside that room again I came up behind
one of the guys operating a machine and he didn't see me and
swore at something that had gone wrong and right afterwards
looked up and saw me. All his mates (or in U.S. buddies)
started laughing and teasing him and he turned red and
apologised—it was just what used to happen when I worked at
Boston Edison. Anyway it was quite funny and familiar. From
there it was down three floors (on the way the supervisor who
was taking me around yelled at a guy who was running up the
stairs because he had recently had a heart attack) to where the
metal page of print is made into a thick semi-circle—almost
like truck breakshoes if you've ever seen them—out of a vat of
molten metal. These are then carried over to the printing
machines themselves and placed on a spinning roller. There a
man mixes the ink (from a panel of about 15–20 adjustment
nobs—almost as complicated as an organ) that sprays onto the
roller that the huge rolls of newsprint (the blank paper) pass over.

The noise in there once the machines start up is incredible. I got there just as they were starting up (about 40 or 50 in all maybe fewer). Just when you thought it was as noisy as it gets, some more machines would kick in and it got louder still. Not sickeningly loud, more on the verge like some fair ride which was fun—I thought so anyway. It did take your breath away though. Every fourth machine or so was a folder so that the stream of flat newsprint went through something that happened too fast to see and came out as folded newspapers which went in little, well almost like train tracks but holding the papers in metal-like things that you make toast on campfires with, and this train of thousands of them wound round about the machines and then (like Santa, finger on nose, was whisked in blink of an eye) straight up two stories and through the ceiling. Bundled up put on trucks sent out to trains to Edinburgh, Glasgow all over. Everyone was so friendly and patient and showed me what they were doing in a very nice way—not paying too much attention to me or too little.

The Managing Director of the company started as an apprenticed printer on the shopfloor and is missing the top two joints on one finger and the top joint on the one next to it. He is absolutely and unself-consciously knocked out about the ancient Greeks. He took his wife to the (I forget the name of it right now but the Greek amphitheatre in stone where the Orestia was performed) and made her climb up the stairs to the top so he could show her that when he whispered from down below she could hear him perfectly. But he's not interested just in the tricky things—I probably chose the wrong example—he reads up on all of it and goes tracking things down in museums with the slightly nosy but totally innocent persistent curiosity of say Mrs. Marple in Agatha Christie. "Oh, Peggy, you should see the beautiful line" (tracing a line from his hip over his head and up his arm) on some statue of a god who was in some eternal trial he said I must see. "But watch out," he said wagging his finger at me, "it will make you weary just looking at it." He had a thick old Scots accent that made the telling of it even more enchanting.

I just realized it's late and I have to finish a labor economics essay (it's not all enjoyable). There were four or five words I was going to check the spelling on but if I go back over and read this I'll never send it. Don't show Mrs. Corette.

I'll probably be in N.Y.C. visiting and looking for jobs, not sure where, in January. Middle term doesn't begin again till late Jan. I'll call if I am in town. I won't call on Christmas probably—my boyfriend is a *pain* about Christmas too—I still like presents wrapped nicely and with bows. He'll oblige though. (yes, there's an "or else" lurking there)

Love,
PEGGY

◄●►

MY MOTHER AND BROTHER came over for graduation. A fancy medieval thing in robes and hats and Latin held in the Sheldonian Theatre. Matthew and Mom were to stay and do a bit of sightseeing with me for a week or so. I was worried about how we'd all get along, but I have to say it was lovely from beginning to end. The other miracle was that it didn't rain for the entire week.

31

Woman Overboard!

❧❧❧

I STAYED ON IN OXFORD TO STAFF A SUMMER PROGRAM for American labor arbitrators. My title was "dean," but my duties were far from impressive, attending to my fellow Yanks' complaints about hard pillows, lack of air-conditioning, and so on. But I did get to sit in on the classes and discussions and meet some terrific people in the field. Toward the end of the course, I was offered a job as an apprentice to an arbitrator in Boston.

When I arrived back in the States, the arbitrator who had offered me the apprenticeship told me that her current apprentice's new job had fallen through so she would be staying on, terribly sorry, but I wasn't needed. I had expected to move back into my old apartment on Marlborough Street, but my landlady said I'd have to wait several months at least because the tenants were suing her about something or other. She would have called me, but she had lost my number and couldn't remember where in England I was staying. I thought that under the circumstances, I might go to New York for a while and stay with my boyfriend, who had just started a big job with an investment bank. Well, when I called to see what he thought, he told me he loved me dearly, but I couldn't come and stay with him. He just couldn't be with me anymore with the level of Sturm und Dräng, or as the Rolling Stones song says, "Nothin' I do don't seem to work, it only seems to make matters worse . . ." Marc was quite right, but I wasn't prepared to see it that way at the time, nor any time probably. No job, no apartment, no beloved; three strikes and I was in free fall over the edge.

Just after my twenty-ninth birthday, and right before Christmas, I nearly died. Sig and Joel (my old friends from ski camp and Woodstock, Liza's brothers) were living in Cambridge and they invited me to stay with them as long as I needed. After a few weeks of staying with the boys, I moved to a dumpy apartment down the street where I was a "tenant at will." I was not doing well alone. One night, at around two-thirty in the morning, I called Marc, woke him up, and tried to convince him that he was making a terrible mistake breaking up with me. Screaming down the phone "I can so be normal!" in the wee hours of the morning is not, as we say in business school, a strategy with a high probability of success. I knew it, but I was in such pain without him that I couldn't stop myself; like a panicked person drowning, I gripped his neck so tightly, I threatened to take him under with me. I felt as though a large piece of me had been ripped from my side, and my head was swimming as if from a severe loss of blood.

I had felt that before when I was eight and I carried my broken arm, across a wide field, staying awake as long as I could, cradling my arm, until too much blood had drained away and I fainted. Imprinted on the deepest parts of my mind as a child was the idea that hospitals are where you go when the pain is so bad you lose consciousness, and there are clean white sheets and people take care of you. Even your mother is nice to you in the hospital.

That night, some twenty years later, when I got off the phone with my boyfriend at three in the morning, knowing I'd driven another nail into the coffin of our relationship, my homing instinct took over. The pain was so bad I couldn't stand it. I felt myself losing consciousness and I knew I had to get to the hospital. But this time there was no blood to show for my pain. So I had to swallow the bottles of pills or they'd be mad at me and call me a liar and send me home. With the "adamantine logic of dreamland," this made perfect sense to me. Never tell a lie.

The first call I made was to Boston City Hospital; I think it was the emergency room. I wanted to know, at 3 A.M., drowning in pain, if someone swallowed a lot of pills and wound up in the hospital, could the newspapers find out the name of that person. I was frantic that the papers might learn that I was Salinger's daughter. My first instinct at this desperate hour was not to protect myself, but to keep my father's secrets, to obey the family creed and avoid anything that might bring the attention of the press.

If, in the midst of telling me not to do anything stupid, the nurse hadn't told me that the papers had no access to that type of information, I don't think I would have taken the pills. I dialed 911, told them I had taken a lot of pills, gave them my address, and then, *after* hanging up, swallowed two bottles of different prescription medications and washed them down with scotch. So they wouldn't think I'd lied to them, and I wouldn't get in trouble.

The ambulance arrived, not what I'd imagined, sort of a square paddy-wagon-looking thing. It was the fire department rescue squad. They let me collect some stuff, which surprised me. They picked up the remaining pills off the floor and put them in their bottles, which I thought was very tidy of them. I realized later that the doctors needed a pill count. I took a small stone carving of an African head that Marc had given me the previous Christmas, and a handkerchief that had belonged to my grandmother. That's all. I was too afraid my teddy bear would get lost. I walked partway downstairs and was then carried on a stretcher. The last thing I remember was a man in the ambulance in my face and yelling at me, "Stay awake, stay with us!"

⬥

IT WASN'T CLEAN WHITE SHEETS. It was a metal table and blinding spotlights in the emergency room. It wasn't like waking up; it was like being struck by lightning. I was sizzling and felt as though I had bees inside my veins. Bees and a thousand cups of coffee. I guess they give you some kind of stimulant to counteract the depressants after pumping your stomach. Something bloody was going on behind the green plastic curtains next to me. Then came the charcoal.

"Drink it. All of it." Quarts and quarts of gritty charcoal in water. Black ashes vomiting out of my nose and mouth, my asshole spewing charcoal. I got some on my grandmother's handkerchief. The stain never came out.

I was shocked to find out how close I'd come to killing myself. Apparently I would have been hard-pressed to pick a more lethal combination than what I happened to have around the house.

I called my soon-to-be–ex boyfriend in New York from the hospital and told him I had kidney stones and not to worry. I called Wayne, one of my best friends from Brandeis, in Washington. He canceled a State Department reception, caught the next plane to Boston, and brought me a blanket because he remembered that I'm always cold. He called our friend Margie in Philadelphia, and she was there a few hours later.

I hadn't seen my therapist since I'd left for England. He came to see me and said, among other things, "Hey, next time use the phone, okay?" Point taken. He was glad to see me but sad to see me there. After some discussion, they let me go home the next day.

When I left the hospital, I went home alone in a cab feeling lousy, but pretty sobered by the near miss. When I opened the door to my apartment, a lovely sight greeted me. Wayne and Margie, both Jews who wouldn't know a Christmas tree from a cactus, had bought a tree and set it up in my room. One of the most oddly decorated Christmas trees I've ever seen, and one of the most beautiful.

32

On and Off the Fast Track

❖❖❖

I HEARD THROUGH A FRIEND that a major international consulting firm, based in Boston, was doing so well that year that they were taking on midyear hires. (Usually these things go with the business-school cycle; if you're not settled by September, forget about it till next year.) I sent them a résumé, and they called me for an interview. It was an offer I couldn't refuse. I told them that my areas of interest and expertise were industrial relations and organizational behavior, I.R. and O.B. as they are known, the "soft" side of business. They said great and placed me on a case team that was evaluating accounting software packages for a Fortune 500 computer firm. I didn't even know how to use a computer, let alone evaluate anything to do with one. At Oxford, although I hear this changed dramatically over the next few years of the program, we had barely switched over from quill pens when we wrote our essays, longhand, on the philosophy of human resource accounting. I spent my first week trying to learn Lotus 1-2-3 on my own without attracting too much attention from the computer whizzes I was supposed to be supervising. Nightmare.

I spent a year trying to "get up to speed," in various traditional "hard" MBA areas such as finance and accounting, but everyone around me had been on a serious fast track from the start. When I had to take some time off to have surgery, it was a relief. The chief of urology at Mass General had examined me for chronic bladder inflammation and pain and told me my urethra was gapped wide open and some other things I didn't quite understand. He brought in another doctor, who asked me some questions about my sex life, all of which I could answer in the negative, half of which hadn't even occurred to me as possibilities. Then she'd like a family history. I called my mother to ask her if I'd had trouble with bladder infections as a child. She said yes, that after she was allowed to take me to real doctors, she was always taking me in for pain "down there," because, she said in a sort of exaggerated whisper, "you *mas*turbated so much."

All I can recall to date is a flashback I have, of sitting in the bathtub, alone, young enough that I was scared to be alone, because usually my mother gave me a bath. I was feeling absolutely excruciating pain in my peepee. I thought maybe I got some soap inside it by mistake when I washed and it was burning me, like soap in the eyes. It hurt so much I couldn't cry. I made a harsh noise in my throat as I drew in each breath, to try to distract my mind from the pain. I sort of rocked myself until the water went cold. Then, my memory goes down the drain.

My father appeared at Mass General the morning of my surgery. I was very surprised, to say the least. He looked green and worried. He said, "You shouldn't have to go into surgery alone." He and Sig and Joel took me home afterward. I was back in my old apartment, the landlady was finally rid of the awful tenants, and there I stayed put till it went condo some ten years later. Daddy liked my apartment. He'd never seen it before.

A few weeks later, I received a call from a headhunter asking me if I'd be interested in a certain job they'd been hired to fill. To make a short story even shorter, I didn't get the job, but the executive search firm for which the headhunter worked offered me a job as a consultant. Same great pay, but decent hours, and talking to people instead of crunching numbers. God, what relief.

My dad came down to visit me at my new job and to take me out to lunch. He liked my business attire a lot, was suitably impressed by my office, which was in a beautiful old building overlooking a splendid courtyard where people could sit outside at little café tables in the spring and summer for drinks and Madame Robert's wonderful French food. Over lunch, Daddy told me how glad he was that I had learned something practical and gone into business. He worried a lot about my brother choosing to be an actor and wished he had gone into some sort of business as well. I felt proud of myself and my position, and I could not have asked for a nicer boss or colleagues; nevertheless, it all felt a lot more like playing dress-up and acting than my father could ever have imagined. I still missed my trucks and cars and work boots, I still missed my libraries and writing, but I was doing the "responsible" thing, being a grown-up and using my degree instead of saying, to misquote a country song, you can take these nylons and shove 'em.*

❧

SOMETIME DURING MY SECOND YEAR of work at the recruiting firm I caught the flu. It didn't go away. I kept trying to go back to work, and my boss, Jack Vernon, a truly decent, kind human being, kept sending me home. Over the next few months, I developed what I called my 100-degree rule: I stayed at my desk and worked as best I could until my temperature reached 101, then I'd give up and go home. My doctor first suspected lupus or multiple sclerosis. I could tell by the tests he ordered, and then he'd tell me when it was ruled out. My blood tests came back very out of whack, white cells in the stratosphere, red cells down the drain, and so on. Something was obviously wrong, but they couldn't figure out what. Meanwhile, I was exhausted, fevered, had constant diarrhea, and felt as if I'd been hit by a bus in all my joints.

My boss finally had a long talk with me and suggested I take some real time off and get better. He assured me my job would be waiting for me when I returned and that I would be of more value to the company if I got well instead of trying to hang in there. I can't tell you what a difference that made to my mental and probably physical well-being. So often people report going through a terrible period before diagnosis where they're suspected of malingering or being a nutcase or just plain lazy. It turned out that I had a classic case of a "new" or newly discov-

---

*I had a book when I was a little girl about a country bear who lived in the woods and wanted to see the big city. He was told, you'll have to wear clothes first, so he fashions a fedora out of a cabbage leaf, two pieces of a hollow log for shoes, quite uncomfortable but de rigueur, and a suit of bark. At the end of the book there is a wonderful illustration of him returning to the woods, kicking off his shoes, tossing his hat in the air with abandon and pure joy at coming home, shedding all those uncomfortable things that just weren't him. (If he'd stayed in costume, he'd have probably gotten sick, too, after a while, just like me.)

ered disease first called Epstein-Barr virus, or CFS—chronic fatigue syndrome—or in England, myalgic encephalomyelitis. When I could no longer safely hold a teacup in my hand without dropping it, fibromyalgia was added to the pot. Some retrovirus was making my autoimmune system wage war on itself. I attacked my own joints as if they were foreign entities, tried to expel ghostly poisons through vomiting or the runs. My whole body seemed engaged in a deadly bout of shadowboxing that left me so exhausted I could no longer walk a block without assistance.

I lived on the second floor, and I remember many times sitting at the bottom of the stairs weeping because there was no way in hell I was going to make it back up. After about a year, I basically stayed in my apartment and neighbors and friends and people from my church helped out with shopping. I can hardly believe how long I was disabled and virtually confined to my apartment. The reason it seems unreal is that I was too exhausted to be bored. I really didn't mind just sitting there as long as I wasn't in too much pain. I wasn't depressed at all, surprisingly; when I felt anything besides tired, it was fear. I was scared I was going to die.

After nearly a year and a half of solid sickness, I started to have days and parts of days where a bit of sunlight, a bit of energy, would break through. My hands had stopped deteriorating, too, thank God; that was something I really couldn't stand. After nearly two years, I felt well enough to be a bit bored and began to devour the contents of the Boston Public Library, subject by subject. A friend would walk me there on a good day and carry the huge stack of books home. I spent several happy months learning about ancient Japanese theater—its art and dance and music—which branched naturally into Japanese religion and religious worship—chanting and liturgical music in particular. This experience was complemented by the church I attended around the corner from me, which presented the entire cycle of the Bach cantatas as part of the liturgy on Sundays, the way they were heard in Bach's time, as an integral part of worship. The church, needless to say, attracted a lot of musicians and music lovers, as well as people in the arts and others who didn't fit into a traditional mold. Nicely, though, we had our share of old Bostonian ladies in hats and white gloves. Emmanuel Church truly welcomes you to come as you are, and to stay that way if you wish. You are welcomed, in booklet and banner, to join in as much or as little of the Episcopal liturgy as your conscience permits, "wherever you are on your spiritual journey." It is not unlike Woodstock, in the way everyone is welcome without having to be *like* everyone else. Music lovers, Jews, Catholics, Buddhists, and nonbelievers share pews with old Bostonian Episcopalians. The liturgy stays the same, the liturgical year goes through its cycle with integrity, and you are permitted to do the same.

❦

ONE DAY I GOT A PHONE CALL from a representative of my disability insurance company. I was ordered to see a doctor hired by and paid for by the insurance company. The state and the company's insurance agency had been paying me a comfortable check each month, and my doctor would periodically send in the results of my lab tests, which confirmed in black and white that *something* was very wrong, though it didn't have a DRG (diagnosis-related group) number yet. The experience of seeing a company doctor was not unlike being in Kit's office once again. Do you know how spooky it is to be examined, clothes off, by somebody who keeps up a steady patter trying to get you to admit or confess that you're malingering? *Enraging, humiliating, powerless,* are a few words that come to mind. Two weeks later I received notice that my disability payments were to be terminated. My real doctor was outraged; he held up my tests and said that what the other doctor had done amounted to malpractice.

The trouble is, that if you really *are* disabled, you're in the worst shape possible to go to court and fight it. Insurance companies are not unaware of this. I feel like a wimp writing it now, that I didn't fight it, but that's only because it's nearly impossible for me to remember or reconstruct the degree of fatigue I suffered. As my friend Marilyn, who has lupus, polymyositis, asthma, and a host of other problems, says, you can't imagine what tired means until you've been there, until you've had to lie there and wet yourself because you're too tired to roll out of bed, let alone make it to the bathroom. I had many, many days like that. Days I was too ashamed to call anyone over to help because I'd lost control of my bowels or bladder again and couldn't change the sheets yet. Now my worst fear was not dying, but that I'd wind up living, destitute, in some state nursing home.

My father, throughout these years, kept asking me if I *trusted* the doctors I was seeing. Wasn't there something more all these Harvard men at their Harvard so-called teaching hospitals could do for me? I went to several alternative-medicine practitioners at his suggestion: a homeopath, a chiropractor, and an acupuncturist for a series of treatments. They weren't cheap, either.

I called and told my father the grave news that my disability payments had been cut off. A week or two later, something arrived in the mail. He had taken out a three-year subscription, in my name, to a monthly booklet of testimonials to miraculous healing put out by the Christian Science Church. He also sent me a hardcover copy of *Science and Health with Key to The Scriptures,* by Mary Baker Eddy. I would get well when I stopped believing in the "illusion" of my sickness.

What began to crack was my belief in the illusion of my father.

33

Weaving My Own Life

❧

I TOOK A LONG, QUIET LOOK AT MY LIFE and decided that if I were to live much longer, I should not waste any more time living someone else's dream. Easier said than done, but framing the intention was a start in the right direction. It was not some quick and easy conversion, I assure you. Those who say that the process of waking up and making one's own way, of slowly tearing down old walls and reintegrating parts of one's self separated by war or violence, ignorance, or neglect, is a "wonderful journey of exciting self-discovery" are the same folks who brought you "The Army: It's an Adventure" and those "fun for the whole family" childbirth films they show you when you're pregnant. Dream on! It's brutal. Like childbirth, though, you do get the best thing in the whole world after the agony. But even then it's still a load of work: sleepless nights, more terror, endless piles of shit (as the joke goes, there must be a pony under there somewhere!), and the privilege of meeting up with one's own terrible twos and adolescence isn't always pretty.

One of the first things I took a look at were all the Salinger "thou shalt nots." Thou shalt not dabble in the arts unless a born genius, thou shalt not study religion unless in a sackcloth at the foot of some foreign guru. Thou shall not set foot in the unclean Ivy League. And for God's sake, for father's sake, never ever take an English class. Thou shalt not do anything unless it's perfect, thou shalt not be flawed, thou shalt not be woman, thou shalt not grow up.

What do I like to do, and given my level of disability, what am I *able* to do? These are the questions I wrestled with. My priest, Al Kershaw, is a wonderful human being to talk to. I told him I didn't feel right making any commitments that I might not be able to live up to. Literally—I can't stand letting anybody down. I think I needed his permission, in a way, to relieve myself of active duty for a while. He said that contemplation was work, too, and suggested that I might think about attending divinity school. I remember looking at him as though he had two heads, exactly my reaction when, years ago, the human resources person at Boston Edison suggested I go to work in the garage. Who, me? I thought divinity schools were places in the Bible Belt where evangelical Christians, people who had it all figured out, went to train to become ministers, places like Oral Roberts U. My priest, an old Kentucky boy himself, laughed so hard he started coughing. When he recovered, he told me about several divinity schools in the immediate area where one could go to explore what one's "ministry" might be, and that plenty of people went who were not considering ordination. Otherwise, he said, it's just another layer of something that isn't you, that isn't genuine.

I knew I couldn't afford the tuition, but I decided to take a look anyway. I really liked the program at Harvard Divinity School; it looked terrific in and of itself, but had, in addition, the wonderful advantage of allowing its students access to Harvard undergraduate courses in any field, as well as classes at Episcopal Divinity School, and the Jesuits' Weston School of Theology just across the Cambridge Common.

I made an appointment with the admissions and financial-aid dean and spilled the beans. I discussed my medical condition and uncertainty, as well as, among other things, the problem of having a famous parent who doesn't approve and will not contribute. The dean said, "We'll see what we can do." A few weeks later a fat package came in the mail informing me that I'd been selected for a merit-based fellowship offered to ten incoming students based on their past academic record. I was awarded a full scholarship and a low-interest loan to provide for living expenses. I would automatically be enrolled in the university's health insurance plan, and the office for students with disabilities would provide me with a tutor to take notes in my classes if I was unable to attend for periods of time, a parking sticker for handicapped students so I wouldn't have to walk far, and an ombudsman should any difficulties arise. There was even a quiet room in the library with a couch if I needed to lie down between classes.

I sent my father a photograph I'd clipped out of a nature magazine that I thought he'd like and told him the news.*

> Dear Daddy,
>   I found this photograph, or rather the fact that this frog exists, very cheering.
>   What a beauty.
>
> Love,
PEGGY
>
> P.S. If you don't want to keep the photo clipping, send it back and I'll find a place for it.
>
> [I enclosed a photo of a (real, living) glass frog. It has transparent, palest-of-green skin, and you can see all its translucent insides, with just one beautiful little red line for an artery.]

The photo was returned with a note agreeing with me that it was a beautiful frog, and perhaps I might like to be a naturalist if such things really excited me. The few naturalists he'd seen on public television seemed to be happy in their work. The field of religion was another matter, however. Except for the rare person who comes around every two thousand years or so, there is little in religion that doesn't come from man's ego and man's need or desire. And still less that doesn't settle into an amalgam of sentiment and dogma, not to mention vanity, ecclesiastical vanity, plus some, evermore plus some. He closed his note by reminding me of Basho's frog poem. Signing off, your merry father.

My mother was excited for me and told all her friends. My brother, I think, couldn't quite wrap his brain around the idea of his sister in the ministry—quite understandably so—but he wished me well.

---

*Holden did not offer much hope of a good reception: "If you want to know the truth, I can't even stand ministers . . . they all have these Holy Joe voices when they start giving their sermons. God, I hate that. . . . They sound so phony when they talk" (*Catcher,* p. 100).

As Joseph Campbell would say, I "followed my bliss" for three restorative years. Sitting, listening, reading, and thinking are things I can do with a tissue-thin level of physical health. Slowly over the three years, with many good days and bad, I crept back to an acceptable quality of life. I still hit the wall where other people get the sniffles and am in the hospital where most people get a light flu. Marilyn and I can forecast the weather by the aches and pains in our joints like a couple of old ladies. I still sleep about eleven hours a night, but when I'm awake, I feel daytime awake rather than like those wretched somnambulists in *Night of the Living Dead*.

On the way through the Divinity School's core curriculum, I had a chance to stop by and visit the Jesuits at Weston for classes in the fundamentals of scriptural exegesis, and a class on the Psalms; Episcopal divinity school for classes on liturgical music; Harvard music department for some wonderful courses on everything from Bach to music theory and composition, ethnomusicology to choral conducting. I audited undergraduate classes on Japanese art, world religions, and even a literature class—sin of Salinger sins—called "Tragic Drama and Human Conflict" taught by (the devil himself!) a member of the psychiatry department at the medical school. It was anything but "a peerage of tin ears" as my father referred to psychiatrists, and though the actors wore masks in the ancient tragedies, I found Oedipus' story a far more undisguised tale than all that business about "the eyes" in Salinger's credo.*

Oh, the things I shut my eyes to so as to remain forever "a swell girl." As I awakened, I'm sure I looked sober enough walking around campus, but secretly I trailed ribbons from unbound feet, dancing my own private May Day celebration through library and classroom. For a time, I fell in love with a satyr disguised as a Ph.D. candidate in ethics and religion, who had a voice like sweet, dark Cuban coffee and called me *"preciosa"* when he growled softly in my ear.

---

*See *Seymour: An Introduction*, pp. 104–5. The "whole ambulance load" of pain that the true artist suffers comes not from a "troubled childhood" nor a "disordered libido." It's the eyes: "Don't those cries come straight from the eyes? . . . the true artist-seer, the heavenly fool who can and does produce beauty, is mainly dazzled to death by his own scruples, the blinding shapes and colors of his own sacred human conscience. My credo is stated."

Takeoffs and landings for me in matters of the heart are still rough. I tried to be careful, but the Glass family tradition of "vomiting the oyster" is still with me. I couldn't eat for about a week after he went on to other nymphs. I made sure I drank plenty of water and tried my hardest to eat, but I vomited before I could swallow even crackers. My priest made a house call and packed me off to the emergency room again with dehydration. They kept me there on IV fluids all night and for most of the next day, when I was finally able to eat something and keep it down. When I told the doctors, who wanted to keep me for another day's observation, that David, my best friend, had flown up from New York and was at my apartment roasting a chicken, they let me go home. What a sweetheart: he'd cleaned the place from top to bottom, singing "I'm gonna wash that man right outa my hair."

Things went rather more smoothly with the last man I dated before I met my husband. Instead of going down with the plane, gripping the controls ever tighter in a rictus of fear,* I ejected. I headed for my friends Henry and Liz and their children for a couple of days to make sure the old stuff didn't come up—gross, sorry. But true. I lost weight that I couldn't afford to lose, though this time, it didn't get serious.

Sometimes that's what getting better means, you learn to work around your disabilities rather than finding the perfect cure. If you know you're going to crash land, you don't keep it a secret; pray to your God by all means, but have a word with the local air traffic controller as well and make arrangements to have the runway sprayed with foam, fire engines standing by, just in case.

<hr />

ABOUT HALFWAY THROUGH THE PROGRAM, the required field placement began to seem within the realm of possibility. I met a chaplain at one of the teaching hospitals who said she thought she could work around my health problems. Most of the patients were moved through

---

*I love science fiction: Have you noticed how in sci-fi novels everybody and his uncle's face contorts into a "rictus" of fear?

the hospital at such a rate that the problem of continuity, should I become unable to work, would not be an issue. Most of her encounters with patients were intense, onetime emergencies. I signed on for a ten-hour-a-week internship. What a unique, fascinating, inspiring encounter with life and death.

When my father called and asked me what I was up to these days, like a fool, I told him. I knew before speaking that we would not see eye to eye about chaplaincy. I knew it just as I knew in eighth grade to ask Jenny not to mention to him our concerts at the nursing home. He asked me about my work and I answered him with stories of patients. This was not what interested him. What he wanted to know, in asking about my work, was about *me*. Didn't I struggle with my own ego, feeling holier-than-thou walking down the corridors of my Harvard hospital? Wasn't it all "ego and ecclesiastical vanity"?

Zooey issues Franny much the same challenge, and she, unlike me, is interested in precisely the same thing. She replies:

> Don't you think I have sense enough to *worry* about my motives for saying the [Jesus] prayer? That's exactly what's *both*ering me so. Just because I'm choosy about what I want—in this case, en-*light*enment, or *peace,* instead of money or pres*tige* or *fame* or any of those things—doesn't mean I'm not as egotistical and self-seeking as everybody else. If anything, I'm more so! I don't need the famous Zachary Glass to tell me that!
>
> (*Franny and Zooey,* p. 149)

Holden, likewise, is preoccupied with the same concern. His sister Phoebe challenges him to name something he'd like to be when he grows up and suggests a lawyer like their father. He replies:

> . . . how would you know if you did it [became a lawyer] because you really *wanted* to save guys' lives, or you did it because what you *really* wanted to do was be a terrific lawyer, with everybody slapping you on the back and congratulating you in court when the goddam trial was over, the reporters and every-

body . . . ? How would you know you weren't being a phony?
The trouble is, you *wouldn't*.   (*Catcher*, p. 172)

To be honest, my "ego" was about the *last* thing I had time to worry about on the ward. That's why chaplain interns meet with their supervisors after work, at the end of the week, to take a structured pause for reflection. I just can't see worrying over one's motivations with the single-minded absorption of an adolescent going at his pimples in the mirror. I'm aware that some saints and other religious persons spend lifetimes in the quest to root out the slightest blemish on their soul. I have to confess, this is something that escapes me, and I say this acknowledging the possibility I may well be wrong; but self-flagellation, mortification, falling "in hate" with oneself, strikes me as much an occupation of Narcissus as falling in love with one's own reflection. Sure I fussed in the mirror the first day, trying to decide what cross to wear: too big, they'll think you're a nun; too small, they might not realize that this relatively young woman really is a chaplain. But to tell you the truth, it makes me smile to remember that, not hate myself like Franny. That good things can come from imperfect vessels, that God can use us just as we are, is something my father and I will never agree on.

Time and again I have had the experience of seeing my meager offering, replete with imperfections, being transformed into something of real use. I remember reading a book of poetry in Spanish, in my own, quite flawed Spanish mind you, to an old man on the ward who didn't speak English and was far from his family. Seeing the tears of joy in his eyes and the comfort it brought is an experience so far beyond oneself, it's humbling. Or figuring out what an old Portuguese woman was raving about in her dread of surgery the next day: "My statues! My statues!" she was crying out. I sat with her for a while and finally pieced it together that she had scores of statues of saints and the Blessed Mother all over her little apartment, and she missed them terribly. They were her family and they'd abandoned her when she needed them most. How small a thing it was to get a little figurine from the gift shop to watch over her through her long night. And how enormous. You pick up your brother's teddy, his bottle, his blankie, and you place them back within reach. It's simple.

I harbor no illusions that I walk on water as I pass down the corridor or sit beside someone's bed. Nor do I have the hubris to think I can call out to the sick and command them to rise from their beds, abracadabra, and be healed. I don't try to fix a person, I don't try to cure his or her disease or to make them "a better person" as a swell girl should. I stay up and watch with a person during the long night in the garden of Gethsemane. If they want to talk, I listen or we talk; if they want to pray, we pray; if they want to hear about the Red Sox—and they aren't at risk for a coronary—I go and find out how the Sox blew it in the ninth from the security guard with a radio.

◆◇◆

THERE WAS SOMETHING ELSE new in my life, but unlike anything "charitable," I fully expected my father would be excited about it. My expectation stemmed from that car ride home from Cross Mountain with Jenny at Christmas so long ago. I had rediscovered the pleasure of singing, only this time, I no longer labored under the illusion of immaculate conception; I had learned the art of practice. I am not blessed with a soloist's voice. But what I discovered is that with hard work, it's amazing how far some fairly basic human machinery can take you. Mine has taken me closer to heaven than I ever dared dream. After three years of auditioning, I finally made it into Tanglewood, the chorus of the Boston Symphony Orchestra. What an extraordinary, shining counterexample to Salinger law—that a mere mortal, one of the crowd, can make music with celestial choirs, Seiji Ozawa conducting.

The night of my first concert with the BSO, I took a cab. I told the driver, "Symphony Hall, please, stage entrance." The driver was an old man, and when I said, "Can I say that again, it sounds so wonderful: stage entrance, please," he was so happy for me. The whole way there, he talked about the operas he'd seen, and the operas he dreamed of.

That Christmas, my mother came to one of our concerts and brought a visiting scholar from Africa in full regalia who thought I was a star. My father had just come back from seeing my brother in a play in New York; he told me over the phone as I was about to leave for a concert. Without reflection, without my guard up, I asked him, "When are you going to come and see one of *my* performances?"

"When I can pick you out of the crowd," he said.

❈❈❈

ONE NIGHT AS I WAS ABOUT TO LEAVE for a performance, the stairs were blocked by a new guy moving into the upstairs "bachelor club," a four-bedroom apartment shared by a bunch of really nice guys, their jukebox, Coca-Cola machine, retro posters, and rock-and-roll paraphernalia. The new guy was a big one, moving a couch up the four flights single-handedly. He saw me in my fancy black-tie symphony wear and with a wide Midwestern grin said, "Well, aren't you all dressed up. What's the occasion?"

"I'm singing in Symphony Hall tonight," I swanned in reply.

"Oh, yeah, that's right. Simon Rattle is guest conductor. I'd forgotten it was so soon. It should be a good one."

Folding my wings beneath me, I introduced myself. Larry knew about the concert because he'd sung with the Opera Company of Boston for the past seven years, until it went bankrupt, and was still friends with singers all over town. He comes from a musical family, although he is the only one with classical training. In high school, he had a voice that could be heard across two counties, which is how he wound up in conservatory rather than working for "Generous" Motors as had most of his high school friends and neighbors in his Michigan hometown. What a change in the building! Instead of being serenaded by the likes of Twisted Sister from the jukebox upstairs, strains of *Aida* wafted through my bedroom window on summer evenings. Not too much later we were engaged, and not too long after that, well, reality struck as accurately as Cupid's arrow, and as the jukebox song goes, "Baby's feeling sick in the morning, says she's havin' trouble gettin' into her jeans."

Unfortunately, this babe was sick morning, noon, and night. Hyper-emesis, vomiting for six solid months. I started out skinny and lost eight pounds in the first six months. I basically held a snail's-eye view of the bathroom floor, because the floor felt cool on my face and because it wasn't worth the bother of moving myself too far from the toilet. Toward the middle of my sixth month I started feeling some relief and tried singing again. In the middle of a concert, I suddenly began to feel faint. I sat down on the riser and the singers to either side moved over slightly to cover me. My chorus conductor from Harvard had come to see us. She said afterward, "It was strange, suddenly you just weren't there." The flu was going around the chorus like wildfire and I was in big trouble.

As I had been feeling better lately, Larry was away on a two-week course for singers and actors. Liza's brother Sig came and picked me up to take me home with him so he could keep an eye on me. Instead, he took one look at me and drove me to the nearest emergency room. They agreed it was probably the flu and said I could go home, but to keep a close watch in case I got worse. I called Larry and asked him to come back right away. We had a major league fight. Phones slammed, don't you ever darken my door again if you're not home by this evening, and so on.

Oh, it appears to be a long, such a long, long time before the dawn.
(Crosby, Stills, and Nash)

※

FOLLOWING IN MY PATERNAL GRANDMOTHER'S FOOTSTEPS, I became gravely ill in the sixth month of my pregnancy. And like my paternal grandmother before me, I, too, was in danger of losing the baby. The following day, Sig, his fiancée, and a fellow chaplain dragged me semiconscious from bed and took me to the hospital, over my delirious objections that I felt too sick to move. I was hospitalized for acute septicemia and dehydration. If I had been a day later, a doctor scolded, I could well have been dead.

After several weeks in the hospital, I was given permission to go home if I had someone to look after me around the clock for a few days to make sure I didn't relapse and lose consciousness. My father had married a young nurse a few years ago, and she offered to drive down and look after me for a while. He was on the other line, so I heard every word he said when he blew up. He said, "What does she need a nurse for anyway? You're just encouraging her invalidism." She said quietly that she'd have to call me back. Sig, who has known my father since we were twelve years old, was in the room at the hospital visiting me when this call came through and was appalled. I was still crying when she called back twenty minutes later and said she'd be there first thing tomorrow morning. She hadn't thought he was going to let her, but she managed to persuade him somehow.

He was *not* happy about it. I thought she was really brave to come. I had seen how he treated her on my visits up there. It was a revelation. I began to understand something that had been a mystery to me for most of my life: how he manages to annihilate the women around him and yet maintain the gentlemanly image of clean hands and correctness.

Colleen, his wife, is nearly fifty years younger than my father. She is pretty in a schoolgirlish way. Soft red hair in a pixie cut, green eyes, and a pretty smile. "Roller-skate skinny," as Holden described his beloved little sister, Phoebe. Colleen looks terrific in a blue blazer. My father should thank his lucky stars. Perhaps in some moments he does, but what I've witnessed is that, instead, he throws stones. He berates her for just those things that make her attractive to him, her age and innocence and simplicity, the same characteristics that allow her to put up with him.

She went to a college in the South where she is from and was a cheerleader. She was also on the bowling team. She is just the sort of pleasant, helpful person one wants at one's sickbed. A bit cheery for my taste, but I can't completely divorce myself from my grumpy heritage. She is by no means unintelligent; she is simply neither interested nor trained in things literary. She is an avid quilt maker and usually sweeps up the blue ribbons at the Cornish Fair, which she helps organize each year.

On a recent tour of the house, my father and Colleen showed me how they'd made over his old study-bedroom, the one with the safes, into a sewing room. I looked at some of her quilting work in progress, and having flunked home economics rather spectacularly myself, I searched for a compliment. Of course I said it was pretty, but I also said I admired the patience and skill it must take to make all those tiny stitches. I said that I've always made such a mess of it when I've tried to do anything that requires that kind of concentration. My father, interrupting my less than elegant attempt, said, "It's been my experience that people who excel at that kind of work never possess a really fine mind." He said it without a trace of rancor in his voice, as if he were simply sharing an objective piece of wisdom he'd attained. It's hard to explain this, but if I'd said, "How can you say such an insulting thing in front of Colleen?" he would have been shocked and incensed at my suggestion that he had said anything insulting to or about Colleen. And furious that I'd accused him of making anything other than a "purely objective" observation; and then he would have gone on to berate women for being such babies and always taking things personally.* He is so clever, so facile with words, that the person he has insulted not only feels insulted, but feels stupid and ashamed for feeling insulted.

What I find most maddening is that I often don't even realize I've been insulted until days or sometimes years later. Then I feel stupid when I think of all the things I *should* have said. I can't count the number of times I've been driving back to Boston from a visit with my father that seemed to go quite pleasantly when suddenly something he said to me sinks in and I'm left saying to my dashboard, "Hey, that wasn't nice."

His comment in the sewing room seemed to sail right past her. All the same, it wasn't nice.

❦

ALTHOUGH DADDY CLAIMED to be terribly concerned when I got out of the hospital, he never came to visit. He called three or four times every single day for the entire week or so that Colleen was with me, asking when she was coming home. I'd hear her side of long conversations about salad bowls and where is such and such in the kitchen and what he ate for lunch, on and on. I remember thinking it sounded more like a conversation between a traveling mother and her two-year-old at home—*some*body wants his mummy and wants her *now*. He spoke to me exactly once. Although he had always been difficult about illness, nothing had prepared me for what was to happen.

He attacked me with the impersonal viciousness of an earthquake. He asked me if I'd given any thought to how I was going to support my child. Thinking this was a preamble to an offer of help, I admitted that I worried about it daily. He said I had no right to bring a child into this "lousy" world that I couldn't support, and he hoped I was considering an abortion.

---

*Joyce, for example, wrote that she wore an old mini-skirt on a day I was to come over for a visit.

"Don't you have something else you can wear?" he says.

"I like this skirt," I say. "You look ridiculous," he says. I start to cry.

"Don't take it personally," he says. "It's a common failing of mankind."

(*At Home,* p. 157)

Nothing he had ever done in the past had prepared me for the unspeakable. I said that I didn't believe in abortion for myself, at thirty-seven, though I had no intention of telling others what to do, and that it was a hell of a thing to say, to suggest that I kill my baby.

He said, *"Kill, kill,* what a silly, dramatic word. I'm only saying what *any* parent of a child in your situation would say."

I don't know where I found the courage—perhaps because I was a mother whose child was being attacked—but I'm proud to say that, for the first time in my life, I let him have it, straight from the gut, unedited. I said, "No, Daddy, any *normal* parent would offer support. All you offer is criticism."

He said, "I've never criticized you. When have I ever criticized you? I've always been there for you when you needed it."

I was totally shocked. I could not believe what I was hearing. I said, "That's absolute crap. You've never once inconvenienced yourself for your children. You've never interrupted your precious work. You've always done exactly what you wanted, when you wanted."

"What about the time I took you guys to England? I didn't have to do that, did I?"

What can you say to a man who thinks the sacrifice of parenthood is a two-week trip to the U.K. when I was twelve?

I said, "That's it? That's all you can come up with? A trip to England where half the reason we went was so you could hook up with a romantic pen pal."

"Christ, you're sounding just like every other woman in my life, my sister, my ex-wives. They all accuse me of neglecting them."

I interrupted, "Well, if the shoe fits, wear it!"

"I can be accused of a certain detachment, that's all. Never neglect. You just need someone to hate. You always did. First it was your brother, then it was your mother, now it's me. You're still seeing a psychiatrist, aren't you?"

"What does that have to do with anything?"

"You *are,* aren't you. You're never happy with anything. You're nothing but a neurotic malcontent."

At this point, the level of his denial was beginning to sink in. I had always thought he justified his neglect because of how important his work was to him. I thought he was at least a little ashamed of himself.

Even when, during this conversation, I confronted him with evidence such as his allowing us to stay with a woman whom he believed had set fire to the house with us in it, he was totally unshaken in his view of himself.

※

As soon as I hung up, or rather, slammed down the phone, I'm not quite sure why, but I wrote down the conversation verbatim. I was outraged, furious, and shocked into intense lucidity where time slows down and one's brain focuses like a laser beam. Who the hell *is* that person I was just talking to, the one I thought was my daddy? I'd always defended him loyally, been a good soldier, but loyal to what, loyal to whom?

I had always thought my father, whatever his shortcomings, would make a perfect grandfather. He peeks into baby carriages in the supermarket line, makes goo-goo eyes, chats with pleasure to any little kid who happens to be around. Just like Seymour and little Sybil in "A Perfect Day for Bananafish," he's a natural with them. I was totally unprepared, blindsided, by the ugliness of his reaction. Instead of being the apple of his eye, I was changed, in a twinkling, into woman: "a body which contains only blood, phlegm, filth, and excreta."

I phoned my mother, stunned, to ask her if she thought he was losing his mind. She became very quiet on the other end of the line and then said, "Peggy, the same thing happened to me when I became pregnant with you." And she began to tell me her story, our family's story. As I listened and began to ask questions, one thought seized me body and soul: This must stop. No more passing on the family inheritance generation to generation unexamined, in silent ignorance of our own past, destined to repeat it. No more reclusion.

My family has a long history of creating beautiful things and hiding them or destroying them with the same hand. My grandmother shrouded her parents in secrecy. What my grandmother left, my father has hidden; what my father left, his children have hidden. My mother tried to destroy her child and herself. My father couldn't begin to introduce his most beloved creation, his "ring-ding *mukta*," Seymour, without killing him off. And those characters he does permit to live must never grow up. They are forever confined to a Salinger Never-Never Land of youth, like boxed butterflies with pins through their bellies.

I want something different for my son. I want him to inherit a connection to where he came from, with all its talent and beauty. I want to pass on a family inheritance rich in intelligence and humor, but without the "four gray walls and four gray towers" we are so good at constructing. I want him to enjoy a future free of the burden of perfection and the urge to destroy anything less.

Most of all I want him to know he has options, that there is a fertile middle ground between perfection and destruction, between heaven and hell. I want him to know forgiveness. I want him to be able to say to himself, "I may not like all the things I do, but I am lovable"; I want him to be able to say to a friend, a partner, a child, "I may not like everything you do, but I love you, and you can count on that." My father is incapable of that. In his world, to be flawed is to be banished. To have a defect is to be a defector, a traitor. It is little wonder that his life is so devoid of living human beings and that his fictional world has such prominent suicides.

34

Awakening

❧❧❧

"So I wasn't dreaming, after all," she said to herself, "unless—unless we're all part of the same dream. Only I do hope it's my dream, and not the Red King's! I don't like belonging to another person's dream. . . . I've a great mind to go and wake him, and see what happens!"

—Chapter 8, "It's My Own Invention"
Through the Looking-Glass, Lewis Carroll

I CALLED LARRY AND SAID we have some talking to do. He said, That's what I've been trying to do for weeks. I showed him the ultrasound picture of the baby they took when they wanted to make sure "it"—now most *def*initely a "he"—was all right. Larry hugged me and cried. With the help of a terrific therapist, and some hard work and will and good fortune of our own, we began to make a real family. "We hope to give our children these two things: one is roots, the other wings." Larry and I want to be like the dream catcher I've hung over my son's bed, letting the nightmares of generations pass through the web, the filter of discernment, and letting the good dreams, his inheritance, run down the feather to where he lies sleeping. We want to make a safe place for him to play and dance with his friends and family in a circle right here on earth, far away from the edge of some crazy cliff.

This is not going to happen by abracadabra, by imagining that when we pull this baby out from inside the cover of my body, he'll be healed like Babe's fingernail and in a safe place rather than in the middle of a battlefield. It was time to roll up our sleeves and get to work. I began to think about a thorough tilling of the soil, and to do some hard digging into places I had always left untouched, covered by weeds and wasteland. I began to open my eyes and look around where I'd always averted my eyes altogether, and to ask questions where previously I'd passed silently by on tiptoes. I had an inkling that this work might grow into a book. I hardly dared think it. When I decided to talk to my mother about what I was considering, she put her hand over her mouth like a Catholic schoolgirl and, with eyes wide, said, "That's sacrilege!" When she dropped her hand from her mouth, though, she was smiling.

Her impulse, her immediate reaction, hit the nail right on the head. Sacrilege. I had no idea how deeply his vision was woven into my being, how much I belonged to my father's dream, until I tried to start untangling myself from it, and to defy the cult of secrecy by writing this book. I use the word *cult* intentionally. Many of my experiences in attempting to "awaken the Red King," to figure out who dreamed what, correspond strikingly to those I've read of persons who have survived leaving a cult, and who took a stand not to pass on such a legacy to their children. I'm sure many went through far worse than I, both in enduring what happened and in the courage it took them to leave, but their stories are the only ones in which I found a bizarre resonance to my own experience. "Dreams, books, are each a world . . . with tendrils strong as flesh and blood." Never underestimate the power of a dream, especially one dreamt by a charismatic dreamer, a speaker for the gods, a man on a sacred mission.

I didn't have much time to think, let alone write, until my son was about a year old. When I tried to begin writing, it was *not* pleasant. I found myself re-experiencing the nightmare world of a terrorized little girl. I had not expected to find myself, once again, at the edge of the cliff. I had an overwhelming, disorienting, vertiginous feeling that if I wrote this book, something terrible and evil would happen to me or to my loved ones as punishment. God or some Powerful Forces would *get* me if I told anyone. Never mind that I don't believe in that kind of theology, even if I *had* been doing something bad. The grown-up person that I am knew better, but it didn't seem to matter. I am at a loss for words to adequately describe the force of this. It was as though I needed a snake charmer or exorcist to release me from those tendrils.

I prayed about it a lot and finally called Marilyn, a sensitive* friend whom the police use from time to time to find missing persons. I asked her to consult one of her spirit guides as to whether I should undertake this project. This is not a thing I am in the habit of doing; I don't even read my horoscope in the paper, I so avoid toying with things supernatural. A few months later she called me and said that a woman had appeared to her in a dream and told her to tell me that I should do it, that it would be important to my son. The point I'm making here isn't about psychic phenomena, but rather that I needed that *kind* of reassurance. I was spooked to my core.

I still couldn't write, the fear of punishment was so strong. Even though I knew full well that it was irrational, I spent nearly a year frozen by the fear that something BAD would happen if I spoke.† Finally, I went incognito—stopping just short of donning funny nose and dark sunglasses—and snuck into the "personal growth" section of a bookstore. I bought a book that contained exercises for getting in touch with one's guardian angel, one's helper and protector. Never mind that I'm paying $85 an hour for therapy! What can I say, it helped. I started to write.

However, with every productive writing session and consequent sense of accomplishment, the nightmares would return. One night my father was in a tractor trying to mow me down. All night long this went on, running in a field, tractor in pursuit. Another night he was stalking me. On and on. But I kept at it, and after a while, reality began to gain some ground, displacing the nightmares.

As I made inroads on the most intense fear, I realized that some-

---

*This is the word "psychics" usually prefer to use in referring to themselves and one another.

†See the previously cited article "Post Mind Control Syndrome" in *Social Work* (March 1982) by Lorna Goldberg and William Goldberg, who co-lead a therapeutic group for former members of religious cults: "Individuals fear punishment for leaving the cult. For example, they fear that the airplane they will ride in will crash or that their parents will be hit by cars. Nightmares are not unusual during the first few months after leaving the cult."

See also *Destructive Cult Conversion* by Dr. John Clark, professor of psychiatry at Harvard Medical School: "To think for oneself is suspect in many groups; to think wrongly is satanic and punishable by psycho-physiological reactions such as migraine headaches, terror and panic, sharp depressions, or gastrointestinal symptoms."

thing else was bothering me that made it hard to write. Although I was plagued by pursuing nightmares, I was also trying to hold on to a dream. It was a dream of lullabies and applewood, where I was cradled in the warmth of my father's love, and the apple of his eye. The dream was tattered and worn, like an old blanket that has been through the wash one too many times, but it was all I had to hold on to. It was faded, but precious, and part of me hoped to find it again someday. I didn't want to lose my perfect daddy entirely.

It has taken all the nerve I could muster to search for who he really is in three dimensions rather than curl up by the fire with a good piece of fiction. It has been hard to let go of the great and powerful man behind the curtain who, if I were only able to do the little thing he asked and remain forever young, forever like him, had the power to take me home. But as the Wizard said to Dorothy, floating away in his hot-air balloon leaving her on the ground, "I can't come back, I don't know how it works."

I am beginning to figure out "how it works," how the man I worshiped as a child came to hide behind curtains and enrobe himself in religious abracadabra. As the great J.D. himself told me many times when I was still a girl, "The old Zen masters refused to accept any false *satoris*—any false unions with the Absolute—any false gods. 'If you see a Buddha,' they warned their disciples, 'knock him down.' " One isn't advised by the masters to beat the living daylights out of a false god and run him out of town on a rail, just to knock down the facade, to look behind the curtain. Doing so is a matter of no small importance—to me, or to anyone else confronted with such a one. History shows us time and again that such figures, humans who would be as God, lead us neither to a sustainable life on earth, nor to heaven; rather, they lead us over the cliff, at the bottom of which you'll find a great heap of dead lemmings.

The exhortation to look behind the curtain concealing those who claim to be godlike, to knock it down rather than follow, is something my father passed on to me (although I doubt he thought I'd apply it to him); something that I, in turn, wish to pass on to my son. There are, however, several nightmarish creatures, misbegotten offspring of my father's conflation of aesthetics, talent, and theology, that I wish to have pass through the dream catcher's web and disappear. My father's belief that perfection of character and perfection of craft are inseparable, for example, drives me crazy. From the leaky Cornish nursery, misconstructed by well-intentioned, unskilled carpenters, to the holy quacks preaching miracle cures, to not allowing me to see regular doctors as a young child, this belief of his could have turned deadly. Can you really live anywhere but in dreamland and believe, for example, that the nicest, most *de*cent man is necessarily going to be the best heart surgeon? I swear to you he'd stake his own life, and the lives of his children, on the surgeon who had a good book of poetry in the office, rather than the one who had the most skill and highest success rate. This may be picturesque in the abstract, but living with it is nuts.

By the same token, his conflation of perfection of character and perfection of work is, I think, a fallacy where it concerns the arts proper. It seems to me that some very badly behaved, morally bankrupt, nasty, egotistical people have created some very beautiful art. And some very good people may wish to bring the velvet Elvises they've painted and the Hummel figurines they've collected as precious gifts for the baby Jesus. "I have reason to believe we all will be received in Graceland."*

Something else happens when he conflates aesthetics and theology. The nature of the work my father creates is transformed—not necessarily qualitatively from bad to good or from better to worse; but rather, the entire category, the structure, the type of thing created is transformed. His work, by the time we get to *Seymour: An Introduction* and "Hapworth," is no longer secular fiction but hagiography.† This is a genre not concerned with time and place, character development, conflict and resolution. Hagiography, given its lack of tension, its lack of earthly focus, and context, is *not* meant to communicate to nonbelievers. They are excluded from the fraternity. Witness his direct address to the elect, the true believers, at the beginning of *Seymour,* who are offered a bouquet of early-blooming parentheses (((()))).

You may say fine, what's the harm, it makes him happy; you don't have to read the book if you don't want to. On one level, this is certainly true. What someone chooses to write about, in a free country anyway, is

---

*Paul Simon.

†Hagiography is a type of religious work concerned with chronicling the lives of saints.

his or her own business. However, any time you exclude certain groups from value, there are consequences. It has been important to me to look carefully at who is excluded, whether it's in religion or any other field. Who gets to play? Who is not allowed on the team? I have concluded that were I not disbarred already by virtue of awakening and growing up, I'd still resign my membership in my father's club.

I don't believe in a path to purity that involves joining an exclusive club that rejects certain "undesirable" elements or groups of people from membership. I have also concluded that I do not believe in my own father's, as well as many of the Church Fathers', attempt to find a solution to suffering through a rejection or renunciation of physical life, the body, and the earth. One cannot spend any time looking at the history of the world's religions and not witness, time and again, that when you exclude or denigrate the body and value only the soul, the lady vanishes. The ancient cult-sacrifice of virgins and firstborn children, whose purity and blood were supposed to please and appease the gods, thought to be humanely and mercifully replaced by a ritual offering of a lamb or the Lamb of God himself, sneaks in the back door.

My father's special blend of "Christianized" Eastern mysticism (not necessarily Eastern mysticism itself nor Christianity nor Zen nor Hinduism nor Buddhism) provides a justification—really a deification—of the sacrifice of the ten-year-old child's emotional life and physical development, to save the adult who is overwhelmed by his own. Behind every good, enlightened man, Christ figure, Teddy, or Seymour in my father's writing, there's a damnation or a demonization of womanhood and a sacrifice of childhood.

The strains of religion that value man and envision woman as temptress and the handmaiden of the snake, that value the spirit and envision the body as a sack of blood, phlegm, filth, and excreta, inevitably, I think, contribute to a world out of balance. Let it pass through the web of the dream catcher into thin air.

I also do not wish to pass on to my son his grandfather's attempt to avoid suffering by joining the great cosmic club of unbeing. This solution to the problem of his beloved Dostoyevski's "hell on earth"—a mental and emotional disintegration from the suffering of being unable to love—is one that I believe should be labeled with a skull and crossbones. For my father, you can't live with others and sustain a kind of balance between merging and separation here on earth, and suffer, therefore, a living hell: merge with the dead.

We first see this solution to life's pain by embracing death in two of the *Nine Stories*, "Teddy" and "A Perfect Day for Bananafish," and then again in Seymour's last words, thus far anyway, from camp in "Hapworth." We are introduced to both Teddy on the day of his death and Seymour (in "Bananafish") on the day he committed suicide. At the end of the short story, Teddy submits, Christ-like, and walks to meet his death in the pool: "Into thy hands I commit my spirit." Seymour blows his brains out, although we don't know how my father will ultimately present this act, since he hasn't yet published what happens between Seymour's childhood in "Hapworth," the "Introduction" of a young man, and his death in "Bananafish." Yet, there are good indications that Seymour's death, like Teddy's, will be sanctified.

Seymour and Teddy, as well as a "great percentage of the Glass siblings," we are told, "have a fairly terrible capacity for experiencing pain that does not always properly belong to them." We are supposed to believe, as their author does, that these characters are saintly sufferers, Christ figures or bodhisattvas, who redeem the suffering of those of us who, like Franny and Buddy, remain, as yet, on earth.

Frankly, I do not see it that way; it is the women I'd like to see elevated and their stories passed down to the next generation. The ones who suffer, it seems to me, are the denigrated Magdalenes he leaves at the foot of the cross, the Echos who waste away, the girls and women who are excluded from the mystical club of Father, Son, and Holy Ghost, i.e., J.D., Buddy, and Seymour. It is the Marys and the Magdalenes who are left to suffer the consequences of the "saint's" sacrifice. It is Teddy's unenlightened sister who has to pay for being the vehicle of his saintly suicide, who is left to weep and mourn. It is Seymour's wife who wakes up to spraying brains and widowhood. It is Mattie and Phoebe who are not allowed to live beyond age ten and who, like Sister Irma, sacrifice their sexuality to the Father.

The living Jesus of Nazareth was, we're told, celibate. The real-life person who was to become the Buddha was married and produced several children before his enlightenment. He renounces them, as Jesus does his mother and father, and goes off to seek God and become the salvation of humanity. On whose back? Who else is sacrificing, probably starving, while he's out sitting under a tree wasting away to nothing in a holy fast? As Lahiri Mahasaya's wife said to him, feeling "forlorn and neglected" (before she came to realize his divine nature and confesses that what she said was a "sin committed against my guru-husband"), "You spend all your time with the disciples. What about your responsibilities for your wife and children? I regret that you do not interest yourself in providing . . . for the family."

The model of marriage that flows from deifying some humans, making them figures of worship, yogi Lahiri Mahasaya and his disciple wife for example, is not one I wish to pass down the feather to my sleeping child. I think that when you set your work up as a mission that somehow exempts you, puts you above any other duty or earthly obligation, there is a grave danger. Or as Euripides said (I know, there is a special place in purgatory for people who dare to begin a sentence "Or as Euripides said"! But he really did hit the nail squarely on the head), "Slight not what is near through aiming at what is far." Or as others have said, charity begins at home. What are you doing that is so much more important than taking care of your kids and family? I've been in several boarding schools full of children whose parents were doing *important* things. Some of the worst abdicators of responsibility to family are those in the "helping" professions, the clergy, doctors, to say nothing of the more stereotypically identified narcissists such as some fast-track businesspeople and artists. To whom are you truly irreplaceable? Your public? Your boss? Your shareholders? Your clients? God can't run the universe without you on duty full-time? One can provide the physical necessities in spades and still have neglected to provide your partner and your children and those who love you with what they needed: you.

❦

I THOUGHT ABOUT THE LAST REAL CONVERSATION I had with my father, when he said to me, "Christ, you're sounding just like every other woman in my life, my sister, my ex-wives. They all accuse me of neglecting them. . . . I can be accused of a certain detachment, that's all. Never neglect."

What I've come to believe in looking at my own life, and at those of the other women in his life, is that, yes, he can be accused of a *certain* detachment. He is detached about *your* pain, but God knows he takes his

own pain more seriously than cancer. When people say that they are committed to living the life they preach—in my father's case, that there
would be no separation between the quest for enlightenment and his
art—it is fair game to hold them accountable for preaching one thing and
behaving in another way altogether. My father's espousal of a doctrine of
detachment and renunciation has a strong strain of "Methinks the man
doth protest too much." There is nothing remotely detached about my father's behavior toward his own pain, in his hemorrhages about anything
personal being known about him. There is nothing remotely detached
about his passionate defense of any felt infringement on his privacy or on
the sanctity of his words and work. If it is all *maya,* all an illusion, why the
continual *shpilkes* (fits, touchiness, as in sitting on pins and needles) in his
own life? The Buddha appears in many "aspects," many forms: the
seated Buddha, the starving Buddha, the lotus Buddha; but never have I
seen a statue or depiction of *der Schlaganfall* (apoplectic-fit) Buddha! It finally dawned on me that my father, for all his protestations and lectures
and writing about detachment, is a very, very needy man.

I think it is this aspect of his work, the intense, borderline neediness
of a cliff walker, that resonates so deeply with the members of his public
who used to mystify me so. People at airline ticket counters, for example, when they see my name and ask if I'm "any relation," time and
again have given me the feeling that they were not talking about a
writer, but a savior. Just touch the hem of his garment and be healed.
Even today, more than forty years since *The Catcher in the Rye* was published, I read in the *Boston Globe* newspaper of some local suburban
high school kids who, after reading *The Catcher* in class, convinced their
teacher to drive a few of them up to Cornish to try to find J. D. Salinger.
They were unsuccessful. The journalist who caught wind of the story
asked one of the girls what she would have done had she been successful, what question did she have for Salinger. She giggled nervously but
finally said, "I'd ask him if he'll be *our* catcher, our catcher in the rye."

Whatever he may be, he is not going to be your catcher in real life.
Get what you can from his writing, his stories, but the author himself
will not appear out of nowhere to catch those kids if they get too close
to that crazy cliff.

AFTER OUR SON WAS BORN, my husband and I went to visit Aunt Doris. I told her what Daddy had said about "all the women" in his life, his ex-wives, his sister, and now me. How we'd all unjustly, according to him, accused him of neglect. What did she think?

She said that if I'd asked her the same question three years ago, before she had her heart attack, she would have given me a very different answer. Up until then, she said, "I thought he was perfect. Sonny demands that, you know. He can't take any criticism. I'm just sorry I'll be dead and won't see that book he's been working on all these years. Not publishing all these years. What a crazy business. It's because he can't stand any criticism. He sure doles it out, though. I love him, my brother and I were the best of friends growing up, you know, but I have to admit that he's a bastard. What can I say? I was all alone when I had my heart attack and he's been useless to me. Visited two, maybe three times. Hardly a phone call. When I had my heart attack, I was sick and alone. That's a terrible thing to be, sick and alone. But anything that interferes with him, with his work, is dismissed."

She made a gesture with her arm of sweeping everything away, of dismissal, and paused.

"He takes any opportunity to dig the knife in," she said, turning an imaginary knife in the air between us. "Do you know what he said, the first thing he asked me, when he called after my heart attack? 'You've gotten so fat lately, did the doctors tell you to lose weight?' I confronted him. I told him he always criticizes."

I broke in and asked, "Was Granny critical of him?"

"Oh, no!" Aunt Doris said, surprised at the suggestion. "He was perfect, he could do no wrong in her eyes."

The perfect artist's eyes. "The whole ambulance load of pain," of the "true artists," according to his credo, comes straight from the eyes. "Isn't he, actually, the only seer we have on earth? I say that the true artist-seer, the heavenly fool who can and does produce beauty, is mainly dazzled to death by his own scruples, the blinding shapes and colors of his own sacred conscience." You may see, as in "De Daumier-Smith's Blue Period," a pile of orthopedic appliances mystically turn into a dazzling vision of twice-blessed flowers, but it still smells like a load of bedpans to me.

IF MY FATHER is to be judged on his own terms, with the moral yardstick by which he measures himself either about his duty in life, or his daily duty, he can meet his maker with his head held high. As Seymour writes to Buddy:

> Do you know what I was smiling at [when they registered to-gether for the draft]? You wrote down that you were a writer by *profession*. It sounded to me like the loveliest euphemism I had ever heard. When was writing ever your profession? It's never been anything but your religion. Never. . . . Since it is your reli-gion, do you know what you will be asked when you die? But let me tell you first what you won't be asked. You won't be asked if you were working on a wonderful, moving piece of writing when you died. You won't be asked if it was long or short, sad or funny, published or unpublished. . . . I'm so sure you'll get asked only two questions. *Were most of your stars out? Were you busy writing your heart out?* If only you knew how easy it would be for you to say yes to both questions.
>
> (*Seymour,* p. 160)

My father has, indeed, spent his life busy writing his heart out. I am not convinced, however, that the way of life he upholds is a well-balanced model of doing one's duty, nor a way to a sustainable peace. Maybe he is wrong, maybe he is right. And maybe he is right and using it wrongly. What I do know is that this philosophy or religion or atti-tude served to justify his living life *exactly* as he wished, others be damned. To get in the way of his work for any reason whatsoever is not just a nuisance or an inconvenience; it is committing an act of sacrilege. Do not stand in the path of a holy quest; move aside or perish. Right or wrong, it fits his narcissistic bent to a T, sanctifying even the most ex-treme narcissism. It's a tricky business, though: one man's narcissist is another man's saint. As Zooey said, "Treasure's treasure, God damn it, and it seems to me that ninety per cent of all the world-hating saints in history were just as *acquis*itive and unattractive, basically, as the rest of us are."

I feel the same way about my father's way of life as Zooey did about Franny's following *The Way of a Pilgrim.* Zooey said to her:

No matter what I say, I sound as though I'm undermining your Jesus Prayer. And I'm *not,* God damn it. All I *am* is against why and how and *where* you're using it. I'd like to be convinced—I'd *love* to be convinced—that you're not using it as a substitute for doing what ever the hell your duty is in life, or just your daily duty . . .   (*Zooey,* p. 169)

Once again, I found Rabbi Fine's guidance to be invaluable in picking one's way through this minefield of a question—as he put it, "How do I know if what I'm doing is good and right?" The rabbi was asked if there were any theological criteria he uses to evaluate the ways of life espoused by "the new religions." He answered:

> Yes, certainly, there are criteria. I'll speak Jewishly. Judaism says there are basically three criteria. . . . First, you have to ask, Am I hurting anybody? Second, Am I adding to what is here? Although there is an intuitive experience in Judaism that is private, personal, and indescribable, you should be able to speak about it in a rational way. Not the experience, but the effect of that experience. Third, Is a positive action modality present in my life? Can I see that I am a better husband, that I'm not as angry, I'm more compassionate, more caring? Those are very powerful value statements. The Jews have ways of serving God which include all kinds of improved interrelationships and interactions. If the quality of life improves after a religious experience, then something true has happened. That includes the affirmation of family and community values. . . . Glaring problems exist in most groups. Nothing is really happening except in the member's "own little world." They're not really doing anything. Ask them why.

I, too, had to give up living in my own little dream world to "ask them why." Nevertheless, in giving up the dream of a perfect Daddy, some of my memories of happy times with my father returned. These are real, and they belong to me. I can, now, take them out and savor them whenever I want to. I don't have to wait for his return from ethereal realms. Similarly, in giving up my pursuit of the heavenly Daddy, the nightmare of the hellish Daddy began to give up its pursuit of me. I am able to see a talented man who, like the rest of us, is neither all good nor all bad. As the Wizard said to Dorothy, I'm not a very bad man, in fact I'm a rather good one, I'm just a very bad wizard.

What I found that is mine to keep and precious is a sense of admiration for my parents' attempt to create a sort of Eden in the rye, a perfect world. I have also found pleasure in the ways in which they succeeded. There is great beauty in the pursuit of a dream even though, in practice, it often becomes a nightmare.*

Being a member of that imperfect society, the Salinger family, has strengths and weaknesses, costs and benefits. There is both a beauty and a danger in attempting to create paradise on earth. To sustain paradise requires perfect people—or dead ones, not mere mortals who are "works in progress," imperfect but forgiven. But the attempt also permits a glimpse of heaven, without which life can be too hard to bear.

＊＊＊

IT'S HARD WORK to find the proper balance, the point of equinox for oneself. My friend Jacobo Timerman told me something nearly twenty years ago, when he was newly released from torture in a clandestine jail in Argentina. To this day, it remains the single most useful thing anyone has ever said to me. I can't re-create the elegance of a lifelong journalist's language, but the gist of what he said to me is as follows. He asked me why I had such sad eyes. I didn't have an answer; that was part of the problem. I felt like an idiot for having sad eyes: I'd not been in jail, I'd not been tortured by the military. He said, It is a very hard thing to find happiness. Hundreds and thousands of examples exist of how to be miserable, and they are everywhere you look for you to copy. It is *easy* to be miserable, he said, millions can show you the way. It requires no thought

---

*The history of the attempt is probably as old as humanity. No less than Plato himself tried, several centuries before the birth of Christ. Plato's unsurpassed attempt in the *Republic* to create a perfect world ended when he came up against the problem of finding persons with perfect judgment, "philosopher kings," to rule such a perfect world. He considered the problem to be an intractable one. He thus moved on to an exploration of the many forms of imperfect society, their strengths and weaknesses, costs and benefits.

or creativity of your own, just following. To be happy is hard, because no one can show you, it is something you have to work out, create for yourself. No one can give you a model to copy, though many will volunteer, because happiness is not off the rack, one size fits all, it is something each of us has to tailor-make for himself or herself.

Up until that point, I had felt ashamed of myself, as well as sad. He took the shame away. When I saw him off at the airport, he gave me a painting of a pasture, surrounded by barbed wire, in the highlands in Argentina. On the back of the painting he wrote, "¡Ánimo! Margarita" (which translates loosely as grab some life, fill yourself with life; it's a cry that urges you on, all that and more).

The last few years have taken the sadness away, the quiet wish I had until recently that, if I had my choice, I'd have never been born. It happened a while ago that the balance between sadness and happiness in my life tilted toward the living, but I didn't really realize it until one moment, shortly after my hellish pregnancy and worse childbirth replete with flashbacks, and unspeakable postpartum panic attacks. I remember looking at my son sleeping in his cradle at the end of a long day and thinking, I would live my life all over again just to have spent this one day with you. Even if he or I should die tomorrow, as I envisioned over and over in my panic attacks, life is in balance, nothing missing, nothing owed.

❦

THE OTHER DAY my son came home from nursery school very upset. He'd had a fight with Katie, one of his best friends, and there had been some harsh words and name-calling. Someone may even have thrown something, but he wasn't volunteering who. Larry and I tried to reassure him; we said, "You have to learn to use your words, and you both will." I said, "Daddy and I fight about stuff sometimes, but we always work it out." He looked at us as if to say, Do you think I was born yesterday? He said slowly and clearly so we fools would understand, "Grown-ups don't fight; only kids do." Larry said, Yes, we do, honey; our son interrupted, "My teachers don't, you and Mommy don't, grown-ups don't fight and that's that." Larry and I looked at each other. We're very different and we sometimes disagree, but we couldn't remember the last real fight, the child's equivalent of name-calling, throwing things, hurt feelings, and so on, we had had. It suddenly dawned on us: boy, are things ever peaceful around this house. I can scarcely imagine growing up with parents who genuinely enjoy each other's company, who are committed to lifelong "learning to use their words," and who think that marriage and children are the best things that ever came their way. It's so out of the realm of my experience that it hadn't occurred to me until that moment just how far we'd come, and how very, very different my son's world is from mine growing up. Now *that's* a keeper, that's a happy ending. Not perfect, but real, and beyond my wildest dreams.

It is so still in the house.
There is a calm in the house,
The snowstorm wails out there
And the dogs are rolled up with snouts under the tail.
My little boy is sleeping on the ledge,
On his back he lies, breathing through his open mouth.
His little stomach is bulging round—
Is it strange if I start to cry with joy?

(Anonymous Inuit mother's poem)

L' Chaim

Afterword

❧❧❧

THE VERY NICEST and most unexpected gift I received after this book was first published was a warm and touching letter from a relative, my father's first cousin, Jay Goldberg. He is just three months older than my father. His mother, Birdie, and my father's father, Sol, were brother and sister, together with siblings Stella, Gertie, and Sam Salinger. I found I have a wealth of cousins, some my father's age, some my age, some my son's age, eager to meet me. I never knew they existed. Over a series of letters, Jay Goldberg has, with great richness of memory and generosity of spirit, filled the gaps in this book and in my knowledge of our family. I think the reader, too, will find it a fascinating, vital addition, both as a portrait of the Salinger family and as a portrait of an era.

One of the things he sent me was a copy of a letter he wrote to my father in 1988, but did not send. He wrote:

> Dear Sonny,
>
> We are getting perilously close to the Biblical age of "Three Score and Ten," which in pre–medical advance days meant that seventy was IT. At any rate, we're not Holden Caulfield's age anymore or even close to it. Without being macabre, I'm old enough to give you my thoughts. You didn't ask for them and you don't need them, but they say catharsis is good for the soul.
>
> I am really proud of you. Just think—the kid I played with in New York in your apartment has become one of the world's

most popular and enduring and important writers. *Catcher in the Rye* still sells hundreds of thousands of copies, after so many years. It is always nice to see the expression on people's faces when they ask, "Are you really J. D. Salinger's first cousin?" All of us in the family, I suppose, have basked in the light of your popularity.

I also respect your great determination to remain utterly private. You have a right to lead your life as you wish, provided you do no harm to anyone.

Having said all that, I will confess that I think you made a touchdown, but lost the game. By that I mean that you neglected to evince any feelings for anyone in the family—except your mother and sister. Fame and adulation are wonderful, but family is also very important. It is vital, I feel, in one's life and in the raising of one's children. . . .

Did your children know anything about the Salingers— their great-grandfather, their cousins, their uncles and aunts? I think it is their loss—and yours.

You obviously turned your back on your heritage. Many Jews died through centuries of persecution. You and I are indeed fortunate our great-grandfather and grandfather had the guts to escape and come to America. It's a very meaningful background, and yet I get the strong impression you have totally rejected it. Here, too, I feel you have lost a great deal. "Zen" may be terrific, but you had a rich Jewish heritage right in your own backyard.

Sonny, I wish you well in the years remaining and I hope your children will have a long and happy life. And I trust they have learned something valuable in this article I have written about who they really are.

Jay

This one of Sonny's children, named Margaret, did learn from my father's cousin Jay something of great value about who I really am— who *we* are—as will my children and, God willing, my children's children. I am deeply grateful for this gift. Jay sent me a copy of our family's history that he had written in 1980 and amended in 1988. What follows are selections taken from his work.

"THE SALINGERS: A FAMILY ALBUM."

These notes will have some words about Sonny [the family name for J. D. Salinger], but it is primarily about the remarkable family from which he and I come. All my life, I have always had enormous pride in the Salinger family. I felt that Sonny's and my grandfather, the late Dr. Simon F. Salinger, was a particularly remarkable man. My gratitude to my grandfather Salinger is great. He had the courage to run away from a little town in Lithuania and eventually make his way to America, I feel deeply that if he hadn't come here, I might not be among the living. (Nor would Sonny.) The Jews from that area were virtually annihilated by Hitler, in later years.

Simon Salinger was born in 1860 in a very small town called Tauroggen, in southern Lithuania. At most, it was about a few thousand people, as even today it is only ten thousand. I was puzzled to learn recently that his citizenship paper (1890) listed him as a native of Germany. In it he renounced "all allegiance and fidelity to the Emperor of Germany." Tauroggen at the time of his birth was under Prussian rule.

When our grandfather, Simon, was twelve, he ran away from home because his father was a difficult man. He went from town to town, literally singing for his supper. He would walk or get a ride on a wagon from a peasant. He had an excellent voice and he managed to get food and lodging in return for being a boy cantor. He was also a highly intelligent youngster with a rare command of Talmudic lore. So he found employment as a scholar, too. In those days in Europe, particularly in that part of the world, studying the Talmud daily was a way of life among Jews.

One day in his wanderings he came to a small village and was put up by a family named Kaplan. There he struck gold! It wasn't the monetary variety, but the gold of human relations. He found a surrogate father, Rabbi Morris Kaplan, and a surrogate mother in Morris's wife. Rabbi Kaplan was a learned man and also a jovial one. He maintained his spirit despite the poverty in the village and the hardship of providing for seven children. One of these was a little girl, Fannie. Although she was only ten, and Simon about fifteen, he noticed Fannie from the start. They would later marry in another far-off land.

Simon and his future father-in-law heard of a pulpit in Manchester, England, and there they went. They worked together in an Orthodox congregation for several years. However, their ultimate aim was always to come to the "promised land"—America. Eventually, their diligence and perseverance brought them to this country, where they landed in 1876. At immigration, it seems, Rabbi Kaplan's name was changed to Copland. They found a congregation in Syracuse, New York, where Simon surely must have been one of the youngest members of the rabbinate in the United States. They moved sometime later to Wilkes-Barre, Pennsylvania. There, in 1882, Simon and Fannie (Sonny's and my grandparents) were married, Rabbi Copland presiding.

A year later, Simon and Fannie became proud parents of a boy, Hyman, who lived only a year and a half. In 1885 the Salingers moved to Cleveland. There, another son, Samuel, was born. Two years later, in 1887, Sol, father of J. D. Salinger, was born. The following year, Simon took Fannie and their two little boys to Louisville, Kentucky, where he became rabbi of a small synagogue called Adath Jeshurun. He set about making some radical changes. In those days, Orthodox Jews separated the men and the women in their places of worship. Simon Salinger was a pioneer in Conservative Judaism, which later became the third branch of the faith, along with Reform. To give you an idea of how revolutionary this was, I, his grandson, was part of a struggle nearly seventy years later to get the two sexes to worship together in a Cincinnati Conservative congregation. Another innovation was that Simon preached his sermons in English, where previously they were in Yiddish or, in some Reform temples, German. He became friendly with Lewis Dembitz in Louisville and this was a decided help to the young rabbi. Dembitz was the uncle of Louis Dembitz Brandeis, the first Jewish Supreme Court Justice. (Justice Brandeis was named to the U.S. Supreme Court by President Woodrow Wilson in 1917 after a long fight for confirmation in Congress.) Lewis Dembitz was a nationally recognized authority on constitutional law, and when Grandpa Salinger came to Louisville in 1888, Dembitz was writing a revised constitution for the state of Kentucky. The two men became close friends. They learned from each other. Dembitz scrutinized my grandfather's sermons and helped him correct grammatical errors. In return,

Dembitz, who was an observant Jew and admired Salinger's vast knowledge of Judaism, was given lessons on the finer points of Talmudic learning.

Simon Salinger taught lessons in Hebrew and Jewish history and customs daily to the children of Adath Jeshurun. He presided over the *minyans,* or prayer sessions, every day at sunrise and sunset. He slaughtered kosher meat. He officiated at funerals, circumcisions and weddings. He scarcely had time to breathe! For all this he was paid the princely salary of $600 a year.

Still there was time to have and raise an ever-growing family. My mother, Birdie, was born in 1889, and a year later another girl, Stella, arrived. He could no longer raise a family on his salary, and at the age of thirty-two, he assumed the rabbinate at the Tree of Life Synagogue in Pittsburgh, a congregation that later would become one of the most prestigious in America. A fifth child, Gertrude, was born, and that same year, Simon Salinger, in addition to his rabbinical duties entered the University of Pittsburgh Medical School—this from a young man with no previous formal schooling.

Things worked out well despite the hardships. Simon obtained tutoring help from a young man who had just arrived in America from Europe. The refugee was highly educated and tutored my grandfather in subjects he needed for the curriculum. In return, Simon obtained a position for the new arrival and housed him. Numerous immigrants were aided over many years by Simon and Fannie. The Salingers helped bring them over and gave them housing and aid until they could sustain themselves. Among the immigrants were both strangers and family, including Simon's only sister, Ada, his brother Barney, and finally his mother. Ada, my mother Birdie recalls, "later married a man named Morris Greenberg. They didn't get along too well. In fact, they had separate bedrooms and didn't talk to each other for forty-two years!" They somehow managed to have three children, however. Barney earned a modest living as a tailor in Indianapolis.

In 1896, Simon was graduated near the top of his class in medical school, having completed the course in three years. He resumed his rabbinate at Adath Jeshurun in Louisville, practiced medicine, and became the medical examiner for Louisville's health department. He was among the first who instituted examinations of children in the schools. He worked these three jobs for ten years.

Sam, the eldest of Simon and Fannie's children, went to work at age twelve to help support the family. He was later able to enter Louisville Male High. He needed two years of Greek to catch up to the junior class and Dr. Salinger called his friend Professor Reuben Post Halleck to seek tutoring for Sam over the summer so he could join the class of his peers. Professor Halleck agreed, but expressed pessimism about Sam's chances, whereupon Simon contacted his old friend Judge Dembitz. Dembitz taught Sam two years of Greek in three months that summer and insisted that he also study advanced Hebrew. This Sam did, along with working in a store for long hours. Sam became valedictorian of his class at the age of fifteen.

Sol quit school at age thirteen and went to work full time. He didn't much like school, although studies came easily to him. He worked for Goldstein's wholesale house in Louisville ten hours a day for one dollar a week. Meanwhile, Birdie was obliged to quit school, at age twelve, much to her disappointment. She was an avid student. She had suffered an attack of typhoid fever. She said, "In those days there were very many fatalities from typhoid fever. It was from the water. The Ohio River was polluted, filled with muck. In the spring, the water was like a sheet of mud. We had to put it in buckets and let it settle. Then we carefully let it spill off into other containers and boiled the water. There was nothing like today's water purification systems." She was not allowed to return to school for fear of her weakened health. Both parents worked with her on home studies, and Birdie started to read all kinds of books—biographies, history, philosophy. She said that the women of her mother's generation who were raised in Lithuania did not receive any formal schooling, even in Hebrew. Her father, however, taught her both Hebrew and German, which she spoke and wrote beautifully, along with English. This thirst for learning prevails even today at age ninety-one. Recently she called me to ask about a point in Plato's *Republic*. I had to confess that I didn't remember it.

She corresponds regularly with the family throughout the country. Her handwriting is as firm as it was at twenty-one. When she spots something she considers wrong in the body politic, she fires off a letter to the offender, be he a Cincinnati judge or the president of the United States. Conversely, when she sees a good deed done, she writes or calls the person involved so he will know the act is appreciated. She has voted in every election since women were granted suffrage. She not only votes regularly, but studies the issues and candidates with a microscope. If something bothers her about a man running for office, she doesn't hesitate to write or call him for clarification. She was the first recording secretary of the Louisville chapter of Hadassah in 1912; one of a handful of young Jewish women who had the foresight sixty-eighty years ago to form this organization dedicated to the re-birth of the State of Israel. She is grateful that after all those years, the dream became a reality. "People thought we were strange back then to work for a Jewish state, to be formed in what was then called Palestine," Birdie recalls. "I guess we were too young to realize how few we were and how arduous the task would be." She was a highly gifted artist and was offered a scholarship at the Chicago Art Institute, but her parents refused to let her attend, fearful that her fragile health wouldn't permit it. She also had an excellent singing voice. Many felt she could have become a top-flight professional singer, but she did not pursue it—again due to parental objections. At age eighty-six she wrote in her diary: "This inability to take advantage of such fine offers remained for many years as a deep hurt. In my more adult years, as I turned to elevating the mind and filling my being with as much knowledge as possible, and with an appreciation of many worthwhile things offered—music, art, religion— my deep hurt was softened, then put to rest. . . . One thing I have found is that if you begin to get sour and start complaining, it works on you. First thing you know, you are not well anymore, and it can affect your mind, too." She married my dad, Lee L. Goldberg in 1912 and, despite doctor's warnings, had two children. The young girl about whom her parents agonized because of ill health is still going strong at ninety-one.

Sonny's and my aunts, Birdie's sisters Stella and Gertie, were going to school and acquiring clerical skills in stenography and bookkeeping. Later, both got very good jobs making $35 a week, which was a lot of money in those days. Their mother, Fannie, contracted Parkinson's disease at age forty and became an invalid. Birdie recalls, "My mother's disposition was a gift from God. Despite her affliction, and constant pain, I never heard her talk against anyone. She didn't bemoan her fate. She always kept a teapot in the kitchen into which she put what little change she could manage. In those days, Jewish people who were down on their luck would come for help, for money. There was always something in that teapot for them."

In 1907, Dr. Salinger took his ailing wife and five children to Chicago. Fannie's six brothers and sisters lived there, as did her father, Rabbi Copland. Simon and Fannie took an apartment upstairs from Rabbi Copland on the teeming west side, where many Jewish people lived. I can still remember as a boy how proud I was of the shingle on the window: "Dr. Simon F. Salinger."

He left the rabbinate for good, to devote himself to medicine and to his wife and family. He practiced from his home and, in this era before specialization, he did everything from delivering babies, to performing surgery, to counseling troubled patients. Often he wasn't paid, as many of his patients were too poor, yet he never dunned anyone. Once a carpenter came to him with three dollars that had been owed for fourteen years. It wasn't unusual for someone to bring him a chicken in lieu of cash. My mother once told me that Grandpa Salinger said to her very often, "I won't leave you any money, but I will leave you a good name." And so he did.

Downstairs, Rabbi Copland, Sonny's and my great-grandfather, enjoyed life to the fullest. Like Uncle Sol, he was a man who savored every moment. Morris Copland had a small synagogue, and every Saturday morning he would sit in the kitchen, no matter how hot and humid, and sip hot tea from a glass. I can still see him in my mind's eye, sitting there with his skullcap on (he never removed it, I suspect, even when he went to sleep!) And *schvitzing* (sweating) with a smile of the utmost satisfaction on his bearded face.

Then he would bathe and put on this Sabbath attire, complete with frock coat and top hat. He would walk majestically several blocks to the synagogue, his wife at his side. She would be dressed in black, very elegant, and she walked *with* him not behind, as was still common for many years to come in Orthodox Jewry.

❦

The Salingers and Coplands were very close. In the early 1900s there wasn't any radio, or TV. Entertainment was mostly of the home variety. The family had a ritual on every Thursday night. They would gather in the spacious Salinger apartment and everyone would do his "act."

Stella and Gertie played the piano. Birdie and Sol sang. Sam fiddled. Mother said, "The children would sprawl on the floor and the older people would sit on chairs all around the room. This was a big family, but we had double parlors with sliding doors between that opened up."

Dave played the banjo and he and his sister Annie used to do the popular dance of the period, the Cakewalk, which included some great strutting. Joe played the violin and Will performed on the mandolin. Uncle Joe Copland not only was a fine violinist, but he also taught the instrument and made violins and cellos. Many of the string players in the Chicago Symphony Orchestra bought their violins and cellos from this gifted man.

"We had marvelous times those Thursday evenings," my mother recalls. "Even Aunt Sarah and Uncle Max performed, and they were deaf mutes. My uncle was a fine magician and Aunt Sarah was his assistant. . . . Then there was Abe Copland. He changed his name to Al. He was the only one who didn't come around very often on those Thursday nights. He was a professional musician and many people considered him to be the best ragtime pianist of his generation. We used to call him 'the genius,' and he played in the leading jazz bands of those days. . . . Abe ended sadly because he was wild."

Dave, the banjo player, proved to be another interesting person in the Salinger-Copland family. Dave met a man named Max Epstein in Chicago. Between them they had $400 dollars. They bought some discarded freight cars and remodeled them and sold the cars for a small profit. They began acquiring more and more cars and soon found themselves in the freight business. After a few years, they accumulated enough money to obtain new cars. These carried oil supplies and other liquid materiel. They called their company General American Tank Car Corp. And today it's General American Transportation. Uncle

Dave, the banjo player, became a multimillionaire. As Harry Golden says, "Only in America."

It was in Chicago that Simon's son Sol met a pretty young Gentile lady from a small town in Iowa called Atlantic (in Cass County). After all this time the entire county today is just sixteen thousand strong. Her name was Marie Jillich and she had come to Chicago, at age seventeen, with only the dress she wore on her back. Her father's name was Frank and her mother's maiden name was Jennie Vincent. My mother remembers cousin Sonny's mother very clearly. "She was a slender seventeen-year-old of extremely modest means when she married my brother Sol. At that time, not long after the turn of the century, it was impossible for the groom to tell his parents about the marriage. How could Sol break the news to his father, a former rabbi? How could he tell his mother, a very devout woman? Then there was Sol's grandfather, Rabbi Copland, who led an Orthodox synagogue."

Sol and Marie kept their marriage a secret. He continued to live at home for two years. One day, after Marie suffered a miscarriage, Sol's brother Sam told him in no uncertain terms that he could no longer keep up the charade, and must tell their parents the truth, come what may.

It was a tense moment when Sol divulged his secret. To his surprise, his mother and father did not cast out the couple, although they were far from being joyful. The young pair could now live openly as man and wife, but first they were married in a Jewish ceremony. (The first time had been with a justice of the peace.) Marie changed her name to Miriam as a placating gesture toward the Salingers, and very few of the family of my generation ever knew that her name hadn't always been Miriam. She went through the conversion ceremony to become officially Jewish, including the *mikvah,* or ritual cleansing bath.

Sam delivered Sol and Miram's first child, Doris, in 1912. The following year, while Sol managed several nickelodeons, Sam went to Vienna for further medical training. Once home, he began to specialize in ear, nose, and throat. He became the first chairman of the Department of Otolaryngology at the Stritch School of Medicine at Loyola University in Chicago. He served as chairman for forty-one years; at the same time he was on the consulting staff at Cook County Hospital and senior attending staff at Michael Reese Hospital. By the end of the First World War he began to work in the new field of plastic surgery. "On Mondays, I noticed any number of people coming in with broken noses from weekend fights and accidents. So, I started fixing those noses. Then I went into plastic surgery of the face—pinning back ears, shortening noses, taking bags out of eyelids, face-lifting, removing scars." He was also instrumental in bringing about many of the techniques that were used in succeeding wars to repair facial wounds suffered by our soldiers in battle.

My parents, Birdie and Lee Goldberg, were close to Uncle Sol and Aunt Miriam. When they moved to New York we often visited throughout my childhood. I recall pillow fights with Sonny in his bedroom while the adults played cards in the living room. My mother remembers Sonny as a child: "He had large brown eyes and he was a very friendly boy and he read, read, read all the time. He always had a book at hand, Sonny was a natural, nice youngster and approachable. He was really a very nice boy."

Sonny, to my recollection, was a normal kid and we got along fine. Also, he used to go in the summer to Sharon, Pennsylvania, when he was a teenager, to stay with our aunt Stella, her husband, Leo Federber, and their three girls. Uncle Leo was an executive with a tank-car company and Sonny was often at their home. In other words, until Sonny grew into manhood, he and his family were quite close to the rest of the Salingers. During the war Uncle Sol came to Cincinnati to celebrate Passover with us. He rose during the seder and offered a toast to me, his sister's son, as I was fighting with the 13th Armored Division in Germany. My father, not to be outdone, stood and toasted Sonny who, unbeknownst to me, was with the 12th Infantry in the same area. My sister remembers my father saying, "Here's to our sons who are fighting Hitler!"

But when Sonny returned from the war, none of us heard from him again, with rare exceptions. Nothing could be clearer than the fact that J. D. Salinger decided to eliminate contact with all of us—grandparents, cousins, uncles, aunts. That was certainly his prerogative. As the old saying goes, You can choose your friends but you can't choose your family.

It would become the standard family "gag" anytime any of the Salinger family met to say, "What do you hear from Sonny?" This ancient wheeze would inevitably be followed by laughter. No one had heard from him.

At a deeper level, it wasn't funny at all, however. I think that the one who was most hurt by Sonny's ignoring the family was Uncle Sam. Sam was always very close to his brother Sol (Sonny's father). He delivered the writer's sister into the world. He was a highly articulate and educated individual. He wrote witty and pungent letters (one of which, to his close friend Groucho Marx, is included in the comedian's book *Letters to Groucho*). Yet his letters to Sonny weren't acknowledged, and it was as though Sam didn't exist. I, too, wrote Sonny five times during the past forty years . . . no reply. Perhaps I didn't have the correct address; I didn't ask Doris or Aunt Miriam or Uncle Sol because the subject of Sonny so clearly made them uncomfortable, but the letters were never returned marked undelivered.

Uncle Sol often visited us in Cincinnati throughout his long life, usually alone. He was always a joy. He had a wonderful sense of humor and was as down to earth as a millionaire as he had been as a boy making one dollar a week. The only times I remember his getting nervous and irritable were when we would ask about Sonny. This was a natural question because the normal thing is to ask about one's family, as to their health and how and what they're doing. Uncle Sol would redden and invariably blurt out, "Oh, he's ok," and hastily change the subject. After some years, I came to realize that this was obviously a painful subject for him. Instead of being able to talk about his son and his son's wife and two children and how they were growing and all the details that doting parents and grandparents love to relate, Uncle Sol was rendered mute—and this from a highly gregarious and family-oriented man. My mother recalls, "Uncle Sol, the complete extrovert, was entirely different when he was by himself than with his own family. He would be at the dining room table (in New York) and hardly utter a word. He was much more reserved than when he was on his own, visiting us in Cincinnati."

It was obvious to us all that the relationship between father and son, and indeed between Uncle Sol and the rest of his family, was strained. "I get the feeling," Birdie says, "that Sonny didn't know that his mother was a convert to Judaism until he was in his middle teens. I think something about learning this traumatized him. My theory, which I can't prove, is that this knowledge changed his attitude. Perhaps he reacted badly because of some twisted attitude concerning his father's part in this. Someday, I think in Sonny's writings, when he dies, it will be revealed why in the world he had this animosity toward his father. As far as I can see, Sol was a good father and meant only good for his son, and I know how proud he was of him. My brother Sol was dear to me, but he never really opened up about this. It was sad. . . . But maybe we will never find out."

Since hearing from Jay, I have had the pleasure of receiving letters from many more Salingers as well as an invitation to a family reunion this summer. As it happens, it falls a few days after Larry's annual family reunion, and it's being held just a couple of hours away in the big Midwest.

This year, for the first time, I, too, get to say to my son, "Have fun. Go play with your cousins." Imagine that.

Acknowledgments

One of the hardest things, for me, about writing a memoir, was the number of people in my life who deserved volumes and received scant mention, or worse yet, were not included at all. This in no way is a reflection of their importance to me—the shape of the book somehow took on a life of its own. I'd like to use this opportunity to acknowledge my love and gratitude for some friends who are unnamed or unmentioned, for reasons of structure rather than of the heart.

Becky, there was no way to do justice to our childhood adventures, and how much your friendship has meant to me without writing another book entirely. Ava, the same thing about our teenage years. Louise Barraclough, the same starting in our twenties. . . . "It's just an illusion." My friends at Cambridge School: Allison and Sara, Revson, Kent, Tremmie and softly falling snow, McCabes all, Brian M., Penny and Tom, Jonathan R., Jane, Ethan, Jocko, Paul B., Larry and his Harley, the late Peter Thompson, Freddy, Aubrey, all the girls in White Farm Dorm who held the walls for me when I thought they were closing in, and Mr. Peirce. My friends at NEC; especially Jay and Amy. My friends at Boston Edison, Local 369 and my boss, the late Kenny Muir. To Ian Frazier and Barbados, "I had the time of my life," I really did. From Brandeis: Professor Jeffrey Abramson, I learned so much from your classes that has stayed with me, and Susan Hardwicke. My friends from Oxford and London: Barbara and Jonson, Penny Stokes, Daniella Israelachwilli, Stephen P., Joyleen, HJWS, Gregor, Rob London, and classmates Elspeth, Terry, and Adrian. My friends from Harvard: Mary Greer, Henry Klumpenhouwer and Liz Pereboom, Mia and Tys, the Music Lounge gang, Lansing, Gabriel, Dean Guy Martin, and John— "If you hear a song in blue." My "godfather" Alan Trustman, who always seems to appear just when I need him.

Dr. Peter Gombosi, my love and thanks.

Dr. Richard L. Goldstein, my general physician, you have made bearable the times I was disabled, and made me feel secure in the knowledge that I always can count on your integrity and skill, and your thoughtful, insightful, honest, *human* care. I am truly grateful.

Dr. Bob Blatman, after five miscarriages, I still like to see your face. I wish we'd had better luck, but your kindness and humanity made all the difference.

David Hirson and family, I love you dearly.

Special thanks to Gracia Trosman and Angella Brunelle.

Here I'd like to thank friends who supported me, morally, critically, and/or financially in writing this book: Mary Greer, Drew Ryce, Phyllis Teiko, Peter Gombosi, Matthew Guerreiro, Kevin Starrs, Marilyn Ross, Jill Hooley, my in-laws, Sig Roos and Ruthie Rhode, Brad Bellows and Jacqueline Berthet, Christine Hemp and Badger, Margery Chaikin, Alex Sheers, Holly and Ric Browde, Ted Lowenkopf, Liza Prior Lucy, Wayne and Adrienne Edisis, Mr. and Mrs. Roos, Lou and Eileen York, Linda Morgan, David Hirson, Henry Klumpenhouwer, and Alan Trustman.

I'd like to thank my agent, Robert Gottlieb of the William Morris Agency. I'd also like to thank his former assistant Amy Ziff and current assistant Lauren Sheftell for their thoughtful and intelligent support. My publicist, the elegant Lynn Goldberg, is beyond compare.

The entire team at Washington Square Press has been phenomenal: Judith Curr, publisher and person extraordinaire; Nancy Miller, I couldn't wish for a more sensitive and intelligent editor, I'm so lucky to have you. May I add that any faults in this book are those I'm sure Nancy tried to talk me out of. Like Nancy, her assistant, Anika Streitfeld, has been a joy to work with and her help has been immeasurable. Linda Dingler, the book looks beautiful inside and out.

Many thanks to my lawyers, Phil Cowan and Stephen Sheppard (at Cowan, DeBaets, Abrahams & Sheppard). For keeping body and soul together, thanks to J.S.N., consummate professional, of Hill & Assoc., and the staff of Gavin de Becker, Inc.

Finally, I'd like to thank my husband and son who are the light of my life.